(later The Red Krayola). David Grub
with the group, is emphatic about th
always refers to The Red Krayola as
rather than a band,' he says. 'When I started playing
of people had already flowed through The Red Krayola. And, yeah, that obviously blew my concept of the "band".'

The Red Crayola's 1967 experimental juggernaut *Coconut Hotel* is unapproachable drone-jazz psychedelia, a mainly instrumental recording that their label International Artists heard, hated, and hurled deep into the vaults. It remained there until 1995, when it was issued on Drag City, thanks in part to the connection Grubbs facilitated between the label and Thompson. '[*Coconut Hotel*] is both thoughtful and freeform,' Thompson said in 1999. 'The improvisational aspects come out of jazz and chance music, like John Cage. The reason it sounds coherent today is we got quite good at it.'

Even more so than The Velvet Underground, the 1960s incarnation of The Red Crayola (Thompson, Frederick Barthelme, Steve Cunningham) staked out a space within rock—psychedelic rock in particular—and then proceeded to dig up the foundations directly beneath it. 'We set out from the beginning to mark our difference from everybody,' Thompson said in 1996. 'We wanted to eliminate everybody, and we wanted to tighten the logic. We wanted to say: is there logic in pop music? And, if there is, if there's a claim for a certain kind of progressive logic or certain kind of developmental logic, well, let's see where it goes. So our strategy was totally informed to some extent by art and avant-garde traditions and those kinds of things. But, our aim was to shut everybody else up.'

Psychedelia was also notable for its heavy use of echo and delay, the far-out sound that fattened up many an otherwise lame record. The fluidity of sound in a stereo space—guitars bouncing from one speaker to another; a creepy, trippy drone; organ on the moon—was a psychedelic principle that found even greater expression in progressive rock, originally an optimistic, catch-all term to signify interest in musical experimentation.

Progressive rock then became prog, which very definitely came with a set of other, less open-minded expectations: elaborate gestures and concepts, theatricality, and a certain aloofness from the grubby commercial business of rock. Post-rock is sometimes compared to progressive rock and/or prog; for example, Bark Psychosis were dubbed 'Punk Floyd', and *Word* magazine, in its 2004 *Definitive Genre Guide*, called post-rock 'prog rock with crippling shyness'. Post-rock's reluctance to show off by no means indicated a lack of accomplishment.

'Quebec is well-known for its love of prog,' says Ian Ilavsky of the Montreal-based Constellation label. 'The Quebecoise population famously were one of the first in North America to embrace Genesis and Pink Floyd. A lot of ink was spilled around Godspeed in this province about why they found such success here as an instrumental band, and so transcending the language barrier, but also fitting right in with the prog rock tastes of the Quebecoise population. But that male prog obsession with virtuosity, that obsession with chops, and showing off, and long, noodly excursions—that was a huge normative no-no in our community.'

Common to both post- and prog rock is certainly a sense of ambition and an interest in new technologies. Kieran Hebden of Fridge remembers seeing Tortoise for the first time at a tiny London venue, the Water Rats. 'Just looking at the equipment onstage was absolutely breathtaking,' he says. 'Crammed on the stage is a vibraphone and a marimba. I'd never seen these instruments at a little concert before. And *two* drum kits. And then there's banks of synthesizers.' ('He was at that show?' says John McEntire of Tortoise. 'He must have been about twelve years old or something! I don't know how we got all that gear on those tiny, tiny stages. It was so hot, so loud, but super fun.')

Although that setup could have been from a prog concert in 1974, the crucial difference was that, for Tortoise, the range of instrumentation was about creating mood, not showboating. If it took *five* drum kits to create that mood, so be it.

fearless.

THE MAKING OF POST-ROCK

JEANETTE LEECH

FEARLESS

THE MAKING OF POST-ROCK
JEANETTE LEECH

A JAWBONE BOOK
FIRST EDITION 2017
PUBLISHED IN THE UK AND THE USA BY
JAWBONE PRESS
3.1D UNION COURT
20–22 UNION ROAD
LONDON SW4 6JP
ENGLAND
www.jawbonepress.com

ISBN 978-1-911036-15-9

EDITOR TOM SEABROOK
JACKET DESIGN GRAHAM SUTTON

PRINTED IN CHINA

1 2 3 4 5 21 20 19 18 17

CONTENTS

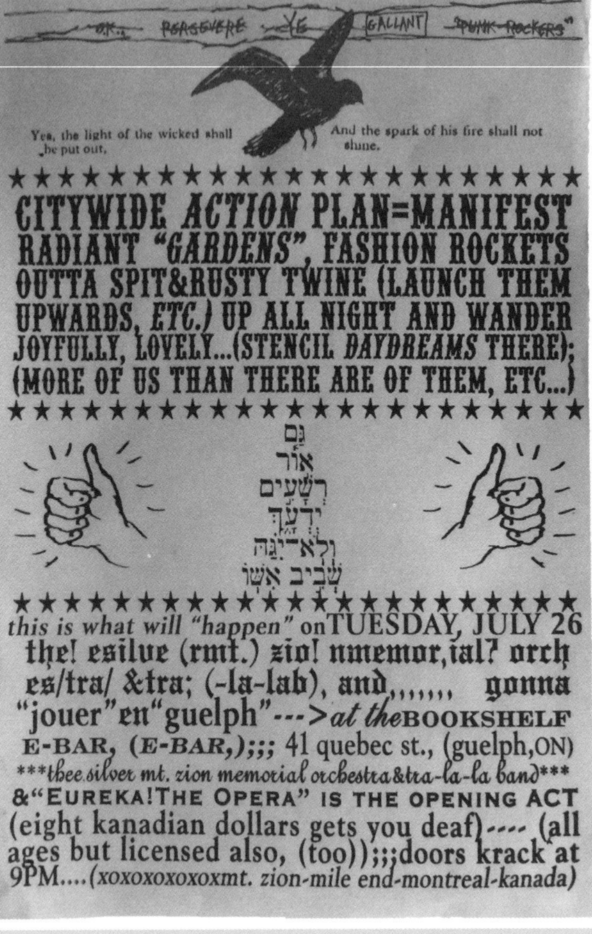

O.K.. PERSEVERE YE GALLANT "PUNK ROCKERS"
Yea, the light of the wicked shall be put out,
And the spark of his fire shall not shine.
CITYWIDE ACTION PLAN=MANIFEST RADIANT "GARDENS", FASHION ROCKETS OUTTA SPIT&RUSTY TWINE (LAUNCH THEM UPWARDS, ETC.) UP ALL NIGHT AND WANDER JOYFULLY, LOVELY...(STENCIL DAYDREAMS THERE); (MORE OF US THAN THERE ARE OF THEM, ETC...)
גם
אור
רשעים
ידעך
ולא־יגה
שביב אשו
this is what will "happen" onTUESDAY, JULY 26
the! esilve (rmt.) zio! nmemor,ial? orch es/tra/ &tra; (-la-lab), and,,,,,,, gonna "jouer"en"guelph"--->at theBOOKSHELF E-BAR, (E-BAR,);;; 41 quebec st., (guelph,ON)
thee.silver mt. zion memorial orchestra&tra-la-la band
&"EUREKA!THE OPERA" IS THE OPENING ACT
(eight kanadian dollars gets you deaf)---- (all ages but licensed also, (too));;;doors krack at 9PM....(xoxoxoxoxoxmt. zion-mile end-montreal-kanada)

INTRODUCTION

fearless.

'That's the thing. When you don't know anything, you're much more fearless about it.' GRAHAM SUTTON, BARK PSYCHOSIS

Trying to encapsulate in a title what unites dozens of artists is difficult at the best of times. But when the subject is post-rock, it borders on the preposterous.

'Maybe the question [of post-rock], in your mind's eye, might have a definitive answer,' says Jeff Mueller of Rodan, June Of 44, and Shipping News, one of my early interviewees. 'But, maybe, then you talk to ten different people and every single one of those ten people would give you a different response.'

For a long time, this book was simply called *The Post-Rock Book*. No working title, no in-joke, no florid author indulgence. Only those few words. They were frightening in their implied definitiveness. What could they *mean*?

'You'll have to define what post-rock is, in this book,' David Callahan of Moonshake warns me, not unreasonably.

It seemed sensible, as a first step, to go back to the source. The term post-rock was meant to be 'open-ended yet precise', or so hoped the critic Simon Reynolds, as he explained the tag he created in 1994. It meant 'using rock instrumentation for non-rock purposes, using guitars as facilitators of textures and timbres rather than riffs and powerchords'.

'I remember seeing [Reynolds's article] and thinking, *ah, he's a clever cunt,*' says Ian Crause of Disco Inferno, one of the original bands cited by Reynolds as post-rock. 'He really knows how to come up with a brand name.'

The artists that predated (or were contemporaneous with) Reynolds's article, on the whole, mind being called post-rock far less than those who came later. 'I never had any issue with it,' says Kirsty Yates of Insides, another band cited in the original Simon Reynolds piece. 'The point was, actually: take rock *up* a level. I understood what he was trying to do.'

The 'post' part, as Yates says, implies that it came after 'rock': that post-rock had evolved from it, and yet was still in a symbiotic relationship with it. For some, though, it also insinuated a bit of snobbery. Post-rock seemed to say that rock was heading for extinction, and this was one reason why a lot of bands rejected the term. They saw themselves as part of a rock—and especially a punk rock—continuum.

'Post-rock is a *pain in the ass*!' says Efrim Menuck of Godspeed You! Black Emperor. 'It's sad, after this many years, that you roll into a place to play a show, and you see the poster, and the name of the band, and afterward, in brackets, "Canadian post-rock". It's still a little heartbreaking.'

'The classic question that we're asked all the time, is, Why did you decide to be a post-rock band? Where do I even start with *that*?' Stuart Braithwaite of Mogwai tells me.

I did find ambivalence bordering on all-out hatred toward the term, but perhaps not as much as I'd prepared myself for. 'Funnily enough, now I've come to accept post-rock,' says John McEntire of Tortoise. 'OK, we were there; we did that. If that's what people want to call it, then we should own it.'

Nevertheless, it took time. Post-rock was not artist-created, nor did many bands wear it proudly. There are no albums called *The Shape Of Post-Rock To Come* or *Post-Rock 1: Music For Airports.*

Part of the problem with defining post-rock is that the thing constantly slithers away from you. It can be either lazily employed or rigorously policed, the worst of 'open-ended and precise'. One moment it's being used to describe virtually all modern experimental guitar music; the next it's used for a needle-eye definition relating *only* to a certain type of instrumental volume-based dynamic music. And God help you if you argue otherwise.

Genre names are frequently created, and most simply fade on the page. All periods of popular music history are littered with pithy journalese that the wider public simply didn't take to (and there are plenty of examples in this book alone). But post-rock clicked for listeners and critics. It became a staple of the modern musical lexicon.

'I used to work as a rock journalist back in the nineties,' says Gen Heistek, a Montreal-based musician whose many bands, including Sackville and Hangedup, were a key part of that city's underground musical community at that time. 'I remember getting in a huge fight over whether or not post-rock actually existed. They maintained firmly that it did, and I was of the opinion that it did not. I still don't really believe it exists.'

Fearless argues that it does. It sees post-rock as an archipelago: islands that may speak different languages and are probably only on nodding terms with one another. But they are in the same sea. And that sea, the one ideological core that unites the major artists covered in this book, is *deconstruction*: a fierce desire to unpick and change predictable channels of expression.

'One cannot get around the response,' the theorist Jacques Derrida wrote in 1967, 'except by challenging the very form of the question.' Deconstruction doesn't necessarily destroy. It takes apart, and then reorders, *using the same materials*.

'We didn't want a guitar to sound like a fucking guitar,' says Rudy Tambala of A.R. Kane. 'You might *think* that's a power chord, but it's not; it's just smashing a guitar against something, dropping it, and then going over and having a smoke, or whatever. But it was really: let's try and tear away, aggressively, any aspect of rock'n'roll.'

Some post-rock artists explicitly and consciously sought to deconstruct rock music; others realised they'd done it after the event; yet more didn't give the process a moment's thought. A lot of this deconstruction was made possible through the advent of the sampler, ushering in a new genre-bending mindset. Most of the post-rock bands used samplers in some form, but even the ones who didn't were influenced by sampling's possibilities for simultaneous structure and chaos. A major reason for the vast bulk of this book being concerned with the period after the mid-to-late 1980s is because it was then that samplers became more affordable.

The attitude of deconstruction was not only related to sonics. Post-rock was usually adamant that it didn't want anything to do with rock's gang-of-mates image. Roles in a band could constantly shift, as musicians changed up instruments, and a single front person or a focal point was rejected. This theory didn't always work in practice, as we shall see, but the idea—to confront the expected spotlights of rock through decentreing both sound and representation—was strong.

'There's a whole way you're meant to interact with the audience,' says Jacqui Ham of Ut, a trio who swapped guitar, bass, and drums on record and onstage. '*Oh, you want us to play this song?* That wasn't our thing. We wanted people to enter into this intensity, to be there totally, none of this interacting with the audience. Our whole philosophy was that we were into shaking things up. Making things uncomfortable. We did not want people to be comfortable. We did *not* want that.'

In many cases, playing live was an ordeal. Post-rock artists generally preferred to shape a sound in the studio rather than prove their 'authenticity' onstage. It could be a challenge to find an adequate way to express their ideas in a live setting, as this is where the entire corporate rock machinery dropped its full force on a band: venues were designed for staring at a stage and emptying your wallet at the bar. There were also the technical limitations of small venues, unused to bands turning up with electricity-hungry samplers and film projectors, or spending fifteen minutes tuning up between songs. Some bands got around all this by establishing their own spaces, some by avoiding gigs as much as possible, some by doing a totally different live set to the record that they were meant to be promoting, and still more by muddling through as best they could.

Why did they do all this, usually to very little reward? They were on a mission. And they were fearless about it.

Fearless: The Making Of Post-Rock winds up in the very early 2000s. By this point, two major and linked phenomena had happened. Firstly, post-rock was now substantially and, it seemed, permanently altered from its original positive and exploratory base.

'For a while, a new record would come out and you didn't know what it would sound like,' says Kieran Hebden of Fridge. 'But unfortunately, after a year or so, post-rock became a sound. It became very predictable.' Certainly, by 2000, the term 'post-rock' had locked anchor and become exactly something that connoted certain (and not always flattering) sonic cues.

Secondly, elements of more conventional rock were incorporating post-rock ideas—sometimes well, sometimes clumsily. But post-rock now had enough creative cachet and visibility to achieve a mainstream breakthrough of sorts. Notwithstanding some excellent individual albums released after the early 2000s, it felt that the most radical period of development had passed, and that post-rock—as a term and as a sound—had indeed been 'made'.

One of the drivers for writing this book was a general sense of frustration at how some discussions around post-rock lack verve, excitement, emotion, and stories. The music is often written about in an overly dry fashion that, at its worst, gets into an obsession with time signatures.

'Someone I know told me, *There's this great song, it's in 7/9 and 8/11,*' says Codeine's John Engle. 'And I was like, that sounds *great.* I can't wait to hear that. I'm not counting when I'm listening to a piece of music. And I would not say, *What's this song about? Well, it's about seven measures of this, followed by eight measures of that.*'

Sometimes a bit of muso chat is inevitable, but I have tried to keep this to a bare minimum, and only include it when it gave a fresh insight into a track, album, or group's development.

The possible ways of organising this book were infinite. In the end, I took a thematic approach. It is broadly chronological, but themes and philosophies always override concerns of creating a rigid linear history: for instance, I discuss Scott Walker's *Tilt* (from 1995) in chapter 4, and Galaxie 500's *On Fire* (from 1989) in chapter 9. I suppose I tried to emulate, in written form, something like Tortoise's 'Djed': building a structure on existing sections, keeping certain elements of what has gone before, while occasionally having to say 'fuck it' and revel in the resulting glitch.

Fearless, after all.

JEANETTE LEECH, LONDON, ENGLAND, OCTOBER 2016

CHAPTER ONE

proto-

'Post-rock, as a term, is relatively new to me. When we were making music, it didn't really have a category. That was the problem.' RICHIE THOMAS, DIF JUZ

The influences on and precursors to post-rock are more divided than united, just like those who came after it, but they all had this in common: they disrupted a continuum. As soon as 'rock' lost its 'roll' in the 1960s, there were those who questioned, and from that fundamentally altered, rock's gene structure. They looked not to Derrida's then-untranslated and obscure theories of deconstruction. They looked to free jazz.

Ornette Coleman was the first modern artist to challenge the way 'improvisation' in jazz was still tethered to formal structure. 'A lot of musicians couldn't really dig his type of music because they were so brainwashed to that same formula—the beginning, you know, then the bridge and the end of the tune; then you solo and take it out,' the drummer Edward Blackwell, who worked with Coleman, recalled. 'But with Ornette it's not like that. You start it and then you're on your own. As long as you're aware of where the music should go, there's no problem at all how it would be. When Ornette starts a tune, there's a certain place he intends to get [to], but there's no certain way to get there.' Coleman's own belle époque, beginning in 1959 with *The Shape Of Jazz To Come*, offered sound with no anchors in musical convention. Any frameworks that did emerge were organic, developed in relation to their own ingredients: repetition, collective insight, feel. He searched for an open-ended approach with zeal, seeing any settling into a 'style' as morally bankrupt.

Ornette Coleman was a divisive figure. Some saw his approach as little more than out-of-tune anarchy, while for others it was an epiphany. Over the next ten years, the inspired minority took Coleman's approach and introduced more freeing elements. Soon, jazz had even more security snatched away by John Coltrane, Albert Ayler, Sun Ra, Pharoah Sanders, and many others. For as well as freeing composition, these pioneers took further the idea that jazz's tools—the instruments—could have their sound and purpose remodelled. For example, saxophones might not sound like saxophones. They might sound like hellfire hollers of rage, or mercury flowing down a glacier.

Lou Reed was a lot of things, including a free jazz nerd who named his college radio show after a Cecil Taylor song and followed Ornette Coleman around town. The Velvet Underground imported and regurgitated ideas of jazz modernism: the rudderless yet overpowering energy, the sense of the *now* and—in particular—the way that the music made sense structurally in relation to itself rather than to outside authorities. Also common in jazz, apparent in The Velvet Underground, and to prove utterly crucial to post-rock, was fluidity in what-meant-what in music. This could range from members being liberated from rigid roles (Reed and Sterling Morrison would frequently swap lead and rhythm guitar) to instruments refusing to obey the rules (Moe Tucker's steady drums dropping out toward the end of 'Sister Ray'). All of these concepts were new frontiers for rock music.

The Velvet Underground managed to be both Roman and the Vandal at the city walls. Wherever there was a binary, they would at least challenge it, if not outright smash it: art/trash, music/noise, meaning/hollowness. Rock was a mere infant, and still The Velvet Underground picked it down to the bones before covering it in entirely new flesh.

'There's no fucking riffs,' says Rudy Tambala of A.R. Kane. 'That dirge-y, drone-y thrash. There's no cock in that rock. You should call it post-cock rock. Seriously.'

Prior to forming The Velvet Underground with Reed, John Cale had played with La Monte Young and Tony Conrad in the drone-based Theatre Of Eternal Music. Their performances, Cale has said, 'consisted of holding one chord for forty-five minutes. It was a form of sense deprivation for all concerned.'

This idea of music as endurance, or at least perseverance and patience, also forms an undercurrent of some post-rock. There was no fear of the beyond, and this was sometimes taken to ludicrous extremes in The Velvet Undeground's live shows. 'Melody Laughter', an abstract improvisation featuring a wordless moan by Nico, could last between two and forty-two minutes in performance. It and the better-known 'Sister Ray' are extreme examples, but the group's entire body of work contains long stretches where instrumentation follows its own wilderness trail, and where vocals are absent, sporadic, or incoherent.

As generally unpopular as *The Velvet Underground & Nico* and (especially) *White Light/White Heat* were at the time, they were certainly better known than the work of the British improvisers AMM. As a collective, AMM had a somewhat fluid roster, but their album *AMMMusic* featured Cornelius Cardew, Keith Rowe, Lou Gare, Lawrence Sheaff, and Eddie Prévost. 'Does group direction, or authority, depend on the strength of a leading personality, whose rise or fall is reflected in the projected image,' the sleeve notes to *AMMMusic* ask, 'or does the collation of a set of minds mean the development of another authority independent of all the members but consisting of all of them?'

Discipline, for AMM, was 'the essential prerequisite for improvisation'. According to Cardew, 'Discipline is not to be seen as the ability to conform to a rigid rule structure, but the ability to work collectively with other people, in a harmonious and fruitful way. Integrity, self-reliance, initiative, to be articulate (on the instrument) in a natural, direct way; these are the qualities necessary for improvisation.'

'AMM music existed before we thought of it,' Keith Rowe said in 1994.

Although AMM did not plan performances and did not talk about what had unfolded in them afterward, they did engage in weekly philosophical discussion sessions. 'Concern about what a "group" meant and the danger of it being a tool for one individual's thinking always lurked beneath the surface,' Prévost reflected in 1988. 'Externally, this fear was justified. Because the world still measured (as it does today) all activity in terms of dominating personalities. The natural collectivist sentiments which our music exemplified were more or less ignored.'

As radical now as they were then, AMM completely rejected the idea of personality and focal point. A difficult battle for AMM to fight—the press would often refer to them as 'Cardew's Group'—it was to be no easier for Godspeed You! Black Emperor, more than thirty years later. 'We were proud and shy motherfuckers, and we engaged with the world thusly,' the group said, in a collective voice, in 2012. 'Means we decided no singer, no leader, no interviews, no press photos.'

AMMMusic and sessions from 1968, known as *The Crypt*, form an extraordinary forward-looking suite of recordings that combine mayhem and discipline. 'The players could, at time, share a timeless immersion in a world of sound, while simultaneously being free to pursue their individual paths,' Prévost continued. 'It was not uncommon for the musician to wonder who or what was producing a particular sound, stop playing, and discover that it was he himself who had been responsible.' Just as with free jazz, it was seldom clear that an AMM guitar actually *was* a guitar, so fluent and alien was the new language they created.

AMM also experimented with primitive loops and sampling, deconstructing an original recording and using it as both starting block and target. 'I used to take things like [The Beach Boys'] "Barbara Ann", take a reel-to-reel tape recorder and make forty or fifty butt-edits of that so it would play for about two hours,' Keith Rowe later recalled of AMM sessions in the mid sixties. 'We'd put that on really, really loud, and that would be the wall and the AMM would try to climb over it.'

Similar in spirit but different in tone to AMM was The Red Crayola

It is, however, to the West German progressive groups of the 1970s that a more obvious musical debt is owed. 'There was such a relief at first not to be called krautrock!' says Glenn Jones of Cul de Sac, remembering when the post-rock label was first applied to his group. 'Ah, finally, something else! But within a year or so I was so tired of the term "post-rock" I found myself saying, *Oh, what I wouldn't give to be called a krautrock band again.*' Indeed, krautrock is a term that attracts similar ire from musicians tagged with it—and it has also proved hard to shift in the popular imagination.

The Düsseldorf groups Kraftwerk and Neu! were interested in electronica, repetition; the *motorik* sound characteristic of them is clearly there in the more accessible post-rock artists. 'I thought of the concept of joining the very minimalistic rhythmic aspect of some of the German bands,' says Tim Gane of Stereolab, 'and combining that with aspects of melody and harmony, which they wouldn't have done.' But it is Can, from Cologne, who are the most influential of all. They even inspired Moonshake to name themselves after a song from the 1973 album *Future Days*.

Both Holger Czukay, on bass, and Irmin Schmidt, on keyboards, had studied under Karlheinz Stockhausen. Michael Karoli was a rock guitarist. Jaki Liebezeit, the drummer, was experienced in jazz ensembles—although by the time Can formed, he had distanced himself from the freer routes it took in the 1960s. Common to all was a desire to deliberately recalibrate their musical training, and to some extent their tastes and interests, into something that was both open-ended and controlled; unbound music that found its own moorings.

'The prog-rock, jazz-rock thing was totally opposed to what we wanted to do,' said Karoli. 'Not impressing people, but caressing them. Sometimes in a rough way, but always as direct physical contact with them.' The main Can vocalists, Malcolm Mooney and then Damo Suzuki, generally used words not as descriptors but as sound art, and could employ a babbling expressionism that had little in common with the expected clarity of a singer.

'The more you learn to play, the more you learn to lie,' Czukay said in 1987, 'whereas if you cannot play, you cannot lie.' Although Can are often characterised as a jam or improv band, Czukay rejects that somewhat, preferring the term 'instant composing'.

'If the idea was spontaneous composition, it still meant that everyone had to know something about the architecture of music,' he has said. 'What Jaki always compared it with was sport. Ballgames like football are the real spontaneous games. The players are trained but they don't know where the ball is going the next minute.'

Can's legendary tightness in the face of all this freedom was largely due to Liebezeit. 'With a cyclical rhythm you cannot change it,' he said, 'you have to obey the rhythmical movement. You can change some things but you must keep the basic shape of that rhythm.' Liebezeit was keen to reduce, reduce, reduce; in a refraction of the Theatre Of Eternal Music, he felt for the pulse of Can and privileged it over all other forms of stimuli.

Nevertheless, environmental factors were important to the group, and Can spent hours, days sometimes, exploring and then customising the nooks and crannies of their studio. 'Every little noise, every sound became meaningful: steps, a chair, a few words, an accidental sound created by touching an instrument,' Schmidt recalled. Most of the time Can recorded live, instant composing with only two microphones and an amplified mixer, and then painstakingly assembling tracks from fragments, drawing on the artistic principles of collage and montage. 'Aumgn', from 1971's *Tago Mago*, is an arresting illustration of this. The zealous attention to detail, the creation of something natural-sounding out of a process that was anything but, and the idea that the studio is as much of a character as any musician would reach mythical status in some post-rock records, Talk Talk's 1991 album *Laughing Stock* being only the most famous example.

Can made music for movies, television, theatre. They were in demand right from their earliest days, with one of their first recorded tracks ('Millionenspeil') intended for a sci-fi TV show; their second album, released in 1970, was *Soundtracks*, a compilation of commissioned tracks. The projects they scored, however, were often low-budget efforts, and not always a meeting of artistic minds. '[The movie *Cream*] was part of this wave of erotic films when it was suddenly allowed to show tits onscreen,' Karoli recalled. 'We didn't know it was going to be like that! It had a different story before. I think the film distributor took all the erotic scenes and threw the story out.'

There was certainly a practical element to Can's soundtrack work in that it allowed them to gain exposure and income. This was to prove increasingly important in the post-digital age, as musicians' revenue streams dwindled; composing for (or syncing to) visuals represented a significant financial injection. Yet, more philosophically, it loaned Can's more outré experiments a narrative.

Post-rock, seldom guiding the listener down an obvious path, would also provide a rich seam for film and TV to mine in those terms, from Mogwai soundtracking the French paranormal horror *Les Revenants* to Bark Psychosis cropping up in Chris Morris's devastating *Jam*. There was even Mouse On Mars's 1998 album *Glam*, written for an American porn film à la Can's experience with *Cream* (although the studio ultimately rejected *Glam*, presumably on the likelihood of it killing the carnal mood).

The West German bands of the 70s were often experimenting with group structures outside of the rock norm; this sometimes related to other forms of non-mainstream living, too. 'It was political by doing, rather than words,' says Liebezeit, with shades of AMM. 'A group with no leader means everyone is leader, everyone is equally responsible.'

Amon Düül, who rose from the Munich communes of the late 60s, were further out still in these principles. 'The idea was, everyone is a musician,' said John Weinzierl, a founder. 'You didn't go along to the concert and watch the band; you came to the event and you were part of it.' Amon Düül were soon to divide into two quarrelsome factions, with Amon Düül II becoming an increasingly professional rock band, and the remnants of the original Amon Düül releasing ludicrously self-indulgent jam records. Still, the era of political progressiveness and idealism, and how it impacted on musical hierarchies, remains an important legacy.

The West German groups caught the ear of one Brian Eno, while he was still in Roxy Music, and the Can-esque tight/free throb can clearly be heard on 'The Bogus Man', from 1973's *For Your Pleasure*. Bryan Ferry, the self-styled leader of Roxy (no West German mushy togetherness *here*), was coddling a bruised ego at the time; the press and public passed over him for the colourful, naturally ebullient Eno. And Eno, with what must have riled Ferry further, was now openly professing a snobbish boredom toward his group.

'Outside the stage door at Roxy shows there'd always be a crowd with these pushy ones at the front, but at the back there'd be two or three more interesting types who were always too polite or proud to bother you, and they were the ones I wanted to talk to,' Eno said in 1990. 'I thought, *how do I get to them and keep these others away*?'

It all ended in a rancorous split and a slight Eno backlash. 'Eno would appear to have rather overdone it,' the *NME* journalist Chris Salewicz sniffed in 1974. 'He is probably the most supreme self-publicist currently among British rock musicians.' At this point Eno was still often seen—despite his work in Roxy, the compelling 1973 prog/*motorik* fusion *No Pussyfooting* with King Crimson's Robert Fripp, and a couple of reasonable solo albums—as a bullshitter yet to prove himself.

To be fair to Eno, he knew why people might think this. 'What happened in Roxy Music was that a particular aspect, a really quite small aspect, came into the open and got an incredible amount of encouragement,' he said in 1977. 'And it sort of blossomed, if that's the right word, at the expense of a lot of other parts of me.' One of these parts, less apparent in Roxy but certainly emerging fully afterward, was his fondness for theorising and pontificating, sometimes grafting on a concept after the event. Looking back on his first solo effort, 1973's *Here Come The Warm Jets*, a few years later, he said, 'In talking so much about that album, I came to examine my methods very closely and began to see what worked and what didn't. In so doing I rejected about half the avenues of approach suggested in that record.'

Eno was already gravitating toward music as a *process*, and an endlessly fascinating one at that. This had deep roots in him. Pre-fame, during his time at the Ipswich Art School, he had a particularly radical tutor, Roy Ascott, who believed that an 'end product'—a painting, an installation, a composition, an album—was almost incidental.

'Give the game away.'

'Repetition is a form of change.'

'Look closely at the most embarrassing details and amplify them.'

'Would anybody want it?'

Subtitled 'Over one hundred worthwhile dilemmas', *Oblique Strategies*, created in 1975 by Eno and Peter Schmidt, is a set of cards designed to confront process head on. Its target was creative stasis, and *Oblique Strategies* helped the user with blocks in numerous ways: hurdling over them, eating them up, breaking them down, or simply backing away from them. Employing chance techniques, such as the I Ching, in musical composition can potentially be very radical. It can trigger counterintuitive decisions, spurring free-associative development down a path that might otherwise have been subconsciously ruled out (or not even considered in the first place). It can also work toward eliminating ego and authorial presence, as it forces submission to chance occurrence. However, it seems *very* Eno that, in order to get rid of Eno, Eno comes up with the *Oblique Strategies*: an Eno-specific process.

During 1975, he was certainly in full philosophical flow. 'We are no longer interested in making horizontal music, by which I mean music that starts at point A, develops through point B, and ends at point C in a kind of logical or semi-logical progression,' he told *Creem* magazine that year. 'What's more interesting is constructing music that is a solid block of interactions. This then leaves your brain free to make some of those interactions more important than others and to find which particular ones it wants to speak to.' He was interested in exploring timbre—the quality or 'colour' of a sound; that which makes the same note at the same pitch and same volume sound different when played on a piano, a saxophone, a guitar.

Eno debated how to use timbre to liberate instruments from their individual sentry boxes. 'The way rock music is traditionally organised is to some extent *ranked*,' Eno has said. 'You have voice, guitar, rhythm guitar, piano maybe—rhythm guitar and piano are interchangeable—bass, and then drums. Then at the bottom you have the bass drum. It's a kind of hierarchy. Partly one of mixing, because normally it was done so that the voice was loudest and the bass was quietest; that was the concept. But that was also the concept of what importance the listener was intended to attach to each of these things.'

The *Oblique Strategies*, the desire to get away from both 'horizontal music' and listener expectation, and months of gorging on Cluster's *Zuckerzeit* came directly to bear on June 1975, when Eno and his musicians entered London's Basing Street studio to make his third solo album. There was no preparation, and no idea of what would come out.

'I tried all kinds of experiments, like seeing how few instructions you could give to the people in order to get something interesting to happen,' Eno later said of the sessions. 'For example, I had a stopwatch, and I said, Right, we'll now play a piece that lasts exactly ninety seconds and each of you has got to leave more spaces than you make noises—something like that, and seeing what happened from it.'

Every day, Eno would come up with an idea or juxtaposition of ideas—'Swing the microphone from the ceiling and hire a trombone', for example—and try to make something of it. But for four long days, nothing usable *at all* emerged. In front of his musicians, Eno kept up a brave face, but privately, his will to work in this way nearly caved in.

Yet he pressed on, in the face of bemusement and mounting costs. On the fifth day, some fertiliser finally seeped into the dry ground. 'His initial guidance would be incredibly vague,' bass player Percy Jones has said. 'There was a tune called "Sky Saw," and the instruction he gave us was he hit a middle A on the piano, and he just went *dun dun dun dun dun dun*, but it had a rhythm, and that was the starting point for the tune. I just started playing *dun dun doodle doodle da da*, put some sort of modulation on it, so we put down that sequence, and that was it, and we moved onto something else.'

From razor-cut snippets like these, Eno gradually amassed a suite of sounds. He also modified and invented instruments. Many were fancifully named but had serious purpose. His 'digital guitar' was fed through a digital delay unit and then back on itself 'until it made this cardboard tube type sound.' Robert Fripp's 'Wimshurst guitar' was so named because its intent was to mimic the Wimshurst machine, a Victorian electrostatic generator. The preparation for 'prepared piano' on 'Little Fishes' was Eno lodging coins behind the hammers and strings. There was a rhythm generator, a precursor to the drum machine that was also used on Can's *Tago Mago*, something Eno then 'treated' to enrich its sonic spectrum.

One instrument used sparingly was the human voice. 'The problem is that people, particularly people who write, assume that the meaning of the song is vested in the lyrics,' Eno has said. 'To me, that has never been the case. There are very few songs that I can think of where I can even remember the words, actually, let alone think that those are the centre of the meaning. For me, music in itself carries a whole set of messages which are very, very rich and complex, and the words either serve to exclude certain ones of those, or point up others that aren't really in there, or aren't worth saying.'

Instrumental tracks like 'The Big Ship', 'In Dark Trees', 'Becalmed', and 'Zawinul / Lava' are not the understated scenery that Eno would go on to advance in his later ambient albums. Instead, they chug and splutter, forming dense fogs of almost-rock illuminated by shafts of hazy pastoral sunshine. If the aim was to make 'horizontal music'—finding a way to construct, de-construct, and re-construct shifting musical states, and to disorder the expected rankings of sound—then, certainly on the instrumental tracks, it was achieved. Sometimes the listener can nearly hear the smug glee of a man realising that his risk of hiring out an expensive studio and packing naught but his hope had paid off.

'I read a science fiction story a long time ago,' Eno said in 1977, of the resulting album's title, *Another Green World*. 'These people are exploring space and they finally find this habitable planet—and it turns out to be identical to Earth in every detail. And I thought that was the supreme irony: that they'd originally left to find something better and arrived in the end—which was actually the same place. Which is how I feel about myself. I'm always trying to project myself at a tangent and always seem eventually to arrive back at the same place.'

Someone else taken with Germany in the mid seventies—its bands, its culture, its turbulent history, and the fact it wasn't cocaine-swaddled Los Angeles—was David Bowie. 'Life in LA had left me with an overwhelming sense of foreboding,' he said in 1999. 'I had approached the brink of drug-induced calamity one too many times and it was essential to take some kind of positive action. For many years Berlin had appealed to me as a sort of sanctuary-like situation. It was one of the few cities where I could move around in virtual anonymity. I was going broke; it was cheap to live. For some reason, Berliners just didn't care. Well, not about an English rock singer anyway.' Bowie had a low profile and, although he had a long way to go in his recovery, it seemed to be suiting him.

Summer 1976, and Bowie, having wrapped up his work on his fellow exile Iggy Pop's *The Idiot* a little early, was bouncing ideas about in a Parisian studio. Producer Tony Visconti was with him. A consummate professional, Visconti had collaborated with Bowie before, and could organise around—and with—the star's sometimes fragile states of mind. He had also brought an intriguing new toy with him. Visconti's Eventide Harmonizer machine, one of only a few in Europe at the time, could shift pitch and delay recorded sound or, as Visconti put it, 'fuck with the fabric of time'. With only vague expectations of something releasable, Visconti and Bowie began to knock about ideas that turned into songs, which then became *Low*.

The sessions with Visconti well underway, Bowie telephoned Brian Eno. The pair were vaguely acquainted and had professed mutual admiration for each other's recent albums. Initially, Bowie thought Eno might lend a hand with overdubbing. But almost as soon as Eno arrived, Bowie—fighting some very concrete legal battles as well as psychological problems—was called away to the Paris courts for four days. He waved his hand for Eno to experiment in his absence, only suggesting he try something slow, even devotional. Eno, perhaps mindful of the same cursed number of fruitless days he'd spent in Basing Street the previous summer, told Bowie to charge him for the studio time if he didn't care for the results.

One morning while Bowie was away, Eno heard Visconti's four-year-old son play a piano noodle; Eno sat down with the boy and joined in. From that, Eno developed a phantasmagorical electronic track, built around a gently undulating central motif. When Bowie returned, he added a chanting vocal inspired by a Bulgarian children's choir, named the track after the capital city of Poland, and didn't issue Eno with a bill. 'Warszawa' launched what was to be the 'ambient' side of *Low*.

'Brian had talked David into this minimalist recording thing—minimal songs, minimal chord changes, minimal rhythms,' Tony Visconti reflected in 1994. 'We decided about halfway through that we liked it and we officially decided to make it an album.'

The other three tracks making up the ambient suite explored Bowie's new home of Berlin: its past glories and its present divided self (in a likely metaphor for the artist's own cleaved mind and uncertain future). The tracks mix optimism, comedown, and the desire to mould a cocoon within a city, one that went about its business whether you were there or not. This strong and intentional sense of place is evoked through subtle aural cues; for example, Bowie's saxophone on 'Subterraneans' was intended to channel the East Berlin jazz scene. Urban sprawl, shitty city conditions, and lost histories are often deliberately summoned in post-rock records, and *Low* is a rare rock record to do this without the explicit aid of lyrics.

David Bowie, in the mid 1970s, was one of the most famous pop stars on the planet. His series of characters had enhanced, rather than hidden, his essential Bowieness. With *Low*, however, a Bowie in need of rehabilitation largely retreated from self and, very deliberately, covered his distinguishing features. He talked of wanting to abandon himself 'to the zeitgeist', of relinquishing control, of embracing spontaneity. 'I couldn't express in words,' he said of his emotions at the time. 'Rather, it required textures.'

Although *Low* was ready in time for Christmas 1976, Bowie's label RCA sensibly thought it more apt for January's misery than December's festive cheer, hanging back on the release until early 1977. This was at the height of punk, and *Low* was often judged in its context. '[*Low*] is an act of purest hatred and destructiveness,' wrote Charles Shaar Murray in the *NME*. 'It comes to us in a bad time and it doesn't help at all. Words like "psychosis", "nihilism", and "anarchy" are fashionable these days, but *Low* is an infinity away from the nihilism of the Pistols, which is at least active, outward-looking and ultimately healing.'

'When it came out, I thought *Low* was the sound of the future,' said Stephen Morris, who would, in August 1977, become the drummer in a group calling itself Warsaw (after 'Warszawa'). Warsaw became Joy Division, and *Low*—as Morris predicted—influenced a cadre of musicians whose music matured after the initial fire of punk had cooled. And Joy Division certainly cooled it some more: they encased it within an arctic palace.

Joy Division and their producer, Martin Hannett, tacitly injected punk with progressive rock's ideas of technical competence, unapologetic intelligence, and studio wizardry, while bleeding out both prog bloat and punk coarseness in the process. When their peers got faster and more colourful, Joy Division got slower and more monochrome.

Hannett drove a wedge between each sound the musicians of Joy Division made, opening up three dimensions around it, and seeming to diminish not only the personalities of the musicians, but shrinking their individual sounds, as they quivered lonely in the space surrounding them. 'A big tom-tom riff of mine would come out sounding like coconuts being hit by matchsticks,' complained Morris (a big fan of Can's Jaki Liebezeit). He, practically speaking, got the roughest end of Hannett's ideology; Morris was not treated as an autonomous musician but as a series of body parts to hit drums.

'At that time, [Hannett] wanted complete separation,' he later said. 'He wanted the bass drum on its own with nothing, no spill, so he could treat it one way and treat the snare drum another way. He wanted it as clean and as treatable as he could get it, which meant you couldn't really play a drum kit because you would get spill. And you could forget playing cymbals. You had to basically take the drum kit to pieces and play each bit separately. At the time I thought he was just doing it to drive me mad—which he did, quite successfully.'

As well as the separation, Hannett used ARP synthesizers and sequencers, their sounds triggered by Morris's drums; he also used digital delay, manipulating milliseconds of time for added snare crispness and, in the case of Ian Curtis's vocals, to effect simultaneous lyrical empathy and alienation. Adding to this Bernard Sumner's stippled guitar and, especially, Peter Hook's melody-carrying bass, Joy Division were a touchstone for dissimilar post-rock artists: Disco Inferno, Codeine, Mogwai.

Analogous to Joy Division in their linking of punk and prog are The Police. 'That was the big joke—half of these bands swearing they were punk and overthrowing the establishment were all prog fans!' Andy Summers, the group's guitarist, has said. And it was Summers, an incredibly schooled and versatile musician, who can claim much of The Police's post-rockish credit. 'I grew up playing jazz as a kid; that was my thing—to be like an American jazz guitar player,' he recalled. 'I wanted to learn the harmonic stuff, which I got by the time I was sixteen. Later on in London I was in rhythm and blues bands. I was listening to a lot of world music, Indian music and Miles Davis, Coltrane. And then I got into Olivier Messiaen and John Cage: so-called twentieth century avant-garde music.' Summers's pre-Police experience in the Canterbury Scene group Soft Machine, combined with his love for dissonance and airy dub patches, resulted in soft-yet-tense moments among The Police's power chords; 'Bring On The Night', from 1979's *Reggatta De Blanc*, is a strong example of his dense, tail-chasing technique.

The Police are barely ever acknowledged as a post-rock influence—their huge success, and the presence of Sting among the group's members, makes shouting about their impact a very uncool thing to do—but Gen Heistek of Hangedup is in no doubt. 'I think if you take the vocals away from The Police, you basically have post-rock,' she says. 'It was there all along, and you just needed to listen better.'

While The Police were being all-conquering rock stars, back at Factory Records, Joy Division were mucking in with label founder Tony Wilson's latest wheeze: gluing together pieces of sandpaper for a record sleeve. Wilson, in common with his contemporary, Malcolm McLaren, got a lot of ideas from the Situationalists. This gang of creative pranksters, whose roots lay in the Parisian civil unrest of May 1968, championed subversive pop culture stunts, and one of said stunts was to house a book in sandpaper to chafe away, and eventually destroy, what was on the shelf next to it.

'I thought it was a bit pretentious,' said Vini Reilly, in 2013, of the sandpaper, for it was his debut album, *The Return Of The Durutti Column*, that had this unusual sleeve. Throughout his career, Reilly has often pointed out his own perceived shortcomings; he is not part of the preening public sloganeering favoured by the Situationists. 'I can't understand why anyone would want to spend two hours in a smoky club watching us,' he has said. 'I can't just see why they don't get bored stiff. I know I would. We are completely self-indulgent, really. No compromise. I think that's why people tend to like us … but all our records are shit, really. Unlistenable shit.'

Reilly cuts a complicated figure. Physical and mental health problems have beset his entire life. 'I first felt funny, I first felt odd, at fifteen,' he once said. 'At that age, I didn't know what it was. I just knew I didn't want to play football with my mates. I finished with the girlfriend that I had. Nothing was good, nothing. Everything was bad.' The death of his father, expulsion from school, domestic violence from his brother, and his own depression snowballed; while still in his mid-teens, he was sleeping rough and had become involved in Manchester's gun culture. 'When you don't care about yourself, you're dangerous,' he said. One morning, seeing no way out, he put a loaded gun in his mouth. Only a jammed trigger prevented his suicide.

If anyone knew anything about Reilly, beyond the personal difficulties and tiny physical frame, it was that he was a precocious and idiosyncratic guitar talent. Although his first instrument was the piano (also played by his father), the guitar clicked with him after he heard the 1963 instrumental hit 'Maria Elena' by Los Indios Tabajaras; he took it up from that point on. Reilly has never followed the easy route to anything, and one of his first public musical endevours now seems especially brave: a guitar/flute duo employing unusual time signatures that he took around Greater Manchester's rough working men's clubs and local talent shows.

'Those gigs taught me so much, because we played to people who were more accustomed to seeing people singing Frank Sinatra songs very badly,' he later said. 'In a sense, that defined my musical stance, and possibly the stance of Factory later on, because I always believed that people would accept a far more diverse music form than they would normally come in contact with.' The energy of punk then ushered Reilly into the band Ed Banger & The Nosebleeds, who released one derivative single, 'Ain't Bin To No Music School', engaged in bitter and violent rivalries with other Manchester punks, and left a clutch of chaotic gigs in their wake.

Initially, The Durutti Column—the name, again, via Tony Wilson's Situationism fetish—was a larger collective; Reilly was the lynchpin, but not its only member. Vocalists came and went. 'I distinctly remember making a telephone call to the singer [Phil Rainford] and being incredibly rude to him. I mean really, really, really horribly rude to him,' Reilly said. Another singer—Colin Sharp, who appeared on The Durutti Column's vinyl debut on the EP *A Factory Sample*—didn't last much longer. 'Dreadful pretentious and portentous lyrics, which bore no resemblance to anything I felt or wanted to say,' Reilly later said of the Sharp tracks. 'Complete and total rubbish, and not me, more importantly. I don't even see them as my work at all. I disowned them.'

'I thought, who needs a fucking band anyway?' Tony Wilson said. 'Vini is the purest talent I had ever come across … why not develop that talent? Why should Durutti Column be anyone other than Vini?' And so it came to pass. Reilly teamed up with Martin Hannett for what turned out to be a fractious three days in 1979.

'I'll never forget the way that Martin was totally impervious to my, let's say, extreme behaviour,' Reilly has said. 'And I was extreme … I was completely out of control, totally suicidal, totally stressed out, depressed, and he just didn't seem to notice. I sat in a chair for two whole days and just screamed and screamed at him while he was playing with synthesizers … spending three hours getting one sound. I mean, he was under intoxication too, so it was all pretty strange. But he just occasionally made comments like, "Well, that's a bit extreme Vini. I think you are being a bit unreasonable there."'

The Return Of The Durutti Column was the first of a dizzying number of recordings from Reilly. His guitar playing is technically innovative and undeniably a thing of beauty, yet more than that, his restraint is so extreme it easily ticks back over into a simmering ferocity. This, too, is an emotional effect found in some of the most powerful post-rock works—lending a savage quality to delicacy—and Reilly was the first to truly pioneer it. Reilly's intricate guitar masked but never completely buried the vicious desperation of The Durutti Column. 'There's definitely a connection between my illness, whatever that is, and my music,' he said in 1989. 'Because I'm often ill, I spend maybe twelve hours a day alone in my room. When life's like that, you go inside yourself.'

While Vini Reilly nurtured his solipsism, another recent ex-punk was finding new friends, allies and inspirations. 'This was the first letter ever that wasn't drooling praise or condemning us,' John Lydon wrote to a fan in the late 1970s, who had asked Lydon for some reggae recommendations. 'Ask for anything out at present by these. None of them ever keep the same label for very long.' Lydon's list was extensive, featuring such obscure artists as Carol Kalphat, Blood Relatives, and Ranking Caretaker. His knowledge was so voluminous that Richard Branson, wanting to add some reggae signings to Virgin, sent Lydon on a scouting trip to Jamaica. 'Reggae was the only other radical music [alongside punk] that was completely underground and not played on the radio,' Lydon wrote in 1993. 'It wasn't played on the air until I did that appearance on *The Tommy Vance Show* on Capital. Then suddenly you'd get Joe Strummer and The Clash say, We always loved reggae.

But those fucks never did. They were never brought up with it the same way I was.'

Serious aficionados like Lydon were increasingly drawn to a subgenre of reggae: dub. 'The technique of dub may well be the most interesting new abstract concept to appear in modern music since Ornette Coleman undermined the dictatorship of Western harmony about two decades ago,' Richard Williams wrote in 1976, in a *Melody Maker* piece explaining the new sound. There was certainly plenty of material for journalists to theorise about, as well as for everyone else to groove on. Dub had its roots in the sixties; reggae DJs would toast, fading tracks in and out and conjuring up spontaneous verse or abstract stutters over the top. This principle migrated into the studio, where producers like King Tubby and Lee 'Scratch' Perry would divest a tune of everything bar drums and bass, then re-add chunks of the original, having subjected it to various effects and modifications. The result was a disorientating yet hypnotic smorgasbord of echoes, distortions, vocal bleats, and swimming instruments. As sounds enter and leave like guests at a party, the effect on the listener is to open up a cavernous yet porous and unpredictable space in the brain.

Lee Perry, like Can, was obsessed with the studio and its reanimation qualities. 'The studio must be like a living thing,' he has said. 'The machine must be live and intelligent. Then I put my mind into the machine by sending it through the controls and the knobs or into the jack panel. The jack panel is the brain itself, so you've got to patch up the brain and make the brain a living man, but the brain can take what you're sending into it and live.'

Dub proved to be a natural nomad, and its influence was soon felt beyond reggae. Singer-songwriter John Martyn, a pioneer of the delay guitar effect, used it subtly on 'Small Hours', from 1977. Recorded following a trip to Jamaica, during which Martyn jammed and chatted with Lee Perry, Burning Spear, and Max Romeo, 'Small Hours' is lengthy and ambient, recorded on a farm under the influence of opium, with sounds of the lake swirling and geese rambling. In New York, Tom Moulton and Walter Gibbons hollowed out disco with dub effects, reconstructing its frippery and reclaiming the dance floor for the outsiders. There was an obvious parallel between a disco 'remix' and a dub 'version'. And in West Germany, Conny Plank—producer and engineer to Neu!, Kraftwerk, Can, and Cluster—admired dub and studied its techniques. Because dub was steeped in a no-rules musical hedonism, it's easy to understand why it echoed well for an artistic vanguard, offering a refreshing freedom at a time when other aspects of the genre could easily harden into caricature.

Few felt more caricatured than John Lydon following the breakup of the Sex Pistols in 1978. 'I'd opened up an entire new genre and way of viewing music,' a humble Lydon reflected in 2014, about punk, 'and what happened when the door was opened? In walked all the flotsam and jetsam, who were very proud of being stupid.' Sardonically fusing a Muriel Spark novel about a narcissistic actress with the idea of a multimedia corporation, this new project was named Public Image Ltd. As well as Lydon, it comprised Jah Wobble on bass, Keith Levene on guitar, and Jim Walker on drums (chosen by Lydon because 'he sounds like Can's drummer. All double beats'). Although Lydon might have felt the burden of his celebrity at the start of PiL, it did ensure attention for the band.

'We used to fuck about with graphic equalizers and customised bass bins, and experiment with putting rock records through the system to see how far you could take the low end,' Wobble has said. 'I loved reggae, the bass line moving around the drumbeat, which you didn't get much in rock music. Rhythm was always more important to me than melody or harmony.' From the off, the combination of characters and abilities in PiL, uneasily united by their interest in dub, eschewed the traditionalism of punk, and stylized themselves as anti-rock.

Virgin Records apparently did not like their debut single, 'Public Image', at first. 'We mixed it to our own requirements,' Lydon said in 1978. 'Then Virgin tried to change it with a special letter to the factory. The complaint was that you couldn't hear the words on the first hearing and that the bass was too heavy.'

The label was also aghast at 'Fodderstompf', nearly eight minutes of dubby punk disco over which the band jabbered nonsense and freely admitted that the track was only there to pad out the debut album, *Public Image: First Issue*. 'They all slagged [*First Issue*],' said Levene, 'because it was self-indulgent, non-simplistic, and non-rock'n'roll. Those are all good points. But that's the kind of music we intend to make.'

Nevertheless, 'Public Image' was a hit, and Virgin kept the faith with PiL; good for them, because it was not the single but 'Fodderstompf' and another track on *First Issue*, 'Theme', that would provide the direction of the next PiL album. But first came another single, 'Death Disco', which combined Lydon's paroxysm of grief at the passing of his mother with Wobble's pummelling bassline and Levene's barbarous re-interpretation of 'Swan Lake'. The twelve-inch took these concepts even further, with a longer '½ Mix' of 'Death Disco' and a new, instrumental version of 'Fodderstompf' (which, without its comedy vocals, turned into an astral workout).

Soon, news of a new PiL album—apparently three twelve-inch singles housed in a cross between a film canister and a biscuit tin—began to leak out. *Metal Box* was released in late 1979, and, when asked what went into its composition, Lydon claimed, 'We take a silly tune and strip it bare and start again.' There were no proper rehearsals before they entered the studio, and many of the tracks were from first or second takes; Lydon said *Metal Box* was about 'compromising the vocal presence.' It emphasises the bass and deliberately muffles the vocals, taking the principles of dub but not relying on its obvious techniques. 'Careering', 'Poptones', 'Chant', 'Graveyard'; *Metal Box*'s multiple highlights might have had distant ancestors in rock, but they have been metamorphosed so far from it that the effect is staggering. 'The idea of [*Metal Box*] was, it would numb you, absolutely flatten your resistance, just wear you out with its omnipresence,' Lydon wrote in 2014. 'I think we got there.'

Although PiL developed musically far more than most others in a very short space of time, it was at the expense of their conceptual ambitions. Plans for PiL to be 'a limited company [that has] access to other things, like video and electronics, and hi-fi and books and painting and, yes, even the theatre' were (according to Lydon) 'piss-arsed about [with] for far too long'; despite good intentions, such grand schemes never properly hit the runway. It was left for others to take this up; notably ZTT, the label founded by Paul Morley and Trevor Horn in 1983, with its communiqués, manifestos, and ample twelve-inch remixes. This enterprising New Pop era—of *Who's Afraid Of The Art Of Noise*, of Frankie Goes To Hollywood's side-long epic 'Welcome To The Pleasuredome', of The Human League and their offshoots—would dominate the childhoods of many British post-rock artists. Morley even used 'post rock' to describe The Human League's *Dare* in 1981.

Green Gartside of Scritti Politti was another key New Pop figure. Cerebral and articulate, he was upfront about his interest in deconstruction (even naming a 1982 song 'Jacques Derrida'). 'All sorts of garbage still surrounds the way most people think about musicians and their work,' he said in 1991. 'I mean, that's why I got out of the indie stuff that I started doing and moved towards the now infamous saccharine pop. It was a deconstructive turn on what was thought to be important and precious about artists.'

Bringing punk, dub space, anti-hierarchy, and textural guitar together, while looking forward to post-rock in the strongest way yet, was the band Dif Juz. One member used to be in Duran Duran; another had auditioned for PiL. 'People couldn't categorise us,' says drummer Richie Thomas. 'It's because it was instrumental music, and it wasn't really at the forefront of people's thinking.'

'Back then, we all thought everything had been said with the punk movement, and we'd just be going over old ground,' says bassist Gary Bromley. 'Everybody else, all these vocalists, they wanted to be the front person, the leader of the band. And we didn't want any leaders in the band.'

Dif Juz grew from the West London punk circuit. Alan Curtis, a guitarist, was in London Pride. 'I watched a gig that London Pride did and afterward, in the toilet, I told the singer that their drummer was crap,' says Thomas, whose own punk band was called The Brats. 'I was taking the piss, but I ended up playing with them.' Meanwhile, the fifteen-year-old Gary Bromley, a self-confessed Sid Vicious clone, also had a band, and could only play the open E string on his bass.

'A couple of years went on, and Public Image's first album came out,' Bromley says. 'I heard Jah Wobble. And when I heard Jah Wobble, it was … wow. He was the first white dude I knew of that played with a reggae sound and a reggae feel.' Inspired, Bromley began to take his bass playing seriously, keen to understand what Wobble did to get that spacious dub noise.

'I auditioned for PiL by accident,' says Thomas. 'I was about fourteen. We were just in the King's Road one day, and there was this Scottish guy who said, Any of you lot drummers? My mate said, He is, and he's really good.' It turned out that PiL were scouting for a new drummer, following the departure of Jim Walker. Thomas went around to PiL's base, Gunter Grove in Chelsea. 'I kept putting my foot in it all afternoon. I got hot and took my jumper off, and I've got the 'Boredom' and 'Nowhere' buses, from the back of the 'Pretty Vacant' sleeve, on my T-shirt. And John Lydon smiled like a rat. He loved it.'

Thomas auditioned by playing 'Public Image'; he was shown how to drum 'Theme' by Keith Levene, heard an early version of 'Death Disco' (which he didn't like), and ate spaghetti hoops with Lydon's brother. 'I never got the job,' he says, 'but it did have a big impact on me. It sowed a seed that I should try and do something.' Later, Thomas found out that PiL had warmed to the teenage drummer but were concerned that his age would rule out an American visa. (The gig eventually went to Martin Atkins, who played on *Metal Box*.)

Meanwhile, Curtis left London and London Pride for Birmingham and a band that would eventually prove one of the most successful New Pop acts of all, Duran Duran. At this time, they were pre-fame, even pre-Simon Le Bon; Curtis's tenure was short, but he was apparently involved with writing an early song, 'Late Bar', which ended up as the B-side to Duran Duran's first single, 'Planet Earth'. The crunch came when new management entered the picture. 'I remember Alan telling me that the managers would come to rehearsals with clothes, boiler suits for the band, saying, We've got some gear for you guys, get into this,' remembers Richie Thomas. 'And they'd be sitting there in rehearsals, saying to Alan, *Can you move?* Alan didn't move. Alan didn't like all that. In the end, they had a falling out, and he said, If you want to spend your money, buy me a decent amp and some decent leads so I can play music, instead of fucking asking me to prance around in a boiler suit.'

Alan Curtis came back to London and started playing with his brother, Dave Curtis (also a guitarist), and Thomas. He told Gary Bromley, who he knew from the punk scene, that he now had a new band. 'You could define it, and say Alan was the lead guitarist and Dave was rhythm guitarist, but Dave's syncopated way of playing was so unusual that you *couldn't* define it by that,' says Thomas. 'Dave was the academic. Alan was really, really sharp. Intelligent, but punk with it. Alan was a character on the guitar. Dave was subtle with the textures he'd create. The two of them together—being brothers, there's arguments, but there's telepathy.'

Dif Juz created music communally from scratch to try and preserve as much instinct as possible. 'We rehearsed every Sunday. Someone would be skinning up somewhere, and we'd jam,' he says. 'We'd play with each others' instruments a bit. I'd play the bass. Alan was on drums—he liked a bit of drumming. I was the youngest, the kid. The nuisance.'

'We went around a few record labels,' says Bromley, 'but they all said, basically, you need a singer. We didn't think so.' Eventually, it was 4AD, a new label founded by Ivo Watts-Russell and Peter Kent, who signed them, initially for a one-off EP, *Huremics*, released in 1981. As well as punk and post-punk, *Huremics* showed the depth of the reggae influence on Dif Juz. The group would pore over new dub acetates, buying, borrowing, or taping them from friends. Thomas also says he was keen on Indian music, especially Ravi Shankar and Ali Akbar Khan.

'We were a bit angry, a bit pissed off with what was going on,' Thomas says of the palpable musical tension in *Huremics* and its follow-up EP, *Vibrating Air*. 'It was a way for us to express ourselves. But it's not so obvious when you haven't got someone singing about it. I really believed that musicians, and people who were artistic, had a fucking duty to make people think.' This tension spilled over into arguments with 4AD; Dif Juz sensed they fell outside of Watts-Russell's inner circle, so released their next two projects, the short album *Who Says So*, and a cassette, *Time Clock Turn Back*, away from the label.

But they returned to 4AD, having befriended the Cocteau Twins. 'They championed us a bit,' says Thomas. 'They invited us to do a tour with them, and we went all around Europe.' Elizabeth Fraser sang on the Dif Juz track 'Love Insane', and Thomas contributed saxophone and tabla to the Cocteaus' 1986 album *Victorialand*. 'They really fucking knew how to party,' he says. 'Don't let the music fool you. You'd think it's a cup of mint tea and early to bed. No chance. Fucking hell, we had some good nights with those guys.'

There was also a one-off collaboration with Lee Perry. 'I can't express to you how much we were totally mystified by Lee Perry,' says Thomas. 'I don't know anyone else who's had the same kind of influence on me, musically. A friend of mine called me, and said, Do you know that Lee Perry is round at Sandra's place? And I'm like, oh, fuck off, don't talk shit. So I went round, and he walked in, and I'm like, *fuck* me, it's Lee Perry.'

Thomas played Perry *Who Says So*, 'And he went, What this? and I said, This is the band I'm in. And he went, I like it! Let's get together! Let's play!' 4AD organised a studio; Perry and Dif Juz recorded five or six tracks, including a reworking of Bob Dylan's 'The Mighty Quinn' as 'The Mighty Scratch'. But Watts-Russell and Dave Curtis were not keen on the end product, and it was never released.

For the 1985 album *Extractions*, there was a very different energy. 'It was a conscious decision to change the sound,' says Bromley. 'They wanted to go away from the dubbier aspects, into more guitar-orientated sounds, more complicated, with more changes in it. I studied the bass more, and I was studying eight hours a day, every day, in my room. I would plan everything out; I studied scales, I learned to read music. I played for forty-five minutes at a time, then I would take a break for fifteen, and get back to it. And I did that all in that time, because they were my mates, and I'd do anything for them. But I wanted them to get what they wanted, and I wanted them to be fulfilled with what they wanted to be fulfilled with.'

Thomas is harsher. 'A lot of stuff we did at rehearsal was so much better than what we ever released on record,' he says. '*Extractions* ... it's OK. It sounds like its coming from half a mile down the road. That fucking saxophone track ["Crosswinds"], I hate that.' Nevertheless, *Extractions* hit a mood that would certainly emerge later for others. It was a stake in the ground that was largely ignored at the time; meanwhile, the group itself began to crumble.

'A lot of stuff brings up pain,' says Bromley. 'There's a lot of pain for me attached to Dif Juz. I was diagnosed with mental illness when I was twenty-one. That, basically, was one of the hardest things for me, trying to relate to the world outside. There was a statement made that the reason why I left the band was that they were upset with me because I was forgetting my bass lines. That wasn't true. I just couldn't be bothered with them.'

'You could see him disintegrating into himself,' says Thomas, of Bromley at this time. 'You could see that he felt he was letting us down. So we got Scott [Rodger] in to do the tour. It's more or less impossible for someone to come into a four-piece instrumental thing. But he learnt the tracks, he was very professional.' Dif Juz were tired and missing Bromley, however, and after another record (the half-compilation, half-new *Out Of The Trees*) they embarked upon a European tour with the Cocteau Twins; that's when things finally cracked. 'It wasn't very healthy,' Thomas says. 'They [the promoters] didn't even want to supply us with food. We were stealing all the breakfast stuff, and having that for lunch. When we came back for the last night at the Kilburn National, the week after that Dave went into hospital for a serious operation. And, basically, he got very disillusioned and said, "I don't want to do this anymore." I think Ivo offered Dave a solo project, which put the nail in the coffin for us.' As 1987 arrived, Dif Juz ceased.

Even more obscure than Dif Juz is the Cornish band Chorchazade, who provide a tense bridge between unruly post-punk and something more textural. 'It was pretty depressing at that time to be a sixteen-year-old boy living in a white bungalow by the sea with his mum and dad,' says Noel Lane, one of the founders of Chorchazade. Huddling together with school friends Chris Williams and Keith Bailey, he formed a punk band: The Panic. 'We went to the Winter Gardens every week. We saw The Damned, The Adverts, The Cortinas, Wire, The Lurkers, and the Sex Pistols. They were all older than us, pale and terrifying, like they'd come from another world. On November 8th, 1977, The Panic did our first, and our last, proper gig.' Bunking off school the next day to return a bass speaker used the night before, the teenagers were caught by the truancy police and told they'd have to leave school if they played any more 'punk' gigs. Lane walked out anyway.

'I formed a group called An Alarm with my brother and his friends, and did my best to come up with music that was different to what the other local groups were doing,' says Lane. 'I was very small-minded about this. I was the singer and songwriter now. I avoided listening to current music and didn't go to any more gigs. If the popular local groups wore tight jeans, we'd wear baggy grey suit trousers, previously owned by old egg-shaped men. They wore cowboy boots and leather jackets, so we wore tweed blazers and tennis pumps. If they were doing fast music we'd do slow music. If they were singing about politics or girls, I'd sing about clouds and yoghurt.' They had nowhere to rehearse apart from the field behind the Lane house, with Noel's brother drumming on plastic food containers.

After An Alarm finished, Lane went up to Huddersfield, where he formed a Fall-obsessed group called Anne Gwirder, with whom he switched to the bass guitar. 'Nobody else wanted to play it,' he says, 'and there were three of them and only one of me, [and] the lead guitarist didn't really like my songs and wouldn't play on them. Hardly anybody came to the gigs, and most of them didn't like what we were doing, so I thought I was still on the right track. If nobody liked the music we were playing, that just proved that it was good, because trendy stupid people liked a load of shit, right?'

The band broke up, and Lane started making quiet, carefully arranged music for keyboard and guitar with Anne Gwirder's drummer,

Clive Shead. Meanwhile, Keith Bailey, now drumming in John Peel favourites Tools You Can Trust, got back in touch with his old friends Lane and Williams, and the three—along with another guitarist, Julian Hunt, decided to form a new band, based in Bristol.

'When I heard Noel's songs I thought I'd found a homegrown genius, to be honest,' says Hunt. 'He used to pick songs out of the air. He'd have these slightly impenetrable lyrics. He was very singular, and he didn't write by fashion or taste or anything. I'd never met anyone who was so outside the bubble, so formed in his own musical world.' Lane called the band Chorchazade in imitation of a collective noun for birds.

Chorchazade, from the beginning, styled themselves as 'anti-rock'. 'We weren't playing power chords and that sort of thing,' Hunt says. 'Chris created landscapes. He developed this thing, on the early songs, of two B strings on the guitar, because he broke the E string and he didn't have any E strings, so he tuned it to two Bs. He used to stick matchsticks in the guitars.' This was combined with Bailey's jazz-influenced drumming and an unamplified composing technique (they wanted it as hushed as possible, so all the members removed their shoes, too). What came out was first captured on the 1985 twelve-inch EP *Crackle And Corkette* and its lead track, 'Ahh You Are As Light As A Feather'.

Fragility, like a frosty spider's web, overlays the 1987 album *Made To Be Devoured*, while quiet-loud dichotomies only serve to enhance the record's vulnerability. Lane's shrouded lyrics came from awkwardness, their abstraction from self-consciousness. 'I watch the telly,' he says. 'That's when I started making sounds with my mouth instead of words, just rolling syllables around, saying the odd word or line here and there. I'd only really write real words on the night before we went into a studio, and I found it arduous and awful. I'd developed a kind of style to write with by then, but I hadn't got anything to write about. I'd been on the dole for ten years, living like a child.'

As well as the sound, the lowercase scrawled handwriting on the sleeve was later to become something of a post-rock shorthand; their audience—'almost totally made up of ugly, short, socially inept, bespectacled young men,' says Lane—would fit another post-rock stereotype.

Chorchazade played with Sonic Youth in Bristol, and when they did get press, they were often compared to the New York group. 'You have to put up with a lot of that,' says Lane. 'You're ripping off this, or that, or things you've never even heard of. Even your best friends do it. People in other groups make a full-time hobby of it. The world is always conspiring to crush your spirit.

'Then we fell out,' he continues. 'My confidence had gone, and it never did come back. The places we played in were either pubs or small gloomy clubs. We lost money every time we played. Apart from cider and beer there were no rock and roll excesses, and a troop of wandering Benedictine lepers probably had more fun than we did. It was all, of course, quite wonderful. We wanted to play every night. It was the only thing that really mattered.'

'Chorchazade, they were failures, really,' says David Callahan of Moonshake, who liked the band. 'They did very slow, ambient guitar music that has a lot of drones. They're fantastic, but no one heard them. They utterly preempted Slint.' (Rumour also has it that Steve Albini was a fan of Chorchazade's sole album.)

Between them, these artists racked up a number of features that post-rock would go on to use, abuse, develop—and deconstruct. But they tended to operate in a vacuum; there wasn't a geographical unity, or an obvious linear progression of ideas. This wasn't so true for a place with a long and proud history of nurturing outsiders: New York.

CHAPTER TWO

bring the noise

'There was no placation.' SALLY YOUNG, UT

In 1989, the British TV arts institution *The South Bank Show* presented a specially commissioned documentary by filmmaker Charles Atlas called *Put Blood In The Music*. 'The film [is] very much a New York artifact,' the host, Melvyn Bragg, said in his preamble. 'You may think that its style and pace reflect the frenetic quality, and the self-consciousness, of that music, and the city itself.'

'I don't know if the programme's exactly *efficient* as an introduction to the New York scene,' Lee Ranaldo said at the time. 'There's no narrative to this programme. Which is why I think we come over in the film pretty well. It's rooted in a fractured aesthetic similar to our own.'

Sonic Youth and John Zorn are the twin focal points of *Put Blood In The Music*. Between performance snippets and cryptic talking heads, Sonic Youth—Ranaldo, Kim Gordon, Thurston Moore, Steve Shelley—speak about the development of their sound. 'We didn't really own any equipment,' says Moore, as he upends his guitar. 'We borrowed a couple of guitars from a friend of ours. And they were really, really, really, really, really, really, *really* crummy guitars, and the only way they sounded good is if we jammed screwdrivers under the neck and detuned 'em a certain way, blah blah blah, rewired 'em, and gutted them out. Such as this guitar *here*,' he chuckles. 'So we started writing songs like that.'

Lee Ranaldo picks up the thread. 'That was one of the reasons why we evolved into having so many guitars,' he says in the film, 'because some guitars that we had early on were only useful for one kind of a thing. You'd string it up a certain way, and you'd get one good thing to come out of it, and so we'd write a song around that guitar. And for the next song we'd pick up a different guitar and figure out what it was good for, and make a song out of it. At this point it's kind of evolved into *really* different tunings for each pair of guitars, or whatever.'

Sonic Youth and their array of guitars were, eventually, the most famous expression of a ten-year trend in the 80s New York underground: to take the rock out of rock. (Sonic Youth would often slip it back again, especially toward the very end of the decade but—for now—rock held a very shifty place in their music.) They didn't just do so on a superficial level: making guitars faster, slower, louder, fiddling with tunings and effects, and so on. Instead—and although Sonic Youth employed all of these techniques—their ambitions had a deeper root. It was about their attitude to the guitar itself. They took out its usual 'rock' purpose: it wasn't for riffing, it wasn't for soloing, and it wasn't for showboating. Sonic Youth's guitars were contemporaneous with, and surely influenced by, the way the city's hip-hop outbreak was using a mash of sounds, jarring sentiments, and expressing a political, if sometimes diffuse, rage. Once rock was shaken by dissonance, collage, and harsh cacophony, it undermined certainties and created space for a whole load of other bandits to wander in.

'It was a small, dense scene,' says Mimi Goese of Hugo Largo. 'So much of it was born out of proximity, immediacy, and grit.' It was no coincidence that it occured in New York with its 'loud, violent, non-stop energy'—well put by Lydia Lunch, who also appeared in *Put Blood In The Music*. For New Yorkers, such conceits were in a fairly straight line from the past. Succeeding The Velvet Underground as the city's premier uncomfortable band was Suicide.

'New York is the grandest shit scene of all time,' the group's Alan Vega said in 1976. 'It's like the Titanic a thousand times over; just sinking away, but it's beautiful.' Suicide melded electronics, minimalism, and the original hoodlum element from rock'n'roll. Like Brian Eno, Vega had studied radical art techniques, and he became involved in direct action to drag museums away from economic conservatism and reliance on dead white European males. Onstage with Suicide, Vega would use his body and a very real sense of threat in performance. 'I get really heavy welts on my leg, bruises, and the whole trip,' he once said. 'It does a three-day number. It goes from red to blue to better. See the cuts on the face?' His heavy, threatening but self-lacerating attitude was a key precursor to a short, abrasive jag in musical history at the end of the 1970s: No Wave.

'We weren't really playing anything as much as hacking away at our instruments,' John Lurie of The Lounge Lizards later said. 'It was just sticking your tongue out at everything.' The hacking at instruments was literal in the case of Lydia Lunch of Teenage Jesus & The Jerks. She rejected playing chords on her guitar, instead rubbing knives and broken bottles on the strings. These objects looked *and* sounded savage onstage, and were characteristic of the confrontational performance art element of No Wave. It had a direct relationship to Suicide, The Velvet Underground, Yoko Ono, and Iggy Pop.

The scene attracted the attention of Brian Eno, who cloaked the No Wavers in one of his more condescending theories: research bands. 'You're glad someone's done it,' he said in 1990, 'but you don't necessarily want to listen to it.' Affecting the pose of an imperial explorer capturing a rare bloom, in 1979 Eno brought together four bands for his compilation *No New York*—The Contortions, Teenage Jesus & The Jerks, Mars, and DNA.

'We very deliberately kept the *No New York* record to just those bands,' claimed Arto Lindsay of DNA. 'We thought it would make sense, and it was a little bit of a turf thing. We convinced Eno that Glenn Branca's band shouldn't be on the record.' Branca's band was Theoretical Girls, also featuring Jeffrey Lohn, Margaret DeWys, and Wharton Tiers, and Branca would later recall a rumour circulating at the time that they had written a song about Eno. ('We didn't,' he said, 'but when he heard "Fuck Yourself" he might've thought that was about him.')

Branca had played with Rhys Chatham, who was then in charge of the music programme at an art and performance space in SoHo, the Kitchen. There was something of a gap between the arty and the scuzzy ends of No Wave, and Chatham—Juilliard-trained, and a former student of La Monte Young and the minimalist electronica pioneer Morton Subotnick—was definitely part of the former. But Chatham was also fascinated by rock music, especially the no-frills, Ramones kind of rock music. Chatham's band The Gynacologists, like Theoretical Girls, had been excluded from *No New York* for being on the wrong side of arty (or, at least, on the wrong side of Arto).

'After working pretty much as a rock musician in various groups for about a year,' Chatham said in 1999, 'I felt I was ready to incorporate everything I was as a musician in a rock context, including my experience as a composer and a piano tuner.' The result was 'Guitar Trio', which Chatham composed in early 1977. 'It was for three electric guitars in special tunings, whose vocabulary consisted entirely of the overtones being generated by playing one chord on the guitar. It was an E minor 7. It was the first piece I made which I felt broke past my teachers and really reflected my individuality as a musician and composer.'

Overtones—sounds heard above a fundamental note—could form thick clouds above a piece of music, and, in the case of 'Guitar Trio', provide unique audience experiences. 'Depending on where you are sitting in the room, each listener literally hears something different,' Chatham said. 'It's to do with the varying air pressure levels in the room one plays in.' 'Guitar Trio' and Chatham's 1982 piece 'Die Donnergötter' are both landmarks of rock classicism, punkishly stripped of the pomposity that dogged other attempts at the same.

Glenn Branca, part of Chatham's 'Guitar Trio', soon made important non-rock guitar statements of his own. 'I had no desire whatsoever to start a commercial rock band,' he said. 'I had no interest at all in going on tour for a year, playing a set every other day, and getting into that whole mentality. None of us were doing it for the money. There wasn't any, and there was never going to be any.' Branca had moved to New York in 1976 from Boston, where he had co-founded the experimental thespian collective The Bastard Theatre. As provoking as the name suggested, Branca's ideas, and the style in which they were presented, would find a primed audience in New York.

After Theoretical Girls folded, Branca formed The Static with Barbara Ess and Christine Hahn. Like Theoretical Girls, The Static were shortlived, but toward the end of their life, Branca composed his first key piece, 'The Spectacular Commodity', for a dance performance.

'When I first started doing the experimental stuff, I still saw it very much in the context of rock music,' he said. 'Because I still loved rock, and I still thought there was so much more that I could do with rock. You could still take the guitar and make it more, without using any digital delay, and reverb, any effects. You could still take it exactly as it was used in 1958, and go somewhere else with it.'

Branca took himself and another three guitarists on tour in 1980, using the same gauge of strings on all the guitars and tuning them all to the same note; he also used volume *as part of composition itself.* The result was the sound of guitars fighting one another to reach the skies, creating a fug of overtones searching for elusive climaxes. And it still retained the primitive bite of No Wave. An album, *The Ascension*, was recorded during this tour and stands as a permanent brutalist monument to Branca's work at this time.

In 1982, John Cage compared Branca's music to fascism. 'I felt negatively about what seemed to be the political implications. I wouldn't want to live in a society like that,' he said. 'It is not a shepherd taking care of his sheep, but a leader insisting people agree with him.'

Branca did always seem a different sort of 'leader' to Rhys Chatham. An experience in the 1970s, while he was playing with Charlemagne Palestine and Tony Conrad, had led Chatham to question the *Il Duce* aura that composers could exploit. 'One concert we did lasted ten hours,' Chatham said in 1999. 'Charlemagne was singing in his Balinese style. Tony played violin and I played harmonium and transverse flute. It was heady stuff and had a profound influence on my later work. It was through my work with them that I broke out of the idea of a composer as a kind of dictator who tells musicians what to do and bosses them around.'

Branca and Chatham crowded the 'rock' out of their guitar immensity, filling any gaps to create overpowering sound. They were also a living challenge to the notion that noise came from a lack of ability; they brought the idea foursquare into New York punk that talent and schooling could *cause* the roughness, the distress. Moreover, between them, Branca and Chatham provided practical training grounds in their ensembles for unconventional guitarists of all hues.

Lee Ranaldo was part of Branca's band on that 1980 tour, and also on *The Ascension*; Kim Gordon had played in a whirlwind art-project band, Introjection, with Branca's Static bandmate, Christine Hahn. Given these ties, and the fact that all of Sonic Youth were Branca fans anyway, it's no surprise that they released their initial, self-titled mini-album on Branca's Neutral label in 1981. In her memoir, Gordon recalls that they asked the engineer to give it a PiL sound; Bob Bert, soon to join the band briefly as drummer, thought that *Sonic Youth* sounded like *Metal Box*, but better.

'The way the band composed songs was pretty much always the same,' Gordon writes. 'Thurston or Lee would usually sing the poppy, more melodic things that came out of all of us playing together, and rearranging until everything gelled. My voice has always had a fairly limited range, and when you're writing a melody, you tend to write it for your own voice. Lee, on the other hand, usually brought in songs that were complete and ready to go.' Ranaldo and Moore, despite their experience, would often defer to the greener Gordon; her fresh ideas, her spare and minimal style, and her art-world ties were all intrinsic to this period.

Confusion Is Sex, released in 1983, is far more nerve-shredding than *Sonic Youth*. With guitars sounding like dolorous bells and Gordon's bass rumbling away, the band had started to explore their treated guitars and alternate tunings in earnest; for 'The World Looks Red', Moore wedged a broken drumstick in his strings, and it sounds as much like an organ in a pagan temple as it does a guitar.

Sonic Youth's guitars were so dilapidated that they couldn't cope with regular tunings anyway, and there was a freedom in that. 'It gave us an advantage that we didn't have to play by the rules of the game,' Ranaldo has said. 'Which was the main thing we were looking for.' As they burned through instruments, their friends would give them old, busted guitars for their arsenal, knowing they'd be put to good use. Tuning up became part of the Sonic Youth live experience; Moore and Ranaldo would come out before the set began, with their guitar hoard, methodically preparing each one. 'It opened up to the audience this notion of what we were all about,' Ranaldo said. 'They'd see all the guitars and the fact that they were all differently tuned. I always thought it was a cool prelude to the beginning of the set.'

The short, gamelan-influenced instrumental 'Lee Is Free' was a Ranaldo tape loop, and 'Freezer Burn' originated from the actual sound of a refrigerator at a local deli. 'Because of our experience with Chatham and Branca, we got a good idea what could work musically,' Ranaldo said in 1988. 'Obviously it's an influence on how we work. But on the first LP, *Confusion Is Sex*, we were still using modal tuning and people think of that as the noisiest. Not until later did we think, ugh, this tuning sounds horrible, but it sounds fine in this context.'

Confusion Is Sex established Sonic Youth as a meeting point between visceral hardcore and something more artistic, sliding very close to pretension but not crossing it. This coincided with the haphazard way it was recorded, with entire sessions wiped by spilled drinks and magnet mishaps.

'Next to our friends the Swans, who were very loud and had a percussionist who pounded metal,' Kim Gordon wrote in 1988, 'we were total wimps.' In 1982, the two bands went on tour together, some of which is preserved on the sound-collage cassette *Sonic Death: Sonic Youth Live*. 'It was raining and sad as hell, and the headlining Swans played their set to six jeering cowboys,' she added. 'Mike Gira, the leader of Swans, introduced a song amid giggles and chants for "Freebird" by saying, "This next song is about getting butt-fucked by a cop."'

Early Swans brought new meaning to the word 'challenging'. Their music was chest-crushing, and certainly—like Branca—employed volume as a key part of composition, but at such a slow pace that it became less a thunderstorm and more a thumbscrew. Their lyrics were loaded with transgression, mutilation, power and exploitation, and lines were often repeated until any shred of humanity was completely expunged from them. Swans were an angry boil of a band: Lydia Lunch on slo-mo down a rusty razorblade.

'I thought the music, *especially* in its, quote, heavy days, was so incredibly, amazingly uplifting,' Gira said in 1999. 'It felt so *good*.'

Swans, too, had firm links to the Chatham/Branca axis. Gira learned bass from Chatham; both he and another early member, Dan Braun, played in Branca's band; and Swans' debut album, *Filth*, was released on Neutral.

'I started working out songs,' Gira recalled of the early days. 'I used chords I made up and usually just stuck to one of them per song, hammering out rhythms, more like a drum than a bass.' Their first New York practice space was a windowless bunker in a former Pentecostal church, adorned with pictures of black snakes and a man on a meat hook. Apparently, one irate neighbour gifted the band a headless chicken in protest at the godless racket emanating from within. 'I just basically at first stuck to the idea of rhythm and sound, without much if any concern for melody or anything else except *rage*,' said Gira, 'and any power I could generate from volume and sound and words.'

Gira has talked of the effect of television on his approach, with its constructed reality and its indifferent flicker. He has also said that he wanted his lyrics to be blunt, almost pragmatic, with the dehumanising effect of advertising slogans. 'It just seems to me that whenever metaphor is used it comes out too poetic and it makes my stomach turn. So I take it out,' he said in 1986. 'I can't understand metaphor.

I guess it's hard to say why anybody's got the need to write like that. Myself, I have increasing difficulty writing lyrics. Each little eight-line thing takes me about a month. It starts off from writing just complete dreck and honing what I can out of it. It's never spontaneous, you know. It never flows out.' Swans removed rock's flexibility and gyration, not to mention its tease. Their sheer physicality was similar to that of dub, but it had none of dub's irresistible sass.

Gira later professed to hating No Wave, but like many of those within it, he had experience of performance art. Before moving to New York, he lived in Los Angeles and worked with Hermann Nitsch, whose *Orgies Mysterien Theater* explored many themes that would become dear to Swans' black heart. 'It was a long, extended performance—not really performances but more like rituals—that took place over four or five hours,' Gira said in 1997. '[Nitsch] would have a lamb's carcass, with each leg attached to a cable, strung across the room. Then a series of rituals would happen where young boys would come out on stretchers and blood and entrails would be poured through the carcass and onto the boys' bodies,' Gira has said.

Swans gig posters of this era came with the Gira quote 'I like the idea of standing in a room full of sledgehammers'. The album *Filth* doubled up on its bass and drums and featured Norman Westberg's annihilating guitar; when he wasn't drumming, Roli Mosimann bashed a metal table with a gaffer-taped metal strap (in the way that had made Kim Gordon feel wimpy). Tape loops of synthesized sounds and slowed-down noise ephemera added to the claustrophobia. The musical and lyrical themes were continued and intensified on 1984's *Cop* and the following EP, *Young God*, which contains the most infamous track of Swans' early career, 'Raping A Slave'. Each of these releases was colossal and felt unrepeatable; they were ugly, expressing a type of misery completely lacking in catharsis, and felt ten times longer than they actually were.

Live, they relished audience walkouts and Gira explored the duality of being both victim and oppressor, in a way analogous to Alan Vega's performances. Gira was into sensory obliteration and 'found total abjection to be for some reason desirable at the time. I thought it was my job as a performer to be as abject as possible'. On one occasion, he proved his point by licking the floor in front of the audience.

The intellectualism and corporeality of 1980s New York was to inspire British fans, and one of them, Paul Smith, started a label to release it. Blast First began in the summer of 1984, named after the early twentieth-century Vorticist literary magazine by Wyndham Lewis. 'It describes how England is kept mild by the warm winds of America, kept in a passive state when there's an impending war happening,' Smith said of the name. 'All that seemed to bear a relevance to putting out a record by an American band which was radical and seemed quite the opposite of passive.' This record was Sonic Youth's *Bad Moon Rising*.

'I wanted to play high-energy music and I wanted to destroy,' Thurston Moore said, 'but at the same time work on sound and whatever.' Immediately following *Confusion Is Sex* and the EP *Kill Yr Idols*, the 'destroy' part of the Sonic Youth equation was in the ascendant. The band would play weekly around New York, and 'killed those songs', according to Moore. 'It was getting to the point where it was much more physical, too, and much more violent, because that seemed like one way to take it, and so the music was getting really crazed, and we were getting totally insane, and it was getting to the point of overkill.'

Their next album, *Bad Moon Rising*, is the 'sound and whatever' half of the Sonic Youth equation, with the band exploring more of the guitar's intricacies as well as its impacts. It's an elemental album, heightening the vertigo of *Confusion Is Sex* but moving away from its bottle-in-the-face violence; the title deliberately harks back to the bitter demolition of hippie idealism as the 1960s ended. The inflamed jack-o'-lantern scarecrow on the cover gives a good sense of the Americana creepiness within and forms a sardonic counterpoint to the use of Lou Reed's *Metal Machine Music* as a background on 'Society Is A Hole'. Yet the band was always reluctant to discuss their specific motivations in public and, it seems, in private. 'We do not try to pinpoint what we do, we leave it open and rely on collective intuition to make it happen,' Ranaldo wrote in his diary, around the time of *Bad Moon Rising*'s release.

The mesmeric *EVOL* was next, and Sonic Youth now featured a bona fide hardcore kid: Steve Shelley, former drummer of The Crucifucks. There was more raga and hum with *EVOL*, its sound plusher, its songs strong, and its approach quietly confident. *EVOL*'s first completed song was also to become its centrepiece: 'Expressway To Yr Skull', aka 'Madonna, Sean And Me', aka 'The Crucifixion Of Sean Penn'. This was a languid yet expressive crescendo of drone, pulling bliss from bloodshed. Its deformed guitars act as guy ropes out of noise and point positively to post-rock's first proper wave.

EVOL is 'just fucking ... too much,' says Rudy Tambala of A.R. Kane. 'Absolutely too much. I still absolutely love that album, nothing can come close, and I won't listen to any of their other albums.' *EVOL* was an undoubted achievement, but it also lit a path Sonic Youth would increasingly follow. Although the vinyl edition ends with 'Expressway' and a locked groove, the CD release features a cute but throwaway bonus track, a version of Kim Fowley's 'Bubblegum'. Fowley's organ-led slice of lounge-y psychedelia was arch and knowing, and this cover is even more so. It had begun to feel as if Sonic Youth's more serious and horrifying sounds were embarrassing the band, and that they were losing their nerve to persist with them; this sense, along with a greater emphasis on the cult of celebrity, less dissonance, and the cleaner recording of *EVOL*, were all signs of the future for Sonic Youth. From this point on, lighter elements that could be taken as a joke, a simultaneous critique of and tribute to popular culture, or at least something more easily slotted into the regular alt-rock record racks, were as much a part of the Sonic Youth world as their adulterated guitar strings.

Swans, too, were calming down, although their idea of 'calm' was probably still most bands' idea of extreme din. The keyboardist and vocalist Jarboe joined in 1986, and she gave a different poise to the group. Lyrical themes widened to explore relationship dynamics that were something other than strictly exploitative or transactional; and Jarboe's strident yet melodic presence dissolved some of the previously unyielding sonic granite. On record, at least, later-decade Swans (and the Gira/Jarboe side project Skin) would even explore serenity, miles away from the barbed trenches of early 1980s New York. Live, however, they remained as pitiless as ever. Stories abounded of their gigs; in Edinburgh, it was reported that it took four men fourteen hours to set up and dismantle Swans' PA (and that, when the band soundchecked, the force of the noise knocked a doorman off his feet). At London's Town & Country Club, the manager had to pull the plug because the police had received so many complaints from the local community. 'They were phoning us as well,' the venue's manager told *Melody Maker*, 'but of course we couldn't hear them.'

In the mid-to-late 1980s, if Swans were popular with the British music press and related alternative tastemakers, then Sonic Youth were all but worshipped. Ranaldo cast a wry eye over this support. 'What it reinforced was the work ethic that American bands had,' he said, of this period of British attention. 'You'd play fifty shows in forty days, and it was really like punching a clock every day in terms of how much time and energy you were putting into it. You'd go to Europe and you'd meet the Mary Chain and they'd play like once every two months and there'd be a big riot and they'd play for fifteen minutes and they'd make a big deal out of how hard it was.'

Soon, Blast First was to fatefully piss off Sonic Youth with the unauthorised release of a live album, *Walls Have Ears*, but for now the relationship was good. Sonic Youth acted as a guarantee-of-quality magnet for other artists to join Blast First. The label put out records by Glenn Branca, Dinosaur Jr., Butthole Surfers, the British metal-influenced band Head Of David, and two other artists significant for the development of post-rock: the guitar anthology that was Band Of Susans and, especially, the complex trio Ut.

Band Of Susans was literally that—at their inception, at least. Susans

Tallman and Lyall were both guitarists, while Susan Stenger was the bassist and a vocalist. Robert Poss brought the total number of guitarists to three, and also provided vocals, while Ron Spitzer drummed and Alva Rogers was yet another vocalist. Although the line-up was flexible, and they would technically become a Band Of Susan when Tallman and Lyall quit, the group never had fewer than three guitarists.

Robert Poss and Susan Stenger were more Rhys Chatham alumni; both knew the power of that approach to music, which was a direct and acknowledged influence on Band Of Susans. 'We use three guitars, each with a different timbre, to create a similar shifting set of different relationships between dissonances, drones, overtones,' Poss said in 1988. 'There's a lot in common with minimalism. The music is scaled down, the structures are very rudimentary and the pop format conventional. But I guess we're more interested in the textures than the songs.'

Like Sonic Youth, Band Of Susans explored tunings and effects, feedback and timbre; they used drone as a means of structure, shifted between layers, and used words as part of the musical stew rather than its meat. They could exude violence, especially when they dropped the vocals; 'Elliott Abrams In Hell', from *Hope Against Hope*, and 'Sin Embargo', on *Love Agenda*, are two good examples of this. But generally, Band Of Susans came up with a tidier, more comprehensible sound than their Blast First labelmates did. Although they were subtle and clever, their multiple guitars interweaving and sparring, their music could often sound a little too controlled, even staid. They certainly didn't have the captivating art-rebel air of Sonic Youth. Instead, Band Of Susans would solemnly discuss E chords and guitar consonance in interviews, baffling and boring journalists who would then seldom write about them in a colourful fashion.

It was a struggle for Band Of Susans on Blast First. At a time when Sonic Youth were still in their can-do-no-wrong era with the British press, Thurston Moore would publicly slag them off ('Blast First would have been a really great label if they'd only dealt with the bands we told them to deal with,' Moore told *Melody Maker* in 1989. '[Paul Smith] signed Band Of Susans and look what happened'). The Susans' second album, *Love Agenda*, was to be their last on the label. Paul Smith reputedly hated it so much he dropped them because of it.

Ut were a different prospect altogether, and a significant force to those in the know; unlike Band Of Susans, they certainly had Thurston Moore's heart. 'I saw Ut's very first gig, when they were a New York band,' he said in 1993. 'It was still totally atonal, a sort of square-wheel rhythm thing. It was at Max's, still during the No Wave, when it was waning. I remember No Wave people coming to see Ut, and they were so hard and weird-edged that the No Wave people left—they couldn't even deal with it.'

Ut could seem just like the ancient sculptures that featured on the cover of their 1987 compilation *Early Live Life*: impervious, graven, unforgiving. Nina Canal, Jacqui Ham, and Sally Young formed the group in New York during December 1978, inspired by their No Wave peers but also by British post-punk. 'PiL, we adored them,' says Ham. 'John Lydon's vocalisms and Keith Levene's guitar really excited us. And then we were really into Joy Division. They were our exact age. The soulfulness, the power, and the beauty. But The Fall … nobody excited us verbally like Mark E. Smith did. Because Sally and me, in particular, had really come out of words.'

Ut had already released records on their own label, Out—the tape *Live At The Venue*, and the EPs *Ut* and *Confidential*—when they travelled from New York to London to support The Fall. 'It was like, yeah, we're going over there for a few months,' Young says. 'All our stuff was in storage. But at the same time as The Fall, we had met this guy, John Loder, who'd come over [to New York] once, and he kind of said, We'll record you when you come to London, and we thought, yeah, yeah, but he came again, he said it twice, and we thought, OK, he really seems serious about doing an album with us. So those two things—recording, and gigging with The Fall—it was a no-brainer.'

'It was also cheap,' Ham adds. 'Nina was from England, and Nina's brother was selling a house in Archway that we could stay in for six weeks. So everything came together.' They enjoyed the community at the Rough Trade shop in Ladbroke Grove, where 'you'd walk in, and they'd all be hanging out, playing their record loud. It was really a fantastic space.' They recorded *Conviction* in London, and again released it on Out. Ut were dedicated to disrupting a central point in their music, stripping away audience expectations. A key way they achieved this was through the swapping of instruments. 'We wanted to explore,' says Young. 'None of us wanted to be just a bass player, we wanted to really explore all these different instruments and different approaches.'

'We were all musical,' says Ham. 'We all had played guitar. None of us had played bass when we started. Sally and me hadn't played drums. So we were all into that together. We were against the hierarchy thing; we were against being stuck in roles. We hated the idea of being stuck. We really wanted everything. And what came from that is it allowed us to experience everything from every vantage point. And that was what was so thrilling. And relaxing. Because if you're always the singer, singing is so nerve-wracking, and it's so nice to just be the guitar player, just be the drummer, and when you're on the drums, you can hear the whole in a new way. When you're on the bass, it's a different mindset again, and it's great.'

Ut signed to Blast First in 1987. While they retained the alienated harshness of their No Wave roots, they now channelled it differently. This suited Paul Smith, who had been fascinated by No Wave and appreciated Ut's particular wayward path from it. The first release for Blast First was *In Gut's House*, recorded in May 1987.

'It was the first record that we actually got given money to go to the studio, for three weeks,' says Ham. 'We had a wonderful engineer, Paul Kendal, who was working with us; he produced it with us. We were very hands-on. By now, we had learned things. We were more experienced. But it was our first experience where we really were in control more than we'd ever been. *In Gut's House* was that very rare, beautiful, collaborative experience, that really was behind that. And also the collection of songs, most of them had been made up a year or so before.'

The improvisational, instant-composing nature was strong in Ut. According to Ham, *In Gut's House*'s 'Mosquito' originated from live performances of the earlier 'Sham Shack.' 'It had been ripened, but it was still young enough. "Evangelist" is one of those songs, and you've heard of this happening, but it was literally made up … I took two bits of words together, started playing this riff, and Sally started playing the bass, and that was it. It took five minutes. The words had an inbuilt structure, so verbally I had a verse; I had a thing. But everything was very automatic, even Sally sang along immediately, Nina played the drums, it was just … we did it once and it was made up. "Hotel" has all these different parts. But it starts as an improv and, Sally's doing this wild bass using a drumstick, then Nina's playing free, and I'm playing a little riff. It was around Nina's singing, her thing, and then we'd stop and re-organised the centre. The structure came, but it was originally improvised. Sometimes some things like that happened in a studio, a song matures.'

Ut was a serious and brooding group, hard for the casual listener to understand. As Ham said in 1989, 'We're not into pacification and there have been a lot of bands, even in our area, who are. Right away they start talking about "entertainment" or "wanting to be accessible". We like being at the edge.' When people tried—as they did, many times—to make an issue of their gender, it found short shrift. 'It was a burden,' Ham says. 'Being female. And we were seen through the eyes of that whole filter. And from the beginning we hated being looked at as a girl band. And we did not choose, we did not design ourselves as a female band. We got together because we were equally into shaking things up, experimenting.'

Their next album, *Griller*, would make for a frustrating finale. 'We had less money, we had less time,' Ham says. 'It felt rushed, and when it feels like that, it just changes everything. I was in the depth of my improvisation and automatic singing stage, which I went through in a very intense way, at that time. So that also was affecting things. But something like "Wailhouse" was worked on, and it was beautiful. It was beautifully recorded, and beautifully mixed. "Dr No" was also a standout production in performance, recording and mix. Those two got the best of us as a unit with [Steve] Albini [who engineered *Griller*].' *Griller* came in for some hardcore criticism. While *In Gut's*

House had bagged a ten-out-of-ten review in the *NME*, *Griller* gained a spiteful mark of one in the same paper. 'Why don't these bitches keep journals?' the *NME* asked. 'That way we wouldn't have to pay for their therapy and question our own stability when we tell the stereo to shut the fuck up.'

'I remember that girl who absolutely slated *Griller* with this idea that somehow we were so *angry*,' says Sally Young. 'I remember thinking, angry? There are people who react to our music, emotionally, in lots of different ways, very drastic ways that I find difficult to understand. To me, we expressed a lot of different emotions. And I suppose, to only see it as expressing anger said more about that person than it did about us. But we *would* bring out these odd psychologies in people.'

Ut broke up shortly afterward. 'We had had a hard tour, some hard experiences that fall, in 1989. Nina moved to California, and we needed a break from each other. It wasn't a break like we aesthetically disagreed, at all. It was more like, god we need a break from *this*. It was a good time for us to split and to check out our own thing.'

Ut played a lot around London, usually in support slots. 'They were important,' says Graham Sutton, who saw Ut many times during the late 80s when he was a teenager, and counts them as an influence on Bark Psychosis. 'It was the freeform configuration of them as a band, the swapping instruments, and the way they brought their personalities to bear on the different tracks they sang. They treated every instrument in a very fractious, non-musician-y way, and there was nothing rock about it.'

'If there was to be spectacle, it was to bring people into heaviness,' Ham says of these live shows. 'It was *not* to entertain people.'

This was consistent, Ham says, with their admiration for Anton Artaud's Theatre Of Cruelty. This was a theory of performance that shared much common ground with post-rock. Artaud saw the Theatre Of Cruelty as a way of unleashing and utilising unconsciousness in performers and audiences; by removing the focus on an individual or group acting performance (in a similar way to how post-rock decentred vocals) and creating equality between the actors and traditional theatrical bridesmaids like lighting, props, and sound, Artaud hoped to tap into new forms of expression for actors and shake audiences from complacency.

From Lydia Lunch's S&M audience interactions through to Branca's Bastard Theatre and Sonic Youth's performative guitar tunings, this kind of provocative and abstract theatricality was ever-present. This was absolutely true, too, of another New York group, Hugo Largo.

'I think the main reason I got into performing and music was the exchange of energy,' Mimi Goese, the group's vocalist, says. 'That's the seduction of performance art, too.' Goese had been to college with performance art pioneers DANCENOISE (Anne Iobst and Lucy Sexton), Jo Andres, and Alien Comic (Tom Murrin). She believed that a performance should challenge passivity, ensuring people 'couldn't hide in the audience, because you'll be confronted for your intent, for staring at the stage'.

Hugo Largo formed in 1984, originally comprising Goese, bassists Tim Sommer and Greg Letson, and violinist Hahn Rowe. 'All Hugo members but me had been in the Branca wall-of-sound band,' says Goese. Sommer had also briefly been in Swans. 'Hahn was our house sound engineer and played violin from the sound desk for quite a while before we were able to get him onstage with us,' Goese adds. Letson left relatively early on, and was replaced by Adam Peacock.

The absence of percussion in Hugo Largo meant they could easily switch between pastoral sunshine, and terrifying night-time open spaces. 'The lack of drums really set us apart,' says Goese. 'Tim had the idea to go drumless. It made it easier to play. It was always my job to turn off the snare drum of the lead act because, in the early days, we always performed in front of the lead act's drum set.'

Despite the apparent dearth of it in their music, however, Hugo Largo were hyper-aware of the role of noise. In this way, they were analogous to Ut's emphasis on heavy emotion, rather than heavy sound in and of itself. 'Me and Hahn especially were interested in hardcore,' Sommer has recalled. 'Hardcore started out intelligent *and* simplistic but ended up too easy. The bands that imitate Sonic Youth and Butthole Surfers think that to be more on the edge, you have to turn up your volume, be more and more offensive. But if you want to be on the edge, why not try to make something that's really powerful and full of tension without the *obvious* statement of turning up the volume. Such a thing would be the new punk, because it's new and it's a reaction to the too simple answers of before.'

'Tim had the uncanny ability to write someone's article for them,' Goese says, about contemporary interviews. 'We got the label "pretentious" so often I would look it up from time to time to digest the definition. I also think we got [that label] because we were a female-led art band, which was unusual at the time in a male-dominated scene. And because we *were* pretentious.'

'We tend to think in terms of the dynamics of the performances, from hard to soft,' Rowe said in 1988. 'We like to maintain a level of intensity throughout the performance, the set as a whole, build it up, rather than just reach climaxes in this or that song.'

When performing with Hugo Largo, Goese would wear multiple layers of clothing, including conventionally pretty dresses and rock T-shirts featuring the names of bands like Metallica and Led Zeppelin; then she would shed layers for each song, confronting and deconstructing the gaze female performers are subject to. 'The stripping of many dresses was a lo-fi costume change to separate the songs, not as a sexy act,' she says. 'We called one tour the *Who's That Girl* tour, because I had the shortest hair in the band, and the brashest personality.' Performances would sometimes climax with knife-play ('to add an edgy, untrustworthy feel against the swooping, dreamy sound'), with Goese running a blade over her face and neck, before appearing to fling it into the crowd. Usually she dropped it behind her back, but once she did follow through. 'At a show in Bath, England, I threw the butcher's knife into the audience!' she remembers. 'Who in their right mind would do that? John Paul Jones [of Led Zeppelin] was at that show. I remember he was running after our van as we left, showing us his just-bought Hugo Largo T-shirt.'

Hugo Largo's two albums—*Drum*, from 1988, and the following year's *Mettle*—are curious and compelling works. They do not rebel against songs so much as shy away from them; structure was still a fascination point for the band. 'It seems bizarre to me that people don't realise that it's more extreme to be quiet,' Sommer said in 1987. In terms of words sung, Goese's voice was coherent and comprehensible; in terms of themes and any kind of logical pathway, however, her songs were disjointed. 'Grow Wild', 'Eskimo Song', 'Second Skin'; these are songs of the elements, cowed and fascinated by the wild side of nature while proudly bookish in their lack of abandon to it. Goese resembled Tim Buckley's ecstatic waywardness in her approach to lyrics and vocals, while Hugo Largo teetered on the edge of the explosive reactions, but always fled from them, knowing the tension and anticlimax to be more powerful.

'Part of the magic of the band was the vibration of two basses with this violin and gymnastic vocal,' Goese says. 'It would hypnotise the audience. They would all invariably sit down on the cigarette-strewn, beer-soaked floor to watch.'

There was a stillness about Hugo Largo's work that had few American contemporaries (although there were Saqqara Dogs, who used folklore and non-Western instrumentation on their album, *Thirst*) until Galaxie 500 explored microscopic changes in mood. In a way, Hugo Largo were more related to something that was underway in Britain. 'I love dreams to death,' Goese says. 'I do! In Hugo Largo, I tried to dredge the debris up from dreams and reconstruct them.'

As No Wave was clearly not a label anymore, journalists—as journalists are wont to do—tried to find something else. In 1984, *Village Voice* critic Robert Christgau coined 'pigfuck' (as an insult) for Sonic Youth. Eventually, pigfuck stood on its own, representing something loud, sludgy, sweary, often repellent in subject matter: Big Black, Pussy Galore, and then Royal Trux and The Jesus Lizard. It travelled, although the UK was a little bit more genteel about it: the preferred term was 'arsequake', because the music's impact is felt in 'neither the dancing feet nor the pensive brain, but [in] the colon.' It also brought another band into arsequake's canal: Public Enemy.

Public Enemy were emphatically *not* part of a scene that spawned Sonic Youth, Ut, and Hugo Largo, but there was no denying that they were part of the complex infrastructure of New York. In the way that Chatham and Branca intellectualised punk, Public Enemy claimed an analogous role in terms of hip-hop. 'Hip-hop may have started in the inner city,' Chuck D said in 1987, 'but it took people on Long Island and Queens to take hip-hop and look at it differently—they dissected it and built it up again.' Public Enemy, in its initial core of Chuck D and Hank Shocklee (in class terms, at least) weren't so far from the suburban backgrounds of the white New York rebel deconstructionists.

Shocklee was part of Spectrum City, a Long Island DJ crew, one of the biggest in the neighbourhood. Chuck D, a graphic design student, began performing with them as a live MC and then hooked up with Bill Stephney, programme director of Adelphi University's radio station. All three recognised that there was a gap in the market for a hip-hop radio show. They decided to fill it.

'Bill had the willing openness to say, Hey, I'm in charge and we're going to play hip-hop, so let's get busy, while Hank and me had the ability to find records and to put together something that would *explode* our community, in our area,' Chuck said. And so it did: the listening figures increased eightfold. Several people who would prove key to Public Enemy soon gravitated to the show: Flavor Flav, Terminator X, Professor Griff.

'It was never a hip-hop group, so to speak,' Shocklee recalled. 'We thought of it like a rock and roll band. Just one that lived in the hip-hop world. In order to do that, everything had to be tactical. I learned a lot from when I used to manage a heavy metal record store. Yeah! I was very interested in a lot of groups like Iron Maiden, Megadeth, Dead Kennedys, Black Flag. Bands like that, everything they did was conceptual.'

In 1987, Public Enemy signed to Def Jam; the label initially reputedly just wanted Chuck D as a soloist. 'What does Flavor *do*?' co-founder Rick Rubin asked. But Chuck and Shocklee—older and more self-assured than most first-time record contract signatories—stuck to their belief that Flavor Flav was as important to them as their motif of a black man in a rifle crosshair. Shocklee described Flavor as a hype man, and he meant it positively. Flavor has the first words on the debut Public Enemy album, *Yo! Bum Rush The Show*, released on Def Jam in 1987.

'I wasn't interested in the business just for the sake of making a record,' Chuck D wrote in 1997. 'I was also concerned with the way rap was being exploited and interpreted.' Any cursory listen to Public Enemy, even a glance at the titles: Chuck's political voice sounds as loud as the siren squeal on 'Rebel Without A Pause'. Practically, a rapper could squeeze in more words to the pound than a singer could, and Chuck D was certainly one who used that density, words viscid with meaning and dynamism.

'Chuck's voice is so powerful, and his tone is so rich, that you can't put him on smooth, silky, melodic music,' Shocklee has said. 'It's only fitting to put a hailstorm around him, a tornado behind him.' Public Enemy's production team, The Bomb Squad (helmed by Shocklee), was so named because of this very reason. Tracks merge abrasive timbres, conflicting rhythms, and samples massing together to form a street symphony. 'I wanted to do something that was not melodic,' Shocklee has said, of this organised noise. 'I wanted frequencies that clashed with each other and created another frequency of dissonance.' Although digital sampling technology was still limited, Shocklee used its boundaries to his advantage, isolating relatively short snippets, divorcing them from their context, and then assembling them to meet the needs of Public Enemy. Shocklee was a pioneer in moving away from hip-hop samples being funky percussion breaks, or grooves for the dance floor. He took piercing jabs of sound and looped them to hammer Public Enemy's music into political and cultural consciousness. This all meant that the idea of *what* could be sampled, as well as how it could be used, expanded; a 'break', in hip-hop, would now be anything that the producer decreed it to be. In addition, to get a tactile quality, he would mix up digital sampling with physical DJing.

Soon, sampling would flex its muscles in rock music, and it was Hank Shocklee's work on *Yo! Bum Rush The Show*, *It Takes A Nation Of Millions To Hold Us Back*, and *Fear Of A Black Planet* that opened it up radically in this direction. He put sounds to new uses, strained the limits of technology, but kept the feel of a careful construct: a black sculpture in the hour of chaos.

'Shocklee, on *Fear Of A Black Planet*, was the first to use sampling to pile on the intensities, rather then just quote obvious riffs,' Kevin Martin of God, Techno Animal, and Ice has said. 'He took the peaks of other songs, like trumpet solos, and layered them densely.'

Kim Gordon was correct when she predicted that people—one subset in particular—would try and quantify all of this activity. 'They seem to have this thing in England,' she said in 1988. 'Like, ever since the Sex Pistols, rock is stupid. So when they see a band that rocks, it can't possibly be rock, so there has to be another explanation for it.'

CHAPTER THREE

you push a knife into my dreams

'You can take drugs, you can do meditation, you can go on runs. There's all kinds of things that release oxytocin, and serotonin, and dopamine, all these different chemicals. It's a potent cocktail for your brain. You feel fucking great. We wanted to make music that did that.' RUDY TAMBALA, A.R. KANE

In 1987, the independent record company 4AD released a compilation album and accompanying video, both called *Lonely Is An Eyesore*. 'The intention of *Lonely Is An Eyesore* was to broaden things, to destroy the myth of a label sound,' 4AD founder Ivo Watts-Russell claimed at its release.

Label samplers, sometimes at reduced prices (although *Lonely Is An Eyesore* was not) were popular with independents in the late 1980s and early 1990s. Joel Leoschke, a founder of the Chicago label kranky, says his label's 1998 *Kompilation* was 'conceived of as a marketing tool by our European distributor as a cheap way to spread the message, and it was a smart idea. Take a single track from a disparate group of artists on one label and sell it for little more than the cost of manufacture. This was before downloads, so it was a simple way to disseminate information about the various artists and the label itself at, hopefully, too tempting a price to pass up. It was not a conscious artistic statement at the time of assembly, but it may well be in an accidental way.'

Lonely Is An Eyesore, however, didn't feel like an economic decision, or one that had anything accidental about it. Here was a carefully curated and celebratory compilation, two years in the making, and one that must have incurred no small cost to the label for its new tranche of music videos alone. Despite Watts-Russell's stated intention, the project achieved the opposite effect: it cemented further the idea of a '4AD band'.

Dif Juz, whose final recorded track, 'No Motion', was a highlight of *Lonely Is An Eyesore*, felt this unwelcome pull keenly all throughout their time with 4AD. 'They were making the label an entity,' says Richie Thomas. 'That's what they wanted to do. We'd made two EPs [for them] and they didn't really seem that interested in us, to be honest. The phone didn't ring. So we thought, *fuck* this. We're a band, we're not a band on a label.'

If anyone was seen as an embodiment of 4AD, it was the label's most successful and artistically relevant group, Cocteau Twins: Elizabeth Fraser, Robin Guthrie, and Simon Raymonde. Fraser could also feel ambiguous toward 4AD. At the time of its release, she described *Lonely Is An Eyesore* as 'disappointing, because of that thing where all the bands get lumped together. People go on about a "4AD house sound". It encourages that.'

Ethereal, diaphanous, *dreamy*: these were the words first out of the press cannon for 4AD bands, the aura of the label always clinging, even in the face of evidence to the contrary. 'It really pissed us off,' said Miki Berenyi from Lush, who signed to 4AD in 1989. '4AD does colour its bands with some sense of artiness. If the Pixies had been, say, on Creation, no one would have thought of Black Francis as being particularly arty or intellectual.'

'It was never very comfortable [for us] at 4AD because they are what they are,' says Rudy Tambala of A.R. Kane, whose tenure at the label started and ended in 1987. 'Very, very precious. And I didn't really get it. They were doing their thing, and it wasn't our thing, and so immediately there was loads of friction.'

The poor experience Tambala and the other core member of A.R. Kane, Alex Ayuli, had at 4AD was particularly galling, since they idolised the Cocteau Twins. 'One night I was watching telly and I saw something,' says Tambala. 'And it was the Cocteau Twins on *The Tube*. I'd never seen anything like it. There was this fucking tape machine and this incredible angel of a woman, and these two guys with big hair, making the most sublime noise. And it had a groove, and it was noisy. It had big drums and Liz Fraser's voice, and I thought, I wanna do that. I *can't* do that, but I *can* do that. It made me ring Alex up, and on the phone he was like, I fucking watched it as well.'

The Cocteaus' performance was of 'Pink Orange Red', from their 1985 EP *Tiny Dynamine*, released almost contemporaneously with another EP, *Echoes In A Shallow Bay*. 'We're thoroughly fed up with them now,' guitarist Robin Guthrie said of these two EPs, a mere month after they'd been released. 'Some of the music goes back to last February. We hate them just the same as we hate the others now.'

Few others hated these EPs, though. Cocteau Twins during their peak—to which 'Pink Orange Red' belongs—were extraordinary. Between the voice and the music, they almost invented a new language, one that had more to do with intuition than communication. Fraser's words, private and indecipherable for the most part, were not difficult to take in because she was being obtuse, evasive, mannered, or mysterious. Instead, she was about emotions and situations so intrinsically ambiguous that the only possible way to make sense of them was to deliver her words in a way reflective of that ambiguity.

'Before I heard them, music was just something I listened to,' says Mark Clifford of Seefeel. 'When I heard their music it was genuinely life-changing. I think partly because I realised I didn't have to be good to play. It was more about making sound. They were revolutionary. Everything about them, the whole setup, the sound, the singing, everything.'

'We never talk about what we're doing. Ever,' Simon Raymonde said in 1990.

Cocteau Twins were prolific in the middle third of the 1980s. *Victorialand*, their fourth album, was released in April 1986; Fraser and Guthrie worked on it without Raymonde, somewhat to his surprise and chagrin ('They could have asked if I minded,' he said in 2013). Although they did enlist Richie Thomas of Dif Juz on tabla and saxophone, the acoustic character and general lack of traditional percussion moved their work onto a different plane. It became even less relatable to a rock or pop tradition, and was freer-floating: about as graspable as vapour, but as meaningful as allegory. The album's title related to Queen Victoria and how, in the name of the monarch, the British mounted a spurious claim to Antarctica; the song titles were lifted from the television naturalist, David Attenborough, and his book, *The Living Planet: A Portrait Of The Earth.*

The Moon And The Melodies was also released in 1986, having been recorded in a fortnight with the composer and pianist Harold Budd. Although this album had Raymonde back in the fold, the band did not see it as an official part of the Cocteau Twins' discography, billing it instead as a four-name collaboration. Budd, part of the original cache of ambient pioneers during the 1970s, had developed a wool-gathering style of piano playing he termed 'soft pedal', which found its most perfect expression on the 1984 Brian Eno collaboration *The Pearl.* Budd's sustained and slow approach, which occasionally tipped over into sentimentality, melded with the Cocteaus' treated guitars on this album: as with *Victorialand*, it all tipped near to ambient and also, to the irritation of all parties, got tagged as 'New Age'. Perhaps this was understandable, given the presence of Budd, and the way the album followed on from *Victorialand*'s environmentalism; but New Age was a loaded term, connoting waffle, misplaced idealism, and weediness.

'[New Age] is a music without form or resistance,' Budd told *The Wire* in 1988, disassociating himself from the tag.

Like most significant artists—and this is probably a reason why New Age was bandied about to describe them—there was no 'right' way to hear the Cocteaus. Yet the way that Rudy Tambala and Alex Ayuli heard them led to something 'life-changing', says Tambala.

'Alex and I had been to school together,' he says. 'I think we met when we were about eight years old. They sat him next to me in school. So this really skinny guy with great big eyes came into the classroom, really nervous. And he sat next to me, and everyone was like, you've got the new boy. But we connected immediately. East London was a funny place to grow up, especially if you were immigrants. *Especially* if you were in a minority of immigrants. Most of the East London immigrants were either Irish or West Indian. Alex's parents were from Nigeria, and there weren't a lot of African immigrants in East London. My dad was from Malawi, and my mum was white and from England. I was in the smallest minority because there weren't any mixed-race kids. So I think that African thing, and being real outcasts, pulled us together really, really tight. We developed our own culture, our own way of dealing with things. And that stuck for years and years and years.'

Ayuli was from a reggae and dub background; Tambala was more soul and jazz. 'And then we both grew up under the punk thing,' says Tambala. 'We both got into things like A Certain Ratio, Factory stuff. Public Image Ltd was probably one of the biggest influences. And in all of these bands, there was this groove thing going on. The dub, and the soul, and the funk, and jazz. But then there was this desire to destroy—even the groove.'

After school, the two friends took different professional routes—Tambala studied biochemistry; Ayuli was headhunted by the advertising agency Saatchi & Saatchi—but they still hung out, and 'our music tastes stayed quite in parallel'. Both owned acoustic guitars, and Ayuli also had a twelve-string electric, but they had never played together before that post-Cocteaus night. 'We didn't decide we were gonna start a band. We just sat there and strummed guitars and made stupid noises.'

Ayuli, as one of London's brightest young advertising talents, was invited to lots of parties, and he would often take his old school friend along. 'It must have been around Christmas time or something. It was like the Roman Empire, [but] in the 80s,' remembers Tambala. 'There was drink and drugs everywhere and it was all free.' Unsurprisingly, both got blitzed and decided, then and there, to start a band. With intoxicated inspiration, they came up with the name A.R. Kane. 'He's a copywriter and I'm a mad wordsmith as well,' Tambala says. 'Alex was really into the movie *Citizen Kane*. And I had been reading *Demian* by Hermann Hesse, which is about the Mark of Cain. We liked playing around with that word, but we thought, we can't call it Kane. So we thought we'll take our initials, A, R, Kane … Arcane! Fuck! *The Garden Of Arcane Delights* by Dead Can Dance. We both loved that. And that was it.'

About an hour and more drugs later, Tambala had a chance meeting with Ray Shulman, who had been in the prog group Gentle Giant and was currently working as a record producer. Tambala immediately mentioned quite literally the newest band going: A.R. Kane. 'And he said, What's it like? and I thought, fucking hell, think, think, think, so I said, It's a bit Velvet Underground, a bit Jefferson Airplane, a bit Joni Mitchell, a bit Miles Davis … . Anything that I'd been listening to, basically. And he said, That sounds really interesting, I'd love to hear your demo.

'About three or four days later I said, Alex, that guy at the party, that record producer, he wanted to hear a demo. We hadn't got a demo. He said, What guy? I said, I don't know what his name was, I can't remember—as you don't. So it just died a death. And then, about two weeks later, Ray rung Alex up and said, Alex, how's your band going with your mate Rudy?'

A.R. Kane bought a drum machine and asked in a guitar shop how the Cocteaus made their signature sound. ('You want delay and distortion pedals,' Tambala was told. He bought them.) They recorded seven songs and sent them to Shulman, who played them to the One Little Indian chief, Derek Birkett. 'Derek said, Yeah … I like that. Can I see them play live? And I was like, *oh, for fuck's sake*.'

Tambala and Ayuli threw together a band with Bomber, an old school friend ('He had a bass guitar but he only played one note, I think it was A'), Tambala's sister Maggie ('She really looked the part, because she's very, very cool'), and drummer Dan Goodwin, who Tambala had been to university with, and who played in the Kitchens Of Distinction.

They pelted the songs on the demo with aggression, verve, and a whole lot of noise. Birkett was impressed, and in 1986, A.R. Kane made their first single with One Little Indian: 'When You're Sad' b/w 'Haunting'. 'Not that you would know their titles from the record cover,' Tambala says. 'When You're Sad' was originally called 'You Push A Knife Into My Womb', he adds, 'but the powers that be at Rough Trade [distributors for One Little Indian] didn't like that. They thought it was about violence against women. But it was about being sensitive. Anyway, they refused to put it out, so we said, Fuck it, we won't put *anything* on [the cover]. So it's known by the refrain, *when you're sad*.'

The single was sensual, provocative, head-blisteringly alive. It sounded ambitious, it *was* ambitious; it used space and noise and both were enveloping. Almost immediately, A.R. Kane picked up press coverage, and were initially characterised, reductively, as 'the black Jesus & Mary Chain'. Their blackness was a real rarity in alternative guitar music at the time, especially in the microclimate of expressive, experimental art-noise. Ayuli and Tambala also came off as intriguing and enigmatic personalities in their early interviews, distancing themselves from 'shambling bands' and refusing to acknowledge any influence bar Miles Davis (not even their beloved Cocteau Twins).

'We were really, really, really arrogant,' Tambala concedes.

No existing genre would do for them. They had to invent their own. Dream pop (or dreampop, as it was sometimes styled, for added visual curves) was less a musical style than a feeling. 'We meant it both literally and metaphorically,' says Tambala. 'Literally in that we dreamt music, we used to wake each other up at stupid hours and say, Listen to this idea, what do you think of these lyrics, what do you think of this imagery? But also [metaphorically], it was the dreaminess of it. It should make you dream.'

One Little Indian didn't hold them for long. 'We wanted to do another single, and Derek said, You have to wait, you have to wait,' Tambala recalls. 'But we weren't patient, and by then we had thirty or forty songs. And we wanted to make an album. So we just said, Fuck it, we're going to go to 4AD, which was our label of choice. We sent Ivo a demo and he said, Yeah, let's do a single. So we told Derek. And Derek sent a whole bunch of skinhead punks down to threaten 4AD.'

4AD somehow managed to survive the skinheads, and A.R. Kane advanced further with their next single, 'Lollita', which was teamed with 'Sado-Masochism Is A Must' and 'The Butterfly Collector'. Robin Guthrie produced them. 'Robin wouldn't accept any of the imperfections that we would have accepted,' Tambala says. 'He was like, no, no, you do that again—but in a Scottish accent, obviously. He was brilliant. He was aggressive and funny and warm and nasty all at the same time. But he could get a performance out of you. He just produced a beautiful record.'

The three tracks were a mix of innocence and cruelty, with A.R. Kane's narrative on women especially disorientating and disturbing, suggestive of mutual misunderstanding and hostility. The single's cover showed an image of a young woman with a steak knife behind her back; there was a spat-out 'bitch' lyric on 'Lollita'; and 'The Butterfly Collector' detailed a possessive male hoarding female power. Violence, whether directed at or experienced by women, men, or society, *was* a key part of A.R. Kane, making them emphatically not a safe or comfortable band to listen to. It was a nightmare they explicitly sought to reflect in the music, as well as in the lyrics. 'You can get really violent on a guitar,' Ayuli commented in 1987.

Elsewhere on 4AD, there was a band called Colourbox. They had released their first single on the label in 1982, the same year of the Cocteau Twins debut, *Garlands*. By 1987, Colourbox weren't one of the label's best sellers, nor were they one of the groups most loved by 4AD aficionados. But they were a band that stuck out there, influenced as they were by electro-house and New York sample culture; their first single, 'Breakdown', is a strong example of sparse synths and cold soul vocals. The core of the group was brothers Steven and Martyn Young.

Tambala, Ayuli, and A.R. Kane bassist Russell Smith joined up with the Young brothers at 4AD's behest, using their first name initials to create the acronym M/A/R/R/S, the slashes indicating tiny fissures that, as it happened, were entirely prophetic. 'They've got their story about it and I've got mine,' says Tambala. The project made one blazing statement, 'Pump Up The Volume'. It caught many trends: samples (over thirty of them), house beats, hip-hop, and bended guitar. It was a massive worldwide hit, and it reached number one in the UK.

'I just know that [the Youngs] went into the studio with a piece of ambient piano, and we went in with "Into The Groove(y)" by Ciccone Youth, the Janet Jackson *Control* remixes, and a whole bunch of dance,' says Tambala. 'And they were telling us that we didn't know anything about dance music, and cutting edge.'

'A.R. Kane have an indie attitude,' Martyn Young said in 1987. 'They don't understand that there's certain things you can never do in dance music, you can't improvise with guitar riffs or play a drum machine out of time.'

'I just got involved inasmuch as Martyn said he wanted to kill these dodgy goths he was working with and would I come over and drop all this stuff in,' said scratcher C.J. Mackintosh, who also featured on 'Pump Up The Volume'. 'No, I'm joking!'

'They got really greedy and nasty around the whole thing,' says Tambala. 'We got screwed out of quite a lot of money on it. My last conversation with Ivo wasn't particularly nice. It only had two words in it.'

'They can fuck off and die,' Colourbox's manager told *Melody Maker* in 1988, after A.R. Kane requested they stop using the M/A/R/R/S name unless Tambala and Ayuli were compensated. 'We're *not* gonna pay them.'

Meanwhile, the royalties for 'Pump Up The Volume' lay in legal limbo. 'Our claim is that they don't have any right to use "Roadblock" without our permission and without paying the artists and the writers,' said Pete Waterman, referring to M/A/R/R/S's use of Stock Aitken Waterman's own sample-heavy track. 'We both have to go to court to decide what the law is on sampling.'

By 1987, samplers were being used in two main ways. The first was widespread, but largely imperceptible to the average listener: the samples emulated conventional instruments, from libraries of sounds, which were then organised by a sequencer. The second type of use, however, was seen as both threatening and exciting—sampling larger and sometimes easily recognisable slabs of recorded music.

The latter was one of those rare cultural phenomena that appealed equally to popular and cutting-edge tastes. On one hand, producers could cut costs and surf the wave with a cheaply constructed hit; on the other, more serious types could use sampling to question ownership, memory, commerce, and cultural overload. It wasn't always clear, even to the artists themselves, which was which during this anarchic time. However, what was certain was that a lot of those who were actually being sampled didn't like it, and didn't care about the sampling artist's motivation. They were just outraged that their work was used without authorization, seeking redress (and compensation) via the courts.

What was creative use of other people's material? What was theft? How much of another track might someone reasonably use and still claim it as a new piece? Was sampling satire? Appropriation? Homage? The whole thing was a mess. It was little wonder that The Justified Ancients Of Mu Mu named their sampletacular album *1987: What The Fuck Is Going On?*

But sampling, particularly via The Justified Ancients Of Mu Mu, Hank Shocklee's work in Public Enemy, and Swiss band The Young Gods, was to provide a crucial creative yardstick to the next few years as post-rock developed. 'I thought the records we were making were basically crap and listening to people like Public Enemy made me genuinely ashamed of them,' says Ian Crause of Disco Inferno, a band that started out with a traditional guitar setup.

A.R. Kane were pioneers in the use of sampling in noisy indie music. It was the way they straddled both worlds of sampling; of course, there was the M/A/R/R/S record and another, lesser-known twelve-inch released in 1988 and credited to ARK, called 'Listen Up!'. But they also integrated sampling into work under the A.R. Kane banner. 'There's sampled stuff on our first record,' Ayuli said in 1987, 'but you can't tell, because it's been done in an A.R. Kane way. With most people, [using samples] is like sticking different kinds of wallpaper together.'

'For us, where the sampler had a great value was that instead of having the option to play things on a keyboard based on some sounds you could find anywhere, we'd sample our own guitar feedback,' My Bloody Valentine's Kevin Shields has said, specifically of the 1991 album *Loveless*. '[Thus], instead of just being one tone, it could be a tone having bends and quirks in it. And then, by using the human voice as well for the top end, you've got these organic things happening, even though sometimes you're using the keyboards to play them. You are letting the organic part be part of the rhythm of the sample.'

With their 1988 EP *You Made Me Realise*, My Bloody Valentine had changed tack: changed their line-up, changed their record label, and changed their hairstyles. Previously, they had come across as jangle-poppers, evoking a forgotten sunny psychedelic band from 1968.

'We really hated the reputation we got,' Shields said in 1989. 'We were always used as an example of how shit indie bands are.' This under-loved era, he later claimed, was a Trojan horse for a sly trick. 'We had this frequency on all the guitars that physically damages your ears,' he said. 'That was the whole point. That it actually wrecked people's hearing. And we sang those songs with really sweet titles about really sordid things. We were too subtle, though. You have to scream "fuck, fuck, motherfucker" and be called something like Rape Everybody to have an impact on extremists.'

The band didn't quite go that far when they relaunched, but with *You Made Me Realise* there was a simultaneous hardening and softening of My Bloody Valentine. Hardening, as the guitars got more raucous, more dangerously meshed, way less approachable; softening, as their tracks gained a spongier quality, away from their earlier buzzy machismo, while the lyrics and the voices that sang them lost clarity and gained vulnerability. They were ferociously protective of their words, not printing them on records and refusing all requests to elucidate their content or meaning. Vocalist and guitarist Bilinda Butcher did say, however, that she left her lines to the last moment, so they may be guided organically. 'I once spent about a month writing some lyrics,' she said in 1990, 'then when it came to the day I was due to sing them they were crap, they were completely wrong and awful. It's just best to leave them to the end, once you've got a picture of what the song's about, the feeling and the atmosphere.'

'Slow', the second track on the EP, was influenced by hip-hop beats and Hank Shocklee's breezeblock noise. Drummer Colm Ó Cíosóig said of it, 'It's just a guitar played really high up and fast with the tone turned right down. You don't actually hear the chords being struck, and there's a tremolo arm bending them, as well as reverse reverb.'

'With the open tunings and guitar bending,' Shields later said of 'Slow', 'what you hear is what is *between* the sound.'

Rudy Tambala remembers hearing 'Slow' at the time and finding it 'stylistically very similar' to 'Baby Milk Snatcher' from A.R. Kane's *69*, released a few months earlier. 'Slow' was, he says, 'a kind of white boy take on noise dub with slide-y guitar. Just as ours was a black boy take on PiL. I remember at the time, Alex and I cracked up and could not believe the cheek of it, some jangly band having a major Kane makeover, to be cool. Maybe. That was our impression at the time—a dirty secret, taboo now. Nevertheless, I take nothing away from their absolute canniness/genius—they sounded awesome and took that vibe to spaces we just did not. And they had a chick with a blade on the cover!'

Live, 'You Made Me Realise' took on gargantuan proportions, as it could extend, Velvet Underground-style, to up to forty minutes of spectral ear desecration, with even the onstage monitors turned outward to the audience. 'Usually, people would experience a type of sensory deprivation, and they would lose the sense of time,' Shields said in 2005. 'It would force them to be in the moment, and since people don't usually get to experience that, there'd be a sense of elation. There would be a feeling of, wow, that was really weird, I don't know what happened, but suddenly I heard this symphony … it was such a huge noise with so much texture to it, it allowed people to imagine anything. Like when you hypnotise somebody, and nothing becomes something. That was what the whole purpose became.'

This was using noise in a way that was superficially similar to (but quite distinct from) how Swans had approached their live shows.

Both groups were interested in corporeal as well as psychological and emotional responses to their music, and this involved stretching stamina to its limit. 'We like to play loud music because we know that once you get above one hundred decibels, that causes a physical change in people,' Shields said. 'Endorphins get released into the system because the body can sense imminent danger.' Yet where Swans would pride themselves on repulsion, daring audience members to leave the venue if they feared for their ears, their acid reflux, or their sanity, My Bloody Valentine's noise battery was about creating new, transcendent states. Throughout the live sonic hailstorm, the band would keep an eye on the audience; as soon as they felt that its hypnosis point had been hit, that 'nothing had become something', the white noise would back down, ringing out once again with the recognisable motif of 'You Made Me Realise', and the show would close.

The earlier incarnation of My Bloody Valentine had *played* with psychedelic baubles; this new version was psychedelic in and of itself, the music now acting as a consciousness-shifting experiment. Kevin Shields was certainly interested in the mental fluidity that occurs at borderline wakefulness, and during recording of the band's 1988 album *Isn't Anything* he explicitly used it as inspiration.

'The *Isn't Anything* phase was big time about sleep deprivation,' he has said. 'I was young enough and strong enough and not into drugs enough. I wasn't smoking lots of dope or anything, because if you smoke enough pot you can't stay awake. I would get off on just having two or three hours of sleep a night and work constantly, and it was very enjoyable.'

Others, however, imbibed a whole lot more chemicals and sought, explicitly, to mimic the impact of hallucinogenic drugs on their music. Spacemen 3 called a set of 1986 demos *Taking Drugs To Make Music To Take Drugs To*, and it was also the group's slogan. 'I'm being totally honest about the whole concept of the band,' Sonic Boom said in 1989. 'That motto is what we are about. I think our music benefits from being listened to while totally out of your head. But, having said that, we appeal to lots of different levels of consciousness, so perhaps it's not an essential prerequisite.' The language of narcotics infused their work and, according to Sonic Boom's frequent and frank admissions, their everyday lives, too. However, the core Spacemen 3 relationship of Sonic Boom and his close friend, Jason Pierce, underlay any altered state.

'[Drugs were] fundamental in the making of that music,' Sonic Boom said in 1996. 'We were taking speed, smack, and dope onstage, but we had a telepathic sense where we knew the time was right to interact with one another. If it felt right to include two minutes of jamming, or if a solo built up perfectly in a minute, that would be it. Drugs didn't stop us communicating like that.'

'When we first started, we were just getting out of our faces and jamming on long continuous bits of music,' Pierce has said. 'But there was something about it that wasn't self-indulgent. We were all playing in the room, until something came through the roof. The sound we were hearing was like from some other planet or something. And that's what Spacemen 3 was. We just found ourselves making this unearthly kind of sound that elevated us.'

Spacemen 3 specifically used monotony to evoke the sensation of tripping. 'It's the same principle as mantras,' Sonic Boom said, 'where the idea is that if you repeat something often enough, it loses its original meaning and yields all kinds of other meanings, which eventually depend on the subjective perception of the individual.' The forty-five-minute live track 'An Evening Of Contemporary Sitar Music' (from *Dreamweapon*) did this by containing no sitars; instead, it recreated the sitar's sound on guitars, in a timbre-bending buzz.

Spacemen 3 were also captivated by 1960s psychedelia, but the difference between them and My Bloody Valentine in 1988 was clear. Sonic Boom and Jason Pierce enjoyed the culture, fashion, and trappings of the psychedelic years, as well as its openness to musical progression. They looked back in a way that My Bloody Valentine did not. Nevertheless, the sheer audacity of Spacemen 3's drone, its ecstasy flux and hedonistic rush, felt modern, even while hearty blues riffing grounded their tracks and promotional videos were splayed with melting, varicoloured period effects.

At the same time as My Bloody Valentine, Spacemen 3 were also trying, musically, to embrace a paradox of size. 'The maximal effect in music is to have the fewest things making the sound,' said Sonic Boom in 1988. 'It's more direct, even dense and textured. We try to do this.' They rejected the flamboyances of progressive rock ('Uuuuuuuurrrgh! GOD! That's the *opposite* of what we want to do! All that King Crimson, Led Zep stuff, too many chord changes, over-elaborate, dull, arty for the sake of it, empty'), and placed themselves within a tradition of minimalist rock music that incorporated early crossroads blues, the Stooges, and Suicide.

Meanwhile, A.R. Kane had freed themselves from 4AD and were now on Rough Trade, looking toward their debut album; it was titled *69*, but not as a throwback. 'We were very, very anti-retro at the time,' says Rudy Tambala. 'There's always something positive, where you can look forward to a better world. Even punk is like that to me. No future, to me, means live *now*.'

Tambala and Ayuli got a bit of cash from their new deal, 'but we didn't go into the studio with loads of money,' Tambala says. 'We built a studio. In Alex's basement. We had to buy all the gear, learn how it all worked, samplers and sequencers and mixing desks and reel-to-reel tape recorders and all this kind of stuff, and record at the same time. And that's why the *69* album sounds quite raw, because it was made in Alex's stinky basement. He put up doors with dirty carpets over them to make a vocal booth, and the ceiling was that low, it would drip back down on you if you were in there for too many hours.'

The psychedelia of *69* is of the same mindset as The Red Crayola, or even some of Sun Ra's most cosmic moments, without sounding remotely like either of them. 'When we'd finished the track "Sulliday", we thought, oh fuck, we didn't put any drums on, let's put them on now. So the drums went on after the track was finished. It made absolutely no difference. It's so deconstructed,' says Tambala. 'When we did tracks on the *69* album, we thought, just let it go. We know how far it can go. It can go really, really, far. It can go *way* further than Sonic Youth.'

Tambala cites the debut album by Cindytalk, 1984's *Camoflage Heart*, as a key influence on *69*. 'There was nothing darker, more sinister, or more beautiful than Cindytalk,' he says, 'and only me and Alex got it, out of everyone we knew. I'd put Cindytalk on when I wanted to empty the party. Alex would stay, everyone else would go home.'

The resulting *69* album was the darkest and most transcendent that A.R. Kane got. Afterward, their material situation changed, as did their outlook. 'I think Rough Trade gave us £25,000 advance on the [second] album,' Tambala says. 'When M/A/R/R/S hit number one, I was living in a squat, with no windows and no heating. And suddenly I was given a publishing cheque for loads of money. I didn't know what the fuck to do with it. I didn't even put it in the bank for two weeks. I was used to digging behind the sofa to get enough money for a bag of chips. And then suddenly I realised, money's there for spending, let's spend it on loads of *stuff*. So I bought guitars and drum machines. We used all these really posh studios where the "top people" went. And hiring orchestras. *Get the fucking orchestra on!*' It was all a long way from Ayuli's sweaty basement. And it told in the tenor and, slightly, in the quality of what came of it.

"i" was released in 1989: a double album, a bit bloated, a bit busy, but still a satisfying second A.R. Kane experience. '[We were] going around with lots and lots of different ideas, and not wanting to be contained,' Tambala says of that record. There were house rhythms and hard rock; messy guitars and sweet backing vocals; summery reggae and even a genuine pop song, 'A Love From Outer Space'. The dub influence was now more cheerful and even conventional, especially on 'Catch My Drift', rather than the scorched-earth open spaces of the first album; only 'Supervixens', with its shrieking spider guitars and lackadaisical vocals, could have nestled comfortably on *69*.

'I think that in retrospect—which is great, isn't it?—we probably could have done with a manager,' Tambala says. 'Someone to say stop. Someone stop us, because we're spending all the money, and we're just having a laugh. And in retrospect I think we could have produced better material, and more concise material. I think *"i"* could make a really wicked single album. Maybe one and a half albums. But not two.'

The house influence that told on *"i"* was being felt elsewhere in British guitar music. 'The new kind of rock'n'roll is definitely house music,' Kevin Shields said in 1990. 'All the young kids everywhere, the way they dress, their attitude towards life, everything. It's like all the previous youth explosions. It *is* that.' In particular, there was a splinter of rave culture that found crossover with emergent post-rock: ambient house. Where acid house tracks were fluorescent and hedonistic, ambient house explored the morning light; it was a helpful sort of music, acting as an aid to sleep, or as a handholding return to stark reality. It often identified with the Polynesian islands on the Pacific Rim, or the Aboriginal mythology of 'dreamtime'; it even quietly crossed over into those dreaded two words, New Age.

'It all happened last summer,' said The Orb's Alex Patterson, in 1990. 'We were clubbing all night, and seeing the dawn in. One day we ended up on Brighton beach at sunrise, recovering. The next day we mixed the twelve-inch.' The twelve-inch in question was The Orb's 'Loving You', subsequently known as 'A Huge Ever Growing Pulsating Brain That Rules From The Centre Of The Ultraworld' (because the lawyers for Minnie Riperton's estate objected to the prominent sample from her famous song).

Also part of The Orb at that point was Jimmy Cauty. He, along with Bill Drummond, had been The Justified Ancients Of Mu Mu; they were now trading as The KLF. In contrast to the brash plundering of *1987: What The Fuck Is Going On?*, The KLF's first album was called *Chill Out* and sampled animals, birds, transport, and Mongolian throat singers.

A canny Cauty explained *Chill Out* in 1990. 'It actually all started off as an accident. We did a mix of a house track, left the drums off by mistake and suddenly realised that the house pads and chords sounded brilliant without the beat. So we decided to do a few more things like that. Then, after we'd recorded several tracks, we began to wonder what to call this sound and how we'd market it if we were a proper record company. The phrase ambient house was basically born out of cynicism, but once we'd come up with it we thought, OK, if it's got to be called something, that's a good a name as any. We knew that people would soon pick up on it—it's the start of a new decade and everyone wants to have something different to talk about.'

The KLF being The KLF, they soon ramped up the *provocateur* aspect of their project. 'We always try to think of an alternative to an ordinary live show,' said Drummond in 1990, 'and for one party we played, Energy at the Brixton Academy, we wanted to build a hill on the stage, cover it with turf, put a fence around it, and let five sheep with The KLF painted on their sides roam around it while we played a track through the PA. We planned to have some equipment up there too with the hope that if the sheep knocked into something it would make a noise and be an added bonus. We thought, *yeah, this is the future of rock'n'roll.* But Lambeth Council refused to let us have live animals onstage.'

'Instead of going to gigs,' says Sarah Peacock of Seefeel, 'we'd be going to all-nighters at the Brixton Academy, taking Es and watching The Orb, and thinking, *how good would this sound if we were to stretch this song out to ten minutes and put a drum machine on it*? And it just seemed to be a slightly more exciting direction from before. We were all up for it.'

Seefeel were not initially considered as contemporaries of The Orb *et al*, however. Along with Moonshake, they were bracketed with the then-scathing term 'shoegazing' on their first releases. The heavy-walled introspection of My Bloody Valentine's 1988 album *Isn't Anything* had set in motion a particular take on its signature sound. Shields's own description of *Isn't Anything*—'it sounds like something loud played quietly'—was ubiquitous in British indie music as the 1980s became the 1990s.

'Over in the States,' Kevin Shields said in 1992, 'they see the Valentines as being on the coattails of Lush and Ride, 'cos they toured [in America] first. It's pretty ironic. And in Britain we've started getting lumped in with other bands who we don't belong with all over again, just like we used to with the C86 bands. We're starting to be seen as just another bunch of rich, lazy, middle-class types who write vague, senseless lyrics and sit around all day doing nothing.'

Initially coined for the band Moose, whose singer Russell Yates had a habit of staring at lyrics taped to the floor during performances, shoegazing came in for a music press roasting. The journalists' complaints were similar to Shields's: this was inconsequential music, played by time-on-their-hands dilettantes, all of whom existed in a metaphorical Thames Valley croquet club. It was briefly tagged as 'The Scene That Celebrates Itself' due to the perception that the bands all knew one another and were engaged in an unofficial competition to boil *Isn't Anything* down to grey mush. While a lot of these musicians *did* come across as earnest and smug, there was a streak of self-aware humour there, too. 'I think bands like us and Chapterhouse reflect these times,' said Neil Halstead of Slowdive. 'Which are, like, complete apathy.'

Moonshake's initial tagging as shoegazers was understandable. Their debut EP, *First*, was released on Creation in 1991, and was only recorded at the time and place it was (the Protocol studio in North London) because of My Bloody Valentine. 'They were already doing *Loveless*, and basically Creation had lots of overtime booked,' says Moonshake's Margaret Fiedler. 'And that's why they put us in there. That's also why they put us with Guy [Fixsen], because he had been doing their sessions.'

'It's a lot better than many of the other supposedly shoegaze-y bands around,' says David Callahan, about *First*. 'But it wasn't what we'd planned to do, and it wasn't what we'd discussed doing. So, Margaret and I were both a bit disappointed.'

'The worst review was "Single of the Weak". W-E-A-K,' says Fiedler. 'And Slowdive were the single of the proper week. It was like: Slowdive, *really*?'

My Bloody Valentine returned, in 1991, and swept away the shoegazing imitators at a stroke. While *You Made Me Realise* had five songs and took five days, *Loveless* had eleven and took two years. 'To Here Knows When', a version of which was first released on the *Glider*

EP, is perhaps their most post-rock statement of all: abstracted to the point of disappearance, with a voluptuous, decaying feel. 'It's the kind of track that'll easily get looked over unless it's shoved down people's throats,' Shields said in 1991. 'There's a lot of things going on. We really wanted people to check their stereos with this on. There's things in it that even the engineers barely remember doing, tons of really subtle inflections. And yet, it's just one guitar.'

As for A.R. Kane, after the release of *"i"* and the inessential *Rem"i"xes* album, all went quiet. 'There was a massive drop after the second album, of just [our] interest in it,' says Tambala. 'Sick of the whole fucking industry by then. I think there's a music careerist approach maybe, where you plot your career, you know what you want to be. We had no idea. It all happened so quickly and we just kept doing it and doing it. And it got to the point where we just weren't enjoying it very much anymore.'

'Once I would have said music was the most important thing in my life,' an unguarded Alex Ayuli said in 1989, during promotional duties for *"i"*. 'But to look back at me even contemplating saying that, seems silly, now.'

'Alex left the country,' Tambala says. 'Our relationship was very telepathic, and I really don't mean that in a John Wyndham *Chrysalids* sense, or even in a hippie sense. I just mean we didn't *have* to talk for so long, because we shared so many experiences, and so many similar things. And we also fought like cat and dog, which is a great relationship. It's fiery. And that was *there*. Then, suddenly, he's in America and I'm sending him floppy discs, and he's putting them into his sampler. And he's writing all of his own songs, and I'm writing all of my own songs … *fuck*. That's not how we work.'

'Because Alex went away, I had lots of time on my hands,' he continues, 'so I built a studio in an old building in Stratford. We hired a unit and we built a studio inside that unit. It had a drum room, a vocal booth. A proper studio, really beautiful. I started engineering and producing other bands.'

Tambala named his studio, and the label that came out of it, H.Ark!

'I was a very big A.R. Kane fan,' says Gary McKendry of Papa Sprain, who would experience H.Ark! first hand. 'I actually thought they were the coolest band in the universe.'

A.R. Kane, My Bloody Valentine, Cocteau Twins—and, in America, Hugo Largo—there was clearly something going on. Dream pop was one tag. Oceanic rock was another, dreamt up by Simon Reynolds and fellow *Melody Maker* journalist Paul Oldfield in 1988.

'"Oceanic" rock, apart from getting away from the turbulences and tantrums of pop's onward march of history, wants to liberate itself from the confines of the self, time, and the "real" world,' they wrote. 'That's why we've spent a year summoning up images of Arctic wastes, the sea, the sky, sleep or the womb.'

From 'When You're Sad' through to 'To Here Knows When' was a period of breakthrough. It looked above and beyond noise, while at the same time using it. To the listener, it was almost as if the music itself dreamt up the sonic rush as a means of expression; to the musicians, this was the result of thousands of hours of meticulous instrument and studio manipulation. 'It was extreme, without being wishy-washy or wet,' Kevin Shields said. 'Anybody can do these things. But nobody has.'

CHAPTER FOUR

spirit is everything

'One note. But you feel the note.' MARK HOLLIS, TALK TALK

One of the great music industry rumours is that My Bloody Valentine's *Loveless* cost a quarter of a million pounds, bankrupting Creation Records in the process.

'I could see my label slipping away,' Alan McGee said in 1999. 'I'd even mortgaged my own house.'

McGee's account conflicts with Kevin Shields's own memories (in short, he denies that *Loveless* spunked *quite* that much money), and there were almost certainly other major issues at Creation that contributed to the insolvency. However, it is probably true that Creation, still an independent then, couldn't bear these kinds of costs like a major.

'£250,000 in debt but we're all smiles,' read a headline in 1984, from the *Standard Recorder*, a local newspaper in South Essex. They were interested in the fortunes of the group Talk Talk, as two-thirds of them came from the neighbourhood. 'Drummer Lee Harris, 21, of Allandale, Thundersley, still doesn't earn as much each week as he did when he was a trainee printer at Leighprint,' the journalist reported.

'But the money's not the point,' Harris told the *Recorder*. 'We are all doing what we want to do.'

Unlike for Creation, this quarter of a million didn't turn out to be much of an issue for EMI, the label Talk Talk owed the money to. For one thing, *It's My Life*, the album that incurred these debts, recouped its costs and more, owing largely to its huge success in mainland Europe. For another, major labels were extremely adroit at gaming the system, being structured not to lose, even when they had so-called 'difficult' or tardy artists on their books.

The advent of CDs was an especial godsend in this regard. Here was a way to persuade music fans to fork out for high-profit-margin consumer products, sold on the concept of better sound quality, durability, modernity, and space-saving. Reissues and greatest hits packages were especially lucrative. They incurred no or low recording costs, and their purpose, so the industry line went, allowed record company investment in the progressive and artistic; without that big artist cash-in, wave goodbye to the future Charles Mingus or Laurie Anderson. However, Steve Albini, in his 1993 essay 'The Problem With Music', explicitly argued otherwise, setting out 'the math [to] explain just how fucked' any future Mingus or Anderson would be on a contemporary major label. Both viewpoints had a logic, given that advances and breathing space were there for visionary projects but, as demonstrated by *It's My Life*, virtually all costs were recoupable by the record label, with risk being shunted onto the band.

Talk Talk left EMI for Polydor in 1990—essentially for money, according to their manager, Keith Aspden, rather than greater freedom—and their former label sought to milk the now-empty husk. This was first done, rather predictably, with the 1990 'best-of', *Natural History*. Its million-selling success then prompted the label to exploit the band's legacy further. So, in March 1991, *History Revisited: The Remixes* was released: a dreadful bodge of Talk Talk's original recordings and tinny dance beats, and it dated even as the turntable spun.

As it turned out, *History Revisited* was also illegal, the band successfully suing EMI for 'false attribution of authorship in contravention of the group's moral rights'. But it was the timing of it that must have *really* stung. For it would only be a few months more until what would be Talk Talk's final album, *Laughing Stock*, was released: perhaps the strongest antithesis of a quickie cash-in job imaginable. In its way, *Laughing Stock* serves as a positive argument for record company wealth accumulation. For without Polydor's resources, this expensive and time-consuming endeavour could never have been made. As galling as it is, *History Revisited* and *Laughing Stock* are two sides of the same industry coin.

'Once upon a time, Talk Talk were a pop band; now they're a law unto themselves,' *Record Mirror* wrote in 1988. This is the common narrative of Talk Talk. That theirs was a gradual progression at first; away from their synth-based first album, *The Party's Over*, in 1982, toward the pastoral pop of *The Colour Of Spring* in 1985. Then there was a dramatic leap into the uncommercial with 1988's *Spirit Of Eden*, with *Laughing Stock* as both refinement and ultimate conclusion of the project. Yet, it could be that *Laughing Stock* was latent in *The Party's Over* all the time.

'What I like about Shostakovich, and music like that, is that total oppressiveness in the force of it and then, at other moments, that pure sort of tranquillity,' Hollis said as early as 1982. 'It's between those two extremes.' For people who had carefully listened to the band beyond the singles, *Spirit Of Eden* wasn't such a shock.

'I hate synths, they're horrible things, but if you want to make multi-textural music, they're a cheap way of doing it,' Hollis said in 1991. 'When you get the opportunity to move on, you take it.' This was consistent with what he maintained at the time of *It's My Life*: that Talk Talk's use of synths shouldn't be construed as trend-cresting but as a way to explore sound possibility. 'We try to use synths from the point of view of unnatural instruments,' he said. 'We try to use a synth sound as you would use a Fairlight or whatever—you don't get a particular string sound where you say, oh, that's obviously a string. You play with the sound and make it into something that hasn't been heard before.' The key influences cited by Hollis—Miles Davis, Gil Evans, Otis Redding, Can, Erik Satie, Shostakovich—barely changed between 1982 and 1991. Nor did his fondness for deeply unfashionable British progressive rock and its ideals.

'Traffic, King Crimson, Spooky Tooth … to me, these groups have been important,' Hollis said in 1984. 'In the late 60s I was thirteen, fourteen years old, a period in a boy's life in which you're very impressionable. My older brother Ed [producer and songwriter Ed Hollis, who worked with Eddie & The Hot Rods] always turned me towards records. Doors, early King Crimson, Soft Machine. Traffic too. Bands who made albums. There were singles, but it was more than two hits and a bunch of rubbish, as it is now. There was a healthy balance between short and long pieces, there was a comprehensive idea in those records.' He went on to name his favourite song as Traffic's denuded epic, 'Low Spark Of High Heeled Boys'.

In the same way that many a high-profile punk had a prog past (John Lydon may have scrawled 'I Hate' on a Pink Floyd T-shirt, but he had unironically owned the item in the first place), Mark Hollis is a fine example of the overlap between prog and punk aesthetics that was such a powerful combination for post-rock. While Hollis was certainly interested in the European classical tradition and believed that music could make grand statements, punk provided a stripped-down energy, a tension, and confidence.

'*Spirit Of Eden* shines for me with the same mentality as formerly punk did; not so much for me to make the same kind of music that punk created, but more a certain attitude,' Hollis has said. 'The technique is not important. It's the enthusiasm that counts for everything.'

The rhythm section, with Harris on drums and Paul Webb on bass, came from a slightly different angle, but was also rooted in something key to post-rock. 'Me and Lee have known each other since fourth year at school in Southend,' Webb said in 1982. 'When all that [punk] scene started, there wasn't anyone interested in being in bands, there was still that rock'n'roll, [Dr] Feelgoods thing. So we gave up for six months and went clubbing.' They were also playing in a reggae band, Eskalator. 'Then [we] met Ed Hollis and tried the thing with Mark. With this band, none of us like rock'n'roll, nor do we like the plastic side of the electronic scene. We want to actually perform and play properly without coming on like a rock band.'

The earliest Talk Talk live shots, and their pre-signing publicity, profess a 'semi-psychedelic' aura. This was more in harmony with the LA-based Paisley Underground bands of the early 1980s, who combined West Coast progressive rock and punk, than with the 'plastic side of the electronic scene' that Talk Talk came to be associated with. A 1979 demo by Hollis, the lilting 'Crying In The Rain', also points to a bucolic interest that he would draw upon, in much more complex form, in 1988.

Another group pegged as pop-synth boys was Japan. But a small scratch revealed that they too loved the early 1970s, and the decade's expansive character ghosted within their career. This time, the pronounced influence was glam rock, especially the decadent, detached, sad poignancy of Roxy Music and David Bowie. Simon Napier-Bell, Japan's first manager, claimed that David Sylvian's early songs 'rambled and got nowhere', so—as EMI persuaded Talk Talk out of their paisley shirts and into white suits in 1982—he steered Japan away from these meanders. 'I decided the only way they'd ever get an audience was if they compromised,' he said. Japan were another group to haemorrhage money, Napier-Bell pouring about £2,000 a week into them at one point.

Sylvian has claimed that the vast majority of his time in Japan was unhappy and unrepresentative of him ('What I feel about the work with Japan is that, at the centre of it, there's an emotional void'). It's true, also, that the press wasn't kind; Sylvian was perceived to be pretentious and aloof. Tensions in the band were both creative and personal (Mick Karn, the bassist, was apparently cuckolded by Sylvian) and they broke up in 1984. Sylvian's first release on leaving the group was *Brilliant Trees*, featuring Holger Czukay of Can, and double-bassist Danny Thompson, who would soon appear on *The Colour Of Spring* and *Spirit Of Eden*.

'We were in Pete Townshend's studio, and I set up my "dictatorphone", an old humming IBM device from the 50s,' Czukay has said. 'David and the engineer were sitting for about one hour in the control room, silent. I tried to get that machine to work properly but didn't succeed. At the end I said, I think we should change my instrument, and over the intercom they said, No, Holger, we want that. They were not only

British gentlemen, they even understood the quality of garbage in a digital age.'

Talk Talk's *The Colour Of Spring*, too, had been unafraid of unusual or archaic instrumentation. The inner sleeve breaks down every single instrument used on every single track. Prominent on the two most understated tracks, 'April 5th' and 'Chameleon Day', is the Variophon, primarily played by producer and co-writer Tim Friese-Greene. On 'Chameleon Day', especially—where it is the only instrument apart from piano and voice—it has a folklore-horror quality, driving the track into an uncanny hinterland.

'It is quite a rare instrument in this country now,' Friese-Greene said of the Variophon in 1986. 'Most people haven't even heard of it, and there are only two in London that I know of. It's basically a very small keyboard, with a breath controller that enables you to put some expression into your playing, so that all sorts of inflections are added to the synthesised sound. The reason we get on with it so well is that it doesn't give you the feeling that it's synthesized. It's basically a woodwind or brass instrument. Its wide range of expression is the main reason that we used it so much.'

'It sounds a bit like a melodica, but it don't sound like a melodica,' added Hollis. 'It sounds right weird.'

The track to most strongly anticipate *Spirit Of Eden* was the B-side to 'Life's What You Make It'; in fact, 'It's Getting Late In The Evening' was bumped off *The Colour Of Spring* album to make way for that famous single. 'In "It's Getting Late In The Evening" there are a lot of references to things that are in the album, from different areas of music,' Hollis said. 'I like the way that there are things in that which are derivative of Ravel, alongside things which are derivative of The Animals.'

'It's Getting Late In The Evening' was based on a gospel song, for which Hollis wrote new lyrics. The track is important because it was, up to that point, Talk Talk's most complete expression of an idea: take as little as possible from many different areas. Tiny fragments—whether from different styles of music or, increasingly, from unique performances and ambient sounds—would be stitched together in such a meticulous way as to be a perfect encapsulation of feeling. In this, it was analogous to Hank Shocklee's work in Public Enemy.

'*Spirit Of Eden* is about construction and destruction,' Hollis said, 'aspects of life that occur simultaneously. *Spirit Of Eden* is all that surrounds us, both what we respect, and what we detest.'

Released in September 1988, *Spirit Of Eden* is a record of vast emotional themes and gravitas, yet without pomp and circumstance. It evokes the inner landscapes of the psyche but is neither inward nor isolationist. The tiny details of life that cause joy and melancholia sparkle and, since voice is sparsely employed, the words feel like haikus woven deeply into the fabric of the track. Hollis has claimed the lyrics 'are three months of my observations, and represent the values in which I believe, on a humanitarian level'. They took so long to write precisely because of their compactness: 'It's much harder to say something in ten words when you have a thousand words at your disposal.'

Hollis's long-held belief that the voice is an instrument with no special privileges over another is realised, as his vocal sounds are on par with Mark Feltham's harmonica and Henry Lowther's distinctive, dissonant trumpet. The Variophon was retired on this album, but there is another unusual electronic sound: the shozyg, a homemade instrument invented by Hugh Davies (who also played it on *Spirit Of Eden*). It comprises contact mics, a chair castor, fretsaw blades, springs, and wire, all surrounded by plywood and foam rubber insulators. The name shozyg came from its original casing: a hollowed-out volume of *The Library Of Knowledge* that ran from *SHO* to *ZYG*; Lee Harris has described it as a 'sort of electro-boffin synth' where 'sounds are made by blowing over strings, moving magnets over pieces of metal, [and] putting your hands in-between "aerials"'.

'As soon as you start using vibrating materials,' Hugh Davies said in 1998, 'you can find some sort of kinship with something that exists already.'

'We learned over the years that giving an "outsider" any hints as to musical approach was almost always doomed to send them off in the wrong direction,' Friese-Greene has said. 'So what we ended up doing, which must have been quite intimidating to say the least, was to get people in and say nothing. That way at least they'd be free to play anything they wanted. Sometimes you'd get a result and sometimes you'd just write the session off and erase them when they'd gone, which happened on many occasions. We became very good at erasing things.'

'The story about how [Hollis] got a twenty-five-piece choir on *Spirit*, got them to sing this beautiful part and erased it, is all true,' says Phill Brown, who engineered the sessions. 'He says things can sometimes be "too perfect".'

This was novel: to erase sound because it was *good*, because it was superb, even because it was heart-stoppingly beautiful. *Spirit Of Eden* wasn't designed for that kind of serene loveliness. It needed tension, ire, and reduction to make it work. Taking things out meant that what was left accrued greater presence. That such lengthy time in the studio could result in something that sounded so still—untamed, even—rather than glossed and flawless was radical for a mainstream band in the late 1980s, although, as Hollis observed, 'We're doing something that's outside the conventional form, and as far as I'm concerned, we only stand out because that form has become so narrow, so constricted.'

Spirit Of Eden wasn't all that inaccessible, but it wasn't particularly saleable, either. It wasn't concise and it wasn't easily relatable. The devotional aspects burned, the silences froze. One almost felt sorry for Tony Wadsworth, Capitol and Parlophone Records' general manager, who was responsible for the marketing of the album. While Mark Hollis undertook interviews as if they were a school detention on a sunny day, Wadsworth spoke up when Hollis did not.

'Talk Talk are not your ordinary combo and require sympathetic marketing,' he told *Q* in 1988. 'They're not so much difficult as not obvious. You've just got to find as many ways as possible to expose the music. The standard marketing route is whack out a single, try to chart the single, and then hopefully on the strength of that, sell some albums. With the way the media is angled, the room you've got to expose adult music—for want of a better term—is very restricted. We've got to do what I believe to be a very heavy campaign on Talk Talk. We've got to go out very bullishly and tell people that this is an album for 1988. That will be the sales pitch—An Album For 1988.'

David Sylvian, on the other hand, didn't need a Tony Wadsworth in interviews. He freely discussed details of his life that the ferociously private Hollis would never have done. 'I've been going through quite a negative time, intense … a lot of things came up about my past which I found very difficult to deal with,' he told *Melody Maker* in 1991, describing how he embarked on analysis, and revealing intimate dynamics of his childhood subconscious.

Sylvian's most notable achievement since *Brilliant Trees* is 1986's double album *Gone To Earth*, the second disc of which is an instrumental shamanic exploration evolved from Sylvian's interest in tape looping. He wanted to create these instrumental tracks at the same time as the conventional album, and so it was agreed with his label, Virgin (although they showed little real interest, and Sylvian ended up virtually self-financing the instrumental half).He gave these tracks quite literal titles describing very visual, concrete scenarios. 'I got the idea from reading about Picasso. When he first started painting Cubist paintings, he said to make it easy for the viewers he gave the pictures very matter-of-fact titles, so they could actually see something within the picture. By just looking at the title they could look at the picture and begin to make the outline of what they are seeing.'

In 1989, Sylvian decided to reconstruct a version of Japan—but on terms informed by his solo career, and perhaps also one that seemed closer to his very early outlook (the one that Simon Napier-Bell had been so keen to bludgeon out of the young group). Named Rain Tree Crow in deference to how different it was from the well-known Japan material, the new band was conceived of as an 'improvisational project' where the members might float in and out of the project in collective fashion.

'We spent a few months hanging out—we'd only talk about the work indirectly—and went into the studio cold,' Sylvian said. 'We hadn't played together since the last Japan tour. Spirits were high. It was a really good time, so much laughter.' Bridges had been rebuilt between Karn and Sylvian, the latter having contributed vocals and keyboards to the former's 1986 album *Dreams Of Reason Produce Monsters*. The idea of Rain Tree Crow, Sylvian said, was to 'open up' the Japan relationships through improvising together, and develop a shared, equal language that they had never enjoyed before.

But it didn't take long to turn sour again. The recording took eighteen months, with Sylvian once again having to stump up his own cash to finish the project. Virgin was also unhappy with using the name Rain Tree Crow instead of Japan. The other members of Rain Tree Crow didn't consider it a shared language in the way as was originally conceived, seeing it instead as another Sylvian project. 'At the end of the day, he's tried to take it away from us,' drummer Steve Jansen (Sylvian's brother) said. 'We [aren't] allowed to go to the mixing because he put up the money, and that for us, doesn't show respect. … I know he believes he's right in what he's doing. He believes in himself to such a degree [he's willing] to abuse his friends.'

'My relationship with the boys in the band has ended,' Sylvian declared in 1991, while promoting the project's sole self-titled album. 'It's not something I feel particularly negative about, but that doesn't mean I rejoice over it. But having made this album, musically we did something on this album that if we had been mature enough ten years ago we would have tackled.'

Rain Tree Crow is certainly a mature work. It's grown-up and tasteful, sometimes world-weary, dismissing energy as a youthful conceit. It, too, was keen on the sculpture method—chiselling away the excess from a track—rather than building it up. 'I find it very difficult to put one note in a composition if it's not relevant for that note to be there,' Sylvian has said. 'To me, that's a bit like putting a soft focus on a lens just to make sure you get a decent portrait out of it.' However, *Rain Tree Crow* engages far more with a classic rockishness than *Spirit Of Eden* does (or even Sylvian himself on *Gone To Earth*); fragile and tactile moments like 'New Moon At Red Deer Wallow' are balanced with guitar squeals, like those on 'Black Crow Hits Shoe Shine City'. Still, Sylvian's excursions into this post-rock space, along with the seriousness of his approach, are an early indication of how it could be attractive to and intelligently employed by figures in the (relative) mainstream.

'I may as well attempt to describe the dawn for you,' began *Melody Maker*'s review of Talk Talk's *Laughing Stock*.

'It's never a thing with any of these albums of knowing what they're going to sound like,' Mark Hollis has said. 'It's more like knowing the kind of feel you want. The one kind of starting point we had this time was just this thing of everyone working in their own little time zone. Really, it's just going back to one of a couple of things—either the jazz ethic or y'know, an album like *Tago Mago* by Can, where the drummer locked in and off he went and people reacted to certain points along the way. It's arranged spontaneity—that's exactly what it is.'

'Silence is the most important thing you can have.'

It starts with that silence, or near to it: twenty seconds of tape hiss, as if the album itself is a found object and has been copied from an antique reel-to-reel. Unlike *Spirit Of Eden*, which shimmers with sunlit optimism among the seclusion, there is a sense of grubby dilapidation right from the opening of *Laughing Stock*. The silences within the album can suggest absences, lack, death, rather than possibility; when 'Ascension Day' abruptly cuts off, it's like a guillotine has dropped.

The work is cyclical and mesmerising, hallowed and tense. The gospel root of 'It's Getting Late In The Evening' grows deeper. 'It's just about virtue, really, just about character,' Hollis has said. 'I can't think of any other way of being able to sing a lyric and actually sing it and feel it unless I believe in what I'm singing about. That goes back to the gospel thing. I'm not saying all lyrics have to be about religion but, in a way, there must be that kind of thing in it.' Hollis's voice, vulnerable, is breath in the frost.

Now, instead of being a band, Talk Talk had become an amorphous, postmodern cell in both form and function. 'The studio was oppressive to the point of unreality,' Hollis said. They recorded in sepulchral light, an oil projector breaking the darkness with kaleidoscopes on the walls, while candles and burning incense further softened the studio's edges (in another expression of the psychedelic thread that has consistently run through Talk Talk).

Hollis's construction/destruction dichotomy from *Spirit Of Eden* is even more central to *Laughing Stock*. He believed that 'the first time that something is played, it is at its finest', so participants were given a basic chord structure and then left to it. To overcome the inherent practical problem in this—that the vast majority of improvisation is 'rubbish', to use Hollis's own word—pruning and arrangement was paramount. Over forty musicians were employed for *Laughing Stock*. Fewer than half of them are actually heard on the album. Of those, often only sections of their performances were saved, rather than the whole, and sometimes just orphaned individual notes. Hollis reckoned that, for every minute of music on the album, an hour's worth was discarded. Those flecks populate and charge *Laughing Stock*, dislocated from their context, fragmentary and disorientating on one hand, imperceptibly sutured on the other.

'So much of what we do is built around mistakes,' Hollis said. 'Either that, or you decide on one or two notes you want and the rest is down to positioning of those sounds in the thing as a whole. That's the most important thing as far as I'm concerned—the space and the placing of sound within that space. It's amazing to think how little you actually need to make your point.'

'I remember thinking: this is the end,' Friese-Greene has said. 'This is as far as we can go. After one note, there's no notes.'

Tracks on *Laughing Stock* referred back, replanting new seeds in their previous work. 'Renee' had become 'Runeii'; 'Myrrhman' was a refraction of 'Mirror Man'. ('I like cross-referencing,' Hollis said in 1998. 'I've had fun doing that'). But there were hints at a possible future, too. Talk Talk released a few extra tracks to accompany the singles from *Laughing Stock*. 'Stump', in particular, was a find: a dissonant instrumental play-around that wouldn't have been out of place on an early Sonic Youth bootleg. At first, 'Stump' sounds like retardation, or at least a parody of *Laughing Stock*'s meticulousness. But it also serves as a reminder that *Laughing Stock*, far from being Talk Talk's logical end point, nurtures within it other, totally different powers—'Stump', for instance, makes explicit the burbling static in 'After The Flood'—and that they still remain unrealised.

Mark Hollis was asked in 1998, around the time of his sole solo album, *Mark Hollis*, whom he might feel affinity with; one name touted by the journalist was Scott Walker. Hollis's response was somewhat lukewarm. 'I only know "The Sun Ain't Gonna Shine Anymore" and *Tilt* and … what can I say? He's obviously someone with a mission, for which I wish him well.'

David Sylvian, on the other hand, was a great admirer of Scott Walker, and sent him a song. 'He asked to meet up,' Sylvian said. 'We chatted and he said he didn't want to record just the one song, how about recording an album together as two vocalists? It didn't strike me as a wonderful idea and I didn't think either of us believed for one second that anything was going to happen, and it didn't. We tried. But Scott's so evasive.'

'He did say that he felt his stuff could use a little more balls,' Walker said, in 1995, of this aborted collaboration. 'He's much more of an ethereal merchant than I am. I'm a man who struggles with spirituality, whereas he's given in to it. My album, and the one before it, is above all a struggle in a Dostoyevskian sense. It's a real fight for me in every line. Whereas he's given in to a state of grace.'

The two albums Walker is talking of are 1984's *Climate Of Hunter* and its follow-up, 1995's *Tilt*. These are brittle, dark records that, as *Spirit Of Eden* and *Laughing Stock* did for Talk Talk, cast the author as a wilfully obtuse property: when once he'd sold, and once he'd pleased, now he alienated. Walker didn't see it that way. 'I've been writing the same stuff since 1969,' he has said. 'Just paring it down.'

'People expect a lot more sales out of me than are generated,' Walker said, acknowledging in 1995 that his material from years back helps at the signing stage of record deals, but not so much at the crunch time of record release. 'So they [labels] are *vastly* disappointed.' Virgin dropped him after *Climate Of Hunter*, allegedly one of the worst-selling records in its history; *Tilt*, interestingly, fared better, especially in the UK. It reached number 27, one place lower than *Laughing Stock*.

Tilt is a record rotted in on itself, buried in the ground and left to decompose into a black mesh of sounds. 'We wanted to record as naturally as possible,' Walker said in 1995, 'so we didn't use any compression. And so because *Tilt* is like a deep focus shot instead of a modern in-your-face noise, you really do have to play this record loud because then it all comes together. Even when the bursts come in, like on "The Cockfighter", you've gotta be brave and keep it loud. Most people go "OHMYGOD! TURN IT DOWN!"'

The words of *Tilt* are like calligrams—the poetry form developed by Guillaume Apollinaire in the early twentieth century, where the layout of letters on a page forge meaning, rather than having meaning solely as the responsibility of language—a fact underlined by Walker's printed arrangement of *Tilt*'s lyrics. And it is language, words, which drive *Tilt* and Walker. 'Everything comes from the songs,' he has said. 'Every single sound in the track relates to the lyric in some way.' The songwriting itself is incredibly considered, Walker's method involving 'waiting and waiting'.

'It comes from silence, most of it,' Walker has said. He will rarely elucidate much on what the lyrics mean, considering explanation to be a cheapening force, although he does sometimes provide context as to their genesis. 'Farmer In The City', *Tilt*'s arresting opener, is rooted in the murder of the Italian filmmaker and poet Pier Paolo Pasolini, while 'The Cockfighter', a dissonant clatter of percussion, is in itself a collision between two different legal trials. The first is of the Nazi war criminal Adolf Eichmann, responsible for organising the forced deportation to extermination camps during the Holocaust (it's there in the faux-locomotive noise). The second is of Queen Caroline of Brunswick, whose husband, George IV of England, tried to rid himself of her through a trumped-up adultery accusation in 1820; this is evoked by a nervous drum heartbeat. The proximity of erotica and death is ever-present in the track.

'Essentially, I'm really trying to find a way to talk about the things that cannot be spoken of,' Walker said in 2006. 'I cannot fake that or take short cuts. There is an absurdity there, too, of course, and I hope that people pick up on that. Without the humour, it would just be heavy and boring. I hope people get that. If you're not connecting with the absurdity, you shouldn't be there.'

'It's a good word, *tilt*,' he added later, in 2013. 'It means so many things today. The way we might feel personally about ourselves, and what we might do, radically. It covers a lot of area and that's what I'm looking for.'

Walker did not record demo tracks, and never disclosed the material to anyone until he was in the studio. *Tilt* was put together in an almost polar opposite way to *Laughing Stock*. 'By the time I get to the studio, it's all written down,' he has said. 'I have to have readers [musicians who can read music] I can work with, because I always want the music to be played together, at once.' Many chords on *Tilt* were unusual and unnamed, bordering on discord, and the musicians had to grope around until Walker's ideal sound was reached. He would also insist on performing his vocals live, without the aid of click or guide tracks, and with minimal if any overdubbing. The result is that his voice sounded both weightily arranged and spontaneous—an effect strengthened by Walker's method-acting approach.

'They're agony,' Brian Gascoigne, who arranged and conducted the strings on *Tilt*, said of the sessions. 'He believes, and I take issue with him on this, that in order to convey very strong emotion in the music, you have to be feeling it while you're making it. Well that couldn't be true, because otherwise the people who are playing Bruckner and Mahler every night would be basket cases by the time they're thirty. And after three or four hours in the studio, he is a basket case, because he lives the thing with such intensity of emotion. I always find writing the strings for Scott very irritating, because they're mostly holding one note for sixteen bars. And yet he will make them go on and on and on, doing it again and again and again, until he gets the emotion.'

This fervour is most apparent on 'Rosary', the album's closer. With just voice and guitar, it gently but malevolently rattles with raw nerves. 'Rosary' is a ballad of sorts, but one to avoid any sort of relief or, indeed, sadness. Instead, it pivots between pure sensation and deadened abstraction, the lyrics so minimal as to be only the yelps of private expression.

'Can we have a lighting change, please?' asked Jools Holland, hosting his *Later* TV show in 1995. Walker was about to perform 'Rosary', to date his final live appearance. But Holland wasn't asking for a darkening of the room for mood purposes. It was sleight-of-hand; to foster the illusion that the audience was still there. Walker insisted on performing 'Rosary' without one, and their cheers were edited in after he had left.

Tilt is a deliberately mysterious album, and because it came out of a period of complete silence, it carried meanings that Scott Walker perhaps did not intend: the weight of his artistic reputation. 'I haven't heard *Tilt* since I made it. The moment I finish, I never listen to it again,' Walker has said. 'Because, look, I've written it over all those years, I've produced it, sung it, mixed it—I produced it with my friend Pete [Walsh], of course. I never want to hear it again. It's a nightmare.'

In many senses, these albums were made during a privileged time and, despite Walker, Sylvian, and Hollis *all* clashing with labels at some point, they had budget, reputation, a loyal audience, and their dislike of playing the media game was indulged. They did not waste their opportunity.

'I worked at it,' Walker said of *Tilt*, 'and [the listener] should work at it as well.'

'I think there's an amount of work you have to do to actually realise what's within those albums,' said Mark Hollis, looking back on *Spirit Of Eden* and *Laughing Stock*. 'Maybe that's not the right word. No, all I mean is, you actually need to *listen* to it.'

CHAPTER FIVE

interested female vocalists write 1864 douglas blvd. louisville, ky 40205

'There was a lot of weird music, specifically Louisville weird music, that wasn't necessarily aggressive or fast or any of that. But it had a punk mentality.' TARA JANE O'NEIL, RODAN

Not everyone rated Talk Talk's way of working.

'Basically, fuck all that,' Steve Albini wrote of *Laughing Stock* on his forum, Electrical Audio, in 2003. 'Snuff the candles, spit on your hands, and make the fucking record.'

'I like noise,' Albini has said. 'I like big-ass vicious noise that makes my head spin. I wanna feel it whipping through me like a fucking jolt. We're so dilapidated and crushed by our pathetic existence we need it like a fix.'

Big Black, Albini's seminal group, had begun in 1981 as a solo project; he possessed a drum machine, and would walk around his college with its beats pumping through his headphones. One Wednesday, Albini bought a guitar and borrowed a four-track; by the weekend he had taken these, plus his drum machine and a cache of songs about angry American misfits, and home recorded the first Big Black release, *Lungs*.

Guitarist Santiago Durango and bassist Jeff Pezzati joined Albini in Big Black soon afterward (and Pezzati was replaced with a stronger player,

Dave Riley, in 1986). Although Albini would claim that his lyrics were often an afterthought, only there to give Big Black the emotion he felt that instrumental music would lack, his words were an important part of their appeal. Big Black ploughed some broadly similar themes to Swans—rage, sexual nonconformity, self-harm, subjugation, psychopathology—but their nihilism was localised, speaking of the boredom of small-town America, and very different from Michael Gira's grand wretchedness. Less raping a slave, more fucking a friend's girlfriend.

Albini revelled in his role as misanthrope, incensing half of the underground scene in Chicago with his gonzo journalism in the fanzine *Matter*; he delighted in personal attacks, and more generally got kicks by pushing liberal buttons on race, feminism, and gay issues. It was one of the walking contradictions of the man—the desire to remain underground and aloof from fame even while he created a persona that seemed designed to draw attention, and Big Black used titles and cover artwork so extreme that they openly invited publicity.

It's hard to imagine Big Black as a delicate flower, but by 1987 the band felt too pure for the global attention they now attracted, and they split. In interviews, they said that this was because Durango wanted to go to law school; less public was the fact that they were feeling creatively bereft (the clues were there: a sardonic message on the *Headache* EP that reads, 'Warning! Not as good as *Atomizer*, so don't get your hopes up, cheese') and that they were finding more success meant more problems. 'As we got bigger, people tried to make plays for the band, appeals to our vanity or our ambition, or tried to coerce us into doing things,' Albini has said. 'And it was obvious that the only way to short-circuit that was just to break the band up. We were never comfortable with the notion that there were people in the audience that we didn't know personally. In the beginning there's a sense of kinship with the audience. As it gets bigger, that community gets diffuse, and you can either accept the fact you're a star entertainer, or you can completely sever yourself from the audience, like we did.'

Albini was a strong, and influential, advocate for independence. '[Big Black] had an ideology about how we dealt with people inside the music scene,' he reflected in 1992, '[and] the way we'd operate as a team internally. We constructed an archetype of a perfect rock band, which we tried to live up to.' They never had a manager or booking agent, nor did they sign a contract. In this, if not directly in their music, Big Black was a part of US hardcore lineage. On a sonic level, 1980s hardcore was by and large very simple: rock-ribbed, alienated, ultra-fast: music lacking in finesse but abounding in the energy of the outsider. However, as a subculture and as a way of life, it was multifaceted, and its workings were influential far outside of its own adherents.

'We wanted to have our own clique,' Ian MacKaye, founder of the bands Minor Threat and Fugazi, and the record label Dischord, has said. 'We wanted to create our own culture because we didn't feel connected to anything. Here was the perfect opportunity for that. You were instantly devoted to others around you. This was the first time rock music was being written by, performed by, shows being put on by, fanzines being put out by, networks being created—all by kids, completely outside of the mainstream music business, for reasons that had very little or nothing to do with economic incentive.'

Three aspects of hardcore, especially, were to be key to the development of an American post-rock. The first was the community. It was the musicians themselves, plus those who felt strong ties to the scene, that not only created but controlled, whether it was the distribution of records and cassettes, the self-publication of fanzines, or putting on gigs. 'That [fanzine] community is part of the same thing,' says Jeff Mueller of Rodan. 'I made some really bad magazines when I was at high school. Really, really awful. Barely worth mentioning, but I know that when we made those, it was nice to be able to exercise those muscles. It gets something out of you that you might not otherwise be able to do.'

An underground network developed. Personal integrity was key (if bands contained assholes or divas, word quickly spread), and there was a deliberate undermining of any kind of 'star quality' onstage. The strident democracy of band structure seen in hardcore was only a small step removed from the explicit undoing of hierarchy that was a common feature of post-rock.

The second was a proud localism, which often extended to commandeering vacant or underused spaces for rehearsals, gigs, and gatherings. During the late 1970s and early 1980s, in troubled post-industrial cities, abandoned properties were common. As there was a sense that the recent past had been destroyed anyway, a future could be forged in the wastelands. Anyway, hardcore bands were often too extreme for existing clubs, and the audience was small; it was easy to make a virtue out of a necessity when reclaiming urban space.

The third was a sense that overt lyrical political statements were less important than an anti-establishment thread, one strong as piano wire. Thus the music itself, and its attitude, made each track *intrinsically* hardcore and anti-rock, whether or not its words reflected it (although they often did). Post-rock took this baseline principle further. Many, if not most, post-rock bands had a political outlook, but they veered away from obvious expression of it. Tracks were political by doing; lyrics, if they were there at all, would not be didactic.

Like any genre, hardcore had an arc. 'Everything [hardcore] set out to be in terms of independence and freedom quickly became such a formula and a book of rules—how to dress, to sound, to act—[that] it wasn't fun anymore,' Jesse Malin of the New York-based Heart Attack said in 2010. When hardcore couldn't get shorter and faster, a way out was to get longer and slower. The second side of Black Flag's 1984 album *My War* consists of three six-minute-plus sludge tracks; the following year's *The Process Of Weeding Out* EP is an all-instrumental jazz-influenced grind, designed to 'weed out' Black Flag fans who desired only to hear adrenalin thrash.

Another characteristic of hardcore was that—often—the bands would be very young. 'I grew up in Louisville, Kentucky, which is a slightly eccentric, midsize city, and I discovered punk rock via the mainstream music press, like *Rolling Stone* magazine, in 1979, when I was twelve,' says David Grubbs of Gastr del Sol. 'Suddenly the field was wide open, and I remember reading interviews with Public Image Ltd and Gang

Of Four, and reading about The Raincoats and This Heat. At the same time, I was taking in the first wave of punk, the Sex Pistols and The Clash. I understood the idea of punk being corrosive toward the idea of entertainment, [that it was] an avant-garde form that was hostile to the institution of rock music. Suddenly rock music seemed like the enemy, which was even more exciting than merely loud music with loud guitars. I was off and running with that.' Grubbs formed a band, The Happy Cadavers, who put out an EP, *With Illustrations*, in 1982, and started a fanzine, *Hit the Trail*.

'There was a very active music scene centred around the Highlands and near downtown neighbourhoods,' says Rachel Grimes of Rachel's, who also grew up in Louisville. 'A unifying factor was actually variety. It was common to have several really different sounding bands on the same bill, and people were open-eared and open-minded about checking new things out. There were several record stores in the area, which were hangout central. The thing to do was just go to a show and discover. Seemed like everyone was in a band, or several bands, and some of those groups came and went very quickly.'

'In the fall of 1982 I started a band called Squirrel Bait,' says Grubbs. 'I'd just turned fifteen years old. Definitely it came out of an American hardcore punk context. Although, by the time we recorded, the tempos had slowed down a little bit, the guitar was a little bit more of a wash of sound than a meat-cutter, hardcore style of guitar. It was already becoming something different.'

Fellow Louisville youngsters Britt Walford and Brian McMahan, who had been in the tween hardcore band Languid & Flaccid (and had to get their parents to carry the equipment as they were so small) were also part of Squirrel Bait, albeit at different points. The band released two albums, *Squirrel Bait* and *Skag Heaven*, and played shows with Sonic Youth, Dinosaur Jr, Big Black, and Hüsker Dü. ('I would say that Squirrel Bait opening for Hüsker Dü when I was sixteen or seventeen years old is still about the most exciting thing that has ever happened to me,' says Grubbs.) The band broke up in 1986, and Grubbs headed off to college, and (soon) formed another band, in Washington DC.

Contemporaneous to Squirrel Bait was Maurice, another project of McMahan and Walford, who had now teamed up with Sean 'Rat' Garrison and Mike Bucayu. Later, an accomplished and schooled guitarist, David Pajo, replaced McMahan. Pajo had trained at Berklee College of Music in Boston, and spent time on little else but practising his craft; he also loved both heavy metal and the Minutemen's guitar clarity. On his arrival, Maurice's sound slowed and its menace increased. 'You couldn't really do anything to it,' Pajo has said of Maurice. 'You couldn't bang your head to it, you couldn't slam to it, 'cos the thrash parts would only be for thirty seconds, then I'd go and do an incredibly slow part.'

Maurice started to fracture, since Pajo and Walford were becoming more complicated in their playing, while Garrison and Bucayu were primarily interested in straightforward hardcore. 'I started getting into this mindset that the weirder it was, the better it was,' Pajo said. 'We'd come up with a part that was in some totally bizarre time signature that was so difficult we couldn't even play it.'

A good friend of Pajo's was Ethan Buckler, who played bass, and with Walford the three broke away from Maurice to explore these ideas in greater concentration. Small Dirty Tight Tufts Of Hair: BEADS played their first show in November 1986 at Thomas Jefferson Unitarian Church, as part of a service; most churchgoers didn't want to hear the growing pains of an experimental band, so they left. However, Brian McMahan remained in the congregation to watch his friends, and he joined up soon after. Small Dirty Tight Tufts Of Hair: BEADS renamed themselves Slint, after one of Walford's fish, and began writing and playing around Louisville.

'Slint was casual, taking about an hour to set up, and had the usual soundchecks and breaks in between songs, but they were still incredibly good and enjoyable,' a local fanzine reported on an early Slint performance supporting Big Black. 'I'm not sure if they need lyrics, cuz they seem pretty OK as it is, but they kind of bore some people. Anyway, Slint was good. Real good.'

'Personally speaking I was into classical music, which maybe had something to do with [Slint],' Walford has said. 'I'd trained in classical, as a classical pianist. But as a whole, I think all of us being into Big Black had the biggest effect—the way their music was hypnotic.'

A mutual appreciation society quickly formed. Steve Albini took a real shine to these precocious kids and became their friend, supporter, and champion. Slint asked him to work with them. Albini (credited as 'Some Fuckin Derd Niffer') engineered their debut album, *Tweez*, in 1987, and enjoyed their mixture of goofiness and seriousness in the studio. 'They were all really conscious of the sound of their instruments,' he said. 'That was a really big thing for them.'

In 1987, Albini was just at the beginning of his career as a recording engineer (his preferred term, instead of 'producer'), something that would flourish and occasionally—this is Albini, remember—prove controversial. Ut recorded their final album, *Griller*, with him in January 1989, and recall the experience well. 'He was great, because his aesthetic was our aesthetic,' Jacqui Ham says. 'We didn't have to say, We need the guitars to sound like that. He knew. He naturally understood the mix, for the most part. He was very good with amps, mics, getting great sound. That's his metier.'

Ut had been a band for more than a decade when recording with Albini, but the Slint lads were still teenagers at the time of *Tweez*. 'This was our first recording,' Ethan Buckler has said, 'and Steve Albini was a superstar. Steve saw us as this goofy math-metal band from Louisville who idolised him. He tried to capture our odd ways and put it on our recording. He was making fun of us, and it worked.'

Post-Big Black, as well as recording others, Albini formed Rapeman, a band hobbled right from the start by its provocative name. The Rapeman was originally a Manga character that used sexual assault as a form of vigilante justice and, when the group adopted it, few could overcome its implications or forgive Albini for using it in the first place. Albini didn't help himself by shrugging when the controversy was raised, or by stoking it further. When a female heckler shouted down Rapeman at a London show, Albini reportedly responded, 'I can't hear you. You've got somebody's dick in your mouth.' (In more recent times, Albini has engaged differently with feminist issues. 'Having been raised male in our culture I have an ingrained male perspective through experience, the same way I have a white perspective, a middle-class one, an educated American one,' he told *LISTEN* in 2016. 'I have tried to cultivate an enlightened perspective, and I try to be an ally to women both in my life and in music. I feel like the female perspective, when adopted by men for song or story, is inevitably a caricature. At worst it's minstrelsy or projection based on cultural norms and exploitative depiction in art.')

If Big Black explored the release of anger, Rapeman was more inclined to consider what happens when that anger warps inward. It was even there in Albini's voice, muted, especially when it seemed to be screaming. 'Budd', from the first EP in 1988, is their best song and an example of when the Rapeman approach is wholly effective. It is about R. Budd Dwyer, a Pennsylvanian politician. Under investigation for bribery and corruption, Dwyer shot himself during a press conference in 1987; the event was recorded by news media, and many US networks chose to show at least some of the real suicide. In Rapeman's 'Budd', the spare sound is jittery with unpredictable drums and stunted phrases, while the track retreats and bursts. 'Budd' is neither elegiac nor grim, but a problematic sound for a problematic subject.

Albini's work on *Tweez* wasn't in this vein. It's a pithy, impatient, and impromptu album, metal-edged, with songs bridged by random noises (one of which was, allegedly, the sound of defecation). However, 'Kent' and 'Darlene' are more considered and episodic, and the best indication of Pajo and Walford's inclinations at the end of Maurice. *Tweez* is also notable for a sweet act on the part of the band: the tracks are named after each member's parents, plus Walford's dog. Indeed, Ron and Charlotte Walford had been especially helpful, allowing their son and his bandmates to practise endlessly in their basement.

Ethan Buckler despised the Albini production of *Tweez* so much that he left Slint after it was finished. Todd Brashear replaced Buckler on bass, while Walford and McMahan went to Northwestern College in Chicago. They shared an apartment. In it was a sort of communal guitar, always plugged in to its amp, where they (and visiting friends) could try out various ideas, recording the interesting ones.

In the way 'It's Getting Late In The Evening' was a bellwether of what Talk Talk would explore on *Spirit Of Eden*, Slint had 'Glenn'. Recorded in spring 1989, again with Albini, it was committed to tape largely because a studio happened to be available; Albini gave his time for free. 'I don't think that we really had a focused objective, necessarily, when we did the recordings,' McMahan has said. Instead, it was to 'seize the moment to spark, or regain some momentum with the band. Just trying to refocus some energy'.

'Glenn' was an instrumental (named after Brashear's father), and Slint's strongest track to date. It took its time to unfurl and, crucially, was Slint's first serious use of volume dynamics—the 'quiet bit, loud bit' that some later and lesser post-rock bands would cleave onto with grim determination. It uses repetition as a form of change, volatility and tension ramped up like Slint had never attempted before.

It and a re-recorded 'Rhoda' lay unreleased. McMahan and Walford were now back in Louisville, and the reconvened Slint toiled *hard* on four new tracks—'Nosferatu Man', 'Breadcrumb Trail', 'Good Morning, Captain', and 'Washer'.

'It was all about practising and working out those details,' Pajo has said. 'You can see how we would spend a couple of years trying to get all the details right. It seemed like even if the most logical answer was the one we began with, we still had to try every option, to go full circle, on every decision. … We could spend three days of practicing trying to find the micro-second between two basslines. It would be a really small detail but it would be important enough to us to spend that much time on it.'

'One thing that seems like a big influence on *Spiderland* was AC/DC,' Walford said. 'Brian and I were listening to *Back In Black* the whole time during making *Spiderland.* It was classic rock, but it was also economic, lean. I think *Back In Black* is for me the best-sounding record ever.'

'The way the writing process was, if one person had a riff, they would play that riff until the end of time, basically, while somebody else was trying to write other parts,' Todd Brashear has said. 'We definitely had a certain mindset to sit there and be able to do that for so long.'

'It made for some really interesting and hypnotic rehearsals,' McMahan added.

Footage from the Walford basement during the *Spiderland* practice era bears this out. Brashear, Pajo, and McMahan all hunch intently over their guitars, while Walford, bare-chested and mouth agape, fluidly smacks the drums, trance-like. Their waxen inertia translated to the stage. When Slint debuted these songs live, in 1989, there was little movement from band or audience; a collective rapture seemed to seize everyone involved.

Unlike *Tweez*'s studio babbles and improvisations, the words for these new songs were much more considered. 'I felt like there wasn't really a storyteller, for lack of a better term, in the band at that point,' McMahan has said. 'Ethan Buckler certainly is a way better songwriter than I could ever hope to be. But once he left, it seemed like there needed to be a humanising element. I perceived my role, at the time, to be one of engagement with the audience that wasn't purely musical—something that was a little more psychic.'

McMahan started to think about lyrics early in the process, as the songs were developing, but the process was private: he recorded these workings-out on a four-track, in his parents' car, parked in the garage, with all the windows up. Words were suggested by the music, rather than being pre-existing plots in McMahan's head. For instance, the sound of 'Breadcrumb Trail', to McMahan, had suggested a loss of innocence; a rite-of-passage story then developed for him of a visit to a fairground, a fortune-teller, and the narrator inviting her away for a ride on the rollercoaster. The words on *Spiderland*—with the exception of 'Washer'—are not sung, and they feel more like stories. 'Good Morning, Captain', in particular, has a strong literary quality. Its understated supernatural hints, the mind's navigation failures, and unreliability of the senses, seem especially related to Henry James's 1898 novella *The Turn Of The Screw*.

'I was a geeky kid, absorbing as much I could living in Louisville,' McMahan has said, 'European art-house classics and the stuff that weird dark teens read. The sort of themes that seemed important to me to address were universal, as far as I was concerned. It was definitely a super-insular experience. The lyrics were never part of our rehearsal. That was not something we ever discussed. Ever.'

Although Slint remained on good terms with Albini, this time, when it came to recording, they looked elsewhere. 'We wanted to do a more straightforward recording,' David Pajo said. 'Even if the songs were more abstract, the production would be really straightforward.' They found Brian Paulson, who had recently recorded the second album by Bastro—the band of their old Louisville mucker, David Grubbs.

'I guess that my mode at that point in time was to record things as purely as possible,' Paulson has said. 'And just let things unfold as they unfold, and not try and get in the way of things that would happen naturally.'

McMahan had been working in a high-quality studio, River North in Chicago, and thus got a discount for its use; nevertheless, the band were squeezed in over a weekend. The basic tracks that would make up *Spiderland* were pretty much recorded live. Through endless honing in the Walford basement, Slint were absolutely on point, and Paulson's unobtrusive method was perfect. In fact, every time they tried to adorn or change a track in the studio, it wouldn't work.

'"Washer" has my one-note guitar solo that I'm so proud of,' Pajo has said. 'I did that a couple times on *Spiderland*; the guys would say, "Do a solo on this part." At that point in my life, if someone asked me to do a solo, I would do the exact opposite of what a solo usually is. Instead of playing a bunch of notes, I would just play one, though I did some decorative stuff around it there.' Along with the four ultra-prepared tracks, Slint composed two more just before entering River North. These were 'Don, Aman', and the instrumental 'For Dinner …' (which was entirely in standard tuning, with no pedals, effects, or distortion).

Comparing the brevity of time afforded them in the studio to their lengthy development, it's unsurprising that the final commitment of these songs was stressful for the group. Brian McMahan checked himself into a hospital when *Spiderland* was finished; in September 1990, he quit Slint.

'Brian came to practice once—this is just a sign of how idiotic we still were—and Todd and Britt and I started playing the *Batman* TV theme,' David Pajo recalled. 'We thought it was so funny; we were jumping into different intervals and making these stupid harmonies. [Brian] said we were doing it for so long and just laughing our heads off that he got frustrated. So he went upstairs and put on some headphones and listened to both sides of Neil Young's *On The Beach*, and when he came downstairs we were still playing the *Batman* theme. And it was at that point he decided he had to leave the band.'

'That was a huge blow,' Walford later said. 'It was very hard for me, really, because I just didn't know what to do.'

Walford, Pajo, and Brashear decided they couldn't carry on without McMahan. A proposed European tour was cancelled. Touch & Go loved *Spiderland* and released it in 1991, but it was a hard sell: the band was already dead. And, all the while, the ghost of Slint smiled from the cover, in a quarry, in black and white, with a cinematic letterbox around them. It was their last picture show, and a mystique was born.

'I really couldn't believe that there were people, who weren't much older than me, who were able to do music like that,' Jason Noble, another kid in the locality at that time, said of Slint. He and his friends had a band, too.

'My first musical project was a rap band,' says Jeff Mueller, referring to King G & The J Krew, which he formed with Noble and another friend, Greg King. 'Our sampler was an effects pedal for a guitar, but it had an eight-second delay sample rate. You would load samples into it and you would utilise them for the song while you're recording it. Then, as there's no memory bank, there was no way to really log the sample. So once it was gone, it was *gone*. It was a very analogue approach to making rap music.'

King G & The J Krew self-released an album in 1992, *Indestructible Songs Of The Humpback Whale*, but it was 'impossible to replicate with live instrumentation, it just couldn't work. So my first punk rock band stemmed from rap music, trying to turn our live recording project into audible versions of these studio recordings. It just made sense to pick up guitars, bass, and have somebody play drums. And once we started playing with those things, the whole idea of the rap project sort of went away.'

Meanwhile, elsewhere in Louisville, nineteen-year-old Tara Jane O'Neil was 'getting out of my suburban reality. I was playing and writing music just alone in my room, but was floating around different social zones, because I've always been kind of a hybrid person. It was a really wonderful time in Louisville, socially and culturally. I daresay that my band, Drinking Woman—we started because we all like to play music, but it was also like, let's do a fucking band, we can do that too. Because we were the only all-female band in Louisville, and I don't think there's even been very many others since then. So it was a social experiment as much as it was bizarre, awesome music experiment.'

Then O'Neil, a bassist, met Noble and Mueller. 'Maybe it was [friend and drummer] Jon Cook who told Jason that I was playing alone in my room, and that they should check out my chops. So I went over with my rented bass, which was hot pink and had a fang headstock. I guess it would be called an audition of sorts, but I just played, and I learned the stuff, and that was it.' Noble, Mueller, and O'Neil wrote songs during the spring of 1992, and—when they had five—played their first show as King Kid International, an offshoot of King G & The J Krew.

'I think the first show as Rodan was at the Maryland Institute Of Art,' O'Neil says. 'That was with the Riot Grrrl tour, at Another Place sandwich shop, with Heavens To Betsy and Bratmobile, and this band Corn Dolly from Illinois.' Rodan gelled quickly; O'Neil quit Drinking Woman and left college, joining fellow dropouts Noble and Mueller.

'I don't think Jason or I really knew how to play guitar when we started that band,' Mueller says. 'We were just muddling our way through it until we could at least play what we had rehearsed. I would never say that we became proficient, but we were able to get our point across, and say what we wanted to say with the songs. Tara had a similar approach musically.'

Jon Cook joined on drums and was also an important factor. 'He could pick up an instrument and suddenly know it exactly, within a matter of hours or a couple of days,' Mueller says. 'He had bought a house with an inheritance, and we all paid rent to live with him. His tenacity and his approach to making music is honestly what I think helped recast and reshape the way that Jason and I approached music as well. And maybe also enhanced what we thought was possible with music.'

Cook's home was called Rocket House, and it became an absolute cornerstone of the Louisville scene. 'Sebadoh, they played at our house, Unwound played at our house, Nation Of Ulysses. Heavens To Betsy, all of these riot grrrl bands,' says Mueller. 'Just having that in Louisville was a really big deal. Holy smokes! It was a pretty good time.'

Cook had been in the band Crain, contemporaries of Slint. 'Crain helped inform how I listened to and played music,' says Mueller. 'The first record is called *Speed*. The second record is called *Heater*. And they're really, really heavy. They're one of the more under-appreciated and uncelebrated bands from Louisville and from that genre of music, and that period of time. They always got thrown under the bus for sounding like other things. People seemed to think they sounded a little bit like Steve Albini music, or a little bit like Bastro music, but I always saw the music independently from those other things.'

'There were definitely a few templates that we all could get into,' O'Neil says of early Rodan. 'And then there was also just youthful exploration. We were all beginning players, in a way the music we wrote was also the device by which we learned our instruments. I can remember, with Jeff, we would just kind of be like, what does this do? Fuck it, let's try that. And with Jason, there was more of a definite arrangement when I would work with him, individually. I know that Jason and Jeff had a lot of the Big Black vibe going on, when they were working, but that was never totally my vibe. There were a lot of things going on socially and culturally that I was a part of and psyched about, but I was also listening to Jefferson Airplane and Joni Mitchell and psychedelic music. And going to Grateful Dead shows! I leaned more toward that kind of stuff.'

Things happened swiftly for Rodan. Lo-fi and impassioned, their first single, 'How The Winter Was Passed', contained 'Milk And Melancholy', a track that incorporated volume dynamics with taut, unhappy spaces. 'Two thumbs up,' said Lee Ranaldo, guest-reviewing the singles for *Melody Maker*. 'Excellent dreamscaping.'

'It's not a premeditated thing,' Noble said of the group's songs in 1994. 'The songs just reflect emotional ups and downs, honest to how the person felt when at the time of writing.'

Rodan also recorded a Peel Session, featuring the incredible muscular ten-minute semi-reggae lurch of 'Before The Train'. The session was 'a really fantastic experience for me', Mueller says. 'That was my first trip overseas, to Europe. And I just remember meeting Everett True.'

'Oh Louisville!' journalist Everett True's 1994 *Melody Maker* feature on Rodan began. 'Shimmering jewel of a city, built along the Ohio River in north Kentucky. Home of the famous Kentucky Derby. Town of leafy suburbs, succulent meatloaf and dusty bookstores. A place where hangovers don't exist, and elephants fuck on the TV with insouciance.'

'He was a complete lunatic,' Mueller says.

Masquerading as the band Truckstop, Rodan were the stars of the underground road movie *Half-Cocked*, 'an inaccurate but charming little timepiece,' says O'Neil. In it, Truckstop steal O'Neil's brother's instruments and van and embark on a road trip, passing themselves off as an experimental band to disguise their musical ineptitude. It's full of quaint touches. O'Neil's brother is played by Ian Svenonius (of Nation Of Ulysses), in a rain bonnet, to preserve his famously fancy hairdo; O'Neil's real-life mother is in it, convincingly John Waters-ing it up; and O'Neil pulls out the Rodan seven-inch, from a record collection in Rocket House.

'We were certainly instructed to behave in a way that was like a younger version of ourselves,' Jason Noble has said, 'like before we had any familiarity with music, but it still has a fair amount of truth to it.

It's pretty light-hearted. And I wouldn't say that our experiences were always light-hearted, especially in Rocket House, but in some ways it's a pleasant thing to look at now, and it was certainly done with a lot of good intentions.'

'Man, those Rodan kids were *cute*,' says John Engle of Codeine, a band that practised at Rocket House in the summer of 1993 in order to develop and rehearse songs for what would become *The White Birch*. 'So I hear this enormous, massive music. It filled the entire house. I'm not really sure what it was, other than that it was enormous, and it just was this relentless sound, and I was trying to figure out which room it was coming from. I knocked on Tara's door, and Tara's in her room, and she's playing this. I asked, *What* are you listening to? And she's just on the bed, and she kind of looks over, and goes, Oh, that's us.'

The song was Rodan's 'The Everyday World Of Bodies'. An album, *Rusty*, soon followed. 'I remember that when we recorded *Rusty*, I was twenty years old, in Steve Albini's studio, and we had two days to record and one day to mix,' O'Neil recalls. 'At that point we had been playing a lot, and we were kind of top game, so that really worked for us. We just rolled in and did our thing, and they captured it—like in a trap. And then, *whoosh*, put it out. It was cool.'

Rusty is both less vulnerable and less ponderous than *Spiderland*, but it's exemplary in how it whips its own energy into new shapes, done within a heartbeat. And it also contains something of the absurdity that bubbled under with Slint, especially on 'Tooth-Fairy Retribution Manifesto'. 'It came out of a joke about being at school,' Jason Noble explained at the time, 'when other kids pick on you. If you punch them, knock their teeth out and put them under your pillow for the tooth fairy, you can get money for it.'

The attention that Rodan received showed the flipside of being in a small, incestuous music scene, however. 'There was a lot of weird stuff back in town, because there were a lot of bands that were amazing,' says O'Neil. 'We were in *Rolling Stone*! We were in *Spin*! We got to go all over the place! And I think for a lot of the community, and the friends, it was difficult for them. When that kind of thing is introduced, it can't do anything but serve to erode a community. I saw that starting to happen, and I saw how some people were very invested in getting the same kind of attention that we were getting, that at the time I either hated, or didn't give a fuck about, or felt it was a real distracting thing. But my friends, who weren't getting the attention, were very affected. The whole thing was shit, basically.'

'We put out our record in the spring of 1994,' Mueller says. 'The first proper Rodan LP came out, and we were done. I think our last show was September 21 1994. But if something has run its course, that doesn't necessarily mean it's failed.'

'Rodan was the one thing that kept us living in Louisville, and some people feel the need to get out of the city,' Jason Noble said in 1994. 'And it wouldn't be … correct if anyone filled another person's shoes. It's fairer to stop rather than fake it.'

'Maybe, at the end, things started fraying and splintering into the individuals,' O'Neil says. 'We had been doing it long enough, and the beautiful fusion of these completely disparate things had started to become more defined. It was cool that we had those couple of years to just be pretty naively open to whatever was coming down the pike, for us. *Oh sure, we'll do that; we'll try this.* And we got to make that body of work, and it got to sound like what it was.'

Jason Noble was already working on a project that would eventually become Rachel's. Tara Jane O'Neil was spending a lot of time in New York; she moved there, to join her girlfriend Cynthia Nelson in the duo Retsin.

'Mueller was the fastest one,' O'Neil remembers. 'He got June Of 44 together a month after we broke up.'

'There was enough drive from the initial short-lived experience in Rodan to push me into finding something very quickly,' Mueller confirms. 'Maybe even within a week I was on the phone trying to find other people to play with. *Let's meet*!'

June Of 44, Rachel's, and O'Neil's next band, The Sonora Pine, would all go on to introduce new elements to post-rock. But Rodan stands unique—scabrous, effortlessly cool, humorous, emotional, lachrymose. 'I think things are supposed to be a little bit of a mess,' Mueller reflects. 'I think that was a part of Rodan. Throwing the plate against a wall, and seeing how many pieces it would shatter into.'

As for the ex-members of Slint, although the band (without Pajo) reconvened as Palace Brothers alongside their friend Will Oldham for 1993's *There Is No-One What Will Take Care Of You*, this was clearly Oldham's project. His lyrics and his voice were its twin foci, and these were more related to folklore than *Spiderland*'s impressionistic vignettes. Oldham was very much a front person, an easy spotlight; Palace Brothers coverage rarely bothered to even mention the Slint heritage.

'Even though *Spiderland* was recorded in 1990, to me it's a pre-90s album,' Britt Walford has said. 'I suppose *Spiderland* was talking about some things that would come to fruition in the nineties, but when we recorded it the 90s hadn't really happened yet.'

But *Spiderland* was the 1990s, and other people recognised it, gradually (fittingly, perhaps). The redoubtable Steve Albini reviewed *Spiderland* in *Melody Maker*, giving it 'ten fucking stars'; this began an achingly slow steamroller for Slint—one that has never really stopped.

'*Please* tell me everything you possibly can about Slint,' a letter to that same music paper asked in 1993. 'I've heard that they split up: is this true? If so, what are the various members doing now? Come on! Please! Slint are/were great!' By 1994, in a review of Rodan's *Rusty*, *Melody Maker* would refer to Slint as 'the most dropped name in indieland', calling them 'the blueprint for a wave of groups who'd rather not grunge or lunge but swoon and bloom and howl at the dawn instead'.

The *NME* was blunter, stating, in a Rodan live review, that Louisville was 'home to the Care In The Community approach to rock of Slint and Squirrel Bait. This means they are alternatively soft and strong, but always very, VERY long and more than capable of startlingly intense slabs of head-crushing noiserock. Unfortunately, it also means they are congenitally incapable of facing the audience, penning a tune, or getting to the sodding POINT.'

It seemed, in some quarters, that the backlash had begun, even before the sound found a name.

CHAPTER SIX

tooled up

'Whatever our different tastes, we were all doing it because we wanted to make things which were as brilliant and uncompromised as possible.' IAN CRAUSE, DISCO INFERNO

'The nineties start here,' read Bark Psychosis's first live review, from 1990. 'Caught in the slipstream of those who want it all.'

'It's this sheer belief that what you were doing was the right thing, and it was just being on a burning fucking mission,' the band's Graham Sutton says.

British post-rock between 1990 and 1994 is one of the most fascinating, nebulous, and forward-thinking periods in music. Almost none of the practitioners found commercial or even cult success (and, if they did, it occurred well after the fact), despite adoration from some influential music journalists. The sound was named—as possible as it was to name such a shape-shifting beast—a *bit* too late for any of the groups to benefit from a 'scene', as such. Although …

'Originally we were part of the Hainault via Newbury Park scene with Bark Psychosis,' says Ian Crause of Disco Inferno, 'because we all lived on that branch of the Central Line [on the London Underground]. That scene lasted for about two or three years. In our heads.'

British post-rock emitted an urban-dread, urban-love, urban-*emprise*; it had a determined anti-retro principle; it could make tranquillity absolutely intolerable; and although its obdurate nature was by no means unlistenable, it was still genuinely anti-establishment and challenging. At the time, doing any of this was a largely thankless task, but a shared belief in it all fostered a certain level of respect between the bands, albeit one leavened by healthy competitiveness and the usual artistic differences.

Sharper ears had definitely clocked that something interesting was afoot by the end of 1992. 'There was the fragile and porcelain Earwig, the ethereal and turquoise Papa Sprain,' Simon Reynolds wrote in the *Melody Maker* review of that year. 'There was the bitter and brooding beauty of Disco Inferno. Best of all, however, were Bark Psychosis.' It was in 1992, three years since their first recorded appearance, that Bark Psychosis released the twelve-inch EP *SCUM*. It was their most ambitious record to date; although their records came out at cathedral-building pace, each was unpredictable, and indispensible.

'John Ling was my very best friend at school,' Graham Sutton says. 'We stuck together through thick and thin.' As well as music, Sutton and Ling bonded over politics: they were heavily into environmental concerns, anti-corporate action, and, especially, Youth CND. 'It was a really big deal, moving forward with it,' Sutton says. 'And that informed a lot of our decisions about how we wanted to operate, and how we wanted to approach the outside world.' Sutton and Ling were earnest, angry, hedonistic, *charged*; and, alongside A.R. Kane and Talk Talk, they loved Big Black, Swans, and Napalm Death.

All the British post-rock bands speak about the influence of John Peel on shaping the breadth of their tastes; a teenage Graham Sutton went so far as to pester him personally. 'I never have any problems listening to a lot of disparate stuff,' he says. 'I loved the programming, because it's how my brain operated, listening to these very different things smashed against each other. I used to phone him up all the time. Because you could. You could call him up while the record was playing. And he'd just chat to you about it.'

Ling and Sutton started playing together—Sutton on guitar, Ling on bass—and almost immediately they were serious about it. 'Doing the band was one of the big reasons for leaving school,' Sutton says. 'I persuaded John to leave after our O-levels, GCSEs. It was, *We're not going to fuck around with this. Let's do it, let's have it.*'

Sutton also left home, initially to a live-in assistant role at a care home, and then he and Ling found a Leyton squat together with Su Page, who contributed occasional vocals to Bark Psychosis. 'It seemed a very sensible way of carving out a bit of space and time for yourself to actually concentrate on what you wanted to do with your band,' Sutton says of squatting. 'It was a real lifeline, and squatting was important for a lot of bands at that point.' Although the squat was pretty civilised, with a toilet and electricity, the three had to mooch down to the local municipal swimming baths for a shower.

Next to join was the older Mark Simnett, found via an advert. 'Mark was into things like Pink Floyd. But in all honesty, me and John were too young to know about that stuff. I knew a bit of Yes at that point. I still really like bits of Yes. There's some cracking shit on *Fragile*.' Later, Sutton considered some parallels with the music of Bark Psychosis and prog. 'The whole thing of allowing things to develop at their own speed, and their own pace. Stuff doesn't have to be chopped down into bite-size portions.'

Simnett's prog heritage found a meeting point with his younger bandmates in their love for Talk Talk, and also in the rave scene. 'You'd listen to five hours of music, where it would gradually change over that five hours,' Sutton says. 'There was no stage, there was no band, there was nothing. You were just with your friends, and you are creating this thing unto itself. So that really fed into it as well. So the whole thing of twenty minutes for "SCUM", it's like, that's pop music by comparison. It ain't a six-hour Orb set, is it?'

Based in Woodford, again on the Hainault via Newbury Park line, was a small record label, Cheree. Its founders were Nick Allport (who wrote the *Sowing Seeds* fanzine) and Vinita Joshi. They had released the debut single by The Telescopes; it had been a success, and it gave them confidence to expand. 'I wouldn't say I was trying to create a scene,'

Allport told *Melody Maker*, in a feature on the label in 1990, 'but there's loads of things going on right in front of people's noses, and they need to be more aware of it, that there's more to life than Mudhoney and all these American bands.' They had put out a flexi in 1989, featuring Spacemen 3's 'Extract From "An Evening Of Contemporary Sitar Music"', The Fury Things' 'Climbing High Falling Sky', and the first Bark Psychosis track, the Napalm Death-influenced 'Clawhammer', which Sutton now disowns. ('It was just done as a favour, really, and at that point it was like, do you want to do a flexi-disc with Spacemen 3 on the other side? Yeah, great! But you don't consider something might still be around even a year later.')

Cheree was cheerfully DIY. 'All scissors and Pritt stick,' says Sutton. 'The evenings I've spent, folding things for Vinita in her kitchen. It was a beautiful thing.' Bark Psychosis were loyal to Allport and Joshi, and Cheree released two twelve-inch singles by the band in 1990, which, unlike 'Clawhammer', *did* represent them: 'All Different Things' b/w 'By-Blow' in the spring, and 'Nothing Feels' b/w 'I Know' in autumn. The tracks offered up a rich palette: from 'All Different Things', which surges and swoops, noise being absorbed and then metamorphosed into blades of light, to 'By-Blow', with a *giallo*-soundtrack black-glove horror, and 'I Know' and its muttered acoustic arc.

It seemed that Bark Psychosis had concluded, in the wake of 'Clawhammer', that noise could dig graves for groups: they sought escape. 'Everyone likes being loud, no one wants to feel quiet,' Sutton says. 'But being loud is a crutch.'

'The moods and the meanings create themselves,' Ling told *Melody Maker* in 1990. 'We don't set out with a particular emotion, and decide to vent it through a song. We couldn't go through our recorded output and tell you what each song is about. The words take shape from sounds.'

Elsewhere along the East London-Essex border (Redbridge, this time) lived another young malcontent, Ian Crause. 'I was fourteen when I decided I wanted to be in a band, and I guess the standard thing of not fitting in and wanting to validate myself was the driving force behind it,' he says. 'By the time the band started to rehearse I was sixteen, and my taste in music had completely changed, not to mention my understanding of what bands were and what kind of musical culture awaited us.' With Paul Willmott on bass, Rob Whatley on drums, and—initially—Daniel Gish adding keyboards, Crause formed Disco Inferno: the name chosen intentionally to be in conflict with their sound.

'Paul and I had quite a lot in common, musically,' Crause says. 'I guess the one "sound" band we both idolised was My Bloody Valentine, who we used to go to see whenever we could, from just after the time *Isn't Anything* came out. They changed my conception of what music was for. Before them, I thought it was about song and meaning. After them, the sound itself could be justification enough. So, I had the idea of sound for sound's sake in my head as a result of this.'

Crause also cites the analytical music journalism of the time as an influence. 'Writers like David Stubbs, and I guess Simon Reynolds to a degree; those two I think set the futurist ball rolling. Had I not read *Melody Maker*, I doubt my interest in working with sound as a language would have happened, and I would really only have been interested in lyric writing.'

Like Bark Psychosis, Disco Inferno put out their early records on Cheree (or its subsidiary, Che): 'Entertainment', the *Science* EP, and the album *Open Doors Closed Windows*. On these records, Crause's guitar is the lynchpin, and the early Disco Inferno material—while more wired with abrasive post-punk existentialism than the bulk of shoegazing records—was lazily bracketed with that discredited genre, if it was mentioned at all.

'The only thing I can even listen to is *Science*, the last EP,' Crause told *Melody Maker* in 1992. 'You must have noticed I'm not the world's greatest vocalist. I'm more interested in what we're about to do. It's gonna involve more sampling, more machine-oriented stuff, more in the Consolidated vein. More political. I'm getting a lot more confident. I really, really want to get up people's noses. I wanna hurt these people. If I had a stronger voice I'd be so fucking loud. No more Mr Oblique Guy.'

Crause had been comprehensively rethinking what Disco Inferno could and should be, particularly in the light of Public Enemy's impact on him. He discussed this with the rest of the group. 'Paul was totally up for [a change] because we were both very taken by the bands making radical sounds right across the spectrum, from rave and what later became jungle music, to stuff like Big Black, Happy Flowers, God, and Extreme Noise Terror.'

Another band that proved revelatory to Crause was The Young Gods. 'It's quite simple,' Franz Treichler, The Young Gods' vocalist, said at the time of their self-titled debut album. 'It's a matter of logical sifting through one hundred years of music—baroque, classical, metal, and punk—then shaking it very, very hard until 1987 leaps out screaming.' The Young Gods called their music New Sonic Architecture. It was constructed from samples, a real drummer, and the cataclysmic bile of Treichler's vocals. While The Young Gods sounded very different to Public Enemy, the groups shared disruptive purpose; the music melted down pre-existing sounds and reshaped them into an anvil for the listener's skull to be cracked upon.

'To me, rock has always been a question mark,' Treichler said in 1992. 'I want to create an ocean of energy and people can surf on the waves. Basically, I would like to give energy to people, like a firework of sounds and words with no specific messages, just a language with no logical interpretation.' It was Frankenstein's Monster music—stitched together, resuscitated, intimidating.

'I had some money in a savings account from my bar mitzvah, when I was thirteen,' says Crause. 'It was about four grand or so, and I had to fight my parents for about six months to let me use a part of it to get the sampler I wanted, which was really expensive in 1991—it cost about £2,500. At that point the record label was having massive trouble with its financial backers and asking for this stuff [samplers] simply provoked a negative response.'

The year 1991 was an awful one for Cheree and its bands. Financial instability had led to corporate men. 'Cocks,' Graham Sutton says.

'They were a nightmare. They were a nightmare that you just wouldn't believe.' The ensuing wrangles left the band haunted, aggravated, and in musical limbo. Eventually their contract was transferred, 'but the people that bought us out of that deal and then took us onto their label, and were managing us at that point, they were cocksuckers as well.' They went to the 3rd Stone label, hoping for a smoother ride.

Meanwhile, Bark Psychosis had recruited a new member—Daniel Gish, who had left Disco Inferno before that group's first release—and were starting to fully explore samplers and digital technology. There was also a new practice place. 'Because none of us had any money, the idea of going to a rehearsal studio, or a rehearsal room, where you're going to pay whatever, forty quid, fifty quid, for a number of hours ... none of us could do that. But Mark Simnett had access to a space underneath the Church of St John The Evangelist in Stratford. We were in the stinky old basements, the community-run network of little rooms in the crypt of the church. It was damp, and *really* smelly, not just mouldy, but it actually smelt of rotting carpet. Really awful. And all the fabric on the amps eventually rotted away. It fucked up all of our gear. But we were incredibly fortunate that we had that space.'

There were a few Bark Psychosis gigs during 1991, and it was clear that the band were evolving, even though, frustratingly, nothing was released. At a gig at the Commonwealth Institute that year, a then-unreleased song called 'The Loom' featured; it was introduced as 'Concept Art'. Other set-list favourites from this period included 'Fast One', 'Slow One', 'Mellow One', 'Droney One', 'Loud One', and 'Bang Goes Our Record Deal'. ('It's showmanship, innit?' laughs Sutton. 'It's showbiz. You've gotta do a bit of that. You've gotta try and draw everyone in.')

'When we play, it's like a really precious thing, it makes me feel better,' John Ling said in 1992. 'It's like an oasis. It keeps me sane. I've stayed poor, I've carried on tolerating the grind so that I can play the music, it's so important to me. Our sound is the communication between four people.'

'There's almost certainly a missing album, in some respects,' Sutton says. The band were set to record an album, but Cheree's financial troubles, which culminated in a time-consuming court case as Bark Psychosis attempted to extricate themselves from the label, prevented it. 'It would have been a document of where we were at the time, and there's very little [by Bark Psychosis] from that period,' Sutton continues. 'It was a lot more band-like back then, but it was just changing so quickly.'

Bark Psychosis had also begun working with one Lee Harris. For Sutton, a long-time Talk Talk fan (he had even written to them at fourteen, asking to help make the tea while they were in the studio), it was barely believable. 'Lee would disappear to make us some "special" coffee, and we would emerge later, feeling pretty strung out,' Sutton has recalled. '[But] Lee's stories gradually got stranger and stranger. His stepbrother had been in Free, apparently. He was wanted for something or other in Australia. By the time he got to regaling us about how he'd once been in the SAS, it all became clear that "Lee" was actually a basket case.'

Sutton wrote a second letter to Talk Talk, this time informing them that there was a charlatan pretending to be Lee Harris; the real Harris then got in touch. 'I was hanging out with Lee and Phill [Brown] a lot at the end of all that,' Sutton says. 'Lee lived 'round my way, and I was getting blind drunk with them all the time in Stoke Newington.'

As for Disco Inferno, they too were looking to leave Cheree. 'Paul had suggested we try to get signed to Virgin, so he was liaising with someone there to see if we could get a deal there, as Bark Psychosis had just done,' Crause says. 'So while he was off doing things like that, and Rob was just working, I spent that six months just going to my supermarket job then coming home and trying sampler ideas through headphones. When we came back to rehearse, in late spring 1992, we went straight into it and tried out all the new ideas I had been working on. Rob had bought digital drum pads, and we had the setup of MIDI guitar and MIDI drums plugged into the one sampler, and Paul playing his bass as before. In all honesty it was a total head-fuck. We basically had to take uncontrollable, and what seemed like unmanageable, sounds and fuse them down into recognisable songs.'

What Disco Inferno did was to link Crause's guitar and Whatley's drums into the sampler by grace of the MIDI software; the instruments were able to spark off a whole vista of ecstasy and dread. 'If I were to put a piano sound, which I have done, on my guitar, and play something kind of conventional, I could create the most incredible harmonies on each different note that you can't do on a guitar,' Crause explained in 1994. 'So you can also do that with sounds from the world around you. I've got six keyboards running at once, one on each string. How many frets are there on a guitar? Twenty, twenty-eight, or something? Times that by six and you've got that many sounds, potentially, in each song.'

'When Ian bought a sampler and bastardised his guitar,' Rob Whatley has said, 'his energy and ideas were really fresh and exiting. He jumped head first into this new idea because, with Ian, it's all or nothing.'

This change was palpable on their next release. The passivity had gone; Crause's downcast self was now the revenge of the dispossessed. 'Summer's Last Sound' spoke of a wretched country and a noxious, bitter future, as the guitar played water and birdsong. 'I have never been a particularly happy person because I have never been left alone,' says Crause. 'So that would come through very strongly in the way I wrote songs: anger and dissatisfaction.' Crause had also moved to Barking, and was rehearsing in Leyton, both of which were very poor parts of London at the time. 'I guess there's a lot more urban noise, and as you constantly look for sounds to sample and a means to create a sort of living sound world through the recordings, this abundance of noise presents itself as a greater part of the palette available to you.'

The *Summer's Last Sound* EP was Disco Inferno's final release on Cheree. 'When the label heard the stuff for the first time,' Crause says, 'they asked why we were doing this when we had been a perfectly good guitar band beforehand.' The criticism was moot: the label had entered receivership. 'Rough Trade had to buy us out,' Crause has said. 'We were lucky [Cheree's backers] heard our music and thought it was unsalable shit, I guess, or our luck might have been even worse.'

RIGHT The original sandpaper artwork for *The Return Of The Durutti Column*, hand-stamped with its Factory Records catalogue number.

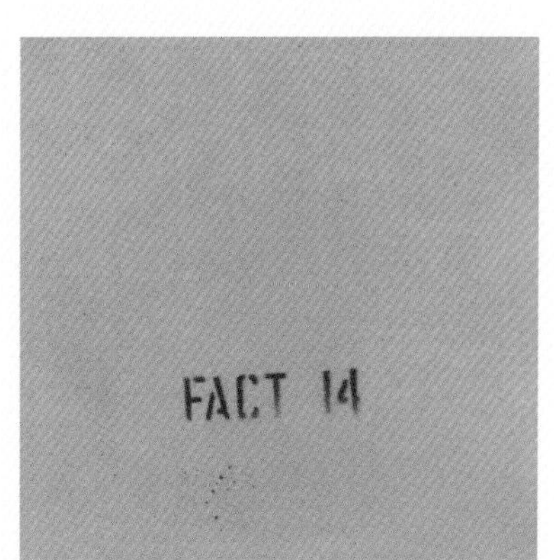

BELOW John Lydon, Keith Levene, and Jeannette Lee of Public Image Ltd. at Virgin Records' London offices, 1980.

RIGHT Ut: Nina Canal, Sally Young, Jacqui Ham, and a flyer for a trio of shows in London in 1984.

BELOW Hugo Largo in 1987. Photo taken in the loft Mimi Goese was living in at 675 Hudson Street, New York.

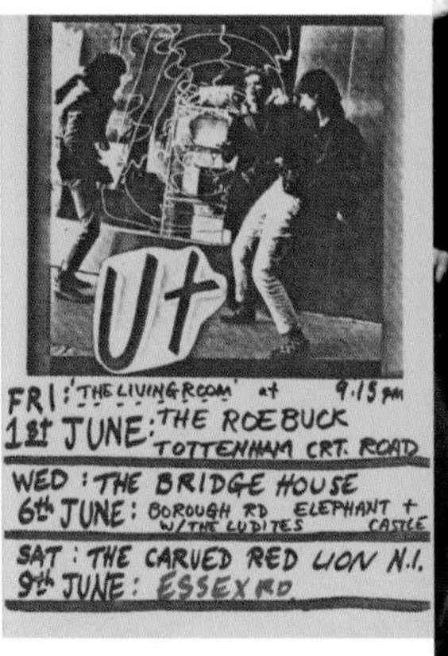

ABOVE Rudy Tambala and Alex Ayuli of A.R. Kane, and the back cover of their 1987 *Lollita* EP on 4AD.

LEFT Cocteau Twins, shown here in a promotional photograph taken for 4AD.

ABOVE The cover art for Talk Talk's final album, 1991's *Laughing Stock*.
LEFT Bandleader Mark Hollis, photographed during promotional duties for the album.

ABOVE RIGHT A set of portraits of Papa Sprain's Gary McKendry from 1992.

RIGHT Slint, as photographed for the cover of the 1991 LP *Spiderland*.

ABOVE Bark Psychosis, the Isle of Dogs, 1992.

RIGHT Disco Inferno's Second *Language EP* from 1994. The direction of the logo changed with each release, representing the band's sound moving in different ways.

ABOVE Seefeel, photographed in 1993, around the time of *Quique*'s recording.

ABOVE Stereolab at the Lizard/Sausage Machine Christmas Party, 1994.

BELOW David Callahan of Moonshake at the same gig. **LEFT** Margaret Fiedler of Moonshake at Leicester's Princess Charlotte in 1993.

Down the road from where Disco Inferno rehearsed, and also taking advantage of the cheap rents in East London caused by its insalubrious reputation, was Rudy Tambala's new studio and record label, H.ark! 'I almost signed Bark Psychosis,' he says. 'They were Stratford as well. And they came down to the studio quite a few times and I was going to sign them, but then they signed to 3rd Stone. It was very, very close. I think they would have had a better home with me.'

Graham Sutton disagrees, believing that the 3rd Stone option allowed the band to have greater control over production. Either way, it didn't matter *too* much, because H.ark! had takers. A pair of Belfast best friends had found their way to him.

'Joe Cassidy got in touch to tell me H.ark! had put an advert in *NME* or *Melody Maker* saying they were looking for bands to produce,' says Gary McKendry, 'so it was decided I would go along with our demos to play to them.'

'Gary, he was very forthright in those days, and very confident,' says Cassidy. 'He met up with Rudy, and played him basically a bunch of the genius pop music that Gary was making back in those days. And then, I guess Gary said, oh, my friend Joe's got a band as well. And he played that to Rudy and Rudy was like, I've got two bands here to get started.'

Cassidy's band was Butterfly Child; McKendry's was Papa Sprain. 'I grew up in the suburbs outside Belfast,' McKendry says. 'Early music in the house was stuff like Miles Davis's *Sketches Of Spain* and *Bitches Brew*; also Buddy Rich and Max Roach. I discovered the hi-fi pretty early as a child, and used to sit in the living room with headphones on listening to any cassettes close to hand, stuff like The Beatles' *Sgt. Pepper* and *Yellow Submarine*; Simon & Garfunkel's *Bridge Over Troubled Water*, or it might have been *Greatest Hits*. Dvořák's 'New World Symphony'; and the *Jacques Loussier Trio Play Bach* or some such … whilst the rest of my family sat nearby eating dinner and watching the television.'

'Nobody in my family is musical,' Cassidy says. 'When "Bohemian Rhapsody" got released, which I think was 1975, apparently I was in the kitchen with my mother, and my mother said that I was humming something. So my mother said, Son, what are you humming? That's not the song! And I said, No, this is what the song should be doing.'

Both were in separate teenage bands, obsessed with Joy Division and New Order; Cassidy then started writing songs and encouraged McKendry to do the same. 'There were no opportunities really in Belfast,' says McKendry. 'No scenes, or at least not when I was growing up. No record companies really, no nothing.' The two friends motivated one another.

While McKendry formed a band—he was the singer and guitarist, with Richard Reynolds on guitar, and Cregan Black on bass—Cassidy almost got pulled in to a major label deal as a musician with a Manchester-based band. On the advice of his mother, he demurred, keeping at his own material instead. 'Probably around the time I was sixteen, seventeen, I started going, I'm gonna do some shows,' Cassidy says. 'But I was very shy and I didn't know what I wanted to do.'

'I went to Stratford,' says McKendry. 'Rudy was there, and I had to wait for a bit for the coin to drop that this was *the* Rudy from *the* A.R. Kane, and he was actually gonna listen to *my* little demos I had recorded in the suburbs outside Belfast between times spent trying to comprehend what made *his band* and *his records* so cool. So he listened whilst I sat trying to look nonchalant, and I guess he must have heard the A.R. Kane influences straight away. I mean, one song, "I Got Loose", was made up from a sample of "In A Circle" from their *"i"* album!'

H.ark! released, almost simultaneously, Butterfly Child's *Tooth Fairy* and Papa Sprain's *Flying To Vegas* EPs. *Tooth Fairy* was both sensuous and innocent, bedroom drift-songs tempered by profane knowledge. *Flying To Vegas* was weirder and dubbier.

'It took about two weeks to record and mix,' McKendry says of *Flying To Vegas*. 'Every track apart from the title track was new. I was getting more into a sort of "let it happen" attitude to recording. Maybe, gradually, I was becoming more confident with what I figured worked. I think this pleased Rudy, and everything flowed pretty easy. I had started "Fizz" with the guitar alone, but it was difficult for me to see where to take it. It was sounding quite listless and wimpy, and then Rudy said I should put a big dirty distorted fuck off bass on top, so I recorded the noise bass.'

'I don't think any of us were trying to say anything, narratively speaking, with lyrics,' says Cassidy. 'It was a very stream of consciousness writing, because I thought that was even more truthful than writing something down and then trying to make it all make sense. Whatever came out, came out, and that was the song.'

Butterfly Child had always been a solo endeavour, really; Papa Sprain now was as well. But Cassidy and McKendry supported one another at shows, and played in iterations that usually involved one another and a mutual friend, Tony McKeown. 'We played as Papa Sprain and then we played as Butterfly Child,' says Cassidy. 'That really freaked out the audience. They were like, *what's going on here? It's the same three guys! They've just switched microphones!*'

This fluidity of line-up, and its challenge to the idea of band as tribe or clique, was an emerging UK post-rock trope; Ian Crause, in the earliest Disco Inferno days, refused to be photographed, while Bark Psychosis were vocal about despising the 'usual reasons' for getting into music. 'Other bands loved the idea of being in a band as a way to gain kudos and attention,' Graham Sutton says. 'People just wanted to be The Byrds or something. Or a gang. Hey hey, we're the fucking Monkees.'

McKendry and Cassidy were increasingly excited by the possibilities of the studio, seeing it not as a way to record their songs *as such*, but as an exercise in manipulation and sound exploitation. McKendry in particular grew to hate touring more and more, soon abandoning it completely, only wanting to 'read, listen and write, record'.

One EP more from each followed on H.ark!—the stripped-down *May*, from Papa Sprain, and the luscious *Eucalyptus*, from Butterfly Child. But Rudy Tambala was growing restive. 'Basically, I had to have weapons in the studio to protect myself,' he says. 'Really scary. In the building over the road, there were hooligans, [who were] doing all the pirate stations. They all had gear, they all had equipment, there were a lot of heavy drug people, heavy football fans doing this stuff all around us and I knew a lot of them, because I grew up in Stratford, and that's where most of them were from. I got a phone call from an old mate from school one day, saying they're coming to get you, they want all your gear. And I thought, this is the time to get out of there.' Tambala was also itching to make his own music again. He shut down the studio and label; both Butterfly Child and Papa Sprain went to Rough Trade in 1992. At that point, their identities became more distinct from one another, and their musical goals diverged.

'Rough Trade didn't have anything that was really bringing in the bacon at that point,' Cassidy says. 'But they had a wee bit of money and I think that they thought we can have kind of a fresh start, bringing in the Disco Inferno boys, bringing in Papa Sprain, bringing in Butterfly Child. It was really rewarding, and it was purely that thing where somebody has got a little bit of money and experience then says, I'll let you do whatever you want to do, because they trust you as a musician and a writer.'

'I think, from pretty early on, Rough Trade started to see me as a liability,' McKendry says. 'Not necessarily in a bad way, but I think they were aware that I was gradually going off the rails.'

Having extricated themselves from Cheree, Disco Inferno's first release on Rough Trade was the fresh 'A Rock To Cling To' b/w 'From The Devil To The Deep Blue Sky'. The A-side sampled chunks of rock music—the first time the band had done so; the B-side was a very strong instrumental excursion. 'From The Devil To The Deep Blue Sky' was live, Paul Willmott has said, 'But it was more influenced by the long song structures that Bark Psychosis were putting together at the time. They had some impact on us giving ourselves the freedom to build something without the parameters of a three minute pop song.'

'We had started getting very good reviews in *Melody Maker* around this time from people like David Stubbs—which meant a great deal to me—and other people our own age, like Neil Kulkarni and Taylor Parkes, who had recently joined the paper and were also looking for new and exciting things [to write about],' says Crause. 'But, at the same time, the audiences who had been into us when we were an indie guitar band were taking one look at us on stage and pretty much turning round and walking out.'

To meet their new mood, Disco Inferno changed things up visually. 'Rob went out and bought a set of multi coloured plastic cymbals which lit up under UV, so we thought it would be an idea to basically paint all our kit with UV paint, which we did before a gig at the Camden Underworld one afternoon, leaving UV footprints all over the floor,' says Crause. 'I sort of Pollocked my guitar with different colours, and Willmott did some sort of thing to his bass and amp as I recall and we just used to play under a black light. Basically I imagine you just stood in the audience and heard this mad sort of sound coming at you very loud, and when you looked at the stage there were just these sort of painted UV objects moving around.'

Disco Inferno's manager was Mike Collins, formerly Wire's manager, box fresh from losing a lot of money for Blur. Collins had also taken on another band: the Brighton-based Insides, formerly known as Earwig.

'When Mike started managing us [alongside Disco Inferno], Ian was a bit, *hmmmmm*,' says Kirsty Yates.

'But what was nice about it,' adds Julian Tardo, the other half of Insides, 'it was like, Oh, here's Ian. He's difficult. He's out there on his own, hating everything around him.'

'I chose to come to university in Brighton, because I wasn't brave enough to go to London,' the Coventry-born Yates says, 'and there were venues in Brighton. There was the Zap Club, and there was the Richmond, and I could go and see bands, and I hoped that I would meet people that liked music. And I hoped that I would be in a band.' Within weeks she had met Tardo and another friend, Dimitri Voulis, and the three formed Earwig.

'All the Earwig stuff was really easy,' Yates said. 'We played a few gigs, someone paid for our first demos, then we played them to Grant [of the La-Di-Da label]. Grant said, Yes, I'll put something out by you; the first single we put out gets played on John Peel, first gig in London gets reviewed in the *Melody Maker*, all stuff like that. That was *really* easy.'

Earwig released the *Hardly*, *Might*, and *Subtract* EPs during 1990 and 1991, all of them solid guitar-based indie-pop, with Yates's unsentimental lyrical tales of relationship paranoia distinguishing them. But it was in 1992, with their single 'Every Day Shines' and the album *Under My Skin I Am Laughing*, that Earwig started to pull away.

'When we were in Earwig we used to play these repetitious things to such an extreme in rehearsal,' says Tardo. 'After you've done something fifty times or something, you just start to forget. You lose your bearings. I remember just really loving that.'

'It was a bit weird,' Yates says, of 'Every Day Shines'. 'We'd open up a gig with it, and just be standing around, waiting. *Der-der, der-der, der-der, der-der* … repetition. Looking at each other. Are we going to get our cue? How does it start? Actually it starts with me singing. Am I going to get that cue? I don't know.'

'We were playing in London, and we were seeing similar bands which we were going to be compared to,' Tardo says. 'We saw Bark Psychosis. So the ideas were definitely in the air. It was at the start of what I see now as a breakdown in all those genre classifications, where electronic started doing things rock, all back and forth.'

University had ended for Earwig. Voulis wanted to join his girlfriend in Spain, and it was clear that Tardo and Yates had evolved. 'We were gradually just reducing everything,' says Yates. 'Like, we don't know where we're going, but we know it's not here, we know it's not here, we know it's *not here*. Which is always easier to do, isn't it?'

The re-emerged Bark Psychosis, now on 3rd Stone, released the *Manman* EP in 1992. The title track was almost tune-free and compellingly so, paying little mind to anything other than its own world; 'Tooled Up' and 'Blood Rush' explored sampling and repetition. Unlike 'I Know', for instance, these tracks seemed fuelled by a lack of compassion; by spite, even. They were airless, with instruments dropping in and out, giving hints to the emotional intricacy Bark Psychosis would go on to achieve.

'When we played together, rehearsing or writing stuff, we'd play for hours,' Graham Sutton says. 'We'd record ourselves, so we were quite used to going back to squats and listening to what we'd done. Bullshit, but *long* bullshit, [in order] to get tiny little bits out of it.'

'It's tension-release-tension-release,' John Ling said in 1992. 'We deploy our music surgically.'

'I had a thing of disliking stuff that was obviously processed to make it sound like it was far away, as opposed to it *really* being over there,' Graham Sutton says. 'I was into the physicality of it. So the biggest thing that I had, at that point in time, was recording in a large space, where you could put microphones really far away from things and get a real sense of perspective, and real depth rather than trying to imitate it.'

SCUM, the 1992 twelve-inch single from Bark Psychosis, explored this sense of environment. 'It genuinely was totally spontaneous, without edits or obvious jiggery-pokery,' Sutton says. 'It was the thing of, OK, we set ourselves ten days to record. And we want a bit of time in a big space. But those studios, the studios with that space to do that kind of thing were stupidly expensive, like a thousand pounds a day. And there's no way we could afford to go in there. So it's like, OK. We've got the church above us. We brought our amps from the room downstairs into the main church, and then ran cables down the main aisle.' They worked on three tracks simultaneously, and a fragment of another survives, used as the first section of what became 'SCUM'.

Since Sutton was now friends with Phill Brown and the *real* Lee Harris, he was able to discuss techniques used on Talk Talk's *Spirit Of Eden* and *Laughing Stock*. Brown acted as a consultant-cum-mentor, advising on types of equipment and offering handy hints; but the direction came from Sutton, beginning now to seriously explore his producer's instincts. *SCUM* isn't scared of deliberation, even stalemate; nor is it afraid to dwell on the easily missed in everyday life, like paper scrunched, traffic undulations, an alarm clock.

'There were a few reasons for the title *SCUM*,' Sutton says. 'There was the Society For Cutting Up Men [Valerie Solanas's 1967 radical feminist tract, *SCUM Manifesto*]. The film *Scum* made a lasting impression on me. And there was the idea of stuff floating to the surface. But, mainly, it looked good written down. At that point I was an angry young man and I liked the idea of making a record with *SCUM* written in big letters.'

Bark Psychosis, Disco Inferno, and the newly minted Insides were all yet to complete their greatest achievements. But the cusp was exciting. 'There was a gig at The White Horse [in Hampstead],' says Kirsty Yates, 'which I always think of as the post-rock Manchester Free Trade Hall gig. It was Earwig and Seefeel playing, and I know that there were members of Disco Inferno and Bark Psychosis there. It was the day before Freddie Mercury died.'

'With a few notable exceptions, we [Bark Psychosis] always felt pretty alienated from everybody and everything, really,' says Graham Sutton. 'We weren't an easy sell. Not us. Neither was A.R. Kane, nor Ian, nor Julian and Kirsty. We were never the cool kids. Callahan [of Moonshake] and the Stereolab kids, Silverfish, the Valentines, those were the cool kids. We were always the dweebs. It makes me laugh now. I quite like it. But people could get quite defensive about it at the time, I think. It was really resented, in some small way.'

CHAPTER SEVEN

too bloody-minded

'Too bloody-minded! Can the headline just read, Too Bloody-Minded?' MARGARET FIEDLER, MOONSHAKE

'Our first gig was in November 1991 at the Sausage Machine, with Earwig, who went on to be Insides,' says Sarah Peacock of Seefeel. 'It was a pretty disastrous gig. Everything went wrong. We didn't really know what we were doing and nobody was there. Paul Cox from Too Pure was running the night, and for some reason saw something in us: *I can see it didn't really go very well for you tonight but whatever you do next, let me know. Keep sending the tapes.*'

The Sausage Machine was the name of the night at the White Horse, North London, and Cox had been helming it for a while. His nights featured a wide range of artists, but two in particular appealed to the British music press: Th' Faith Healers and Silverfish. A slapdash genre was duly fabricated for them. 'Enter Camden Lurch, christened in these pages after a night out watching Th' Faith Healers,' Simon Williams and Steve Lamacq wrote in a co-authored 1991 *NME* feature. 'The Lurch took its name from the erratic, jerky dancing which people lapsed into at the Camden gigs—a sort of lunging from the hips, accompanied by a dramatic shaking of the head.'

'The whole point was to be as loud and as obnoxious as possible,' Joe Dilworth of Th' Faith Healers has said of that period. 'All of a sudden you could make an awful racket and be completely socially unacceptable—which was great.'

If musicians think the term post-rock is bad, they should be glad they weren't saddled with Camden Lurch, one of the least convincing genres of all time. About the only musical definition advanced for it was mixing 'melody with a tense, sometimes fucked-up guitar onslaught—and a rhythm that jerks back and forth like a drunken metronome.' The 'movement' barely lasted until the following week's issue. It didn't matter. '[It] was basically just a tool to get Th' Faith Healers and Silverfish in the *NME*,' Steve Lamacq later confirmed.

'It really was a good time to be in London, just seeing lots of different kinds of music,' Tim Gane of Stereolab says, 'and you saw them every night, five nights a week, six nights a week, you'd see the same people either playing or in the audience. People love that term incestuous, but we were just all friends, you know.'

The energy that was put into these nights at the Sausage Machine, onstage and off, was contagious. It was also expansive and welcoming. 'I got Richard [Roberts] down to see a lot of the bands, and we both felt something was happening,' Paul Cox said in 1993. 'There were a lot of good bands around, a lot of which were being ignored at the time.' Cox and Roberts took action: they founded a label, Too Pure, in 1990, and as its first release put out a selection of live performances from the Sausage Machine: *Now Thats Disgusting Music*. It (probably unconsciously) set out the label's ideology of supporting obstinate and hard-to-categorise bands, many of which garnered sizeable cult followings.

'If we sign a band, we believe in that band, and we want to take that band as far as we can take them,' Richard Roberts said in 1993. 'It's as simple as that.'

'We always had a good relationship with Too Pure,' Mark Clifford of Seefeel says. 'We weren't being shepherded around in expensive cars, we weren't making a load of money or that kind of stuff, but just in terms of doing what we wanted to do. I guess it was all really happy. I don't remember it ever not being happy. The bands were really good, there was always really good camaraderie between quite diverse artists.'

'There isn't a Too Pure sound as such,' Roberts has said. 'Our philosophy is, we want to release records by bands that don't sound like anyone else.'

'It didn't really occur to us that Too Pure was a cool label and maybe we should be on it, until we ran out of options,' David Callahan of Moonshake says. 'It was kind of ludicrous really. We should have gone to them in the first place. They turned down Sebadoh and Pavement. They were *that cool*.'

Moonshake had just emerged from Creation records, following on from the *First* EP, and were a little bruised. Although it had been their decision to leave, it was clear they would be dropped anyway. 'The record had been disappointing,' Callahan says. 'It had been dissed in most quarters. We were stuck in rehearsals, and it all seemed a bit aimless, and we were depressed and down. But then it turned around. I was waiting to be picked up by Mig [Moreland, Moonshake drummer], and I started playing a bass guitar that was just lying around. I played the bass line to "Secondhand Clothes". And so when there was a lull in rehearsals, I just picked up the bass and started playing that. Everything fell into place.'

Moonshake had formed a couple of years earlier when Callahan was growing dissatisfied with his previous group, The Wolfhounds. 'It all got a bit laddish, and we wanted a female guitarist, if possible,' he says. '[Also], the last couple of Wolfhounds records had used the odd sample, a vocal sample, or a saxophone sample, here and there. It was very tentative. But when I'd seen what a sampler could do I was there for a couple of years saying, "I wish I could get my hands on one."'

'I came to London, and within a few months I met Dave,' Margaret Fiedler says. 'I was advertising in *Melody Maker*, he was advertising in *Melody Maker*, and Moonshake was formed by me answering one of his adverts. We were both looking for different people to work with, and people we didn't know. You just put things up on the biggest noticeboard possible, which was *Melody Maker*.'

Fiedler was American; she had been musically active since she was a small child, and had been in bands since her teens, including one with her friend Moby. 'He had this band called AWOL and their bass player quit. And he said, "Well, you play the cello, you can play the bass." He just lent me a bass guitar, and it was actually really easy to play. But what turned out was that he had had some demo time booked. It was going to be $375, and I found out is that what they *really* wanted was someone to put in $125.'

The band went through a number of name and personnel changes, and for Fiedler, 'what it made me also realise is that the bass player doesn't really write the songs. The guitarist writes the songs. And I just thought, I want to write the songs.' She took up the guitar soon afterward.

Fiedler and Callahan made an initial connection. 'The Wolfhounds were playing at the Camden Falcon, with Gallon Drunk, and Dave said come along, so I came along. I didn't know who was onstage, and I watched all of Gallon Drunk, and left. And I was like, they were great, but … I really don't know why they need a female singer. But when I spoke to Dave on the phone [afterward], it was painfully obvious that I'd seen the wrong band. I was like, that's off to a great start, then.'

'By then, I'd become really frustrated with The Wolfhounds,' Callahan says. 'The last LP we did [1990's *Attitude*] I thought was pretty good, but it did the worst of all our records. I rang up Margaret and I said, Look, I'm fed up with doing The Wolfhounds, it's too indie-guitary and that kind of thing, and would you like to do something with samples and that's dubby? My original idea, which never happened at all, was like *Metal Box* crossed with The Byrds, so there'd be harmonies over the top. But when I met Margaret, I knew that wasn't what I was going to get with her. But she was too talented not to work with.'

John Frenett joined on bass ('I found him because he had an affair with my then-girlfriend,' says Callahan), then Mig Moreland on drums, recruited through the more prosaic means of the *Melody Maker* classifieds, and finally 'this Roland four-second sampler. It had these little computer discs, maybe an inch and a half across. I used to do things like play records at 78rpm so you'd get a longer sampling time.'

'Public Enemy crossed with Can crossed with Kraftwerk crossed with ... I don't know,' says Fiedler. Moonshake had begun.

'I think there was definitely a feeling around that time of shaking things up,' says Tim Gane. 'Friends of mine like Dave Callahan, who was in The Wolfhounds ... we did lots of gigs with him. Later, when we began Stereolab, he began Moonshake, so there was a whole thing of trying to break down a little bit the more straightened stuff that had been going on before, with whatever means you could, basically.'

The parallels between Callahan and Gane are striking. 'The band I was in, McCarthy, was coming to an end,' says Gane, 'and although I'd written a lot of the music for that band, I was getting a little bit disillusioned. I was kind of tiring of the sound. I think everyone in the band was.' Gane had recently met Laetitia Sadier, a McCarthy fan from France, and the two had fallen in love; Sadier then contributed vocals to the final McCarthy album, *Banking, Violence And The Inner Life Today.*

'I took about a year just to think about what to do, because I'd been in a band, a band that possibly thought it would be popular, and I'd really got a bit tired of that world,' Gane says. 'So I thought, I don't want to start a band straight away just to be in a band. What would be different? And I did think about what would be different.'

Gane, a huge fan of *motorik* as a Peel-listening teenager, re-found those influences; he also believed My Bloody Valentine and Spacemen 3 offered a route out of an indie-pop warren. 'The idea was to create not exactly a fusion, but a kind of combination, [one that] would hopefully get more knock-on effects and create something even newer. It was very stripped down, minimalist music, one or two chords, but with melodies and harmonies.'

'I was always trying to make Stereolab pop,' Gane continues, 'but our version of pop. There wasn't a concept to make it avant-garde, and there was obviously no post-rock [term] then. It was just kind of to make our own version of something, to reclaim a bit of pop music.

For good or bad, I was trying to find out different kinds of music, and I was always very enthusiastic to speak about it. I didn't have any side of me that wanted to hide influences, and in some ways that can cause problems, because from the beginning I remember getting a lot of criticism of being diluted avant-garde.'

On *Super 45*, Stereolab's first EP from 1991, taut open chords ascended and curled, layering and spraying like a waterspout. 'I was very interested in repetition, but repetition to enhance the possibility of melody,' Gane says. 'The more you strip down the notes of a chord, the wider the possibility of adding notes in other ways. The more complicated the chord, the more restricted you are.' Stereolab thought carefully about the tools to make that music, as well, employing an array of vintage electronic equipment. 'You can't look for easy options,' Gane says. 'To me, that leads the way to settling for whatever works, and I don't find that's a good way to do music. But other people would say I was retro. [Those comments are] from people who don't really understand quite what they're saying. *You just like that sound*, or *You just like this because it looks good*. It's not, it's really not.'

The 'retro' accusation stalked Stereolab at the very beginning; their very name, from an offshoot of the 1960s folk label Vanguard, suggested they were interested in the future primarily through the tempered lens of the past. Yet while it's true that Stereolab were more willing to overtly reference musical history than Moonshake, for example, Stereolab was not a nostalgia project, because never did it solely seek to reproduce prior trends. Rather, theirs was a postmodern collapse of past, present, and future.

Listening to Stereolab, it was clear that they didn't put too much store in verses, choruses, guitar fetish, standard rock dynamics, or so-called *authenticity*. A fluctuating line-up was a strong Stereolab principle from the start, designed for open-endedness and dissolution of a power centre. 'I'm taken by the idea of [New York label] Shimmy Disc, where the bands swap over musicians, or having a backing band like Nancy Sinatra or Bob Dylan did, where the personalities of the backing band alter the way you present a song. It creates a sense that everything is constantly evolving,' Gane said in 1991, in one of Stereolab's earliest interviews.

'The original idea was to do our own label,' Gane says today. 'We started the label, Duophonic, and the group, Stereolab, at the same time, and they were deliberately started together.' Gane's experience at the end of McCarthy was marred by record-company interference, and he wanted to definitively 'break from this whole stifling way, having to redo tracks, having to get them approved. I didn't like it at all. It wasn't that bad, but even a little tiny bit of it was annoying to me.' The idea with Duophonic was flow and scatter, spontaneous recordings with minority appeal, which would then be released quickly, in limited amounts, exactly as the band (or like-minded others) intended.

'The Too Pure thing came because our drummer at the time, Joe Dilworth [of Th' Faith Healers], was helping us out,' Gane says. 'His band was on Too Pure; they'd come to see us, and they liked us, so we decided to do a record.'

'Stereolab we came across because I reckon Joe from Th' Faith Healers is a bit of a cheapskate, really,' Richard Roberts said in 1993. 'It was my birthday, and they [Stereolab] had done a single which he'd played drums on, and we didn't know, and he gave me a copy of it. He said, Hope you like this, it's something I've been doing. Then he came up to me a week later and said, They're looking for a label, what did you think of the single?'

'Young enthusiastic people are much more exciting than working with people who've done it all before,' Gane told MTV in 1993. 'Too Pure were just starting then, and we were like the second band on the label. And, for us, we were just finding things out about ourselves.'

It was starting to really happen for Too Pure. Although Th' Faith Healers were popular with a North London pub-going cabal, they were not especially profitable. This new breed was different, though. Stereolab picked up press almost immediately—quite a feat for a group selling their singles primarily through mail order. Another new signing, P.J. Harvey, held considerable promise, too. And then Moonshake were on the table, bringing with them a fearsome live reputation.

'We were a very aggressive band, live,' says Callahan. 'And Margaret probably more than me, I think. There are photos of her just glaring at people from the stage. And she was much more likely to stop a gig and yell at the soundman than I was, or refuse to play because there was nothing in the monitors.'

Moonshake also had a startling new demo—they'd put 'Secondhand Clothes' with a new Fiedler track, 'I'll Bring Tears' ('It was an eight or nine minute long segue of these two songs, with feedback and noise linking them,' Callahan says). Too Pure was *very* interested.

But there was a problem. Talent was one thing; hard cash to put records out was quite another. Ivo Watts-Russell, founder of 4AD, was impressed with the roster at that point and, particularly, did not want Too Pure to miss out on releasing the debut P.J. Harvey album, as he sensed a lot of interest in that group from elsewhere (he wasn't wrong; P.J. Harvey decamped to Island Records soon enough). Too Pure was £10,000 in debt and Watts-Russell's cash injection, along with setting Too Pure up as a limited company, helped the label stabilise and continue. Its newly swollen coffers and the relationship with Watts-Russell also allowed the label a little more flexibility. 'We know that we're never going to be judged by sales,' Roberts said in 1992. 'The bottom line is that the guy has never told us what to do and he's never stepped foot in the office. But he's put in some money and given us the opportunity to continue.' A golden chapter of records followed. March 1992 saw the release of Stereolab's *Peng!*, P.J. Harvey's *Dry*, and Moonshake's *Secondhand Clothes* EP. The EP was careful and considered, and had both time and money properly invested into it, having apparently cost twice as much to make as *Dry*.

'Secondhand Clothes', says Callahan, 'was dubby—it had both our vocals on it, it had the possibility of samples being added to it, which Margaret did, and it had weird guitars. It had a bit of urban angst. Everything was in there, basically. It was a proper calling card.'

'It was everything,' says Margaret Fiedler.

Full of prole ire—the title referred to a type of working-class snobbery, where the characters were comfortable with violence and degradation, but 'won't be seen dead in secondhand clothes'—it was a massive record, strikingly unfamiliar, throbbing and danceable, a stinging slap to the indie-rock consensus. 'It wasn't really big like a big rock record,' says Callahan, 'but it had a really low bottom end, a really high top end, and loads of space between everything. All the guitars, there's chords here and there, but most of the guitars are lead bits so they've got their own space. There's no filling it out, like a lot of indie records do.'

Although the *First* EP had sold well, this was despite—rather than because of—support from the band's label at the time, Creation, whose involvement came almost to the point of near-sabotage. 'Creation had told us that they weren't going to make a video because they didn't think the record would sell very well,' says Callahan, 'and the next thing we knew we were in the top ten of the indie chart. It sold so well that a snippet was played on British TV—or, at least a version of it was. *The Chart Show* wanted to have us on TV, and we've got no video.'

'The most hysterical thing,' says Fiedler. 'And so we all tuned in … '

'*We're gonna be on TV this morning*!' adds Callahan.

'They used to actually play the chart things on vinyl, on the TV, and they played our record at the wrong speed.'

'With just a black-and-white promo shot of us.'

'And it sounded like some death metal. It was actually … I was kind of quite pleased.'

For 'Secondhand Clothes', Too Pure coughed up for a cheap but effective video.

'*Secondhand Clothes* did pretty well,' Callahan says. 'And because of that, and other records that Stereolab, and Th' Faith Healers were putting out, Paul and Richard managed to get their records distributed in the States. Matador ended up putting us out.'

'Things started snowballing for us then,' Callahan continues. 'It was almost like being in a proper indie-pop band, but doing this weird music. You couldn't have planned it better, really.' By now, Moonshake were rehearsing long hours every day, hyperconscious about ensuring rhythmic tightness, and so were well placed to start an album—which

Too Pure gave them a month to record. By this point, Guy Fixsen was their producer and engineer, and the band were delighted with how he understood their intent. Terry Edwards played trumpet and saxophone. The generous studio timescale allowed gestation and ongoing constructive critique between band members, as well as the maturation of a concept.

'We were very obsessed with Dr John's *Gris-Gris* album,' Callahan says. 'We had this theory about urban voodoo, how you could make everything spooky and magical, but it would be to do with [our] city, not New Orleans. It was a constant subject of conversation between us for a while. That you could do this city voodoo.'

The finished *Eva Luna* is bilious with urban sickness, 'where the rain smells dirty as exhaust'. Callahan's lyrics, barked out in pointed aggravation, deal with the scummy and vicious—from parochial hatred ('Wanderlust') to murderers and their nameless victims ('Mugshot Heroine'). Fiedler's words, hushed, menace in a different way: 'Bleach And Salt Water' and 'Little Thing' are ambiguous songs, suggestive of self-administered abortion, or smack withdrawal, or anorexia; city tales ending in anonymous ignominy. Even when the album is at its most thrashy—'Spaceship Earth'—it collapses in on itself, a landslide of broken electronic consumer goods clogging up the city's arteries. Samples are plentiful but not gratuitous, and communicate with the live instruments in a fine balance; 'Mugshot Heroine', for example, is underpinned by samples of bhangra music played at differing speeds, while Terry Edwards's trumpet spurts hostility over the top. Dub is then used to ramp up the tension—the rout of 'Seen And Not Heard'—until the whole thing is rigid with dread. The music of *Eva Luna* took London's temperature in the way The Bomb Squad had expressed the New York of Public Enemy.

'There'd be a vibe you got from us, and that vibe would be unearthly, but down to earth at the same time,' Callahan says. 'Spooky but real. We were doing some kind of alchemy with electronics and guitars, the whole thing. That was the idea, really. Making gold out of shit.' Released in September 1992, *Eva Luna* was the first significant album of 1990s British post-rock.

Meanwhile, Stereolab released a handful of singles, the album *Peng!*, the compilation *Switched On*, and, most textural of all, *The Groop Played Space Age Bachelor Pad Music*. They used electronic sounds in a way that was dualistic, absurdist, and alienating, echoing their concerns about the fractured societies under modern capitalism. The sweet, near-blank vocals of Laetitia Sadier and (from 1992) Mary Hansen, and the hint of ersatz exotica, seldom made the listener consider post-Marxian economic analysis, or the ideological state apparatuses of society. But they were there, in the lyrics. 'We need a shake and therefore demand more than the cold conclusion of reason / The only impossible thing is to delimit the impossible', from 'Au Grand Jour', is just one of many examples.

'I could write a nice little happy song about Tim to this nice little happy tune, but who gives a fuck about how happy Tim and me are?' Sadier said in 1994. 'We're made to believe we're the centre of the universe and I'm trying to correct that.'

'I really had a determination to avoid genres. We even wrote records about the subject,' says Tim Gane, referring to 'Avant Garde MOR', 'Ronco Symphony', and—in a bone-dry take on the band, 'The Groop Play Chord X'—from *The Groop Played Space Age Bachelor Pad Music*. 'We *had* avoided any one specific genre, but then we had about four or five that were mainstays, and we were that to different people,' he adds. 'It was krautrock, it was lounge, even shoegaze-y in the early days. Post-rock, also.' Stereolab were striking and popular, crossing over into the near-mainstream—they even appeared on *The Word*, the pre-eminent British post-pub Yoof TV show of 1993, playing 'French Disko' (and bringing David Callahan along for the ride: 'I volunteered my Moog services at a party,' Callahan says of this appearance, 'having never touched one in my life').

Although Stereolab were hardly pinnacles of professionalism, they did generally use their unusual musical toys in a melodious way. Others threw them wholly out of the pram. 'Pram have some fine haircuts,' *Melody Maker* said, on reviewing the support band for one of the final Ut gigs, in 1990, at the Camden Falcon. 'They look sallow and uninvolved and play asylum music. The whole odd affair is held together by seriously deranged drum rhythms that sound like they're being played on one of those noddy Chad Valley drum kits.'

Rosie Cuckston, Matthew Eaton, and Andy Weir all came from Harrogate and went to school together; although Cuckston and Eaton had relocated to Birmingham (forming the creditable jangle-pop band Friends Of The Family) and Weir was in London, the three remained close and then began, along with Sam Owen, the band Hole in 1988. They self-built a theremin, accumulated a cache of toy instruments, changed their name to Pram (to avoid confusion with Courtney Love's group), and performed locally.

'There was never any discussion at that time what the group would sound like,' Eaton said in 2011. 'We appropriated some of the working methods of Can and Faust after reading about them, and of course listening to some of the great records—particularly *Tago Mago* and *Faust IV*—at the same time we'd develop songs with more conventional structures. We'd think nothing of twenty minute improvisations or playing for an hour—the aim was generally a song though, even if it came about in an unconventional manner.' They were also inspired by the joyous experimentation of The Raincoats and The Slits, but 'we were never that cerebral about it though, and it would be wrong to claim there was a master plan. It was all about new sounds and new ways of writing a song.'

Gash, a mini-album released in 1990, set out a Pram signature. This music was a vessel for quashed memories and violent primitive instincts, evoking temporarily emancipated trauma from the amygdala: the centres of emotional memory in the brain. 'There is a theme of childhood running through a lot of the songs,' Cuckston has said. 'I think you see things from a different perspective when you're a child—you sense things more. I like that perspective.' The tinny toy keyboard and nerve-jangling percussion—drums fed through a vocal harmoniser, saucepans being thrown down stairs—increased the feeling that *Gash* was the inner concert of a serial killer living on a sink estate.

'When you're a kid, if a tall man walks into the room, you run and hide,' Cuckston has said. 'Everything's disproportionate. So it's a good way of utilising your own experience—using your own memories from childhood to make something really stand out, and give it a bit of a sinister edge.'

Gash was recorded in a congruous environment. 'It used to be a home for juvenile delinquents,' Cuckston has said, of the Birmingham house Pram recorded in. 'It had been empty for about six months, and then some people we knew squatted it. We were looking for somewhere to record, so we went there. We found these papers there from the kids who used to live there—arrest warrants and so on. They were all in for trivial things, and a lot of the reports were really funny—"The defendant said 'Bollocks' to the policeman", and things like that. The spirit of juvenile delinquency haunted the record.'

'The new Too Pure signing (which hasn't been unveiled yet) is much more extreme than we are,' Mig Moreland told the *NME* in 1992.

By the time Pram had joined Too Pure, the return-of-the-repressed bedlam of *Gash* was tempered by an arcane, uncanny ambience ('film, animation, children's TV, *Play For Today* and public information broadcasts all lodged their spirit into our songs,' Owen has said.) Cuckston's vocals remained wilfully disagreeable, but now it was as if her voice had been distorted through a bent radio aerial. The songs were now harder to pin solely to a carousel-from-hell motif, although their tracks, peppered with grotesquery, gave Pram's macabre humour a warm air; different from the alienated brutality of Moonshake and the icy Situationism of Stereolab.

The *Iron Lung* EP came first. 'I've always liked music that takes you into another world,' Eaton said in 1993. 'So this record is full of a kind of storytelling. And some of the tracks are fairly strange to listen to.'

'The music is more ambient than *Gash*,' Cuckston said at the time. 'I suppose it does lull you into a false sense of security, and then give you a jolt. It's more like being in the cradle than being in the pram.'

'A typical day in the *Gash*/*Stars* era might involve rehearsing, jamming, taping it onto a four-track, breakfast of coffee, taping tapes and records, clubbing, phoning promoters, endlessly hassling for gigs, sending out tapes,' Eaton has said. 'I did a lot of listening to music, lots of reading, occasional visits to the job centre.'

The Stars Are So Big The Earth Is So Small … Stay As You Are, the album that followed, was also recorded in a domestic environment. ('Typical Pram clutter,' Owen has said. 'We need it to function! Leads everywhere, running from cellar to attic, all of us huddled around, punching stuff in, playing. We'd come out of our bedrooms with ideas and then go down to the cellar to put them all together.') Written and recorded in a month, happy accidents were retained, and the album's centrepiece—'In Dreams You Too Can Fly'—was recorded in one take, according to Owen (two takes, according to Eaton). 'It came out wrong, wonky, but that was us. That was Pram.'

It was vastly different from *Gash*, and illustrated Pram's interest in, and ability to incorporate, jazz motifs. '*Journey In Satchidananda* [by Alice Coltrane] is still, to me, the most perfect piece of music,' Owen has said. 'There was a lot of discovering music by swapping tapes at that time—I think that one came to me from the direction of Godflesh, via a friend of a friend.'

Live, Pram made a visible virtue of their cheapness and artlessness, Cuckston behind an ironing board with her keyboard on top. ('It was just the cost at first,' Eaton has said. 'The keyboards were £20, so you don't want a £100 symbol of professionalism to put them on.') Whether by intention or design, the use of housework contraptions chimed well with Pram's lyrics—'Cumulus', for example, was a locked-groove elegy for bored housewives and the fantasy life they can indulge in. Their very lo-fi and homemade approach would precipitate a strand of post-rock yet to come.

'Too Pure invited us to their Christmas party [in 1992],' says Sarah Peacock of Seefeel. 'Pram played, and I think it was Th' Faith Healers. Richard Roberts pulled me aside at the end of the night [and asked], Did you enjoy tonight? [I said,] Yeah, it was brilliant. And he just said, Oh, you're part of it now. And I wasn't sure how to take it. Because he hadn't actually said, Oh, we want to sign you, but I just remember going home that night and thinking, does that mean they want to sign us? And it was just the *thrill*, the thrill of it.'

Like David Callahan and Margaret Fiedler, Sarah Peacock had been actively looking for people to work with in the music press. Her advert read, 'People wanted to form band. MBV, SY, etc.'

'Mark rang me up and said, We've kind of already got a band going, [but] we need another member. Would you be interested in joining a band, rather than starting a band?' she remembers. 'He then said, Do you like the Cocteaus as well? and I said, Yeah, of course I do.'

Mark was Mark Clifford. 'I've made music since I was about fourteen or fifteen,' he says. 'I was at Goldsmith's College, and when I left I didn't really know what I wanted to do. I don't know whether it was a complete desire to make music or just because I had nothing better to do.' Peacock, meanwhile, had learnt classical piano and flute growing up, and in her teens she picked up the guitar.

'I guess by the time I was about sixteen, I thought, I really want to be in a proper band,' she says. 'Play guitar and shout. I never had a lesson, and still would freely admit that I'm a fairly rubbish guitarist, technically. But that's the way I like it.'

When Peacock joined, the nascent Seefeel was Clifford and Justin Fletcher—nephew to John Mayall, so of blues heritage, but a mad dub fan as well. 'They already had a demo, of four songs, which Mark sent me,' Peacock says. 'I really liked it, but it was very indie. Like a gentler My Bloody Valentine. Mark was singing.'

'I hated singing,' Clifford says. 'I didn't really think I could sing. I was just mumbling like Kevin Shields or something, but in the wrong context. Sarah joined on bass but soon after she gave me a little tape, which was called *Tiny Bits Of Sarah*. She'd done loads of little recordings at home. And she'd done some vocals on some of them. I just thought, yes, she should be singing. She couldn't play bass anyway, so it didn't matter.'

'I went along to meet them and we tried jamming some songs,'

Peacock says. 'I started playing bass, but I wasn't really very good at it, so I moved to guitar, and took over singing. [Mark and I bonded] over music and over ambition, and what we wanted to do and where we wanted to take it. And other things, personality-wise, didn't really matter at that point. Well, they did come along later.'

Seefeel began hanging out, writing, and rehearsing together, at first using Mark Van Hoen as temporary bassist before recruiting Daren Seymour in early 1992. They found their horizons expanding significantly from that first demo, through rave music and culture; they kept experimenting and, soon, the song 'More Like Space' emerged, 'the first track where we all kind of looked at each other and knew we'd done something a bit more special,' Clifford says.

Peacock borrowed Clifford's four-track. 'I used it to record some soundtracks for my film, the final film I did for college,' she says; she was studying animation. 'I invited Mark and Daren: Do you want to come and see my film? I was showing off a bit. When the two bits of music that I'd done came on, they were like, *what are they*? And I said, They're just a couple of things I wrote on your four-track, and I passed the tapes to them. One of them was on a lost demo, and the other one ended up being "Time To Find Me". We made another demo that had "Time To Find Me" and "More Like Space" on, and that was the one that people picked up on.'

They sent the demo out to Creation, 4AD, and Too Pure, remembering that ill-fated gig with Earwig at the Sausage Machine. 'The words I always remember Richard Roberts saying to us were, I don't really get your music, but there's something about it that I really like, and I don't know what it is,' Clifford says. Seefeel signed with Too Pure, and the label's commitment increased the band's optimism and energy.

As with Disco Inferno and Bark Psychosis, Seefeel gravitated to the cheap spaces of East London, rehearsing three times a week in a 'scuzzy little room in Stratford', says Peacock. 'I was finding that soft singing sounds better than belting it out. It was almost a knock to my confidence of trying to [sing] in the traditional way that led me to do it in the way that I did. We did a studio session where it was literally, *let's see what you can come up with on the spot.* It was absolutely terrifying. And I just scribbled down a load of stream-of-consciousness stuff, went in and sung it, and it was awful, horrible self-pitying rubbish. Everyone was being polite, but we did that song, and it was never mentioned again. From then on, the lyrics became less and less, and the way that I enunciated them became more and more vague and hazy. I've got a lisp and I've always been a bit conscious about that, so I would avoid singing words with an *s* in. So, I arrived at [something] I felt comfortable with.'

An EP—*More Like Space*—was released in the first half of 1993, with a showcase gig set up in a recording studio sound booth for an interested thong of journalists and tastemakers. It was a clever move; there was a 'Statement Of Intent', which guests could pick up on the way in, which held the gig's aim to be 'using technology as a live instrument'. It was clear that Too Pure was getting more sophisticated in its launching of bands.

More Like Space gained a lukewarm reception, but it was followed by the shining *Plainsong* twelve-inch, named after the monophonic liturgical chant; its reviews often mentioned several diverse reference points, especially in conjunction with the B-side, the slowly intoxicating 'Minky Starshine'.

'"Plainsong" I have a real love-hate relationship with, because I love the sequencing and the vocals, but I *hate* the rhythm on it,' says Clifford. 'I really agonised over the rhythm.'

'There were literally about thirty mixes,' says Peacock. 'And we'd be sitting there, and Mark would be playing us one after the other. *What's the difference? I can't be arsed with this!*'

Sessions began for their debut album, *Quique*, in Camden, at the time just as much of a shithole as Stratford was. 'We had a really nice time recording it,' Peacock says. 'We'd written most of the songs before. There'd be four or five of them constructed in the studio, like "Charlotte's Mouth", "Through You", other bits and pieces like "Signals", which is a thing that Daren had sampled off shortwave radio, which is why he gets a credit for playing the radio. "Polyfusion", "Industrious", "Plainsong" had all been written in the rehearsal studio. It was beautiful weather, we'd go into the night and then we'd drink, and it'd be really nice. We were all getting on well and having fun, and loving the way it was turning out. Everything was sounding really good.'

'[The title] doesn't really mean anything,' Clifford says. 'It's purely that when we were in the studio, when we were mixing the album, I used to put strips on the mixing desk, [because] there were so many channels when you're mixing, and you have to be aware of where everything is. Occasionally you'll go, oh, where's the kick gone? So we used to give them names. "Quique" was "kick". And it wasn't like we'd made it up, it just transformed into that over a period of weeks. *Kik*, to *Kiq*, to *Qiq*, something like that. All the instruments started to have stupid names. But *Quique*, just the sound of it, it seemed to reflect what we were doing somehow. And I don't really know why, it just the way it looks, the sound, it was quite crisp but also quite soft. Lots of curves.'

'On *Quique*, we had one track that got left off, and it had some chords on that I'd written,' says Peacock. 'When I was doing the sleeve layout, late at night, frantically trying to get it together on our publishers' computer, [the rest of Seefeel] rang me up and said, We're leaving this track off. It was the only one, so it was I had to grudgingly go back to my credit and put "Sarah Peacock—vocals", and not guitar as well. I felt, I'm really cheating myself here. The bastards, they've done me out of that. I am now just the singer, even though I still play guitar live. I felt I deserved more than that, [but] there's a certain kind of martyrdom that women put up with. I certainly did. I should have just left [the credit] in there, because who cares? But I honestly can't do that; I feel I've got to be a martyr and I've got to be truthful. And when you do shout and stamp your foot, you don't get away with it as well as a bloke would.'

Released at the very end of 1993, *Quique* was received positively; it revived the 'oceanic' trope for critics, and there was much talk of submarines and depth charges. Seefeel found that their elusiveness with genre emitted strength, most journalists scrabbling to pin down the wind; they acknowledged the influence of techno and rave, while unable to shake the presence of guitars. Seefeel were a crosshatch of so many things, and you couldn't see any of the joins. They even positively affected the shoegaze they were so keen to distance themselves from—Slowdive's 'Souvlaki Space Station', from 1993, is their best song, and it sounds directly influenced by Seefeel—or, at least influenced by what had also fed into the making of *Quique*, such as dub, and Aphex Twin. (Kirsty Yates of Insides, who toured with Slowdive at this point, remembers that they 'made a point of talking about how they'd bought some samplers. They wouldn't have been happy with what people were writing about them. They would have wanted to get away from that as fast as they could.')

The early Seefeel period was 'very productive', Clifford says. 'It was like a tap.'

Moonshake, too, kept their work rate and profile high. 'Beautiful Pigeon' was lifted from *Eva Luna* as a single. 'Margaret and the band thought "Beautiful Pigeon" would be a good A-side, so they staged a little bit of a coup,' Callahan says. 'And Margaret had her first A-side. But it's good. I didn't have a problem.'

During this time, Moonshake were playing live virtually constantly. 'I was doing it all the time, at the expense of everything else,' Callahan says. 'At the expense of relationships and friendships, and at the expense of financial security. I loved doing it, but we were in each other's face for all that time. So we had tiffs and things.'

The dynamic tension between Callahan and Fiedler in Moonshake was, in a strange way, a mirror to the volume dynamics in Slint, even though the two groups sounded utterly distinct from one another. Just as Slint's noise-and-release wasn't binary, but rather highlighted the two elements' uncomfortable interdependency, Moonshake never relied on superficial contrast based on male/female, harsh/quiet, rock/sampling. Rather, Moonshake sucked those binaries in and spewed out a new, restless sound.

'The thing with Moonshake,' Callahan says, 'is that it was emotionally fractious. It wasn't like we were *just* in a band. We were always on the verge of an emotional breakdown. There was always anger, and a load of emotional stress going on. By then, it was almost getting to where

Margaret working on her stuff, and I was working on my stuff. There wasn't a lot of meeting in the middle. But it wasn't just because of how we were as people. It's also because, when you're working with a sampler, you can't really jam. You can't really write too much together. The only times we did write together, Margaret would probably get some music, and I'd add the vocal or a bass line to it.' Two of these rare collaborations, 'Beeside' and 'Home Survival Kit', appeared as bonus tracks on the *Beautiful Pigeon* EP.

Moonshake went back into the studio to record a mini-album, *Big Good Angel*. This was less dramatic than *Eva Luna*, but arguably more wracked with oppressive torment. 'I was always jealous that Margaret could get a lot more sex in her lyrics than I could,' Callahan says, referring especially to Fiedler's heady 'Flow' on *Big Good Angel*. 'It's hard for a man to write about sex in a harsh, critical tone without it sounding like you're some kind of sexist idiot.'

'I think it's interesting that the female gaze can be more acceptable,' Fiedler says.

Big Good Angel gave a sense that Moonshake were turning inwards, directing their attention to inner space more than toward the London fields. The band sounded hemmed in and vertiginous, and when the music spilled out, it arranged itself in curious canted structures.

'We are a remix without the original being heard,' Mig Moreland said in 1993.

'I'd done "Capital Letters" and thought, I've got the best track on this,' Callahan says of *Big Good Angel*, 'and then she came back with "Two Trains".'

'Yes, "Two Trains", that's a doozy. I love it, I love it,' Fiedler says.

'Fortunately, when it came to doing a video, "Two Trains" was almost unfilmable,' Callahan says, 'so we had to do "Capital Letters".' It was filmed near to the Hackney high-rise where Callahan lived at the time. 'None of that's there anymore. It's all been destroyed. The estate, and the band, has been knocked down.'

As 1993 was nearing its end, Too Pure had lost Stereolab—through mutual agreement, and in recognition of how far the band valued their own Duophonic imprint—but retained Moonshake, Seefeel, and Pram. But more splintering was afoot.

'The whole Too Pure thing was a very exciting time,' says Tim Gane.

'Until it inevitably went tits up, Too Pure had really great taste,' says David Callahan.

'Paul Cox just always seemed like a really good guy,' Kirsty Yates says. 'He loved what he was doing, and he'd take a chance on stuff, even though, after P.J. Harvey, he probably had the opportunity to go, No, I'm not going to mess around with this stuff anymore, I'm going to concentrate on stuff that sells. He could still be bothered to do the gigs. He didn't need to.'

'We didn't leave Too Pure because it wasn't happy,' Mark Clifford says. *Quique* was to be Seefeel's only album on the label, as they followed P.J. Harvey and Stereolab out of the door. 'But they were a budget label. Although they gave us the money we wanted, I felt terrible even asking for it. We had to, though. We had to remaster *Quique* because I wanted to change two tracks. And they gave us the money to do it, but I felt really bad.' As 1994 dawned, Seefeel moved to Warp—a label that gave them a new identity but also new problems.

And, as Seefeel were bedding down in their new home, 1993 also found someone who was to play his own part in the post-rock story—the journalist Simon Reynolds—testing out ground. Citing Seefeel, Disco Inferno, Main, Stereolab, Papa Sprain, Insides, and Ice in his review of that year, he referred to these artists as 'post-rock and post-rave stuff'—and 'the stuff worth cherishing in 1993'.

CHAPTER EIGHT

1994: the year post-rock broke

'Nietzsche says, somewhere, that it's harder to make an ending than to make a new beginning.' GARY MCKENDRY, PAPA SPRAIN

Almost as soon as post-rock was named, it was a curse. Bands were dropped, friendships were ruined, mental health was compromised, and *absolutely no money* was made. Post-rock seemed to inhabit and then annihilate its first generation, as if it were a malign superbug.

The term's creator had the very best of intentions. Simon Reynolds was analytical, his knowledge of musical history vast, and he had a logophile's vocabulary. (And, perhaps a wicked sense of his own indulgences too: he once memorably described a Papa Sprain concert as 'diamante detonations, spectral rainbows, a fluorescent blizzard, scintillations and tintabulations, the discharged light of phosphorescing marine organisms congregating in dense shoals like a succession of submerged haloes.')

As the 1990s edged toward midlife, Reynolds's type of writing was increasingly marginalised in the weekly music press, the kind of bands it tended to champion ghettoised. Whereas once a *Melody Maker* reader might find The Young Gods, Public Enemy, and A.R. Kane on the cover—multiple times!—coverage of such bands was now downsized or eschewed completely. The knock-on effect was that artists like Disco Inferno (who would certainly have received a good-sized feature a few years earlier) languished in squibs and reviews, sustained chiefly by the individual journalists who happened to like them.

Many of the more thoughtful music writers, Reynolds included, were now also writing for *The Wire*. This monthly magazine, far more serious in intent than the inkies, had relatively recently expanded its remit from its origins as a pure avant-jazz magazine to cover all types of 'music from out there'. Reynolds's writing could really stretch out in *The Wire*, and it was here that he properly debuted 'post-rock' in May 1994. It was a concept he had been playing with in reviews and features for a good few months.

'What to call this zone?' Reynolds asked in that *Wire* article, 'Shaking The Rock Narcotic'. 'Some of its occupants, Seefeel for instance, could be dubbed "ambient"; others, Bark Psychosis and Papa Sprain, could be called "art rock". "Avant rock" would just about suffice, but is too suggestive of jerky time signatures and a dearth of melodic loveliness, which isn't necessarily the case. Perhaps the only term open-ended yet precise enough to cover all this activity is "post-rock".'

As far back as his 'oceanic rock' term of the late 1980s, it's clear that Reynolds had been divining for a name to pinpoint what he saw going on. In 1993, he had called both Insides and Seefeel 'post-rock/post-techno', relating their music to liminal space between and beyond both genres; but it was Bark Psychosis to whom he first gave 'post-rock' as a standalone term, when positively reviewing their 1994 album *Hex* for *Mojo* magazine. In this piece, Reynolds rehearsed much of what he would go on to develop fully in *The Wire* two months later: textures and dynamics; the influence of Eno, A.R. Kane, Can; the role of techno and dub; the primacy of the studio; a lack of concern with rock's traditional signifiers and trappings. 'The future of rock is looking more buoyant than it has for a while,' he concluded, 'thanks to Bark Psychosis and their "post-rock" ilk.'

'I was never really aware of [the term] until much, much later,' says Graham Sutton, 'because I never read any reviews of *Hex*. It was probably about the year 2000 when someone pointed it out to me. But at the time the album came out … we had put so much into it. The last thing I wanted to know is if some cunt hates it. Or even if some cunt likes it.'

While most of the musicians that occupied Reynolds's post-rock purview appreciated what he was trying to achieve, few accepted it completely. Sometimes it was the 'post' that rankled; sometimes the 'rock'.

'I had thought, if we had a name, it was post-pop,' says Ian Crause.

'We viewed ourselves as a rock'n'roll band,' says David Callahan, 'in terms of: this is what rock'n'roll should sound like *now*, rather than the clichés. We figured that's where rock should have evolved to.'

What really *did* resonate for most of the artists, however, was that they were not usual bands with usual ambitions. Post-rock, Reynolds suggested, was opposed to notions of 'collective toil' and 'authenticity'; instead, it used musicians for a 'palette of textures' and, in doing so, rejected the ego of rock. Later, Reynolds would go further, claiming post-rock had 'given up the idea of mass success or even indie cult-hood, and accepted the idea of being marginal, forever'.

This wasn't quite true. No one enjoyed the grinding penury—as David Callahan says, 'I didn't want to be obscure, I wanted to take these weird things into the chart, and to headline big venues'—but there was, in every single case, an especially prominent dislike of compromise in order to achieve success. This marked these artists out from a growing neoliberal consensus in the music industry.

'I couldn't have expressed it with any eloquence at the time, as I lacked the intellect,' says Crause, 'but what did come across was that our generation of musicians seemed to be first and foremost on a career tip and shamelessly so, bragging about their material ambitions in interviews. I imagine in past times musicians kept their ambitions balanced with all sorts of other concerns, such as trying to be brilliant at what they did, for one, and it would have been a rare case where someone was openly venal and materialistic, not least because it would be seen as something tasteless and could damage their perceived sense of integrity. What happens, though, is by the very fact of *not* being seen to prioritise material success in a society where it is quickly becoming the only yardstick by which to measure things, far from being perceived as having integrity, you are perceived as being losers who aren't prepared to make the necessary compromises to make your business work.'

Simon Reynolds is also remembered as being an advocate, ally, and critical friend for artists. 'I used to correspond with him, for quite a while, whilst I was at university,' says Julian Tardo. 'I just really liked what he was doing. So when we had a record out, and he reviewed it, I think he was easy to get on board.'

'I remember Simon Reynolds saying—and this was probably a big thing [for us]—that the quieter stuff works better than when you go for onslaught,' says Kirsty Yates. 'And having that mirror held up … we adore Simon Reynolds, so that's quite nice to have [him say] actually, the way you're developing is pretty good. He called *Euphoria* "easy glistening". And it was lovely to be referred to in those terms.'

Reynolds, and other journalists at *The Wire*, gave smart, meaty features to many of the British post-rock artists during 1993 and 1994, equivalents of which were almost entirely absent from the weeklies. However, *The Wire*'s readers were older and more serious; its circulation was less than that of the *Melody Maker* or the *NME*; its writing could be impenetrable and lacked a sense of fun; and, being monthly, it found the exciting churn of new bands much harder to capture. Some of those bands, many of whom had grown up on *Melody Maker* especially, were upset that they had been sidelined.

'There was just massive disinterest from all and sundry,' says Graham Sutton, recalling the music press's response at the time of *Hex*'s release. 'I'd heard that there aren't going to be any features on us, not going to be anything in the press about it at all. Couldn't get arrested for it. It wasn't even that everyone hated it. It was complete disinterest.' In Bark Psychosis's case, this was pretty striking. Along with Moonshake, they had been the greatest beneficiaries of press interest in the preceding couple of years. But then …

'What happened?' *Melody Maker* asked in a live review. 'Bark Psychosis 1994 bear no resemblance to any previous incarnation.'

What happened indeed?

There was a gap of more than a year between *SCUM* and *Hex*, the album released on Valentine's Day 1994. 'It was a lot more extreme, or a lot more noisy, whatever you want to call it, before,' Sutton says, 'and then we cut all that stuff out. And I think some people were confused, or disappointed. Or expecting something different, certainly. But I saw it as a natural extension of what we had been doing.'

Nothing illustrated the new Bark Psychosis more than the transformation of 'The Loom'. From its early incarnation as 'Prologue' into the 1991 live version sardonically named 'Concept Art', it's a ringing, intense, instrumental, guitar-based track, frothing into volume dynamics, tension-release foreplay and malicious brood. By the time of the *Hex* version, it was completely post-guitar; the piano motif that opens it introduces strings and minimal, wistful lyrics, while the drums are in a hemisphere all of their own, hectares of space around them, before crunching distortion brings the track to a close. Slow shifts had become part of the Bark Psychosis *raison d'être*, as had the technique of creating a disembodied sound that could seem tranquil, but would—often due to Ling's bass—have the unsentimental pummel of a migraine.

Sutton had always been interested in how records were constructed—he pored over Talk Talk credits as a teenager—and he had become completely absorbed in arranging, re-arranging, paring, listening to tiny segments, hearing sounds in different contexts. 'I suppose [it was] not wanting to adhere to a conservative way of putting together a piece of music,' he says. 'Just wanting to do something on our own terms, and with our own language, and with our own particular take on things.' This took time, and headspace, and concentration.

But such concepts were difficult to access for Sutton, due to all the record label and management troubles the band had suffered throughout 1992 and 1993; calm was also rare in the Leyton squat. 'I overdid it a bit when I was squatting with John [Ling],' Sutton says. 'I had a nervous breakdown. At that particular point in time, I was seen as a rogue element, [one] that could in some way upset the equilibrium of their outlook; that the lifestyle wasn't necessarily all peachy keen. I was pushed to one side. I was seen as a threat to a state of mind and a way of life that we'd all been having for a long time—which was really burning it at both ends, and everything in the middle as well. So I moved out.'

Initially, he went elsewhere in London, and then further away. 'I was down in Brighton and controlling everything, directing everything, saying that it should be like this, like that … when you're young, you have very strong ideas about things. I don't feel bad about that,' he says. Bark Psychosis got together to record in Sutton's Brighton flat, in studios in Bath and London, and in the Stratford church, and the album was finally mixed at the expensive RAK studios, in a move that meant the band couldn't afford to eat. Sutton tirelessly developed the *Hex* sound, absolutely obsessing over the whole thing.

'It was really something, to get that record made,' Sutton says. 'I think about it now, I think about the hoops, and the dealing with bullshit. It was unbelievable that it managed to get made as it did.'

Sutton's vocals and lyrics on *Hex* intensified and matured the 'SCUM' technique of short, non-narrative stylings; but, now, anger and cynicism had given way to solemnity and rue. 'You're going out to raves, and you're listening to the pieces, and you're thinking, OK, we're having these experiences, how does this assimilate?' Sutton says of his lyrics. 'Memories of hearing these slogans, they're very simplistic: *we're all free, everybody's free*, all that sort of stuff. Of how you approach words, and vocals, or whatever.'

Hex charts a brutal, protean comedown in its words, with no clear path or healing. 'It was important to feel, in some way, really exposed,' he adds. 'It was all quite fragile stuff in some ways. It could collapse any second.'

'The album is about the power that people and places have over you,' Sutton said at the time of *Hex*'s release. 'How they keep drawing you back even though you know they're destructive.' The 'hex' was their bewitching force; it could have also doubled as explanation for the enslaving pull of the album itself on Sutton. He acknowledges that the rest of the band probably saw him as a despot during the making of

Hex ('Pendulum Man' was titled after his epic mood swings), and knows that the album killed off the band.

'It's one of the worst things that ever happened to me,' he says. 'And it's something that I'm still sore about now.' The first casualty was keyboard player Daniel Gish, but all the band members were feeling the financial strain; despite being on a major label, they were still signing on for unemployment benefit. After Gish left, there was one track left to do: 'Big Shot'. 'John started it by programming a bunch of stuff, and then he passed it to me, and I programmed a bunch of stuff. That was done in a very different way to all the other tracks,' Sutton says.

The gruelling process of making *Hex* finally over, a battered Bark Psychosis needed a break at the end of 1993, for the new year would herald more work: the album's release, a short tour, and promotional duties. 'We got together to start rehearsing. We hadn't played together as a band for most of the previous year, because we'd been making the album, and I remember it vividly. We'd set everything up for doing the tour. It's quite a bit of work to make it all happen. We got [to the rehearsal space], and John just sort of literally sat in the corner, foetus-like. Refused to play the bass, wouldn't pick it up. Nothing. So after a whole afternoon of it, I was like, you might as well go home; this is awful. So he left. And he never came back.'

It was a crisis, and it felt 'extremely personal', says Sutton, as the ten-year Ling/Sutton friendship derailed and ended. 'As for the tour, we could have pulled the dates, but that wouldn't have helped either, really. We managed to get a session guy in, and another friend of mine, Paul Thomas, helped out, and we managed to pull it together, somehow. It was horrible. Awful. But we still managed to pull it off.'

They toured with the stop-motion animated film *The Secret Adventures Of Tom Thumb*, a Jan Svankmayer-inspired, grimy fairy-tale horror, and the theme of a naïf literally trampled underfoot by an urban nightmare unsurprisingly struck a chord, as did—as always—not taking the expected 'rock' path to gigs. 'Why should it be that you pay a certain amount of money, and you go to the bar, you trudge through three different bands?' Sutton says. 'We wanted to find a brand new film that hadn't been released. It was almost like a pre-release screening, running a little film festival.'

Sometimes, however, *The Secret Adventures Of Tom Thumb* couldn't be shown. This was symptomatic of the square-peg ambition that post-rock had in a live setting, and the round-hole venues it was forced into. While a gig wasn't seen as the 'authentic' way of hearing the music (and many post-rock artists, through personal shyness as well as ego erasure, feared or hated them), they all did it, and sought to transform it to some extent.

'You realise when you're setting up your gear that you need electricity for *this*,' says Julian Tardo. 'You've got films showing *there*, and everything is all over the place. "Where can we plug in?" "Just in that room around the back." And you go in there, and there's sockets with loads of four-ways coming off them.'

'Playing live was really stressful back then because we used a lot of technology and it wasn't like now where everything goes in a tiny little box,' says Mark Clifford. 'We were carting unreliable equipment around. Soundchecks were nightmarish. Certain things wouldn't start. It was really hard work.'

There was also the question of who to play *with*. For every Disco Inferno / Insides double-header, there were dozens more uninspiring setups. 'You're still playing the indie circuits, you're still doing the inappropriate support slots, and we did some *incredibly* inappropriate support slots,' says Kirsty Yates, remembering how Insides supported the conventional indie-pop band Kingmaker. 'There I was, in my silver leggings, and red dress … I remember there were some kids at the front going, look at her, look at her, while we were playing for our fifty quid.'

'For the first album, we decided to tour with The Wedding Present,' says David Callahan, 'which is the most heinous tour I've ever been on.'

'David Gedge, what a twat,' says Margaret Fiedler. 'That's *on* record.'

'There's one particular show I remember,' says Callahan. 'We did the

Brixton Academy with them, four thousand people, utterly sold out, and I swear at the end of every song there was almost silence.'

'Having stuff thrown at us and abuse shouted was pretty normal, as was people getting into it on occasion, but the silence thing, that was special,' says Ian Crause. 'When I got a Stratocaster for *Second Language*, we got that painted in a UV sunburst from blue through green and yellow to red, like a sunset, with a clear scratchplate. Once, we supported Spectrum [the new project of Spacemen 3's Sonic Boom] in St Helens, near Liverpool, and were playing the *D.I. Go Pop* stuff to a crowd of indie types, sort of Smiths fans. And we came onstage in close to total silence, which was normal. I guess they were looking at our UV-spattered kit and wondering what they were in for. Then we started, and played the first song. When it finished, the silence was total. No sound at all in the whole place, which was something I don't ever recall having heard. But no one was getting up and leaving, the whole place was just sort of sitting staring at us. So we carried on. Total silence after each song.

'About four songs in, [Paul] Willmott and I looked at each other and started laughing. We'd never had this before and it was novel, to put it mildly. After another song I heard someone talking so I looked into the audience, and about six rows back I could see a guy cupping his hand to his girlfriend's ear and whispering into it. I could hear it from the stage. And still I couldn't see anyone get up and leave. They were just gawping. So we finished the set and packed our stuff up in total silence. That's pretty much the definitive gig for me.'

Disco Inferno were also the only post-rock act of this era with a logo: a circle and three curved lines representing transmission, and it changed direction with each release. 'One of the first things our manager did when we signed to Rough Trade was to approach FUEL, the graphic design company, who he had seen in a *Sunday Times* feature,' Crause says. 'Up until then, I had been involved in the sleeve artwork to varying degrees. As soon as they got involved, they took control of it completely, which was both a joy and a relief. It was obvious they were the best and so we just gave them complete control. I remember one meeting where I suggested something to them as an idea, and was told if I wanted to do the art I could just get on and do it and they would not be involved. If we wanted them to do it then we had to leave them to do what they wanted. Because we had had a few sleeves by that point, and knew how good they were, I just let them do it.'

Graham Sutton had designed the sleeve for *SCUM*, but he got another artist in, Dave McKean, for the 1994 single 'A Street Scene'. McKean had illustrated the 1989 graphic novel *Arkham Asylum*, casting the Batman story into fine-art *tableaux*; Sutton felt this impressionistic technique resonated with *Hex*'s fabric. However, for *Hex* itself, Sutton retook the reigns. 'I was told I was useless at art from a very early age, and they were quite correct,' he says. 'But I'm a good graphic designer.' *Hex* featured a lurid sky over Leyton Goods Yard, an image so representative of the micro-apocalypses in the album's narrative.

Moonshake's artwork, a salmagundi of handwriting, obtuse angles, and surreal imagery, was an appropriate visual metaphor for how the band used samples. 'I don't think I ripped off people's music by sampling it, because part of the sound I was sampling would have a skip in the record,' David Callahan says. 'It would have dust on it. It would all be part of the noise. It's almost as if it was a de-tuned radio. It is like collage; you're not just cutting out bits of photos and sticking them together, you're fading them, colouring them, shrinking them, expanding them, flipping them over, distorting them.'

It was also, sadly, uncomfortably close to the collision now engulfing the band. 'At least for two years, we were thick as thieves. Artistically, we were very close,' says Callahan, of himself and Fiedler. 'But we were pulling apart all the time. Doesn't that say everything you need to know about men and women's relationships? You have to be together, but you're always pulling away. I think that's why it worked. There was some glue and some abrasion. But neither of us were very good diplomats with each other. We knew we had something, and it worked, but we were never very good at talking about it in a rational way. We just reacted very instinctively. There were probably a few simple steps we could have taken at the time, but neither of us was willing or able to do it.'

During and immediately after *Big Good Angel*, there was a sense that compromise in Moonshake was becoming insurmountable: Fiedler, Callahan says, looked to consolidate and improve on the sound of *Eva Luna*, while Callahan wanted to abandon it for a change in style. Tensions reached a head while they toured America, as lack of sleep, drink and drug use, emotional stress, and constant close quarters sat with miserable dead weight upon the band. Tempers chaffed and sparked, and the Callahan-Fiedler partnership completely broke down.

'As I recall it, Margaret had said to me that she wanted to go and record, hire out a whole studio, have two different rooms, and she'd work with Guy [Fixsen] in one room, and I'd record with the house guy in another,' Callahan recalls. 'I remember being really offended by that. Probably because I was hoping we'd be able to put it together again. But I wasn't doing anything to do that. If anything, I was probably making it worse.'

A decision that Callahan had taken back in the Creation days became significant. Without telling any of the others, he had copyrighted the name Moonshake, partly out of insecurity that the rest of the band would quit after they left Creation. 'I'm not going to say that was a nice thing to do,' he says, 'but when we were breaking up, I knew I was on safe ground to some degree. It was doing that cowardly thing of, oh, I'll go out with someone else before I break up with this person. I know Margaret was very upset about the whole thing.'

'Yes,' she says.

'But I also thought that Margaret was set up, because she'd been going out with Guy [Fixsen], and had this live-in workmate, really, and everything was set up, in a way.'

'Yes,' Fiedler says. 'Sort of. It's hard to say. I was really upset. All I can say is, I was super-upset. I found it very hard not to be working with him. I missed him.'

Callahan and Fiedler put a brave face on it for the music press, which also reported that Mig Moreland was to stay with Callahan, while John Frenett and Guy Fixsen were throwing in their lot with Fiedler in an as-yet-unnamed new band. 'I am a little upset that Dave's continuing with the name Moonshake, because I did write half of the material,' Fiedler told *Melody Maker* in late 1993, as the split became public, 'but that's the only aspect of it that wasn't amicable.'

'Part of me was getting used to striking out on my own, part of me was going, *shit*, that didn't turn out how I wanted,' says Callahan. 'I would say I shot myself in the foot a bit, because in my own arrogance I didn't realise what effect it would have on me. I lost self-esteem, and self-belief, and confidence, after that. This whole edifice had been built up, and then it had gone, and I thought I could somehow fly in the air like Wile E Coyote over the canyon. But I suddenly looked at the camera, and *wooosh*.'

Now the *de facto* leader of Moonshake, Callahan surveyed the wreckage. Initially, he looked for a 'new Margaret'—approaching Rose Carlotti of The Heart Throbs (who 'stopped just short of telling me to fuck off, to be honest')—but soon dumped the idea entirely, opting instead for a roster of guests and a completely new band, which was to include a horn player. 'I was very taken by what Terry Edwards had done on *Eva Luna*,' Callahan says. 'I wanted to explore that more, [especially] horns with effects on. I basically thought, it's time to do *Trout Mask Replica*, it's time to do *Dragnet*, it's time to do the lo-fi extremity thing.' The horn player Callahan recruited was Ray Dickaty, who straddled free-jazz, improv, and Gallon Drunk. He used a number of effects on his saxophone, including delay, reverb, and distortion, and borrowed Callahan's 'whammy' pitch-shifting pedal (as used with guitar on *Eva Luna*) to make it 'sound like there's several saxes playing at once'.

Now the sole writer, Callahan was inspired by folk-art and urban myth, as well as by the fissures in interpersonal relationships. 'I've always been fascinated by detachment, the detachment in people's lives,' he says. 'Sometimes I'm *detached* from that detachment, and other times I feel it myself.'

This is most striking on 'Just A Working Girl', a spontaneously written track. 'I got drunk and wrote the whole thing in my bedroom after the pub,' he says, 'and woke up about lunchtime the next day, and put the tape in. I had turned the sampler off without saving the samples, I hadn't written the words down. It was recorded like a drunk would on a four-track. But I thought, *that's one of the best things I've ever done.*'

Callahan had been buying lots of records from the 1940s and 1950s, primarily with the intention of sampling them, but 'I actually started really getting into them, listening to them for pleasure. I got into all sorts of standards and easy listening arrangements. It had a big influence not so much on the music, but on the lyrics.'

'Just A Working Girl', which combines Brechtian estrangement with a modern underground film-noir feel, was inspired by the direct experiences of people Callahan knew. 'I've had friends who have worked in the sex industry, and unless there's a real bastard, they don't really judge their clients,' he says. 'A friend of mine who was stripping in Belgium said to me, I looked out and half the men there looked like they could have been my friend.' Polly Harvey's incurious vocal—sung while Callahan narrates the backstory of the prostitute's customers—conveys this well.

When it came to recording, Callahan found that he missed not only Fiedler but Guy Fixsen as well. Moreover, since Too Pure now unexpectedly found itself with two bands that needed recording costs paid, the label economised, cutting Moonshake's studio time to half that of *Eva Luna* and shunted them to the cheaper Blackwing studios. Problems with the studio's engineer and owner, which resulted in personality clashes, obstructions, and the occasional severe mistake—including the time the engineer wiped a Polly Harvey vocal—had left Callahan exhausted. 'I think the reason I don't have good memories of the time after Margaret is because I was trying to do everything on my own,' he says. 'I'm surprised I didn't have a breakdown, really.'

The Sound Your Eyes Can Follow is a highly distinctive album, unflinching in its blocks of atonality and pugilistic lyrics, and offering few havens. 'I *meant* the percussion and drum samples to go slightly out of time, so they're woozy,' Callahan says. 'I *meant* them to jar.' Guaranteed guitar-free (it said so on the cover), it was congested with everything else and, while the album generally received middling-to-poor reviews that were aghast at its perceived incoherence, *The Wire* got its intent, placing *The Sound Your Eyes Can Follow* in the lineage of Public Enemy, as an aural 'inversion' of jazz through sampling that sought to both reflect, and arm city dwellers against, their environment.

Meanwhile, Fiedler formed Laika. 'It was kind of developing my half of Moonshake,' Fiedler says. 'It really was as simple as that. It was developing it, and developing it with some different people. And, also, growing as the technology grew. Because when Moonshake started, we were pretty much totally analogue. The sequencing and the sampling was super, super-basic, because that was the technology that was available. And we focused more on the rhythm. There was less guitar. Dave, in Moonshake mk 2, he was anti-guitar. And I wasn't anti-guitar, but there was actually no room for it.'

Laika's first salvo was the *Antenna* EP, a funk-flow that opens with 'Marimba Song'. 'We were quite into our time signatures,' Fiedler says. 'I've never really liked techno or house, and I cannot, and I will not, do anything with the four-on-the-floor bass drum. I can never do it. Ever. If we did do something in 4/4, it had to be not straight 4/4. "Marimba Song", we wanted to write something in 7/8. And we liked marimbas.'

The combination of exoticism, licentiousness, menace, glitch-less electronic flow, and percussive density found full electronic head-rush in the album *Silver Apples Of The Moon*. Fiedler particularly liked the opening track, 'Sugar Daddy'. 'It's really evocative of the sort of "found sound" stuff,' she says. 'We were living in Kings Cross, and it sounds like it sounded with our windows open, with the buses, the old Routemasters wheezing to halt at the red lights right outside our flat.'

Laika seemed to absorb their immediate air and spit it out as a mass of tangled wires. The album's most distinctive moment is 'Coming Down Glass', an even-more-explicit take on sex and exhibitionism than Fiedler had previously explored within Moonshake. 'It actually happened, in Grand Central Station,' she says. 'I was waiting for the 130 train, which is the last train out to a place called Bronxville in the suburbs, and I thought, I'll phone somebody from a phone booth. And, yeah, I heard this knocking on the phone booth, and I thought, maybe somebody needs to use the phone. Then I saw that all the other phone booths were empty. And I turned around, and this guy was masturbating.' And he came—down the phone booth glass.

Fiedler had a philosophy degree, and Laika felt, somehow, like philosophical music; theories joined together to shine new lights on old certainties. It was clever and subtle music, easy to like but hard to truly understand. Laika were undoubtedly a more attractive commercial proposition than Moonshake had been, and certainly more so than Moonshake were now. *Silver Apples Of The Moon* set Laika up for the future; *The Sound Your Eyes Can Follow* set Moonshake teetering.

'I delivered *The Sound Your Eyes Can Follow* to Too Pure, and when they heard it back, there was silence,' Callahan says. 'And then Paul Cox said, It's very brave.' Just before Moonshake were due to tour, they were dropped from the label, Cox and Roberts citing poor sales and high recording costs. Rejection elsewhere followed.

'A lot of people who worked at Creation and some of these other labels, for a while they thought they'd missed out on us, because they heard "Secondhand Clothes" and *Eva Luna*,' Callahan says. 'And then, for a lot of people on the commercial indie side, I'd completely blown it.' A drunken, insecure tour around Europe followed; the doldrums weren't far behind. 'I know it sounds stupid, you're meant to be all, *I'm an artist, I'm in your face, I believe in what I'm doing*, but actually I got very upset that no one seemed to understand what I was doing. It undermined my confidence. To be quite frank, I was lost.'

Eventually, Moonshake found a home on C/Z, a label based in Seattle, which released the final Moonshake album *Dirty & Divine* in 1996. It betrayed more of an exotica—and swing—influence than the previous two records. 'Things like "Nothing But Time" are really slowed down, glitchy,' Callahan says. 'There's always surface noise and things like that.' More relaxed than *The Sound Your Eyes Can Follow* but less conceptually solid, the album 'utterly flopped here. And then I felt we had our arms twisted into doing some remixes.' This led to the album *Remixes*, which the band disowned.

C/Z was a very different, more glitzy operation than Too Pure. Big, long tours, label showcases, and a Lollapalooza stint meant Callahan was 'living on whatever the equivalent of Pro Plus is over there. Trucker speed. Sleeping two or three hours a night.' Finally, a tour with Meat Beat Manifesto was proposed, and the mere idea of it proved too much for a weary band missing home; they rebelled and insisted on a return to Britain. 'I looked at the tour itinerary and I thought, this could make it for us, but everyone wanted to go home. I was nearly in tears. We'd been working so hard and I didn't know what to do, but I really think we should have stayed there that month.'

After *Dirty & Divine*, Callahan moved to New York. 'As the line-up of Moonshake had changed every record since *Big Good Angel*, I figured I could just start another band, as I'd be writing the stuff with samples anyway,' he says. 'And then I went there and immediately got a massive artistic block. I did write the odd bit of stuff, but I couldn't break through this feeling that I had run it into the ground, and I couldn't do it anymore.'

Despite Margaret Fiedler's departure, Moonshake always retained a strong female voice and personality through its female guests; along with Pram, they would delve into the grotty visceral mess of being a woman. Fiedler's 'Blister', for example, was about premenstrual tension, and Pram's 'Pram' was about unwanted pregnancy. For a genre commonly considered male-dominated—and which certainly *was* in other iterations and phases—post-rock of this era featured near-equal female creative presence, true also of less significant groups such as Passing Clouds and Shiva Affect.

It wasn't always easy or pleasant for women, though. 'I can handle booze, I can brush off the sexist comments. I can come back and I can hold my own,' says Sarah Peacock. 'But there were a lot of situations where I was the only girl in with a whole load of blokes, like on the Chapterhouse tour. Their drummer was a session bloke, and he was a proper rock'n'roll monster. He was telling dirty jokes and stuff. And I was the only girl there. "Hang on, I am here, you know."'

'It *was* very serious and chin-stroking,' says Kirsty Yates. 'Which reference have you got, and all of that stuff. It was a very masculine world, and I definitely think that we were regarded as less serious.' Insides were perhaps the band to go furthest into exploring non-binary, deconstructed language with polymorphous *jouissance* and evanescent torment on their album *Euphoria*.

'The Earwig thing, for me, was becoming more and more minimal,' says Julian Tardo, 'and the Insides thing was rejecting rock completely.'

Insides were signed to the Guernica imprint of 4AD, a neither-fish-nor-fowl label that had a bizarre policy of only releasing one release by any particular band, forcing structural insecurity on artists. ('There was a hint of desperation about the whole Guernica thing,' says Tardo. 'That was Ivo going, I don't know how I can continue to be like an indie person.') At any rate, Insides were not an Ivo Watts-Russell priority. Partly this was due to his intractable problems elsewhere on 4AD; partly this was due to Yates and Tardo being awkward about accepting guidance and sharing works-in-progress.

'We've always had a really, really small world, and everything we did became insular,' says Yates. 'When we were on the dole, [we would] have tedious days. The same loop, over and over and over and over. Oh, it's time for *Neighbours*. That's lunchtime. Then, over and over and over. Oh, it's time for *Neighbours* again. That was our life. Let's go to WH Smith and read some magazines.'

'I think, as well, we were also quite comfortable with that,' Tardo adds. This fostered an interest in repetition: 'That moment when you're locked in and you know what the next thing's gonna be. There's a series of structures that you know you have to step through.'

The insularity and circularity of Insides was not simply about the insides of these people; the closer the mirror was held up, and the more Yates *seemed* to reveal, the less penetrable her psyche was. Fear, duplicity, violence, betrayal; all were eroticised and then suspended in the air, almost blankly, on *Euphoria*. 'When you start, you start massive, and then you edit and edit and edit,' Yates says of her lyrics. 'And try and say as much as you can in as few words as possible. I think I thought if I hone this down, I'm being quite mysterious and quite ambiguous. Actually I wasn't. I was being very, very concentrated.'

'At, the time, there was an album by this woman called Lesley Winer,' says Tardo. 'She had been an assistant to William Burroughs. She did this album with Jah Wobble, under the name ©, called *Witch*. Just before we did our album, I was listening to that album a lot.' *Witch*, on boards of dub, scattered breaks, and evacuated samples, contains Winer's hyper-intense, hyper-*intimate* soul-poetry, in the tradition of Wanda Robinson's *Black Ivory*, or Peggy Lee's 'Is That All There Is?'

'I remember thinking, if it was a camera, it's too close-up,' Tardo continues. 'That was something we definitely tried to get when we went up to the studio to record it. We tried to get the closest delivery. Soft and keeping things simple. It wasn't heavily layered. Because I always thought that what My Bloody Valentine did, it was hugely influential on me, but once they'd done it, I don't understand why anyone else tried to do it. By layering things, you take the detail out of it. Taking out the humanity, the sound, so it's no longer boy-girl, it's like this *thing*. And I thought, let's try the opposite of that. [*Euphoria*] is completely exposed, and you can hear every little creak.'

Although they had two weeks booked at a studio for *Euphoria*, Insides found themselves racing through the process; it is a sparse album, and—in combination with the pre-programming, there were only a few guitars and vocals to record. 'On the first day, we finished two songs,' Tardo says. 'We were thinking, we should just start taking our time.'

'The whole Talk Talk *Laughing Stock* [recording ethos] was big around that time, that you have to be in a dark room with a candle, and you shouldn't have any preconceived ideas,' says Yates. 'Well, that's fucking great if you've got loads of money.'

'Everyone else seemed to be experimenting, and we weren't experimenting,' Tardo says. 'We were minimal. We were *econo*. We turned up in a Sierra, put down our sequences, and we were out by 5pm.'

Tardo and Yates seemed to react musically against interiority on their next release, 1994's *Clear Skin*, which arose from their desire not to play with other bands and—like Disco Inferno, Bark Psychosis, and Seefeel—to disrupt traditional rockist gig-going. When launching *Euphoria*, Insides composed a long work to 'support themselves' in a live setting.

'I've never particularly enjoyed talking to other people in bands,' says Yates. 'Even if people wouldn't admit it, it is quite competitive. Everyone's claiming their space. I don't even want anyone's opinions. I don't want that confrontation. So, partly it was, we don't want to share this with anyone. Partly it was paranoia. This is *my gig*. I don't want the support band to be better than me.'

From such impulses came probably the most post-rock piece of music that Insides would create. 'Clear Skin' builds; it's not an episodic work, *per se*, but one where new elements lattice into the structure like falling and interlocking snowflakes.

'We only spent four, five days doing that piece of music,' Tardo says. 'It wasn't really something we put a lot of thought into. There was *way* more thought into *Euphoria* and the Earwig album.' However, like Bark Psychosis's 'SCUM' (which Tardo cites as an influence, along with Steve Reich's *Systems Music*), it simultaneously embraced notions beyond 'the song' and implicitly critiqued splits between neatly marketable concepts like 'single' and 'album'. It was never really intended for release, but then Watts-Russell said he liked it.

'I always regretted it, because I felt like we'd put it out [just] because Ivo offered to pay for it,' Tardo says. 'We were on the cusp of the whole digital age. At the time, to get thirty-three minutes of music, you couldn't physically record thirty-three minutes. You had to do it as sixteen-and-a-half minutes, and then pick up the back end of it, and *then* you had to take it to a digital studio, another studio, you'd mix it in two bits, on to two tapes, and then you'd take the two tapes to a state-of-the-art digital suite, where they'd join them together magically. And it would cost a fortune to do it.'

'Clear Skin' did shift perceptions of Insides, who previously had rather been painted as the indie Fleetwood Mac, due to their fascination for MOR rock (song titles included 'Carly Simon' and 'Don Henley', the latter the original title for 'Darling Effect') and because Tardo and Yates had been in a romantic relationship; they had broken up and got back together again.

'Actually, after *Clear Skin*, I got a virus and I couldn't hear for about a year,' says Yates. 'So that affected me. Even if I was going to get off my arse, I couldn't. Then, after a while it occurs to you: this is going nowhere. This is going *absolutely nowhere*.'

'I kind of felt like the whole Insides period, that whole dole culture thing, by 1995 I was done with it,' says Tardo. 'It's fucking hard, psychologically draining. I wanted some structure. I'd grown up. I was twenty-five, twenty-six, and I just felt like I was starting to know who I actually am. Anyway, I think [after *Clear Skin*] we were sort of feeling that we were being pushed into a trance-y thing. I suppose that was a more welcoming atmosphere than the Camden Falcon.'

'I just remember, when we played "Clear Skin" live, we had crappy equipment,' says Yates. 'We used to really pride ourselves on having some of the crappiest equipment next to the hi-tech stuff. So we had these keyboards from Argos.'

'Disco Inferno would turn up with their latest advance all spent on the latest Roland samplers,' says Tardo, 'and we'd come with PSS-80s, two of them from Argos.'

Better technology wasn't always a guarantee of reliability, says Ian Crause. 'The MIDI info as it flowed from the instruments to the sampler was too much for the routing to process, so it used to overheat, especially in hot clubs, and it would scramble the notes,' he says. 'To be fair, people said they couldn't tell the difference half the time, so when you heard that you just sort of shrugged and thought, oh well.'

Geoff Travis of Rough Trade had asked Disco Inferno to make an album. 'It's ironic that people assume we were very hi-tech and computer driven when, really, *D.I. Go Pop* was a more rough-and-ready recording than most guitar bands at that time were doing, simply because of the sampling and triggering technology we were using,' says Crause. 'We would run through the track until we were happy, and then I'd redo the vocals. It really was that simple.'

The smell of *D.I. Go Pop* was the fetid dung of Britain. Inspiring Crause was the retrogression of the solid working class into a stigmatised underclass, the simmering violence of (sub)urban streets, and a prescient sense that—still—things will find a way to get worse. Crause feels that *D.I. Go Pop* was when he began to turn his lyrical concerns outward and 'away from my navel. There's also a level of irony there, because I guess I was young and thought I was a lot cleverer than I really was. So you tend to treat heavy emotions ironically, something using the sampling made easier as it created a fractured, postmodernist colour to the sound.'

The album also gives off an end-of-pop-history air, where 'going pop' is an oxymoron, leaving a sampled trail of God, U2, and Miles Davis as it burns out with nowhere to go.

The scrabbled sound did not denote a chaotic loss of order, but a stringent organisation of noise into mini-narratives, sounds twisting around Crause's low-mixed, shady vocals. 'I found that [sampling] took some strain off my having to try to convey all the meaning through the words,' he says. 'From the beginning, I tried to fuse the lyric and sound as much as possible.'

Disco Inferno's decentred sound also seemed reflective of a thought process distorted by constant interruption and self-doubt. Crause described his intent at the time as 'ambient music where you've got a snapshot of an environment, then bits of the environment come to life and start playing tunes. So you've got a man walking down the street and a bus going past … but in 3D, like a real thing in your head.'

'To be honest, I was devastated by *D.I. Go Pop* bombing and getting absolutely nowhere,' he says. Like *Hex*, like *Euphoria*, like *The Sound Your Eyes Can Follow*, *D.I. Go Pop* did very little, sales-wise. 'Everyone expected *D.I. Go Pop* to be a critical hit and get us an audience, which it didn't, so Geoff [Travis] suggested holding off on the next album and making more singles for a year or so. From then on, really, it was just songs in smallish batches.'

During the post-*Science*, pre-*D.I. Go Pop* period, EPs had been a good way to keep the momentum flowing of a band erupting with ideas; now, succinct units were done through expediency. The EPs *Second Language* and *It's A Kid's World* came out in 1994, following *D.I. Go Pop*.

'We had great fun using a newly acquired sound library,' Paul Willmott has said of the mournful 'At The End Of The Line'. 'Samples such as biting an apple, corking a bottle, thunderstorms, and a pitched sheep's *baaa* on the bass. We also borrowed the main melody from a *Professor Playtime* children's cassette, which is in the background on the chorus.'

'A Night On The Tiles', from *It's A Kid's World*, was especially notable for Disco Inferno because it used a prominent famous sample—Edith Piaf's 'Non, Je ne regrette rien'—to kick off a sound-story that progressed from clinking glasses, through drunkenness and dancing, to a blaring siren at the end.

'What used to be the case was that artists would start small and grow slowly for years, only eventually mushrooming out and making lots of money,' Crause says. 'Rough Trade told us this was how they saw us, too. They were prepared to wait until *people caught up with us*, as they would put it.' Disco Inferno signed a five-album deal with Rough Trade toward the end of 1994, 'and it was decided we had better just get another album done, so the last few batches, which were recorded intermittently between gigging and touring, became *Technicolour*. I had originally envisaged "Second Language" as the start of *Technicolour*, so that's how long the period dragged out for.'

Disco Inferno saw out 1994—despite longstanding personal tensions in the band—but broke up just before *Technicolour* was released in 1995. 'Rough Trade were forced by their backers, Mayking Records, to drop us before *Technicolour*'s release in 1995, but Geoff went to other labels to try to get us another deal for it, almost getting us in with ZTT, until they changed their minds.' ZTT would have been an intriguing prospect, as Disco Inferno were, in pop ideology terms, almost a hereditary version of what the Art Of Noise were doing on 1986's *Who's Afraid Of The Art Of Noise*; and *Technicolour*, given the right exposure, was accessible enough to have spawned a hit.

'We slogged our guts out for six years, trying to develop, evolve, create with very little reward,' Willmott has said. 'Ian was exhausted creatively and ran out of steam. We needed to take time to take stock and to spend the next twelve months working up new material. Ian couldn't bear to be in the same room with me and convinced himself that I was the sole reason for most of his woes. He suggested that he write and record the next album his on own, and Rob and I should write the album afterward in readiness. An idea that I thought was bizarre and unworkable and created a way out for him.'

'Had there not been problems between us we would have carried on,' Crause says, 'especially with Geoff batting for us as our A&R man, but with all the personal stuff and getting dropped, I just woke up one morning, got a train over to West London, and told Geoff I had had enough and that was it. And it felt good.'

The hoped-for revival of Rough Trade hadn't really happened. One of the label's bright ideas of this period was a seven-inch singles club, established in 1991, 'to preserve the unique thrill of rock's simplest incarnation by supplying a swiftly-produced one-off record every four weeks, recorded by artists ranging from the talented but unknown to the highly collectable' (or so the promotional blurb went). Butterfly Child had put one out in 1992; Papa Sprain did so the following year.

'Lyrically, I was interested in using words to say the *nothing*,' Gary McKendry says, 'a sort of post-disinterestedness. Not to tell or command with strategies, but to express the void-emptiness-nothingness-meaninglessness-aimlessness … I hadn't read any Samuel Beckett then, but now I totally get what he was doing with, say, *The Unnameable*. I wanted language to be bland but original at the same time.' This first—and as it would turn out, only—Papa Sprain release on Rough Trade contained the phonetic iron lung of 'See Sons Bring Out Some More Tomb We Enter' alongside 'Tech Yes' (an attempt to expand on Lou Reed's guitar solo on 'I Heard Her Call My Name' at the point after he sings, 'And then I felt my mind split open') and 'Noise Lessons', a short, but completely free piece.

'By "Noise Lessons" I couldn't see where to take freeform noise further,' he says, 'and I couldn't go backward. So what could I do?'

As well as becoming more focused on improvisation, McKendry was keen on exploring different philosophical ideas in the structure of his music. This wasn't new—*Flying To Vegas* was an allusion to Umberto Eco's *Travels In Hyperreality*—but it became far more intense, and more difficult to understand Papa Sprain's music without an insight into these doctrines.

'I thought I would try and get into philosophy,' McKendry says. 'It was something I was always drawn toward, but never got round to finding out about in any depth until then. Its fuzziness seemed a good place to start from, so I started reading Nietzsche and Heidegger, and books about structuralism and post-structuralism. For me, it led to thoughts about capturing events—how small ideas occurring on the edges could be expanded upon to create something—new? Bigger? Also, maybe [I had] thoughts about how the object, or the objective, would be interpreted by the audience. I started thinking that the original meaning I intended was beyond my control anyway especially when the object entered the market space.'

This was by no means the end of it. McKendry was also influenced by theories of Buddhism, abstract expressionism, Dada, Zen, the Enlightenment, meditation, Kant's 'Observations On The Feeling Of The Beautiful And Sublime,' Artaud's Theatre Of Cruelty, William Burroughs's tape cutups, historicism, postmodernism, deconstruction, irrationality, Schoenberg's Second Viennese School; he wanted to tap into 'unconscious art', letting loose all sorts of psychic pandemonium on the music he was now making.

'I was reading James Joyce's *Finnegans Wake* pretty constantly through 1992—purely as a relativist [experience], and not trying to follow the narrative—and also, later, getting into rap and hip-hop,' he says. 'Rap seemed interested in the power of words too, slang and the like, and I thought why not try and make new words up, and new sentences—as an un-Intentional thought, something I was absent from as a creative agent. So I cut up through the *Wake*. I pretty much know all the phrases [I constructed] and can still remember them.'

Part I starts:

> riv* to the and what kill of s tru x you go for next this to to sand the blighting
> chris bell hurr horn rock kish heling I sum sing for pike lip this on is all will bawn lists bar of half boy hag me red him the hopes am in blood how rise for floote him sit bossed of sound …

'All I ended up using to record the whole thing was a microphone, a distortion pedal, and a four track recorder,' he adds. 'There were no electronics like reverb or even graphic equalization, apart from the bass and treble built into the recorder itself.' He sped up his vocals, rendering his usual soft stoned burr unrecognizable.

Finglas Since The Flood, the album McKendry made through this method, has four parts. It is more post-*music*, or even post-~~music~~, than post-rock; a juddering experience that leaves a listener concussed. Lucidity *does* emerge on repeated plays, along with a distressing sense of being privy to mental arrest. The gabble finally ends up becoming more addictive even than Papa Sprain's previous material.

That Rough Trade would be unhappy with such an extreme artistic statement ('don't think *Finglas* was what they were expecting') was predictable. But McKendry, too, found the results oppressive. 'Conceptually I loved it, but for some reason decided it was too true even for me. So, I self-censored and didn't release it, and that hurt me a lot. I was mentally exhausted and racked with indecision and self-doubt, and eventually I fell to pieces and had to spend the next ten years or so being lovingly reconstructed by NHS psychiatrics. So, sadly, [*Finglas Since The Flood*] has faded into some sort of Papa Sprain mythology.'

McKendry, like most of the post-rock artists, was a reserved personality type, and not much interested in 'hanging out' in 'a scene'. But he did strike up a friendship with Graham Sutton. 'I think Bark Psychosis were the only one of those [post-rock] bands I had seen live. I even almost collaborated with Graham in 1993 but it didn't work out. Totally down to me and my breakdown,' McKendry says.

The final Bark Psychosis release—for now—was *Blue*, whose title track was, for Sutton, 'a pretty pop thing', albeit one with the sardonic sadness of Soft Cell. 'It felt very important to keep moving forward,' he adds. 'At that point, I'd moved back from Brighton to London, and I wanted a clear demarcation. What could be better, after everything else, than doing a stupid poppy sort of thing?' It was written and recorded in three weeks, catharsis after the breakdown of a romantic relationship and hoped-for new start in Brighton, the loss of his friendship and musical partnership with John Ling, and for the way *Hex* and Bark Psychosis had been overlooked in the music press. Given all that, it was little wonder that the B-side to 'Blue' was the track 'Hex' (not on the album), its tarpaulins of white noise eventually giving way to a breezeless ambience. It was as if the series of shocks had necessitated a huge expulsion, and then a long period of quiet to ever make the world seem OK again.

'You know, I was saying about the album that people were confused because it wasn't noisy at all?' says Sutton. 'Well, we played the ICA, tripled the size of the PA, and quadrupled the number of bass bins. And our first thing was we'd do this twenty-five-minute version of the track "Hex", like a Whitehouse number. It was absolutely insane. Eyeballs would wobble.'

One of the final acts for Bark Psychosis as a band was to perform at the Britronica festival in Moscow, in April 1994, alongside Seefeel, Aphex Twin, Autechre, Ultramarine, Banco De Gaia, and others. 'First and last time I've been to Moscow,' Sutton says. 'It was an absolute fucking nightmare. Got over there, Richard James was carried off the plane with food poisoning that he'd got from a bunch of bad cheese on the flight over. So he was immediately off grid.' The hospital lost James's clothes and locked him in a room. The rest of the artists went, Sutton remembers, to 'a weird greeting thing. It was immediately apparent that it was a mafia-fronted bullshit thing.'

Organised by British promoter Nick Hobbs and Russian

entrepreneur Artem Troitsky, Britronica was indeed financed with mafia money and took place at a time when the country was mired in governmental corruption and administrative chaos. 'It was held over three or four different venues,' remembers Sarah Peacock. 'One was called the Palace Of Youth. It was this massive modernist building with relief statues of the workers. And then there were a couple of other places that were like nightclubs. Mafia all over those places. We got there and we got picked up and driven from the airport through, probably, about fifty miles of monolithic tower blocks, what a place, blimey this is grim. In fact, as soon as we got to the airport they were having to bribe people to get trolleys so we could get our gear off the airport and into the van.'

'Vodka like paint-stripper,' says Sutton. 'There were these little booths on the high street, and you'd get these bottles of vodka called Terminator, with a picture of Arnie, with half his face in metal. It'd be a litre bottle, and it would spin you out. Also, we weren't fed at all. There was no food, and no one had any money.'

'And then there was the night we threw a sofa off the hotel balcony,' says Peacock. 'Everyone was so pissed on vodka and so stressed and traumatised by what was going on.'

Performances went OK, if subject to cancellations and underwhelming attendances (and history can thank Britronica, because it saved live footage of Bark Psychosis and Seefeel), but DJs like Bruce Gilbert and Paul Oakenfold were abused at gunpoint for playing insufficiently poppy music.

'But we met some really cool kids,' says Peacock. 'A few of them were hanging around outside, kids who had been listening to Peel on the World Service and knew about us, and knew about the other bands who were on. But they couldn't afford to get in, because they were skint, and so we had to smuggle them in through the back.'

On the final night, artists were tired, hungry, spun out, and in no mood to go to another mafia meet-and-greet; the mafia responded by seriously assaulting the promoter. 'Then, there was the whole thing about getting people's equipment back on the plane,' says Sutton. 'It was a real mission. We had to bribe the airport officials. And *then* it was a really, really bad flight. People were crying. As soon as it touched down, everyone was *waaaa-heeeeyyyyy* because we'd got back home.'

And what *of* back home? Britain was undergoing a rebranding exercise, in the process of becoming 'Cool Britannia', which was a key external reason why post-rock—in 1994—was stillborn in the country.

'People were singing "Parklife" all the time,' says Graham Sutton.

'Mat, the bass player from Suede, was a nice bloke,' says David Callahan, who met him while both were recording at the Protocol studio. 'Suede had this single that sounded like "I'm In Love With A German Film Star" by The Passions. And I said, That song really sounds like The Passions. And he said, It does, doesn't it? I'm going to tell the others. He came back ten minutes later, and I said, Did you tell them? and he said, Yeah. They don't care. If somebody came up to us and said we sounded like a particular song, we'd be in tears. It would have been the most wounding thing you could say.'

'I remember meeting with some guy who worked for some agency,' Julian Tardo recalls, 'and he said, Why can't you be a bit more like Oasis?'

In contrast to the abstract thought needed for post-rock, Britpop was feet-on-the-ground, salt-of-the-earth rock stuff in a clear and comforting tradition, and it came with a corrosive 'irony' get-out clause to cover for dollops of sexism and xenophobia. *Select* magazine's 1993 'Yanks Go Home!' cover feature, featuring Suede's Brett Anderson pouting in front of a Union Jack, summed up the reference points: 'Sid James, proper football, Pulp, the BBC, The Kinks, The Jam, a decent bus service, bhangramuffin, chips in curry sauce, pubs serving real beer, *One Foot In The Grave*, raving, the National Health, black cabs, John Shuttleworth.'

The 'city as lover' of *Hex*, the London voodoo of Moonshake, the cruel indifference of Disco Inferno; all were drowned out. Britpop was also a gift for the weekly music press, solidifying the trend toward more populist and less challenging content. The work that Simon Reynolds did in this atmosphere—including recalibrating his *Wire* piece for another article, this time in *Melody Maker*, 'R U Ready 2 Post-Rock?'—is thus even more to his credit. He stuck with his term, and with the artists he saw as part of it.

His dedication paid off—just not for the bands. By the end of the 1994, or year 1AD of post-rock, Bark Psychosis were broken and felled, Insides were in retreat, Disco Inferno were uncommunicative and sullen, Papa Sprain was faraway, and Moonshake were chopped into pieces. This was not deconstruction but destruction, plain and simple. The only real victor in the mess was post-rock itself—which now had press presence and marketable kudos (.O.rang, the band formed by Talk Talk's Lee Harris and Paul Webb, were defined as post-rock on the press release accompanying the *Spoor* EP late in 1994).

Musicians did not ride to success on the back of post-rock, it seemed. Post-rock rode to success on the back of them.

CHAPTER NINE

the slow-down

'We're not very tough, but we can be annoying. We can be resolute.' STEPHEN IMMERWAHR, CODEINE

Britpop, as much as it may have irritated the first wave of British post-rock musicians, was likely largely ignorant of post-rock's existence. But what Britpop *was* aware of, and what it partly defined itself against, was American: it was grunge. A favourite Britpop sport, indulged in even by the biggest hitters, was to reduce grunge to MTV angst, smack, and checked shirts. 'People make the most absurd claims for Nirvana,' Dave Rowntree, Blur's drummer, argued in 1993, 'but what have they actually *done*? Basically turned soft American rock into slightly harder American rock. Big deal.'

There was a good point buried in Rowntree's dismissive rhetoric. Grunge was 'authentic' and—just like Britpop, in fact—could be placed within an identifiable rock heritage. Grunge seemed to have a largely uncomplicated relationship with the guitar, valuing putting in sweat and effort to gain a rock sound, albeit with a skuzzier veneer. The reason Simon Reynolds called his post-rock *Wire* article 'Shaking The Rock Narcotic' was to reference Joe Carducci's 1991 book *Rock And The Pop Narcotic*. 'Grunge—the fusion of punk and metal into an all-American hard rock—happened after [Carducci] finished the book,' Reynolds wrote in 1996, while interviewing Carducci, who was promoting a revised edition. 'In the revamp, it provides the punch line, the absolute vindication of Carducci's creed.'

The energy and fire of the early grunge scene was effectively captured and sold to the wider world by Sub Pop. They deliberately shaped a 'Seattle sound', which became eminently exportable in the late 1980s and early 90s. 'We got to kind of cultivate our own scene but as a lot of musicians know, you can create really good music but convincing people that they should check it out is oftentimes a difficult job,' Sub Pop co-founder Bruce Pavitt said. 'And I think Sub Pop did a really great job at letting the world know that this music was really special.'

Sub Pop played up regionalism—in a conscious reprise of Detroit's Motown and Southern California's SST (interestingly, Joe Carducci had been an A&R man and producer at that label)—and targeted Europe, particularly Britain, in selling Seattle as the grunge capital. Consequently, there was an expectation of what a 'Sub Pop band' would sound like.

John Engle of Codeine remembers some of these preconceptions. 'When we played, you could see a certain percentage of the audience immediately go, "What. Is. *This*. I'm going to the bar, what beer do you want to drink?"' Sub Pop bands were not *all* of a type, then.

Codeine were a bunch of sonic introverts who treated words like seeping wounds, crippled their tempos, and created space enough for agoraphobic despair. Codeine's small body of work took the tautness of Slint and the fastidiousness of Talk Talk, added in a punk-not-punk sensibility ('How slow can a punk go?' jokes Stephen Immerwahr), and created music for the existential dread found in everyday life. Codeine's timing and tone was the basis for a post-rock-influenced 'slowcore' sound—something that adopted their tempos and subject matter, yet which usually simplified their queasy and complicated approach to rock music.

The clear separation of sounds—especially of drums—was just as important to the feeling of disconnection as the inert tempos were. One root of this was Joy Division. Codeine began, and indeed ended, their tenure with Joy Division covers, and they had an important immediate predecessor in that regard. 'We've played a lot of Joy Division songs over the years,' Galaxie 500 drummer Damon Krukowski has said. 'We've learnt a lot from that band.'

If A.R. Kane defined dream pop in the UK, their nearest US equivalents were Galaxie 500. They were as spare and as chimerical, and certainly could be as fuzzed and dubby. But while A.R. Kane's dreams were surreal, quixotic, and sometimes even *fun*, Galaxie 500's were in a perpetual cycle of pensiveness and uncertainty. They traded A.R. Kane's buccaneering air to be the defeated misanthropes rocking to themselves in the middle of a field. Galaxie 500 found strength through timidity, completeness through cutback, momentum through languor. 'I think if people are prepared to work at listening to bands like Sonic Youth then they'll be open enough to hear us,' bassist Naomi Yang said in 1989.

'I like people who go out on a limb, on a whim, and construct these elaborate theories which are easily debunked,' Krukowski said in 1990. 'I think most of the things written about us are just theories slapped on us because we're handy to support them. But I hope people carry on thinking them up. We all love reading them!'

All three members of Galaxie 500—Yang, Krukowski, and guitarist/vocalist Dean Wareham—had attended the same school in Upper Manhattan and then gone on to Harvard University. 'To be perfectly honest, when they first came in and played for me, I thought these kids must be lying,' said Kramer, head of the Shimmy Disc label, owner of the Noise New York studio, and Galaxie 500's soon-to-be producer. 'There's no way they went to Harvard; they sounded so fucking retarded! One chord for an entire song, played that slowly? Come on!'

'We had been listening to a Half Japanese record produced at Noise [New York],' Krukowski recalled, referring to 1987's *Music To Strip By*. 'It sounded very spacious. All the other Boston bands were turning out a very heavy, dense sound. We were looking for something else.' Krukowski asked Kramer whether he could get that drum sound for

Galaxie 500; Kramer assured him he could (he actually had no idea how to replicate it).

As befits a trio of Harvard graduates, Galaxie 500 were a cerebral band in their inspirations and executions. 'Our sound is a Hegelian synthesis between the abstract and the concrete,' Wareham said in 1990. Wareham's melancholic, sometimes sardonic lyrics (which he likened to Zen poetry in 'the way they focus in on tiny details'), were delivered by him in a racked voice. It replicated the discomfort of the subject matter, while his unschooled, direct guitar gave the songs innocence and inexperience.

However it is the bass that tent pegs the sound, adding real emotional heft to what might otherwise be self-pitying material. 'I always thought of the bass lines as alternative melodies, or countermelodies,' Yang has said. 'I picked up the bass without knowing how to play it, and took a few lessons where the teacher was showing me how to play the bass "properly", but that just seemed totally boring. I had all these melodies going around my head and I just decided to play bass that way. It seemed more natural, and it seemed to add more to the song than what I was "supposed" to play. I usually played only on the top two strings of my bass, as that mirrored my vocal range.' Krukowski claimed that, when Galaxie 500 played live, he kept Yang's bass overwhelmingly loud in his monitor—at the expense of everything else. This strong and melodic bass approach of Yang's allowed Wareham to employ minimum chords to create an understated mood.

'To play less notes is sometimes more challenging than to play a whole lot of them,' Wareham has said. 'You play a whole lot of them when you don't know what to do.'

Galaxie 500 might have shared Talk Talk's 'one note' philosophy, but the way Kramer captured the band was more allied to Steve Albini's snuffing-candles approach. *Today*, the first album, was recorded in three days; *On Fire*, the second, in ten. 'Quick doesn't do Kramer's system justice,' Krukowski has said. '*Next!* No second takes. We had to come in very prepared. Any mistake you made, you knew it was going to end up on the record. Kramer loves mistakes.'

Problems were depressingly swift to establish themselves within the band. Yang and Krukowski, a couple, briefly quit due to a row over the first album's track listing and songwriting credits. In a theme that was to reassert itself, *they* felt Wareham's ego was running riot, while *he* felt they were ganging up on him. Yang and Krukowski re-joined on this occasion, but the mirror had been cracked, and trust was never fully re-established.

In 1989, the band signed with Rough Trade, and the label released the second Galaxie 500 record, *On Fire*. Steeped in browns, greens, and dusty gold, *On Fire* celebrated disenchantment; it watched trees decompose and TV on its own. It yearned for help, but put high barriers up to actually receiving it. It was miserable but eschewed miserablism.

Recording the third album, *This Is Our Music*, proved a rancorous experience, and the result is patchy. Nevertheless, it yielded the Yoko Ono cover 'Listen, The Snow Is Falling', a pristine melancholic crystal and also a conscious attempt to emulate Can. 'Outside the music, things had definitely deteriorated,' Krukowski reflected in 1997, six years after the band split. 'Naomi and I had developed a strong distrust of Dean, which in the end turned out to be not nearly strong enough. We were blindsided, despite our misgivings about the person he was becoming and the ways in which he was dealing with our modicum of "success".'

Yang and Krukowski believed Wareham to be deliberately hogging the spotlight, sometimes literally, as he stepped downstage into a beam of light during a show in LA while they were supporting the Cocteau Twins. 'Apparently, this had been arranged with the sound and lighting people beforehand,' Krukowski believed. 'Nothing, but nothing, like that had ever been done at a Galaxie 500 show, and it completely freaked me out—I remember struggling to keep the beat while it happened. I was so surprised. In retrospect, I noticed that Dean chose the LA show to launch this new trick, when the audience was full of music industry people.'

'The lighting director (probably an employee of The Cocteau Twins', but not someone I had ever spoken a word to) turned a spotlight on me,' Wareham writes in his 2008 autobiography. 'Why Damon thought this came about because of a secret deal I had made, I don't know.'

Whatever the truth, it didn't matter. An impasse had been reached. Wareham ended up blurting out that he was quitting when Krukowski rang him with a question about flights for an upcoming tour. 'No explanation, just *there's nothing more to talk about*, and that was it,' Krukowski said. 'A lot of years of friendship, not to mention the band, down the drain in a minute flat.'

'It really felt like he had killed the creature that we had all invented together,' Yang added.

'The suggestion is that I broke up Galaxie 500 for the money,' Wareham has said. 'No, it was not the money. There was no money. I had a hundred reasons, ranging from petty annoyances to major structural problems in the band. The bottom line is I quit *because I couldn't stop thinking about quitting*.'

Galaxie 500, for all their shambolic feel and lack of formal training, had seemed very much in the New York avant-garde musical intelligentsia tradition, from The Velvet Underground to Hugo Largo. Codeine were also, originally, from New York. However, they felt more allied to early Swans; the death-march tempos were a strong similarity, but it was also to do with a similar fascination with disconnection. Michael Gira could stretch out words to emphasise the detachment of human from human, and Stephen Immerwahr did the same. However, while Gira used words like 'degrade' or 'pain', Immerwahr would emphasise the cruelty of the everyday, as he atrophied 'understand' and 'realise' like a loveless heart. Gira, certainly, appreciated Codeine; he personally sought them as opening act for Swans in 1994 (not realising the band had broken up by then).

'You want to be incredible as a band,' says Immerwahr. 'And I really *had* to do Codeine, and I had to do it with John.'

John Engle remembers being approached by Immerwahr, who went to Oberlin College with Engle's brother, to play guitar. As Immerwahr explained what he was after in terms of stillness, Engle's response was, 'Who would want to play guitar in a band like that?'

'When we started, we had a few other songs,' Engle remembers. 'We had a very up-tempo song, and a few other songs that we felt would give some variety to our performance. And I think, after the second show, and when we had a prospect of a third show, it was like … *who are we*? We really *are* those slow songs. Those other songs that we use for variety, they're not us. So we culled anything that wasn't Codeine, and only Codeine remained.'

Also at Oberlin College was Sooyoung Park of Bitch Magnet and Seam. 'Sooyoung was one of the first people I knew, perhaps even *the* first person, to write stuff on four-track cassette recorder,' says Immerwahr. 'Sooyoung was writing a ton of cool songs, and he and I passed cassettes back and forth, scraps of four-track stuff.'

Park and the rest of Bitch Magnet were interested in manipulating tempos to emulate particular states. 'We find the power through slowness idea a lot more effective than going real fast, sure,' Bitch Magnet guitarist Jon Fine said in 1991. 'That's the appeal we really want to have—an unbelievably *powerful* groove.'

'Then my girlfriend broke up with me to start dating Sooyoung. That was kind of tough,' says Immerwahr. The girlfriend in question was Lexi Mitchell, later the bassist of Seam, who 'had impeccable music taste,' Immerwahr says. 'She was the person to really turn me on to the Marine Girls, and one of the first people to have The Jesus & Mary Chain's "Upside Down" seven-inch. The influence of Jesus & Mary Chain on my songwriting cannot be overstated. There was a B-side of theirs, "Just Out Of Reach", that's just devastating in its simplicity, in its repetition, and for me, at least, in its emotion.'

Sooyoung Park was also effective at geeing up Immerwahr. 'Sooyoung was like, we [Bitch Magnet] have an opening slot, are you guys going to put your band together? And the reason we got Chris [Brokaw] is because we said, We're playing in Boston and we need someone to drum for us—and Chris was in Boston.'

Brokaw had played in hardcore bands and was impressed with

Codeine. 'I hadn't played with anyone before who could discuss parts of a song with such a total lack of ego,' Brokaw has said. 'It was extremely codified and, in a way, very experimental—almost like a science project. We spent a lot of time discussing the purpose of a single bass note; the various effects of eighth notes on the ride cymbal versus sixteenth notes; the placement and use of feedback … we were really dissecting the whole thing and trying to determine what role each instrument took in a particular way.'

'We had just played one show,' says John Engle, 'in the August of 1989. Nothing, absolutely nothing, happened for months. Then Steve went on tour, in Europe, with Bitch Magnet, doing sound, and they told him, *we can't pay you anything*. Steve said, all right, well, you can make it up to me: any time anyone asks you about up-and-coming bands, just say Codeine.' The label Glitterhouse read one of these interviews and sent a fax to Bitch Magnet to find out if Codeine were still unsigned.

'Somehow it actually worked,' says Immerwahr. 'That just seems ridiculous.'

Codeine posted off a tape to Reinhard Holstein at Glitterhouse, containing 'Castle' and 'Three Angels', which Engle and Immerwahr, along with drummer Pete Pollack, had recorded a couple of years previously, in a twenty-four-track studio—'so it sounds a lot larger,' says Engle. 'Reinhard was like, oh, I'd love to put ["Castle"] on a compilation. Holy shit! Sure!' Glitterhouse paid Codeine $500, and 'Castle' appeared on *Endangered Species*.

The band used the $500, and the further offer of $750 to record a single for Glitterhouse, to hire equipment and the services of Mike McMackin. 'We talked to Mike, and we basically recorded the first side of the *Frigid Stars* LP,' says Immerwahr. 'We sent a tape back to Glitterhouse, and they were like, this is great. And we were like, well send us some more money, and we'll do a full-length record.'

Frigid Stars was recorded in McMackin's basement. 'It was a great production,' says Engle. 'That's where all the reverb comes from. The guitar sound I was using, I think I used Mike's Stratocaster … it sounded a little plinky, but with all the reverb on it, it sounded very, very distant.'

'The three of us were playing and recording,' Engle continues. 'It was all fairly minimal and skeletal, and it was done live where Steve played bass, Chris played drums, and I played guitar. Chris added a second guitar. Steve sang. And when it was done, I remember saying to Steve, All right, so when are we going to do the extra parts for the record? When are we going to add in the stuff in the middle of the songs that do things? And he said, No, that's it. Steve looked at me like: *Yes, do you understand what we're doing here?*'

In emulation of Joy Division, Codeine used four tracks of their eight-track basement setup for drums. 'One of the best things for me, one of the reasons why mechanically and logistically Codeine could work, was because I could only remember guitar enough to record one song,' says Immerwahr, on how the *Frigid Stars* songs developed. 'Then I'd give the tape to John, and I'd be like, *you have to figure this out.* Because I just couldn't. That was an early pattern that stayed constant.'

'"Old Things" was barely a song,' says Engle, remembering that track's four-track inception. 'Steve was obviously inebriated. It was just some notes played over, and he'd be like, *and throw … oooooIlddddd thinggggggs awayyyyyyy*, and this huge expanse of noise would pour in, and then it would be silent again. And he does the song for three verses, and at the end of it, it's just Steve hitting a snare drum with a pedal delay on it. And it just seemed like a perfect sense of resignation. I thought the four-tracks were all great.'

'I think the other part of why Codeine managed to work,' says Immerwahr, 'was that John had that four-track cassette recorder. Not only that, he had guitars, he had basses, he had compression, and echo, and a chorus box, and a couple of microphones. And even some drum-type stuff that I could use. It was great to be able to stay at his house, which I did for a bunch of months. Pretty much, every single song we ever did was first created on a four-track cassette recorder, and then taught to the band.'

Early in 1992, Codeine started work on the next record. 'I think we were able to do the first record without actually being a band,' says Immerwahr. 'But the second record, by the time we were doing that and

I'd already been through the process of making a record with Codeine, and I was actually listening a lot more to other bands' records, and what their performance on record was. I wanted a lot more for the next record.'

Now contracted to Sub Pop for the next release, Codeine planned it as *The White Birch*, and started recording in Harold Dessau studios, Manhattan. 'Steve came in for the first day of recording with a huge mango, and said, "Now, before we play, we will share … the mango!"' Chris Brokaw has recalled. 'He spread a newspaper on the floor, cut open the mango, and it was rotten and horrifying inside, practically crawling with parasites. I think it cursed the sessions.'

On the very first day at Dessau, that curse started. 'Steve heard frequencies,' Engle says. Nobody else could detect them, but Immerwahr swore they were there. 'I was having some problems, I think,' he says now.

Codeine abandoned the upscale Dessau, scrapped the work, and relocated to a Boston studio. It became clear that a full album was still a way off; instead, they cobbled together a mini album—*Barely Real*—from the salvageable parts of recent abandoned projects and sessions. Given this, *Barely Real* is remarkably cogent; it's especially notable for the piano ballad 'W', which began life as a deliberate Slint rip-off named 'Slintstrumental'.

'Actually, part of the crisis for me about the second record was really that I wanted us to be tight like Slint,' says Immerwahr, 'and there was no way, because that kind of tightness would not work for Codeine. But I was really impressed with what Slint were doing, and they had a lot of power, and I think part of that came from Britt [Walford], who's a wonderful drummer, and also from their background in metal. We have *no* metal knowledge.'

For the piano on 'W', they turned to another Louisville person: David Grubbs, then playing in both Bastro and Bitch Magnet. 'I really had a guy-crush on David Grubbs,' says Immerwahr. 'He was and is a really wonderful person, and I was very much fascinated by him.' ('W' would prove an interesting harbinger of Grubbs's approaching interests, too.)

The cover of *Barely Real* was an image of the Belvedere Palace in Vienna; Immerwahr used it because it reminded him of the rigid visual aesthetic and ambiguous narrative of the film *Last Year In Marienbad*, and 'the emptiness of upper-class lives'. It was also, in its hues, an echo of what Codeine had planned as the cover for the abandoned *The White Birch*: an 1896 painting by Thomas Wilmer Dewing. 'That painting was summer energy, just wild, big green force, and there's this tiny sliver of a white birch and there's these two thin women who are either blending into it, or they're just observing it,' says Immerwahr. 'Green power. That was the record I was envisioning in 1992. But we did end up with a cover [for *Barely Real*] that was blue-y, and had more green to it. And then by the time we actually got to *The White Birch* it was a different *White Birch* entirely.'

One of the reasons for this was a change in personnel. 'Chris came to a Codeine practice with a cassette of Come demos,' Engle has said, 'probably before they'd played any shows or had a name. So he plays us "Submerge", and when the guitar solo starts we think, OK, that's great. It's great to hear Chris playing [guitar] and it's very good. About a minute and a half later, a second guitar solo starts and I think, Chris is not staying in Codeine over this band. Not a chance.'

'For the last year or so, I've been drumming with Codeine,' Brokaw told *Melody Maker*, in one of Come's first features. 'They have a very clinical approach to music, which is fine. But with Come it feels like we have the option to try a lot of different approaches.'

'It's funny, because Come were actually the things we weren't,' says Engle now.

Brokaw juggled Come and Codeine for a year or so, but it was an untenable situation, especially when Come were offered a lengthy European tour. Josh Madell temporarily replaced Brokaw, allowing Codeine to fulfil their upcoming obligations.

'I had heard that Chris Brokaw had left Codeine to pursue playing guitar full-time in Come,' Doug Scharin says. 'I called John Engle. Woke John Engle up at one in the afternoon. I thought, damn, it must be good to be in a band that puts records out.'

Scharin is ambidextrous, although with a preference for his left hand, and he learnt to drum on his brother's (right-handed) kit. 'Naturally, I played with my left foot, so I played a downbeat with my left foot on the hi-hat instead of the kick drum,' he says. 'So, everything on the kick drum was an upbeat to me. I was playing downbeats with my left hand, but upbeats with my right foot, and immediately, something clicked. That was the basic rhythm that I built everything off of. It was this opposite rhythm on the kick drum. But I could get into that.'

'Doug was a different drummer to Chris,' says Engle. 'Chris was throwing the beat in a little late. But Doug was just somehow *playing* so slowly. His whole body would get slowed down. And he would keep in tempo. I'm not saying it was better or worse than playing with Chris, but it was a little easier to follow Doug. And he was also a really *powerful* drummer. When Doug joined, me and Steve sort of looked at each other like, *woah*, are we really going to do this? First audition, we were playing "D" and Doug was … holy shit, it was so powerful.'

'Codeine could never have happened without Chris. But Doug really changed the band a lot,' Immerwahr adds, 'and the band also changed. We had really become full-time.'

Codeine moved to Louisville in early summer 1993; they had strong links with the place already through David Grubbs and Immerwahr's then-girlfriend, Cathy Bowman. Moreover, before Codeine had properly started, they had recorded 'Pea' there, which Bitch Magnet used as a B-side to their *Valmead* twelve-inch. While they stayed in Louisville they practised in Rocket House. 'We just rehearsed six, seven hours a day, pretty much, for what seemed to be an eternity,' Doug Scharin says. 'It was a month, maybe more, a good long time.'

They started to rehearse against a metronome, much to the dismay of one Britt Walford, whom Engle was staying with. 'I remember telling Britt, Steve has us using a metronome,' Engle remembers. 'Britt was like—in his soft voice—*that's not a good idea*, and I said, I know, Britt. I know.'

'There would be a click,' says Engle, 'Steve was changing the weight of the metronome, pulling it further down. It was just getting slower and slower. He finally said, Gentlemen. These will be the tempos.'

Codeine relocated again, this time to Chicago, where they went to Idful studios to begin laying down *The White Birch*. 'We got all set up to go start recording basics, and I think we got to the first take, and then I think there was maybe an overdub that had to be done, and the machine wouldn't sync, couldn't overdub. Something was jacked,' Scharin remembers. 'So for two days we just hung out in Chicago instead of recording *The White Birch*. I'm sure in Steve's head, and in John's, too, it seemed like it must have been the record that cannot be done, that is not *meant* to be done.'

Codeine were forced to record on ADAT instead, but according to Scharin, 'Thankfully, that room [in Idful] was such a great sounding room, and Mike McMakin really knew the material well. The basics, regardless of whether they were done on ADAT or not sounded good, and we did everything we had put together at that point.' Finally, *The White Birch* was growing.

Immerwahr kept a journal; in the past, songs had originated there, germinated on four-track, and then been fleshed out by the band. But for *The White Birch*, he had started to view lyrics in a more conscious way. 'I wanted to have lyrics that were a little less rhyme-y, and a little more poetic,' he says. '"Sea" came from watching this terrible band at this club called Tramps, and just having a vision of something very, very different. For "Vacancy", an uncle of mine had written a bunch of novels using cut 'n' paste technique. He'd mostly done them in the seventies. They never were published, and they were kind of difficult to publish, partly because of they're like a bunch of clipped sentences on pages. But the one that I liked the best was this very existential, very minimal, sparse, and self-referential detective novel called *Vacancy*. And so that was the inspiration, at least for the title. I think dreams were also part of it, but mainly just feelings. "Smoking Room": there were smoking rooms at the college library where you could go and study and smoke. That's a pretty pedestrian title, but it was consistent with the non-histrionic vocal thing, being non-epic, more like the reality of or the presence of meaning. We live our lives as our lives. My life doesn't feel like elaborate drama.'

There were some literary influences, too, both with a convalescent as a central character: Thomas Bernhard's *Concrete* and Thomas Mann's *The Magic Mountain*. Immerwahr also cites the 1964 Michelangelo Antonioni film *Red Desert*. 'At the very beginning, there's this long shot of people walking out from the factory,' he says, 'and there's a bunch of factory noise. It looks like people are talking to each other, but you can't hear it because of the factory noise. That movie spoke to me a lot.'

Immerwahr booked a studio in Middletown, Connecticut, to finally finish the album off. 'It couldn't have contrasted any more from the Idful studio,' Scharin says. 'Idful sounded great; this place, 3-Communications, was like an old office with dropped ceilings. It sounded horrible, and I hated playing in there.' Nevertheless, finally, it was done, over a year and a whole load of stress later than planned.

'We couldn't get the painting [*The White Birch*] for the cover,' says Immerwahr. 'Anyway, the record had gotten more bleak, and less organic.' Sub Pop had held a catalogue number for *The White Birch*—SP166—since the planned release. *Barely Real* had been SP205, and Sub Pop's current release schedule was at SP244.

'[Immerwahr] always seemed really highly stressed out to me,' says Scharin. 'We didn't get along very well, and I don't know if that tension, that he had imagined something and he was trying to achieve that *so* much [with *The White Birch*], and I thought maybe I didn't quite fit into the mould of what he had imagined that record was going to be. So, I sort of backed off. And once we finished the record, once we finished mixing it at Mike [McMackin's] place, Steve's face changed completely. Once the record was done, it was like this total weight lifted off him. I just remember him turning to me with this big smile and saying, Man, you did such a great job on this record. It was—*whew*. So I imagine that record was a heavy, heavy load for him, for whatever it meant to him, those songs, and wherever it was coming from.'

Immerwahr has said that those songs came from 'some intense states. It's a desire for emotional connection in the face of impossibility. Like there's a chasm between you and what you want to be close to. And that feeling is in some of the songwriting and singing. It's not necessarily depressed, but it certainly is a little bit resigned. In terms of themes of what the lyrics were—yes, it was anger. But one way to deal with anger is to turn the thermometer down so you're freezing it, containing it by turning down everything else—whether that's emotions, edges, or tempos.'

Almost as if they personified a song on *The White Birch*, Codeine as a group found only the barest relief of tension; the problem with frozen anger is that it can thaw at any time. Immerwahr had now lost impetus for new material, so when the tours came around to promote *The White Birch*—especially a lengthy and poorly co-ordinated slog around Europe—there was a sense that they were a zombie band without fresh meat to nourish them. Plus, less existentially, no one was enjoying themselves anymore. 'It ended in the UK,' Scharin remembers. 'It just got ugly by the end. Stephen and I were not getting along *at all*. And I was, *I'm done with this. I can't take it anymore. I quit.*' Scharin agreed to see out the remaining dates on their West Coast tour. 'We started out in Seattle, went all the way to San Diego, and back up, and didn't talk the entire time. It was rough, man. It was not a fun trip at all.'

'Wow, that person then,' Immerwahr says of himself. 'Shit. Being in a band with that person must have been fucking awful.'

Down to Engle and Immerwahr again, Codeine didn't look for a new drummer. 'We had disintegrated in 1994,' Immerwahr says. 'I was trying to figure out *what*. What can we do? Maybe we could be an instrumental band. I think I was just heartbroken and basically I never wanted to sing again. But the instrumental stuff never really took off, and the band breaking up was … yeah.'

'We had envisioned Codeine as a limited thing,' says Engle. 'Lyrically, sonically, and emotionally, it was pretty prescribed. There was a narrow space. And, sure, you could have just said the same thing over and over every song but, given the narrow parameters, how further on could we realistically consider going?'

'There's some kind of paradigm in psychology,' says Immerwahr, 'where the tools that you develop to protect yourself as a kid are the things that sink you as an adult. In some ways, the thing that gave us strength might also have been the thing that kept us from going a whole lot further.'

Codeine might have been done, but the sound they pioneered certainly was *not.*

Otis Coyote had begun before Doug Scharin joined Codeine, when he was living in Portland, Maine. 'I was sharing a rehearsal space with a group of guys, and went down there to practise drums one day,' Doug Scharin says. 'Curtis Harvey was outside the rehearsal room. He had just come back from Europe, and he was getting back to playing. I knew guys who knew him, but I didn't really know him. And he was there with some other guys who were coming to play, and they were starting something. And I was like, come on inside, let's just jam until they get here. And that was *it.* It took about ten minutes. The bass player showed up, and we wrote like four songs in a few minutes. It was *bam.* And all the while, we look over at the door, and there's their drummer, standing there on the floor, and his jaw is just *open.* Looking at us, going, *errrrrrr.*'

Harvey was a friend of Chris Brokaw. 'Curtis was like, let's go down to meet Chris, and see this new band he's in called Codeine,' Scharin remembers. 'We saw their first show in Boston and we were just, this is some cool shit. Our tempos got way slower after we saw them in that first show, for sure. That record [*Frigid Stars*] made a big splash on us, [as did] the second Slint record.' It was also through the Harvey-Brokaw friendship that Scharin found out about the drummer vacancy in Codeine.

This incarnation of Otis Coyote didn't last too long, as Harvey got wanderlust again and left town; Scharin moved to New York and joined Codeine. Otis Coyote, now named Rex, picked up again in earnest after Scharin exited Codeine, and their first album, comprised of tracks recorded to cassette on a four-track, was released in 1994.

'It wasn't a band that had played together and written all these songs,' Scharin says. 'We just recorded and made up this demo tape, what we *thought* was a demo tape, which Southern loved, and thought it would just be a perfect record.' Rex took the 1994 Swans support slot offered to Codeine. 'Swans hated us,' says Scharin. 'For the entire tour, they wouldn't move any gear off the stage, so we played in the tightest of little areas.'

For the second Rex album, *C*, the group went to Chicago's Idful studio and recorded with Brian Deck from Red Red Meat. Rex were more expansive, in terms of their instrument range, than Codeine had been, bringing in cello, tambourine, and accordion, and there was a sniff of allying themselves to bar-brawl country. Harvey described their final album, *3* (which features Bundy K. Brown on sampler), as 'headphone music for when you're coming down—from a heavy meal, heavy night, whatever. If you're still awake when it's over, all the better.'

Bedhead were originally a Texan group that closely adhered to principles of recording spaciousness, and had been built around the Band Of Susans-esque three-guitar stipple of brothers Matt and Bubba Kadane and Tench Coxe. However, and in stark contrast to Codeine, they did not navigate various studios and agonise over a finished product. Instead, Bedhead consciously evoked the simplicity of old jazz and classical material. *4songCDEP19:10*, recorded in Kessler Community Church, was the best expression of this.

'We just really worked the idea—four songs played straight through—into regular practice, and then Trini [Martinez, drummer] and Matt, and I worked out the tempos, the approach—basically the overall feel—in a few extra practices,' Bubba Kadane has said. 'By the time we got to the church, we were running late because of various disasters, and we really didn't know if we would be able to pull it off. We played half of the first song a couple of times to get levels and adjust the instruments in the room for desirable balance, then we played the whole thing. Once we started, it took nineteen minutes to record.'

The final track on the EP was a cover of Joy Division's 'Disorder'. Chris Brokaw was a fan of Bedhead; he wound up inviting Bedhead to play with Come in Boston and New York. Later, Brokaw would join the Kadanes in a project, The New Year.

There was also Bluetile Lounge, curious outliers from Perth, Australia, who were early adopters of slowcore. Their two albums—*lowercase* and *Half-Cut*, from 1995 and 1998, respectively—went almost entirely unnoticed outside their immediate circle. 'Howard [Healy] and I started with Joy Division covers,' says guitarist and vocalist Dan Erickson. 'Galaxie 500 was a bit of a changer in confirming a plan to play slow and quiet music, [which was] later cemented by Codiene, Slint, and Red House Painters, but we also always liked more loud and loose stuff too, especially the quiet bits of Sonic Youth, and wonky stuff like Polvo.'

Like Bedhead, Bluetile Lounge was concerned with big space. 'We aimed for an expansive sound,' says Erickson. 'I think we were trying to react against lo-fi at the time and recorded it in a huge room in a Masonic Lodge in Fremantle. There was a portrait of the Queen on the wall. We tried to use the room as much as we could, including an old tonky piano, and used these guys who had a mobile studio in a van to record and engineer it. We did lots of noodling in the background while overdubs were done which you can hear sometimes. Often it was just trying to hold the sound and overtones of a chord for as long as we could.'

'Originally, [playing slow] was totally to annoy people,' Alan Sparhawk of Low said in 1996, 'but that changed pretty quickly and became a powerful connection live. Some of our favourite shows have been where people are literally throwing stuff at us. We'd rather get that than the same old apathetic indie reaction.' Low took Codeine's 'anger freezing' and extended it to all emotion; the line 'She used to let me cut her hair,' from 1994's *I Could Live In Hope*, summed up the desolation and personalised mourning that Low excelled at. Their funereal drumbeats and minor chords left a music so sparse it was almost empty. (*They* also covered Joy Division, this time 'Transmission', on a 1996 EP.)

Like Bedhead and Galaxie 500, Low recorded quickly—'a week-and-a-half tops,' Sparhawk said in 1999. 'We don't spend a lot of time dawdling around in the studio. I like the way it captures the moment.

We've made a record in a week, and here it is! It's like a live performance. It may not be perfect, but at that moment in time it was right.'

Low's *Songs For A Dead Pilot*, from 1997, is perhaps the fullest—if that's not a contradiction in terms—expression of slowcore. Tracks are devoid of almost everything save the barest minimum of ebb and flow; it's as sad and curiously violent as that dead pilot, laying there, bleeding slowly, the heatless sun low in the sky and casting an icy shadow of his body.

Galaxie 500 also anticipated a certain strand of moody space *motorik* rock, which was tinged with both psychedelia and the stoned Spacemen 3 end of dream pop. The sound often employed vintage instruments—Moog, Farfisa, out-dated guitar pedals—emphasising drone and reflecting what Dean Wareham said in 1989: 'I guess we do take inspiration from a lot of 60s music. But it doesn't actually sound like it's from the 60s.'

Early Jessamine, Bardo Pond (and their pun-loaded side project, Hash Jar Tempo), Windy & Carl, The Azusa Plane, Fonn, Füxa, Transient Waves, the first Bowery Electric album; all were of this ilk (Jessamine allegedly wanted *Don't Stay Too Long* to recapture 1972), and deconstructive of rock to a lesser or greater extent. Bardo Pond's 'Amen 29:15'—the number relating to its length—was perhaps the *Songs From A Dead Pilot* of modern spacerock. A four-track home recording, it contains no percussion to ground it. 'We're more interested in rhythms than melody,' Michael Gibbons of Bardo Pond said in 1995. 'We're trying to get to that point where we lose ourselves, and by the most minimal means. That's when you find yourself surrounded in emotions you can't quite pin down and, because it happens unconsciously, it's far more resonant than anything you sit down and plan out.' This attitude misses conscious dismantling and re-building, and lacks the radical edge of post-rock, even though it was often grouped with it. (And this in itself was perhaps an early indication of how flexible the definition would become.)

Damon Krukowski and Naomi Yang, too, explored modern spacerock, especially with the expansive 1996 jam record *Secession96*, their final album as Magic Hour (a band Yang and Krukowski were in with Wayne Rogers and Kate Biggar). However, it was the first album as Damon & Naomi, *More Sad Hits* from 1992, that was their Codeine-esque evocation of complicated and simple feelings brought out at the demise of Galaxie 500. One track in particular, 'This Car Climbed Mt. Washington' (which originated in 1990 from another Yang and Krukowski project, Pierre Etoile, that Wareham had declined to be involved with), was a case in point. 'It's peculiar, but those lyrics came to me way before Dean had said he didn't want to make the EP,' Krukowski said in 1991. 'They just came to me one day, and I thought I better write them down. Looking back now, it's some weird premonition. Really creepy. It's about other things too, but in retrospect it's overwhelmingly about the band.'

These bands were often brief in lifespan, and are among the most fervently loved of all cult bands. 'Back in the day, when we got the money from Glitterhouse to have "Castle" on that compilation, we set up a post-office box so we had an address,' says Stephen Immerwahr. 'We started getting letters. One of the first letters we got, it was just super. "Our band heard your record and we broke up." And I wrote back, and I said, "More bands should form. And more bands should break up."'

CHAPTER TEN

vertical flux

'Those were years of growth, no question.' DAVID GRUBBS, GASTR DEL SOL

Two-thirds into 'Djed', the side-long track on Tortoise's second album, *Millions Now Living Will Never Die*, a short, attractive, ringing gets crunched up by a harsh electronic glitch. It's an arresting moment. The first time it's heard, the natural reaction is to check the equipment: surely the needle is bouncing over the track, the CD player has got jammed on some fluff, the internet connection is breaking, the radio has been interrupted by an electrical storm?

But no. It's *there*, woven into the track, and—since the rest of 'Djed''s psycho-geographical travelogue deals in gradual overlaps—it's an especially effective strategy. It's also an appropriate metaphor for a particular attitude that emerged from, but was not confined to, Chicago in the 1990s. It was disruptive, tearing through a linear narrative, although it created pockets of lucidity in its wake.

This music was 'vertical'. In a philosophical sense, it rejected expected structure (although it still could be *highly* structured), and did not move laterally from stage to stage. In this, it resembled the ideology of Ornette Coleman, because the music made sense according to its own terms, and there was no real way of knowing what was coming (nor, often, was it easy to comprehend what had just passed). It was interested in the margins of thought, creating meaning by stacking up spaces between gestures and overlapping perspectives on a moment in time, rather than having a story or a static focus. In terms of musical theory, too, it was vertical: it tended to explore the 'colour' of sound, the timbre. The plethora of sounds layered and interlocked to draw attention to harmonic differences, with less emphasis on the 'horizontal' melodic line. Finally, in a very literal sense, there was an absolute explosion of records released by an eye-watering array of projects: piles upon piles of physical product teetered upward and colonised the shelf space of the devoted.

However, and as literate as its practitioners usually were in musical theory, muso chops weren't ultimately needed to appreciate it. 'If the idea is exciting, the way that you choose to express it, with what instruments you use, or the timbres and the textures, is not so important as the initial thing,' says Tim Gane of Stereolab. 'As soon as you hear an idea, you go "eek", go crazy. It goes into your head straightaway.'

Chicago was a city with major pedigree in non-conformist music: Sun Ra, The Art Ensemble Of Chicago, Big Black, Frankie Knuckles, Phuture. 'I guess the air in Chicago might have affected the way we are a little,' Tortoise's Johnny Herndon said in 1998. 'There's a lot of weirdness there, which might be what attracted us to the place originally.' The artists orbiting this Chicagoan aura during the mid-to-late 1990s include Tortoise, Gastr del Sol, Stereolab, and their myriad associated projects formed a remarkable collection of voracious musical and cultural *bon vivants*. There was no Balkanisation of genre. At once, they could sustain a mood on a pallid pinpricked sound, or expand into a colourful, complicated sphere of remixology.

'To me, that was totally normal,' says Tim Gane. 'You'd see Tortoise, and they'd play this kind of music, and everything was included. It was a bit like the world of hip-hop where everything's included; if they can use it, it doesn't matter what the music is.'

A seedling for this musical Babel was Bastro. 'Bastro had a slow start, and then picked up a little steam when John McEntire joined the group,'

David Grubbs says. 'John McEntire is three years younger than I am. I met him when he was a college freshman [at Oberlin Conservatory, Ohio], when he had just turned eighteen and I was probably twenty-one. And I immediately found him as a simpatico person. He was an incredible drummer. High-school state marching snare drum champion, and a musical omnivore.'

McEntire had just enrolled at Oberlin's TIMARA programme. 'Because I'm from Kentucky, I pronounce the word TIMARA as *to-morra*,' Grubbs adds. 'I assumed it meant "artists of tomorrow". But it stands for Technology In Music And Related Arts, and I didn't understand that until a couple of years later, because I'm a fucking hillbilly.' McEntire was honing his skills as a studio engineer, and Grubbs was learning alongside him; they were also enhancing one another's musical taste. 'John was playing early Xenakis, and Stockhausen electronic pieces. And I just couldn't believe my ears. That these were figures taken seriously, people who produced scores and so on. People studied them at college, and the music itself was unprecedented, sonically.'

The two Bastro albums, *Bastro Diablo Guapo* and *Sing The Troubled Beast*, were released, along with a handful of EPs and singles, on Homestead (which had also put out Squirrel Bait's records), and are fine examples of tinderbox post-hardcore. Contemporary Bastro interviews do give a sense of what was to come; it was clear that this group was above the fray of lunk-headed Big Black copyists. 'The lyrics must go hand in hand with the composition,' Grubbs told *Melody Maker* in 1990. 'And, since the music is climax after climax, so the lyrics similarly are a series of peaks, a series of very strong images.'

'I remember at the very end of Bastro feeling like we did one thing and we did that thing well, of playing this loud, muscular post-punk power-trio music,' Grubbs says. 'And I recall that there were some places where we played where it sounded wonderful, it sounded amazing, and there were some places where we were much too loud for the space, or unable to respond to the acoustics of the space. It just seemed inflexible. All of a sudden it seemed weirdly inflexible, and we needed to go back to the drawing board.' Playing in the final iteration of Bastro was Grubbs's roommate, Bundy K. Brown, and this period seeded electric sketches of many songs that would soon be subject to thoroughgoing deconstruction.

'In 1991, when Codeine toured with Bastro, I thought they were amazing,' says Stephen Immerwahr. 'John McEntire is an incredible drummer to watch, and to listen to. And there were definitely some non-rock elements, or more avant-garde things that people were interested in. Grubbs was into it, and I was into it. He turned me on to lots of interesting things, and I really dug his interest in doing stuff on piano.'

'Bastro burned itself out kind of quickly,' Grubbs continues. 'I was juggling school and being in a band, and I'd started a graduate programme in literature. Tortoise had just started, which quickly became John's main thing. And it just seemed a good moment to reassess. To reassess the idea of being in a group with fixed membership, to reassess being in a group that had two rehearsals a week, and to reassess being in a group that only did one thing, no matter how well it did it.'

Gastr del Sol, in its first performances and recordings, had the same membership as Bastro, but 'it was a bit of a unilateral disarmament,' says Grubbs. 'Instead of practice space, with the amps always set to maximum volume, Bundy and I started writing music together in the living room. I'd never really played an acoustic guitar before. I just remember at the time, this idea of "human scale" and working without amplification.'

'Human scale' relates to measurements of the physical, sensory, and mental proportions of a human; as opposed to, say, light years or the subatomic scale. Amplification, therefore, goes beyond what a human can produce on his or her own.

'I'd grown up playing piano, and suddenly the sound of acoustic instruments became really, really of interest to me,' Grubbs says. 'When Bundy and I, and then Bundy and John and I, and then Bundy and Jim O'Rourke and I were meshing acoustic instruments, particularly acoustic guitar and piano, with electronics, we didn't really feel that we had role models for it. Squirrel Bait could always measure itself up to the slightly older generation, but I really felt that we were travelling without a compass at the early stages of Gastr del Sol.

'I recall the very first time that we recorded, recording this stuff that was on the record *The Serpentine Similar*, and recording the song "A Watery Kentucky",' he continues, 'and just lying on the rug on the studio after we recorded it and thinking, this is unbearable! It's unbearably slow, tempo-wise, the rate of it unfolding, it's so long, what the fuck are we doing? It was one of those things where I think we had enjoyed so much crafting this sound in the living room, and then actually going to the recording studio was a total shock, you know, that was the one moment where I thought, *we have absolutely lost our minds*. We need to get back into the practice space, plug into the Hiwatt amp; what the fuck are we doing? Now I listen to it, and actually it seems kind of brisk! But at the time, I just remember thinking, oh my god. How could anyone listen to this? It's just the sound of water from a dripping faucet.'

The Serpentine Similar, the first Gastr del Sol record (Grubbs and Brown, with McEntire on percussion), is also clearly linked with Grubbs's growing fascination with words and their non-narrative functions, which he had tentatively expressed at the end of Bastro. 'Very few verbs in the early Gastr del Sol lyrics,' he says. 'It was imagistic in that way, and broken. And obviously it didn't rhyme, it didn't scan, line lengths tended to differ.' Writing the music and the lyrics were completely separate processes, 'then stretching one, or warping one, to fit the other, [until it] yielded a satisfying result. And that kind of distortion, whether its distortion in the delivery, in the timing, where many words need to occupy a small space or, conversely, where few words need to occupy a much larger space ... to me, that's compelling.'

In 1993, when *The Serpentine Similar* was released, Grubbs had another 'instructive moment'—meeting Mayo Thompson and starting to play in The Red Krayola, further deconstructing the idea of a 'band' in his mind. 'And there was something about going back to graduate school, and Tortoise happening, and wanting to do something that was more flexible and responsive and nimble and fleet, and could respond to the situation at hand,' he says.

'Tortoise is about being flexible enough not to be like a regular rock band, and to do things that wouldn't normally be in their repertoire,' Doug McCombs said in 1994. 'Our thing is outside the realm of rock.'

Flexibility was the watchword for both Gastr del Sol and Tortoise. It seems that all the innovations to follow flowed from this basic attitude. 'One of the reasons we started the band, actually, was so we could have a space to just do something that would give us a platform to maybe showcase some of the stuff that we weren't able to do necessarily in other, more traditional projects that we'd been in,' McEntire says.

McCombs and Johnny Herndon were the founders of Tortoise; membership and contributions came as and when. Bundy K. Brown and John McEntire were interested in what they were doing, as was Brad Wood, the owner of Idful studios—where Codeine had recorded—and he invited their new project to come in and use the facilities during dead time. Tortoise recorded and released two seven-inch singles, 'Mosquito' and 'Lonesome Sound', from these sessions; feet-finding exercises as they unpicked what being 'outside the realm of rock' might sound, look, and feel like.

'Things really changed through having McEntire on board,' Herndon said in 2001. 'His studies of electronic music really opened up that whole area.'

'Where with Gastr it was this real cerebral music, with Tortoise gigs, in the early days, they were like dance parties,' Brown has said. 'It was very rhythmic and people were into that vibe we were throwing out. I've been listening to hip-hop my entire life. But that just didn't really come into play in Bastro or Gastr. But to be able to do this stuff that was more informed by reggae or dub or hip-hop was refreshing. We used to do Isaac Hayes covers.'

Next to get involved was Dan Bitney, who had long drummed in the art-punk band The Tar Babies. The idea of doing something more rhythmic appealed to him. 'I had never played in anything like that,' he has said. 'I just knew I was kind of sick of dealing with guitar players, you know what I mean? It was reactionary. Nirvana was blowing up, and we were like, *OK, let's do something else …*'

The funkiness of Tortoise was evident on their debut album, *Tortoise*, released in 1994. It was indebted to all sorts of things—Can, *My Life In The Bush Of Ghosts*, *Spiderland*, Steve Reich, hip-hop, jazz, dub, the

Paris, Texas soundtrack—but it didn't really sound like any of them. It was indeed outside the realm of rock, and perhaps this is why the still-young designation 'post-rock' was so readily applied to it. For it was Tortoise who first inspired journalists to broaden post-rock's designation away from the British school and steam it across the Atlantic.

'In the beginning, we pushed back against [being called post-rock] pretty forcefully,' John McEntire says. 'Because, for myself, it just seemed so lazy. *Oh, I can't figure out a better way to describe what this is, so I'll create this category that doesn't really mean anything.*'

'The problem I always had with [the term] is it basically had to reduce rock music to clichés in order for it to even have any platform to stand on,' says Jeff Parker, at that point a fan and friend of Tortoise. 'For me, rock music, it was never just about three chords or no rhythm. What was most interesting to me was when the music used to kind of like *whoosh* together and become indistinguishable. At least the musicians I admired and liked, who I was inspired by, were always blurring these lines. And I kind of saw our band as being in the tradition of that more than anything.'

Members of Tortoise were extremely interested in dance music culture and, at that point, the dominant innovative form was jungle (and its younger sibling, drum'n'bass). 'Last year, when we came to England, I was sort of introduced to pirate radio stations and the drum'n'bass thing going on,' Johnny Herndon said in 1996. 'That just blew my mind—just the whole idea of … the music, I thought, was amazing, but the whole idea of people taking over the airwaves for themselves was incredible. I think that has left its mark on our music.'

They weren't the only ones.

At this point, Graham Sutton had picked up the pieces from the messy breakup of Bark Psychosis and recast himself as Boymerang, although the transition was more gradual than first appears. 'The band had kind of disintegrated after doing *Hex*, but we'd been offered to play the Phoenix Festival,' says Sutton. 'OK. We didn't have a band. And typical me, it's like, *fine, I'm just gonna go down there and play a load of jungle.* So I knocked up a set with Daniel Gish, who was back around. It was really really good fun, *and* it was fresh.'

An amended version of this set came out as the first Boymerang twelve-inch, on the Leaf label, in 1995. 'I just really got it in terms of hearing the two speeds of stuff happening at once. You're really moving and responding, mentally and physically, to the half-speed as opposed to the 160bpm. It's like drums have been moved, because they've been sped up, and trebilised, they turn into the percussion element. And more than anything else, it was just the genius rhythmic feel that I hadn't actually heard before, and it was so exciting. Plus, [in the jungle scene] you were just really accepted. There was no question of who are you, where do you come from, what's your musical background. No one knew anything about me at all. I loved that.' Most jungle / drum'n'bass artists had wide tastes and a keen ear: Omni Trio's Rob Haigh, for example, grew up on The Fall and Can, while Goldie shared a love for hip-hop with a passion for David Sylvian. Like post-rock, jungle was a broad term and could encompass ambient comedowns to hardcore, bad-boy floor-fillers.

Goldie's *Timeless*, an episodic work dealing with 'inner city life, inner city pressure', shared many traits with post-rock: environmental awareness, space, exigent tension, the use of dub techniques, and the evocation of feeling with minimal lyrics. 'It's alright taking these kids into euphoria, into a dream state, but you have to come back to reality,' Goldie said in 1994. 'What I'm providing is that comedown. We're dealing with a subculture that took a lot of drugs. Rob [Playford, co-producer] and I know how to tap into their heads. When you're on drugs, don't go near *Timeless*, 'cos it will take your soul out, take it on a fuckin' journey, and hand it back to you, smoking.' It used the key junglist technique, 'timestretching': a process where a sample is sped up to fit any tempo, without the pitch changing, here resulting in chaotic disorientation and an eerie, empty texture.

Kieran Hebden, just at the point Fridge were starting, remembers the impact of jungle well, and how it interacted with his burgeoning love of post-rock. He saw Tortoise play with The Sea & Cake at London's LA2, and says the DJ was 'playing jungle records in between the bands. And that was a real moment. You could see that [Tortoise] were all interested in what was going on in London. They were desperate to come here because of all that was going on. And I was desperate for them to come here because of what they had going on in Chicago.'

Tortoise's interest in dance music and culture was apparent on the remix album *Rhythms, Resolutions And Clusters*; it remains one of their most fascinating projects for its *savoir faire* in engaging jungle, electronica, and bass so low it slithers in a leaden skin. Most tracks are only distant cousins of their original *Tortoise* sources, as underlined by the change in titles. 'I don't think any rock bands or indie-rock bands put out a remix record before we did,' Brown has said. 'If I'm going to claim anything that Tortoise did, we brought that whole idea of it being cool to have these electronic dudes tear it apart and redo it. I remember even approaching [Steve] Albini to do a remix on the remix record and he was like, "What the fuck are you talking about?" And he was one of the most talented recording engineers I know, a master of tape editing. He knew all of this stuff that guys had to do to become competent remixers in the era before samplers. He's really great at all those things but his whole perspective was, *Remix? What are you talking about? The record's the record.* And I was like, *No it's not. We're on the verge of the twenty-first century here.*'

In fact, the Albini remix—'The Match Incident'—is less a reworking of its source, 'Ry Cooder', and more a tactile self-referential version of it. Albini turns a non-narrative piece of music into a story, complete with environmental sounds of television dialogue; 'Ry Cooder' itself then dominates, eventually becoming over-exposed and distorted.

'I knew Tortoise a bit,' Tim Gane of Stereolab says. 'We'd played with them the first time we played in Chicago, we played with John [McEntire] and Jim O'Rourke, they were the support band, and we started talking about Farfisas and stuff, and we just became friends, quite quickly. And, later on, we played with Tortoise. They came to England, and we asked them to do a single. They said yeah. And we thought they would just send this little track for a seven-inch, but then they sent this track and it arrived—on cassette, of course, in those days—and it was an amazing track ["Gamera"]. It was *so* good sounding that we couldn't quite believe it. Suddenly you're thinking, *wow*; you're entering a whole new world, a new level, now. And that was OK, because it really kicked off in Stereolab as well a period of rethinking about what we're gonna do, and in the end that resulted in *Emperor Tomato Ketchup*, which was an album that did push us a bit to another phase.'

By this point, Stereolab had already worked with Nurse With Wound's Steven Stapleton on 1996's *Crumb Duck* (and would do so again, the following year, on *Simple Headphone Mind*); these records reflected, in their own way, *Rhythms, Resolutions And Clusters*. 'When we did those records together, [Stereolab would] record a lot of stuff, then [Stapleton would] take it away,' Gane said in 1997. 'We're not there with him. He comes back and it's always a surprise, always a surprise, which is not true of a lot of remixes. He takes what we've given him as a basic sound palette and mixes it with other stuff he's found.' On *Simple Headphone Mind*, most of the original material 'wasn't used at all', Gane added. 'He just used a couple of peripheral things, made it into something completely different.' At this point, Stereolab had a very strong and individual identity and, to the band's frustration, it *wasn't* seen as flexible. They were often typecast for their use of drone, repetition, retrofuturism, and political lyrics.

'Around the time of *Mars Audaic Quintet*, which was 1994, it was a very difficult process,' Gane says. 'I went through a period of—not depression, but musically just being lost. Because, basically, I had explored the initial stage of that sound, which was the minimalistic, open chords, basic two-note chords; I couldn't see a way to explore it anymore, and I didn't know what else to do. So, for the period between *Mars Audaic Quintet* and *Emperor Tomato Ketchup*, there was about a year, and the only two songs I wrote were two terrible tracks, and I completely lost where to go.'

The answer for Gane was a movement away from the horizontal and a new focus on 'melody cells'. A cell is an indivisible unit (unlike a musical figure or motif) and a clutch of these cells can be used to structure an entire piece of music. Still interested in repetition, yet struggling to move on from the way Stereolab had used it to date, Gane found that melody cells 'built up as very simple elements. And then I got the idea of just having loops of things. Now, instead of making the minimalism lateral, in terms of chords, [I could] make it more joined together, and build it up. And that then led me to write the songs that were on that album. For me, that was liberating, because I wrote the whole record very fast once I got that idea. Maybe in two days.'

Tracks on *Emperor Tomato Ketchup* are more bass-driven and build at a slower pace than Stereolab were previously associated with, especially on the Hitchcockian 'Monstre Sacre', with lyrics by Laetitia Sadier about her mother's death and the power of forgiveness. 'The big influence on me, for that record, was Sun Ra, and the way that he made jazz very modular,' Gane says. 'Very simple elements are joined together to make something more complex. I don't like the word sophisticated, but you join two elements, then the third element, you make a third, or fourth, or fifth. It's basic simplicity leading to complex simplicity. The idea is that everything's very simple, but it's just in the way you organise it, the way you put them together. So that thing was key to what I needed, and for sure that's definitely influenced by new music, some of the Chicago bands in particular, plus I was a big electronic music fan.' The tracks 'Les Yper Sound', 'Tomorrow Is Already Here', 'Monster Sacre', and 'Anonymous Collective' were recorded at Idful in Chicago, engineered and co-produced by John McEntire.

The next Tortoise record, *Millions Now Living Will Never Die*, was written outside of Chicago: in Vermont, on retreat, in the summer of 1995. It's a more consummate record than *Tortoise*; perhaps because the band was now functioning more as a group, aware of people's interest in and expectation for them. (Bundy K. Brown certainly was; he left after *Tortoise*, as the band became more well-known, unhappy with the prospect of a long tour, and disgusted by the way some aspects of the music industry operated.) It was different from the earlier years of grabbing spits and spots of time together, since it was now other things that had to compete for time with Tortoise. Replacing Brown was David

Pajo; he was inspired by Tortoise, and Tortoise admired his work with Slint. 'Glass Museum' is a Pajo-led track.

'I think I tried to play—or thought of—the bass as I would a guitar,' Pajo has said. 'Everyone switched up instruments anyway: onstage, at the beginning of a song; during recording, if you wanted to. That was encouraged.'

While in Vermont, Tortoise had lots of fragments along with more cohesive tracks. 'Doug came up with the intro bit, and he had the krautrock section, too,' John McEntire says of what was to become 'Djed'. 'And then I came up with the organ mallet thing. And we didn't know if they were going to develop more substantially into their own things. Or how to treat them. So, I don't know, maybe we had the idea when we were there that we would make a kind of collage with the stuff that's not really related and that we didn't have to put a whole load of pressure on ourselves to actually write more stuff. We would just use those fragments as seeds for extrapolating as much material as we could without being too heavy-handed about it. It was really fun and interesting to put that together because we just recorded the sections all separately, and I'd do a mix of something, and then I'd do an alternate mix, and a third alternate mix, and so *then* we had all these things that were still existing in their own world. *Then* it was a matter of figuring out how to make the transitions. And that was kind of a painstaking process … OK, these things are totally unrelated, in tempo, in key, you know … so it was like, there was one part where I had to vari-speed the tape down so it would match the tempo of the next section, and weird stuff like that. It was definitely a learning experience.'

When the seismic glitch occurs, it's because McEntire—infuriated by the experience of finding an edit at that point—snatched up dozens of discarded fragments, said 'fuck it', and physically, randomly, joined them together. 'Djed' remixes itself; it's a further refinement from *Rhythms, Resolutions And Clusters*. It dismantles and piles sounds up again while the track is actually in process.

It all became even more *meta* with a series of three twelve-inch singles released in 1996, offering subtle-to-radical re-workings of Tortoise tracks (including two versions of 'Djed'), often in collaboration with more electronica-identified artists whom Tortoise strongly admired: Oval, UNKLE, and Luke Vibert. This was different in itself from getting Steve Albini and Brad Wood to remix tracks. Furthermore, the twelve-inches were a strong visual proclamation. Prior to 1996, most of the Tortoise singles had been seven-inches, and the first two, especially, fit in with the US underground aesthetic of the time: coloured vinyl, wraparound poly-bagged sleeves, retro-tinged artwork.

These 1996 Tortoise twelve-inches, in bright die-cut yellow sleeves, were 'a statement, in a way', says McEntire. 'The whole remix phenomenon did not exist until the mid, late 1990s. I guess it was a way for us to say, OK, we're embracing this whole concept. And the formatting played a big role in that. Even though none of them—well, a few of them—were dance mixes.' Putting this material *only* on a twelve-inch (there were none of the usual accompanying CD singles) was a conscious shop-window for Tortoise's current ambition and, perhaps more pertinently, an indication of what they *didn't* want to be identified with.

The collaboration with Oval, in particular, reflected Tortoise's interest in the glitch—the 'fuck it' moment on 'Djed'—which was now becoming an electronica subgenre in itself, as pioneered by Oval on 'Do While' from *94diskont*. Oval had sabotaged CDs by slashing them with knives and spattering them with paint, before reconstructing the sickly discs into loops of melody, which the pockmarked, skipping CDs punctured. This all created a hypnotic lure of its own, and Oval brought this to bear on 'Bubble Economy' and 'Learning Curve' from the third Tortoise twelve-inch.

Bundy K. Brown, meanwhile, was in a different mood. 'It was weird for me to quit this group [Tortoise] and then see them become huge and hear people talking about them as being on the forefront of some movement that I just didn't see as a movement,' he said in 1997. 'I was like, *fuck post-rock. This is a load of horseshit. I'm gonna make a fuckin' rock record and the first song is gonna be this tune I ripped off from The Allman Brothers*. That was part of what motivated me to make a record that was more rooted in more basic and roots-orientated stuff.'

'James Warden was Bundy's roommate in college,' says Doug Scharin, 'and James taught Bundy some of his first chords on guitar. I think that he and James had some things that they had put together in James's basement, and they sent me a tape.' Scharin—by now drumming with both Rex and June Of 44, and engaged in a dub-focused solo project, HiM—thought the cassette was good. He had common ground with Brown. 'My musical education was listening to records, and that's what Bundy's was,' Scharin says. 'He wasn't ever that comfortable with getting in a room and jamming with folk, because he started playing so late, as I did.'

A fuckin' rock record may have been the initial idea for the 1996 album *Directions In Music* by Brown, Warden, and Scharin (and it certainly wouldn't be the last time that an artist branded 'post-rock' railed at the label and argued for a straightforward 'rock' instead), but it wasn't the result.

'I don't think *anything* came out as I initially heard it, or practised it,' says Scharin. 'It has a particular sound from the time, and rhythmically you can hear some Tortoise in there, some chord structures and stuff that Bundy had written. There are similarities with what he wrote [in Tortoise], but a lot of it just happened at Idful. Bundy was a regular engineer there, so had the keys to it, and we just kind of went when we could. Being in a studio with a load of cool-sounding gear, great-sounding microphones in a great-sounding room. We threw a lot of ideas down on tape, and had fun experimenting with them once they were down. A lot of it wasn't preconceived. It was cool groove stuff, a sense of rhythm, lot of studio experiment, lot of flipping the tapes backwards, and hands on the mixing board … *numbers* of hands on the mixing board at one time. I think that's why the record sounds like it does. I guess it just flowed.'

Brown—as he had been with Tortoise—was wary of how this record might be (mis)construed. 'I wish we had been able to do another album, but that's a peculiar fellow in Bundy Brown,' says Scharin, 'and he's very particular about how he wants to approach records. And we could never get [another album] off the ground. We tried, a couple of times, but I think he had a notion not to make it this *band*, as an ongoing thing.' Brown made one more record under the name Directions—the *Echoes* twelve-inch, released on the UK label Soul Static Sound later in the year—but stuck to his idea.

'I don't know if that sounds pretentious or what,' Brown said in 1997, 'but that was just the concept; it's just going to be this thing and it's going to have music on it, and hopefully people will then be able to deal with it on the level of what the music is about.' The press release stated that there would be no group photos, no tour, and no names for the songs or the group itself. This principle—expressed slightly differently but with a lot more force—would soon surface again in post-rock.

Scharin's HiM had begun just after the first Rex record, after Southern had given the band money for equipment. 'I had this great loft in Brooklyn that had these huge twenty-foot ceilings that were tin, and wood floors,' says Scharin. 'I was paying $450 a month to live, and I could play music whenever I wanted to. I started learning how to bounce from cassette four-track to the reel-to-reel, physically cutting tape together and putting it back, back and forth, recording bouncing, those early experiments with that became the first HiM record.' For 1999's *Sworn Eyes*, Scharin recruited Bundy K. Brown on bass, Rob Mazurek on cornet, and Jeff Parker on guitar. 'We went into the studio for two days,' he recalled. 'I had some real basic sketches and Rob and Jeff really changed the direction and made the form on a few of those pieces just because they play together so well. The original tracks for that song ["A Verdict Of Science"] are really different. Like Bundy's bassline, I had marimba parts which were offsetting from the drum part, all these different grooves, and he put on all this 9/8 shit. So I had to cut his bassline up … it's all really cut up.'

Meanwhile, since Brown and John McEntire had migrated from Gastr del Sol to Tortoise, David Grubbs found a new partner: Jim O'Rourke.

'The whole basis of almost everything I'm interested in is to point out things that are taken for granted,' O'Rourke has said. In his early teens, he had developed his prepared guitar technique—using bottles and other domestic ephemera to strike the strings—'as a way to avoid having to practise the stuff I'd been given'. He had been intrigued by Pierre Boulez and Karlheinz Stockhausen while in his teens, but 'it wasn't until I grew up, got in the world a bit, and started having to develop aesthetics and morals, as it were, that I started to find these people a bit repulsive. My fascination with them earlier on had to do with that sort of insecurity that these people feed off, the hierarchy they create, like a godhead. As I became increasingly more upset with these ideas, it also tied in with the sort of cult of personality idea about "the great musician", "the virtuoso".'

Initially, O'Rourke was involved in live work with Gastr del Sol, but according to Grubbs, 'Because he's such a polymath, and works so quickly—when he chooses to do so—the next thing I knew I was making a record with him.' This was the EP *Twenty Songs Less* (also featuring McEntire and Brown): 'Essentially a tape music piece composed of fragments, little musical fragments, that I had composed but Jim recomposed, through recording and editing,' says Grubbs.

O'Rourke had come into Gastr del Sol with an already-swollen discography and numerous collaborations under his belt; one of the most notable was being part of the improvisational found-sounds group brise-glace. brise-glace would improvise in the studio and O'Rourke would physically splice the results together (he's credited with 'razor blade' on their 1994 album, *When In Vanitas …*).

'I was afraid,' O'Rourke has said of that period. 'I still didn't think I had anything to say that was worthwhile enough to bother people with. So the way I approached the brise-glace record was that it was a tape piece, but instead of car doors slamming I decided to put these four people together [O'Rourke, Darin Gray, Thymme Jones, Dylan Posa], just to see how they worked and almost make a documentary about that, like a tape piece. It was like something I could hide behind a bit, a concept to divert attention from me. I still didn't feel comfortable with having a band, but I did feel comfortable with presenting a band that wasn't a band.'

Because O'Rourke had already experienced a number of academic, rarefied, and improvisational settings, and was still green in the world of rock, he initially wanted to take Gastr del Sol in a more 'sludge-rock' direction. 'We did play once [like that], with Warren Fischer from Fischerspooner playing bass,' Grubbs says. 'And I think Thymme Jones played drums. And it was a sludgy rock band, and we played once or twice like that. Jim was really a shy person at this point ... and then the personality just fluoresced.'

In a very real sense, Grubbs's musical trajectory was heading in the other direction to O'Rourke's—he had begun in much more straightforward rock settings, and was now exploring the more esoteric. It was this crossover tension that made their first album as a pair, *Crookt, Crackt, or Fly*, such a fine balance of warm rock balladry and the deliberate sabotage of that simplicity: 'Work From Smoke', for example, resembles less a song, more an experimental film of a small-town community experiencing alien abduction.

'I would say that each [Gastr del Sol] album was really considered as a distinct project,' says Grubbs. 'So, for instance, *Upgrade and Afterlife*, we knew that there would be this firewall at the beginning of it [the dissonant, discomforting "Our Exquisite Replica of 'Eternity'"], that people had to decide whether they were going to scale, or wade through.'

The final album O'Rourke and Grubbs made together was *Camoufleur*, released in 1998. 'I think there was that sense with *Camoufleur* that it would be more song-centred,' Grubbs says. 'It could have a breezier, lighter feel to it. That was unprecedented for us. "The Seasons Reverse" was such a weird snapshot of everything we were listening to at the time. The guitar part sounds like Tropicalia; it sounds like Caetano Veloso, the singing sounded a little bit *more* like Caetano Veloso; the guitar part, which was the nucleus of the song, came from that. There's all kinds of weird dub techniques on the snare drum that Jim was doing, they certainly came out of this milieu that would have included John McEntire and Tortoise, stuff like that. There's various kinds of free playing from Rob Mazurek on it, music concrete, and Markus Popp from Oval is bubbling up in there somewhere.' Popp's presence is particularly noticeable on 'Blues Subtitled No Sense Of Wonder', which has a buzz of a broken CD player continually disrupting its melancholic mood.

Jim O'Rourke left Gastr del Sol in 1998, in not altogether felicitous circumstances. 'When you're presenting yourself as someone trying to make "creative music", I think you have an obligation to the audience to trip yourself all the time,' O'Rourke told the *Chicago Reader* in 1997. 'I've been shocked by how many people don't do it. I do it by making myself uncomfortable, and for that reason I should have quit Gastr a year ago. It became too much of a full-time thing. It's not that I get bored, but I don't believe in doing something over and over again.' The two halves of Gastr del Sol immediately became apparent as soon as the duo stopped working together. Grubbs's next release, *Banana Cabbage, Potato Lettuce, Onion Orange*, was three long solo elegies (one on piano, one on untreated electric guitar, one on acoustic guitar). As for O'Rourke, while continuing to release limited-edition work within avant-garde circles, he took the sun-washed pop element of *Camoufleur* and made *Eureka*, a singer-songwriter pop album that has a feel common with the elaborate framings of Van Dyke Parks or Jimmy Webb.

There was also concord between Gastr del Sol and Stereolab; the former supported the latter in Chicago. 'I remember being taken aback at the quality of what they were doing,' Laetitia Sadier said in 1997. When Stereolab arrived back in Chicago to record their next album, *Dots And Loops*, and with the encouragement of John McEntire, they tried a different approach. 'I tend to write songs just on a four-track cassette, and in their four-track cassette guise they were not massively dissimilar to the ones on *Emperor Tomato Ketchup*,' Tim Gane says. 'But when we arrived in Chicago ... we didn't plan to do it on computer, in fact I think I only heard about it a bit before. We got there, and John said, Ah, we're gonna try it out with ProTools; and we were like, all right. And we thought it was great because it was like a toy. You could record, and you'd just have to do a little bit, and then you could just loop it, and so on, and so on. But we saw it only as a positive thing, then. And it totally changed our approach, because we did the recording in a week.'

For *Dots And Loops*, Stereolab were not only working with McEntire but with Andi Toma and Jan St Werner of the German group Mouse On Mars. 'I don't think he remembers this, but [St Werner] made faces and heckled me at one of my shows,' Jim O'Rourke recalled in 1999. 'It was where I played a blues solo or something, just two notes for an hour. He was shouting *Bullshit*!'

Mouse On Mars, like Stereolab, put out their earliest records on Too Pure; they always seemed more irreverent than—say—Seefeel (who they had a deep admiration for, and in fact joined Too Pure in part because of that). Their music was often blemished with video game sounds and giggles; 'Distroia', from 1999's *Niun Niggung*, has all the restraint of a sugar rush. Yet St Werner thought that the ultimate musical moment was the feedback guitar on Talk Talk's 'After The Flood', and the group was certainly capable of calm beauty, as evidenced by the 1997 album *Instrumentals*. 'It's about the spaces, what's behind the obvious,' St Werner said in 1995. 'About setting *obvious* information to communicate other information; it's about structures, space, grooves, perspectives, seeing things from lots of different angles. It's not about melody or harmony. Those are tricks, like shaking hands. When you meet somebody, you shake hands to say: I touch you, I accept you. This is what the music attempts. The "song" offers a way in; a way of organising, of communicating.'

'The album's not a very rock record,' Tim Gane said at the time of *Dots And Loops*' release, 'but it would have been a miracle if it was, seeing as how we haven't listened to rock music for the last five years. We didn't really feel like using distorted guitars—the only reason for us to have done that would've been if we couldn't think of anything else to do.'

'Maybe that's why we're not considered part of the 90s in the way that Oasis are,' Laetitia Sadier added, 'because we're not backward-looking, and this is such a fucking nostalgic decade.'

'With the computer, it did change things,' Gane says now. 'It changed the dynamics of the music, and how to integrate things. It was a way of almost cross-fertilising between different DNA groups. Cross-pollinating with plants and humans to create a human-plant. Crossing the species barrier. I thought that was really fascinating and I really loved doing it. The track "Miss Modular" never would have been able to exist, or it would have been a totally different kind of song, because you could really lock in on very specific things in the rhythm, and change it. It was fascinating; it really was fascinating. But I think after that record was done, I decided that we didn't want to do it like that anymore. We wanted to have a hybrid of using the computer to do extra-human things, but be more in control of the initial input. And that was the album *Cobra* [*And Phases Group Play Voltage In The Milky Night*], which I think is probably the most accessible of the combination of using computers and playing live. We wanted to reclaim a little bit of, I suppose, the live attack of the sound, but use the computer to … I would say tart it up, in some ways. Opening the possibilities of doing such cosmetic work that you couldn't have done before really, with tape.'

Stereolab were also similar to Tortoise in that they expanded, contracted, and wandered off into other identities. There was the *Turn On* project with long-term Stereolab collaborator Sean O'Hagan; there was Laetitia Saidier's Monade; and there was Uilab, who—on the *Fires* twelve-inch—covered Brian Eno's 'St Elmo's Fire' from *Another Green World*. This was Stereolab in collaboration with the New York-based group Ui, a trio of two bass players and one drummer who augmented their all-out rhythm with samplers and, occasionally, folk- and classical-identified instruments such as banjo and cornet. Bassist Sasha Frere-Jones, a native New Yorker indeed, grew up on early hip-hop radio, hardcore, and the punk-funk of ESG and Liquid Liquid; he taught himself bass by playing along to Grace Jones's 'Pull Up To The Bumper' and Afrika Bambaataa's 'Jazzy Sensation'.

'When I was young there were no guitar bands,' Frere-Jones said in 1997. 'The ones that were around were like Bad Brains. The first time I heard "Pay To Cum" it was like the hardest hardcore ever. I couldn't believe it when I found out they were black. Again, everything—reggae and hardcore—was being thrown together … I know it's sad, but I just want to recreate my high school experience.'

The Ui albums *Sidelong* and *Lifelike*, plus a host of EPs and remixes, were full of drum 'n' space, and incorporated muscular rhythmic thud ('The Fortunate One Knows No Anxiety'), low-key dubby sketches ('Painted Hill'), and junglist groove ('The Sharpie').

Frere-Jones *hated* Ui being called post-rock at the time; he even got into a newsprint scrap with Simon Reynolds about it. 'He wrote a piece, ironically saying basically that American bands suck, Britain has this great new thing called post-rock,' Frere-Jones said in 2008. 'I mean, it's ironic, because the bands he mentioned all suck. Bands that were supposed to be interesting for five minutes and never were. And then my band ended up being called post-rock, and I wrote a piece back saying, no, American bands suck; it wasn't that great an exchange really, I'm sure it wasn't his best piece and it wasn't my best piece, but then the [*Village*] *Voice* asked me, we're going to do a post-rock section and you're in one of these bands, will you write something for it.' (Frere-Jones went on, from that piece, to a career as one of the US's most prominent music critics.)

'There's so much good music in Chicago that doesn't seem to get out of the city,' Tim Gane reflected in 1997. 'When we recorded there, there were jazz bands playing and everyone played in each other's bands as well.' He was not wrong. Take Brokeback, for example: this was Doug McCombs's project, and the debut *Field Recordings From The Cook County Water Table* featured John McEntire and Johnny Herndon on percussion, and Stereolab's own Mary Hanson on vocals.

Slightly less fluid in terms of membership was The Sea & Cake. Sam Prekop and Eric Claridge 'were in this band Shrimp Boat that broke up, and [Rough Trade, Shrimp Boat's label] were like, we'll give you this money to do something else,' Prekop has said. 'And I had no idea if I could pull it off. I had no experience of trying to come up with stuff on my own. I think it was like two weeks before we were scheduled to record that I called Archer.' Archer Prewitt was in The Coctails, who had taken instrument swapping to its logical conclusion; they actually rotated them to *ensure* chaos. Prekop was a visual artist, too; it is his painting that is used for the cover of *Tortoise*. John McEntire also joined The Sea & Cake, on drums.

'Each record has been a little different to the last,' Prekop said in 1997, at the time of the album *The Fawn*. 'The only thing they have in common is a soul approach. By that I mean the vocals and music have to compliment one another.' The Sea & Cake (the name is a corruption of the Gastr del Sol track 'The C in Cake' from *Crookt, Crackt, or Fly*) were more song-based than Tortoise, and used vocals in a more linear way to Gastr del Sol. They were also keen on bleeding between 'dance' and 'rock' boundaries, most notably on their 1997 *Two Gentlemen* EP, featuring a remix of 'The Fawn' by Bundy K. Brown, retooled as 'The Cheech Wizard Meets Baby Ultraman In The Cool Blue Cave (Short Stories About Birds, Trees, And The Sports Life Wherever You Are)'.

Tortoise existed as long as people still wanted to do it; David Pajo moved on, but in came Jeff Parker. 'I was kind of trying to figure out my own way with music,' he says of this time. 'To figure out my own music, my own original ideas, I was making my living as a local, working musician in Chicago, which means playing jazz in restaurants, playing at weddings, playing at parties, birthday parties, but I was also touring with a lot of mainstream jazz artists, from New York. I was coming to Europe and playing jazz festivals. I had a very, very wide, broad collection of music that I was forced to confront every day. And at that same time I was beginning to play with Tortoise and Isotope 217°, and there was incredible amount of, at least for me, information, musical information that I was processing.'

Isotope 217° was Parker, Dan Bitney, and Johnny Herndon, plus Rob Mazurek, Matthew Lux, and Sara Smith. 'Sara and I were friends in college,' says Parker, 'and we had a group that we moved from Boston to Chicago, called The Last Kwartet. The Last Kwartet turned into Isotope 217°. We had just started to play, and we got a steady gig every week at this place called The Rainbow Club, and we played every Monday. I think we played for maybe two years, and it started as more of an improvised group, and turned into more of a workshop, and eventually we recorded an album.'

Isotope 217°'s first album, *The Unstable Molecule*, contains 'La Jeteé', which Tortoise would also record (as 'Jetty') on their next record, *TNT*.

'I was buying a jacket recently,' Johnny Herndon related to the *NME* in 1998, 'and *TNT* was playing. The guy was showing me jackets, saying, This one is warmer, but this one is cheaper—oh my god this music sends you to sleep—and let me show you this … And I was like, [looking crushed] I don't want to buy jackets anymore.'

TNT, released in 1998, did not receive the rapturous welcome that *Tortoise* and especially *Millions Now Living Will Never Die* enjoyed. It was a double album, and for some this gave automatic licence for them to claim it bloated and egotistical; but it also felt muted, in the way that their previous releases had not.

Lukewarm reviews meant the mood in the Tortoise camp was defensive. 'It's not an easy record to just sit down and listen to,' John McEntire said in 1999. 'I'm certainly not trying to blow my own horn or anything, but I think it demands a certain amount of attention. There's a lot going on within it. I think another thing that put so many people off is that it's so long and there's so much detail in there. There's a lot to take in one sitting.' *TNT* was the first Tortoise album to be entirely created on a computer, using ProTools, and the group spent a year making it, picking down into ever-tinier details.

'Tortoise, in many ways, is in its own world which is why we've been called pretentious and self-indulgent,' Dan Bitney said in 1998. 'But being self-indulgent and creating art that nobody but you can enjoy isn't necessarily a bad thing. Miles Davis could have been described as self-indulgent, but his music was unique. It was created from his vision for himself, but that genius drew people in.'

McEntire was right; *TNT* takes a dozen, or even more, concentrated listens before its full power is achieved. What at first seemed undemonstrative is revealed as slow-building loveliness; where there seemed to be naught but empty intent, *TNT* knows what it's doing all along. Structurally, it doesn't hold a listener's hand, but then, after

Millions Now Living Will Never Die, it shouldn't need to. It also feels that, on certain tracks, the influence of Stereolab's breezier moments can be heard; a ray of Tropicalia is also apparent (and, in 1999, Tortoise would back Tom Zé on a series of live dates, and Zé has said that 'the guys manage to play samba that not even the Brazilians could complain about'). 'Almost Always Is Nearly Enough', the most glitched and jungle-influenced track on the album, also anticipated the next round of Tortoise twelve-inch remixes, this time by Derrick Carter and Autechre.

The cover was perhaps unsettling, too—almost a rebuke to the earlier lush LP artwork—as it was an off-the-cuff doodle by Herndon. 'We were working on *TNT* and I went to Johnny's room to look for him one day,' says John McEntire, 'and I could see he'd taken the CD-r and made that *thing*, and I was like, that's the fucking cover.'

In very stark contrast to the meticulousness of *TNT*, Tortoise were then asked to contribute to the *In The Fishtank* series, the pet project of Dutch record distributor Konkurrent, where a band or two—in this case, Tortoise and The Ex—are given a very limited amount of studio time in which to create an album, and are not allowed to bring in any existing material. It was 'very stressful,' McEntire says. 'I mean, it was fun, we loved those guys as people, they're wonderful, but it was like, OK, we have to do … what did we have, three days or something? And that's really not the way we work. *At all*.'

In The Fishtank stands as a peculiar aberration in Tortoise's catalogue, recreating a garage-band sensibility, where the first take is best, and a studio is viewed exclusively as a functional place to capture a spontaneous moment. But perhaps it was apt that, after *TNT*, the wheels screeched in the other direction, albeit temporarily. And, in a small way, it did feed into what would emerge on their next album. For now, though, it didn't alter the general mindset or the outside perception. After all, these artists had remixed and produced and watched and performed alongside one another for five or six years, they had become bywords for experimentation and, at that point, synonymous with the term post-rock. It counted as the term's second phase.

CHAPTER ELEVEN

splitting the root

'This is how we learn things in life, you know?' GLENN JONES, CUL DE SAC

Sometimes, to move forward, you go back.

'It's interesting, isn't it,' mused Warren Ellis of Dirty Three, 'that people think instrumental music is some kind of novelty, when it's been around for ages.'

When post-rock interacted with the techniques and traditions of 'roots' music—country-blues, acoustic fingerpicking, vaudevillian wanderers, folk, all manner of oral history—it didn't seek to replicate it. Instead, it critiqued it, paid homage to it, dismantled it, or provided a detached *reportage* on it.

'At the level of its basic material, our music depends upon organic sounds,' Drew Daniel of Matmos has said, 'whether they come from an acoustic instrument like a banjo or a guitar or "natural" sounds found around us: breathing, pages turning, the cherry of a cigarette burning, latex clothing, or, as we have recently captured, the sounds of a surgeon giving someone a nose job. It comes down to perversity—I don't like the "purist" approach.'

A figurehead was John Fahey. The style of guitar playing that Fahey had pioneered in the late 1950s was dubbed 'American Primitive';

it combined country-blues music with interests in non-Western folk influences and dissonance (Fahey being particularly attracted to the composers Sibelius, Bartók, and Charles Ives). Through his compositions, Fahey channelled anger, depression, death, in close quarters with joy, calm, elation; and he ripped conventional guitar tunings down to frayed strings to achieve it. But American Primitive was about something more philosophical than guitar techniques. It took in American myth and legend, concurrently expressing weird and harsh realities, wordlessly channelling the chaos of poverty and the hope of deliverance. It was born of roots but was severed from them, too. In fact, American Primitive had a very similar relationship to roots music as post-rock did to rock. It was unsurprising, therefore, that there were shared sympathies. 'Fahey's weirder tunings were a real secret influence on early Sonic Youth,' Thurston Moore has said.

John Fahey accompanied his music with garrulous, parabolic sleeve notes, presenting an embellished take on how his albums came together. The song 'Wine And Roses', he writes in the notes to *Dance Of Death And Other Plantation Favorites*, 'is a graceful minor melody learned by Fahey from an old Indian he met while visiting the Mississippi Monner Monument Coffee and Gift Shop in West Heliotrope, Maryland. He was given to understand that the song was an anthem used by the Indians in their heroic struggle on Capitol Hill in the early 1930s against the political entrenchment of the brief alliance of the Episcopal Ministry with Captain Marvel and the Mole Men.'

'I bought every album by him I could find,' Cul de Sac's Glenn Jones has said of John Fahey, 'and was soon enveloped in the esoteric world he invented in his liner notes. All very mysterious, obscure—and very sexy.'

When Fahey played, he used the concept of a 'buried tune' to incorporate familiar but deconstructed elements of existing tunes, working them into his new world order of invented tunings and guitar intuition. The four-part 'Requiem For Molly', a conscious attempt at *musique concrète* on 1967's *Requia And Other Compositions For Guitar Solo*, buries Charles Ives, Charley Patton, and The Mamas & The Papas inside fairground mania, brass orchestras, children's cries, and Nazi propaganda recordings.

'I've always really thought of myself as a spiritual and psychological detective,' Fahey said in 1995. 'I'm always trying to get to a fuller understanding of myself through my music. I felt so alienated from the culture around me, like I was from a different planet, like I wasn't really a member of the human race. I had two heads; one just wasn't visible. So I was looking for another path of music. I didn't really know what it was. I didn't care what it was, and I still don't.'

'I spent so many years playing improvised music,' Jim O'Rourke said, in a revealing conversation with Fahey in 1998, 'that I've been slowly trying to incorporate that into this [fingerpicking] style of playing.'

'We're kind of opposites,' Fahey responded. 'You've got all this improvisation and now you're going into more structured stuff. I'm going in the opposite direction—from highly structured stuff. Believe me, I'm sick and tired of structure, but I didn't know you could get away with what you get away with. I'm moving into what you do. A lot of it is random.' O'Rourke laughed at the backhanded compliment.

While O'Rourke and David Grubbs pulled in opposite directions as Gastr del Sol aged, one thing they had in common was an interest in American Primitive, although O'Rourke has said that he 'actually started that fingerpicking stuff' after hearing 'Horizons' by Genesis, from *Foxtrot*. 'That's where I learned to fingerpick from, more from Genesis than Fahey.'

Grubbs says that his own interest stemmed from when, in around 1997, 'Smithsonian Folkways reissued the Harry Smith *Anthology Of American Folk Music*, and that really spun me around.' Blind Lemon Jefferson's 'Black Horse Blues' and Fahey's 'Dry Bones In The Valley' were two notable songs Gastr del Sol covered. Both Grubbs and O'Rourke would go on to incorporate these influences more in their solo records, and O'Rourke would also produce one of Fahey's albums: 1997's *Womblife*.

That same year, Fahey also recorded an album with the Boston band Cul de Sac. 'The collaboration with John Fahey was completely emotionally debilitating,' says Glenn Jones. 'It was a psychodrama.'

Cul de Sac are one of those outlying post-rock bands—like a Labradford, or even a Chorchazade—where there was no Louisville, Montreal, or East London scene to encourage and support them. 'I don't know whether it's that "prophet without honour in his own country" thing or what, but we never really had much of a following in Boston,' Jones says. 'While there were people that came to shows we did, we were very much taken for granted here. There was very little in the way of local press. We got modest airplay on some of the college radio stations, but I don't feel like there was ever a Boston scene that we were part of, or a Boston community to support us.'

Cul de Sac formed in 1988: Jones, Robin Amos on synthesizer, Chris Fujiwara on bass, and Chris Guttmacher on drums. 'I was particularly into the so-called American Primitive guitar thing,' Jones says. 'Robin and I were the same age and had grown up with all those krautrock records. We were big Captain Beefheart fans. We listened to Stockhausen and electronic music. So the band was really a way to synthesize a bunch of influences in a way that we hoped was unique.'

As well as guitar, Jones played a Contraption, which he used throughout Cul de Sac's lifespan. 'It was a Hawaiian guitar that was mounted on top of a box with drawers and lights and effects pedals inside, and was played with various kitchen utensils,' he says. 'There were two reasons I created it. One, I wanted to have an instrument that I couldn't play technically. It was basically just a noisemaker, tuned at random, something I could only play emotionally, or intuitively. But it was also a way to use a lot of various effects pedals, to manipulate them on the fly at the same time as I was playing guitar. You see people with their effects pedals on the floor, and you'll see them kneel down, twist a knob, and have to get back up again—I wanted them up where I could reach them! All of this paraphernalia was enclosed in a big wooden box that sat on top of an old person's walker. I figured if a walker could support the weight of a human being, it'd be strong enough for my needs. Then, I wanted to make it look beautiful and mysterious, so I put lights inside it, and decorated it inside and out. For me, it was a very good thing. It was nice to set the guitar down for a while and go to the Contraption. Sometimes, mysterious and beautiful and unpredictable things came out of it.'

Cul de Sac's 1991 debut album, *ECIM*, remains a favourite of Jones's. 'By and large, it's a very good first statement, I think,' he says. 'Certainly the first song on there, "Death Kit Train", that song continued to evolve, and we were still playing a version of that song all the way through to our end.' They also continued to play 'Nico's Dream' and 'Lauren's Blues'. On there, too, they arranged John Fahey's 'The Portland Cement Factory At Monolith, California', one of the earliest times that a then-untrendy Fahey was covered in an experimental rock context. 'That was one of the first things we worked out in the band when we formed,' Jones says. 'It became part of our set for a long time, and I occasionally play it at my solo shows to this day.'

ECIM also features Dan Ireton, aka Dredd Foole, a fellow Bostonian. 'Dan was part of our idea of what a singer should do, or could do, in a band, but he wasn't ready to commit,' says Jones. 'He played live with us a few times and guested with us on a couple of songs on the album. Dan uses his voice like an instrument, like a saxophone or something.' Ireton sings the Cul de Sac original 'Homunculus' and a cover of Tim Buckley's 'Song To The Siren'; he was soon to go on to use his weeping freeform strange-folk voice on his first solo record, 1994's *In Quest Of Tense*.

Cul de Sac evolved over the next few years. 'I don't know that we ever said, the next record is going to be this or the next record is going to be that,' says Jones. 'I mean, we basically just continued to write songs, to create new pieces of music, we tried very hard not to repeat ourselves, and when we had enough for a new record, we'd record.' Their life wasn't always smooth—they had troubles with their record label, Thirsty Ear—but their albums were consistently good. *I Don't Want To Go To Bed*, a collection of spontaneous improvisations, and the more structured *China Gate* were both released in 1995.

Glenn Jones had been a friend of John Fahey's for years, and by the mid 1990s, Fahey was in a bad way, plagued by ill health, alcoholism, and poverty. Fresh from a ruinous divorce, he was surviving on reselling thrift-shopped albums while living in a series of run-down welfare motels; things hit base when he pawned his guitar and moved into the Union Charity Mission in Salem. However, there was now renewed interest in his work from a younger generation—as the Gastr del Sol cover illustrates—and Cul de Sac, backed by Thirsty Ear records, were interested in recording an album with him. After a bit of to-ing and fro-ing, terms were agreed, and work could begin.

Fahey was an erratic presence from the moment he arrived in Boston. Missed flights, forgotten medication, contract arguments, and cancelled studio bookings made the project immediately stressful. And then rehearsals started. 'For a week of rehearsal I struggled to teach Fahey some of our material, and learn some of his that I could teach to the band,' Jones recounted. 'This was a mistake. In trying to be Fahey's conduit to the band (and vice versa), I managed to piss off both the band and Fahey.'

They had nine days to record and mix the album. Fahey had 'no interest in making the kind of record I'd envisioned', according to Jones. 'He attacked the material, said it would be disastrous for his career to be associated with it.' Cul de Sac would want to redo tracks; Fahey usually thought the first take was the best. First the heating and then the lighting broke in the band's accommodation, and *then* Glenn Jones's bed collapsed. Fahey, staying in a nearby motel, was unmoved by the band's privation. ('Sorry,' he reputedly said, rather too breezily.)

Thirsty Ear was nagging for product, but nothing they'd done so far was usable. Jones was on the verge of quitting. It was the producer, Jon Williams, who urged him to stay but to … *let go*. 'In scrapping what we'd started, the process of making a record together became a part of the record itself,' Jones recalled. 'The sessions became more challenging. The mood of the music was often dark, mysterious—at times almost morbid. But, as we and Fahey got into it, the sessions became more spontaneous—more fun.' Fahey brought in a bizarre ceramic object, which he named the Great Kooniklaster, and it became a totem that watched over the sessions. It smashed of its own volition as soon as they wrapped.

The album, *The Epiphany Of Glenn Jones*, is an effective mélange of Fahey's past with his newer interest in the 'random', rubbing against Cul de Sac's economy and feel. For the cyclical 'Gamelan Guitar', Jones recorded a torent of different items (fava beans, lentils, pinto beans, dried rice) pouring onto the strings of four guitars lying face-up on the floor and into various ceramic and glass bowls; there are such haphazard sounds and artless moments everywhere. *The Epiphany Of Glenn Jones* is the sound of people with nothing to lose, and what's more remarkable is that it's consistently balanced between disharmony and clear-eyed beauty. It finishes on two surreal spoken-word tracks that give some insight into the tension of the album sessions. 'What does Cul de Sac mean? What does Cul de Sac mean? WHAT DOES CUL DE SAC MEAN?' Fahey asks Jones, as he strums his guitar in increased agitation.

'The magazine *Ptolemaic Terrascope* asked me to write like a tour diary, only a record diary, of what it was like working with John,' says Jones. 'And my writing of it was a way to exorcise all the horrible feelings I had about John, about making that record; a way to deal with my feelings of inadequacy, doubt, and failure. But I didn't want John to feel that he was blindsided by the article, or to feel angry that it came out. So I mailed him this thing, writing, *Some magazine is thinking about publishing this as an article, but I wanted you to see it first*. John called me from Oregon as soon as it arrived, which was the first time we'd talked since the sessions for the album. He said, Glenn, these have to be the liner notes of the album. And I said, Are you kidding? Because none of us come off very well in the telling. And he said, It doesn't matter, it's true.'

The sleeve notes to *The Epiphany Of Glenn Jones* became a bastard grandchild of Fahey's own past liner notes, but this time they were sired by Jones. 'There was kind of a postscript to *The Epiphany Of Glenn Jones*,' he continues. 'I guess it was around 2000 that I visited John—it was the last time I would see him before he died—out in Oregon, ostensibly to interview him for the project that became the boxed set, *Your Past Comes Back To Haunt You*. And this was the first time I'd spent any time with John after the—well, what was *nearly* the debacle of *The Epiphany Of Glenn Jones.* John, his then-girlfriend, Melissa, and I were driving around. We'd just had dinner at a Chinese restaurant, and John was sprawled in the back seat, eating the leftovers. Melissa and I were in the front. And Melissa just kind of made a joke, like, *John told me about the record you guys made together—I could have predicted that that wasn't going to go well!* And John quickly chastised her, but not in a mean way. He said, Melissa, you don't understand; what Glenn did, you couldn't have done, and I couldn't have done.

'And it made me feel two ways. One was, it's a little bit like when you go to a softball game or something as a twelve year old, and your team loses, and your dad tries to cheer you up as he's driving you home. *Well, you lost, but you pitched a good game.* It was supportive, but in an uncomfortably parental way. But at the same time it also made me feel really good that John clearly recognised how difficult he had been, and how difficult a situation he'd put me in. He recognised that I wanted to run away from it all, and he understood that impulse. But if I'd quit the project just because my feelings were hurt, we wouldn't have had this experience, and we wouldn't have had this work of art. It was a very loving and kind thing for him to say. I don't know. It's not just about music. It's about life and your expectations. Things that you never could have predicted when you said, hey, let's start a band and play music. Who would have ever thought you go down some of the roads you end up going down?'

Quite.

'That one recording session really changed everything for me,' David Pajo has said. 'By the time we came to make *Spiderland*, we had started listening to old country music, Delta blues, Leonard Cohen, Nick Cave, all this stuff. We started to take more of a purist approach to recording—more of a documentary style of recording. It just let the music speak for itself. We didn't have any time to do to much in the way of production, even if we had wanted to.'

An early post-Slint project was with their friend Will Oldham, as Palace Brothers, on the album *There Is No-One What Will Take Care Of You*. Featuring Britt Walford, Todd Brashear, and Brian McMahan among his musicians, Oldham took a *Straw Dogs*-esque approach to rural America, where the wilds were full of incest, bloodshed, gallows humour, warped emotions, debilitation. It was recorded in two remote locations: a house near the banks of the Ohio River, and a cabin in Meade County. Oldham's words are the focus of *There Is No-One What Will Take Care Of You*, although Walford, Brashear, and McMahan are an important part of that record's discomfort (Walford's impending-doom drums on 'Riding', for example). David Pajo, and to a lesser extent Brian McMahan, would carry a strain of this distorted blues onward.

Brian McMahan's The For Carnation introduced itself in 1997, somewhat obliquely, as 'a non-profit organisation serving members of the elderly community involved in revitalisation of local cottage industries'. McMahan initially conceived of The For Carnation as a kind of enhanced solo project, where a revolving cast of musicians might provide the spokes to his hub. At the beginning, Pajo and Walford were part of it; Walford left before any recordings took place. It was a line-up of McMahan and Pajo, with Doug McCombs and John Herndon of Tortoise, that created the *Fight Songs* EP in 1995. Pajo had gone by the time of the *Marshmallows* LP the following year; and by the time of 2000's *The For Carnation*, Walford was back as a guest drummer on 'Being Held', John McEntire contributed synthesizer, and Christian Frederickson of Rachel's arranged strings on two tracks.

'I would never think of trying to do stuff by myself,' McMahan has said, 'and the reason that I play music is because I love getting together with all the people and making it happen, but it hasn't been a solid band until this record [*The For Carnation*].' For it is *The For Carnation* that carries with it the weight of American Gothic: 'Emp. Man's Blues', 'Tales—Live From The Crypt', and 'A Tribute To' all plunder fable, injecting into it the echoes of cracked bell tolls. McMahan's growl is alternatively foreboding like a seer, or intimidating like a person to leave alone at a bar.

As for David Pajo: 'I think you can hear the things I worked on before, in Aerial M,' he said in 1998. 'There's a learning curve. I want to keep on moving.'

M Is … , Pajo's debut EP as Aerial M, contains 'Wedding Song No. 3', 'the first and last multi-track recording of a live band that I ever did on my own,' as he put it in 2004. 'The sound quality is suspect, but I didn't know any better; I was too hopeful to care.' Hope was the watchword of *M Is …* , but it is even more apparent on the Aerial M self-titled LP. Its fragility is folkish, personal, and introverted; there isn't the tension of Slint, nor is there much of the dub of Pajo's work on Tortoise's *Millions Now Living Will Never Die*. The backward looping of 'Compassion For M' is a key exception, Chicago haemorrhaging rhythms into Pajo's quiet folklore. This was developed even more on Aerial M's *Post-Global Music* in 1999, for which Bundy K. Brown dissected 'Wedding Song No. 3' and then retitled it 'AttentionSpanDeficitDisorderDisruption'.

Using a new *nom de plume*, Papa M, Pajo released *Live From A Shark Cage* in 1999, which includes the ringing 'I Am Not Lonely With Cricket', recorded with Stereolab's Tim Gane, and the psychedelic raga 'Drunken Spree'. These recordings are aligned to what would be dubbed 'New Weird America': the underground lo-fi folk music as pioneered by Dredd Foole's *In Quest Of Tense* and epitomised by The Tower Recordings' 2000 album *Folk Scene*. Probably because of his heritage in Slint, Pajo's work as Aerial M and Papa M was seldom considered in this light. Still, he was interested in exploring music of the hills and earth. 'I chose the banjo for some songs because I didn't want it to be far out, cerebral music,' he said. 'I wanted to find some sort of middle ground space, total weirdness, but still kind of rooted somehow. For some reason, banjo and harmonica grounds it again.'

Like Will Oldham, Pajo would eventually cease using aliases and put out records under his real name; he also, literally, started using his own voice. The cover version 'Last Caress' (after The Misfits) on 1998's Aerial M *October* EP had its roots for Pajo pre-Slint, as Maurice used to cover it, but Pajo's execution of it owed little to his former bands. 'Last Caress' mutates from shock-schlock paean to violence into a backwoods killer's lament. *Papa M Sings* followed in 2001, featuring songs written by Jerry Jeff Walker and Gary P. Nunn.

'I listen to a lot of country music,' Pajo said in 2000. 'I grew up in a town where country music's really popular. You absorb it growing up there.' When he was a youngster—and this is where 'Last Caress' really starts to make sense—his interest in country interacted with his love for metal. 'Like most Midwesterners, I grew up a metaller,' he has said. 'We were sort of over the top, immature, play-as-fast-as-you-can.'

As well as his M material, Pajo was in demand pretty much everywhere as a guitarist, which included popping up on a record by Californians Matmos. They had been tagged intelligent dance music (IDM) but fought very strongly against it. 'If you consider the sociological origins of contemporary electronic dance music in black and gay clubs in Chicago and New York and then consider the overall "whiteness" and "straightness" of the average IDM artist and fan it all starts to look kind of sinister, like people patting themselves on the back because they are so much more advanced than those savages who leap about to their wild drums or something,' Matmos's Drew Daniel has said. 'When we made *The West* we didn't know about the term, but we knew that we were sick of lazy reviewers comparing us to Autechre and we wanted to ditch all those comparisons and reflect the fact that we love Robbie Basho and Hawaiian guitars.'

Matmos are a duo (and a couple), Daniel and M.C. Schmidt, who from their earliest days had a fascination with sound art and never wanted to be confined to electronica. 'There's a hybridness to what we do,' Daniel said in 2001, 'because even though its based on the objects, it's subjected to so much filtering, editing, chopping and slicing that we do have a signature rhythmic set of tendencies that is the music as much as the object. But I do think it's at least 50 percent what the object does, because different objects and different sources suggest what sort of song they want to be made into and they put some limits on what can be done.'

For *The West*, sun-cracked guitar strums burn into Matmos's objects—cigarettes, dice, a bible, all suggestive of a rugged outlaw caricature—then glitches, and catches in loops. David Pajo played on three tracks, and 'Tonight, The End' is especially redolent of an electronically scrambled Aerial M demo.

Australia's Dirty Three incorporated roots music in a far more straightforward and consistent fashion than did Matmos. 'We never really had an idea of the band,' Warren Ellis, the band's fiddle player, said in 1995. 'It just evolved out of playing. I guess the main thing is that now we're going for the melody and playing tunes. Originally we were just looking to make dynamics—I guess we still do it—trying to make as much of a variety as we could with just a few instruments.'

The Dirty Three are an interesting case because they seem to be bracketed as post-rock primarily by virtue of them being instrumental. Their music exudes last-drink passion and woe; live, the band are more akin to Jimi Hendrix or The Who than a static post-rock band. 'It's celebratory,' Ellis has said. 'It usually rises. People often say that it tends to pick them up. A lot of our songs tend to swell and build up and up ... then the whole thing falls out of them. I don't think we're a bunch of miseries.'

As for Cul de Sac, they picked themselves up after the John Fahey experience, but the band members weren't altogether happy. 'We've probably all been in a situation like this where you've had a partner, in your younger days, who is just so great in bed that you just stop looking at all the other stuff,' Jones says. 'The music in Cul de Sac was fantastic, you know. But it's sort of like, outside of the bed, everything else ... you couldn't agree on anything, everything else was frustrating, and there were so many things working against you.'

Their 2003 record, *Death Of The Sun*, 'set the stage for me going back to acoustic instruments, and going off on my own,' Jones says. '*Death Of The Sun* is so highly processed and treated and sampled, that in the course of making it what I found stood out the most were acoustic instruments, not electric instruments. So I got more into acoustic guitar on that record that I had on any previous Cul de Sac record. Most of the guitar parts on there are played on acoustic instruments. It was that, and also hearing people like Jack Rose and Chris Corsano, these younger musicians—younger than me, anyway—who had a range of similar influences.'

For an art form as determinedly anti-nostalgic as post-rock, this fascination with a particular aspect of the outlaw American past, so often steeped in dewy-eyed romanticism elsewhere, initially feels jarring. But what resulted was an unreal version, speckled with modernity; it had a complex relationship with the soil that was less about preservation, more about desecration as assumptions about authentic and ersatz disappeared. Or maybe it was just sharing a more straightforward frustration. 'Post-rock is like American Primitive now,' Jones concludes. 'It's just a categorisation that has almost become meaningless, because it's applied to so many different kinds of players and I'm hard pressed to see what they have in common at certain points.'

CHAPTER TWELVE

sharks & courtesan

'It's probably something that you could go to sleep to, or hold and kiss a loved one to. It's music to love by!' JASON NOBLE, RACHEL'S/SHIPPING NEWS

King Kong—a buoyant indie-pop band that dealt in songs about interspecies love triangles and time-travelling trains—seemed an unlikely post-Slint adventure. Formed by Ethan Buckler in 1989, after he left Slint following *Tweez*, King Kong debuted with a single, 'Movie Star', that credited *all* the members of Slint—David Pajo, Brian McMahan, Britt Walford, and Buckler. Pajo even contributed the cover art (a drawing of a gorilla, far from Slint's photorealism).

King Kong was an early lesson not to take anything for granted in Louisville. 'People talk of the Louisville Sound—which they associate with a fairly small number of bands,' Jason Noble wrote in 2012. 'The biggest strength of this city for me is that there's so much totally different music happening. And people really support one another.' It seemed every time a breadcrumb was dropped by a Louisville resident, the spores of the city would settle on it, and a band would grow. But it would be in some new mutation. Past style was rarely a guarantee of future direction.

'The main reason we were coming together to try these songs was as an alternative flavour to being in a rock band,' Rachel Grimes of

Rachel's says. 'Not to replace that experience, but in addition to it, something we were excited by and could explore.'

'It's not rock music at all,' Noble said of Rachel's in 1994, 'but then I never felt Rodan was rock music.'

What Noble had started exploring with Rachel's, even before Rodan was formed, was dark neoclassicism. He was taken, in particular, by the Australian group Dead Can Dance. Here was a sound that had its ancestry in rock, but had intentionally morphed into something very different. 'Around the time we started recording for *Within The Realm Of A Dying Sun* in late '86,' Lisa Gerrard of Dead Can Dance said in 1994, 'we came to the realisation that the standard band format of bass, guitar, and drums wouldn't be adequate to express our musical vision. We had been learning classical theory such as baroque structures, and were no longer interested in a strictly contemporary style of music. This required a whole new array of instrumentation backed up with synthesizers, which could give us many additional sounds.' (Dead Can Dance were also huge Joy Division fans, going as far as to incorporate Ian Curtis's lyrics in their songs.)

Dead Can Dance considered themselves as expansive, with no set line-up of musicians other than Gerrard and Brendan Perry, and an open mind to all different sorts of artistic practice and inspiration. 'We started working together when we were seventeen years old, and we basically went through a lot of cathartic experiences and came through the trenches,' Gerrard said in 2012. 'Our art was a guider on our foreheads, it was like a crown, it was the most important thing we possessed and it represented everything of who we were and where we were going. When I work with Brendan there's a lot of literature and painting and philosophy and discovery, you know? It's not just music—it evolves into that but there are a lot of things on the palette before we arrive at a finished work and before it can become that so sometimes it can take two to three years.' Another key feature of Dead Can Dance, especially around the time of *The Serpent's Egg* in 1988, was the debt to the intimate feel of chamber music.

'I met Jason [Noble] at a party in college, maybe in 1990, and then we both started running into each other at shows,' says Rachel Grimes. 'When he found out I was also a piano and composition student, he was eager to share a tape he had made of his keyboard songs that had string arrangements. That tape was called *Rachel's Halo*.'

While away at art school in Baltimore, Noble had become friends with violist and Peabody conservatory student Christian Frederickson. Noble already had some ideas for this new project; Frederickson helped him to dictate keyboard parts into string arrangements, and the pair then gathered a group of musicians together to record them. Noble produced one hundred copies of the *Rachel's Halo* cassette (named after Sean Young's character in *Blade Runner*), and this was what he gave to Grimes. She enjoyed it.

Grimes and Noble started to devise piano experiments 'for fun', which they then arranged for a larger group of musicians. 'We were consciously trying to stay free of the hierarchy of vocalist/band with the emphasis on message/lyrics and verse/chorus,' Grimes says. 'Instrumental music offers the potential for more options. We loved the film music of Glass, Morricone, Nyman, and the Kronos albums. The idea was that somehow we could step into that realm by combining keyboards, guitars, sampler, strings, and drums.'

Noble was also a big fan of Talk Talk's *Laughing Stock*, introducing Grimes to it. 'We just got lost absorbing that visceral, earthy, intimate quality of the mix, the ease and grace of the drums, the multi-dimensional guitars and trumpet, the voice that weaves in so effortlessly,' she says. 'It felt so free and yet so deeply structured all at the same time. We shamelessly tried to cop that sound quality and style on several songs over the years.'

'I remember very specifically the first song on that record,' Noble said in 2009 of *Laughing Stock*, 'the only drum part is the drummer setting up his drumset. You hear this rattling around through the whole song, of stuff. It was such an appealing thing that they let the quietest song set a mood.'

After the success of Rodan's *Rusty* the label that put it out, Touch & Go (on their Quarterstick subsidiary), was interested in the *Rachel's*

Halo cassette, and let Noble know that it would be open to releasing something in this vein. *Rachel's Halo* became Rachel's ('foreverafter creating seriously unintended and immense confusion, and a confounding and at times ferocious focus from the print press about the origin of the name,' sighs Grimes), and the time to properly explore it came around for Noble soon enough.

'End of September [1994], Rodan breaks up,' Jeff Mueller says. 'I call Fred, call Sean, call Doug, say, let's meet in New York, and practise for a week and a half, or two weeks, and then record. And we were like, *what?* We had all been in bands that spent a year, maybe even two years, trying to create a full family of music that would make sense on a record together.' Sean Meadows was playing bass in Lungfish; Fred Erskine was fresh from the break-up of Hoover and now in The Crownhate Ruin; Doug Scharin was in Codeine and Rex. 'All of their schedules were very, very busy,' Mueller says, 'whereas my schedule was trying to survive. I was like, I have to do something to make my life work. So let's make this band, let's do this, and let's just see what comes of it.'

'As Rex were probably finishing our first record, Jeff Mueller called me and said, Hey, I met this guy in Tennessee and this other guy in DC and I'm thinking about recording these songs that Rodan never finished, and wondered if you were interested? And I was like, Absolutely, man, I wanna play. I was ready to play; I just wanted to play and not get a job again. *At all costs.*'

Mueller, Meadows, and Erskine went to Scharin's Brooklyn loft, got up early each day, had coffee and breakfast, and played together for the rest of the time. 'Every day, for ten days,' says Mueller, 'and whatever we get, we get. And my theory was, if we can do that, then I can bring it home, and I can finish it.' June Of 44 recorded *Engine Takes To Water* in December 1994 in a jam-together-and-make-it-fit approach.

'That was supposed to be the end of it,' says Scharin.

Instead, a few shows were booked. It started with New York, and then in New York and Chicago (where Touch & Go were based, so June Of 44 could deliver *Engine Takes To Water*), and *then* in New York, Chicago, and other points in between. 'By the time we got to Chicago, we finished a show at The Empty Bottle, and I remember sitting at the bar, talking,' Scharin says. 'It was a lot of fun. And we were *all* like, that was a lot of fun. Let's do it again! It wasn't *supposed* to be again.'

'It wasn't that anyone was unhappy with their [other] respective projects they were pursuing,' says Mueller. 'Fred was certainly happy with his bands, and so was Doug, and so was Sean, but there was also like this really crazy amount of good stuff happening in a short space of time, so let's cultivate that, work at that, pick it apart.'

As well as June Of 44, Mueller had taken on a day job. 'A guy graduated the year before me [from college in Kansas City],' says Mueller. 'His name was John Upchurch.' Upchurch was part of The Coctails along with The Sea & Cake's Archer Prewitt; he also owned a letterpress business, Fireproof Press. 'I had zero letterpress experience, but I needed a job,' says Mueller, 'so I said, you're my friend; you should hire me. So he did!'

'I was looking for ways to package my music that were interesting, and less plastic-y, I guess,' Mueller continues. 'I liked the idea of a paper-y, cardboard-y package on recycled stuff.' Fireproof had just put Shellac's *At Action Park* to bed; when Mueller joined, one of his first tasks was to work on the sleeve for *Tortoise*.

This type of artwork would be a strong visual symbol of post-rock, and typically something that, later, bands that were *trying* to create a post-rock ambience would ape. There had been one significant precursor to Fireproof—Independent Project Press, founded in 1983 by the founder of Los Angeles noise/anthrological band Savage Republic, Bruce Licher. 'I was looking for an artful and unique way to create a cover for the [Savage Republic] *Tragic Figures* album,' he has said, 'and wanted to make a record as if it were a limited edition piece of art.' This concern was also in Mueller's mind.

'I felt that, when you got that first Tortoise record, when you got Shellac's *At Action Park*, or when you got the first Rachel's record, it was packaged in something that was so careful, and so conceived, and so realised, I felt that might inform how you might open it up and listen to it,' says Mueller. 'It felt like it meant something a little bit more to the people who created it, that it wasn't an afterthought, or something that came in a jewel box and that just had some artwork slapped on. That's not to say the music was any better, or more important, but to me what that said was that somebody actually put some thought into it. And that's going to engage me, and compel me to want to participate a little bit more with the project. I'm going to want to listen to it, whatever it is, because it looks like something that's important to someone.'

The second June Of 44 album, *Tropics And Meridians*, came with a set of postage stamps and sixty of the records were even housed in a wooden box. 'We started with the intention to make two hundred [boxes],' Mueller recalled. 'A friend forged a brass branding iron that sorta worked, but it failed after the first ten. I ended up lightly screenprinting the design as a guide for a wood-burning tool, handwork galore. After fifty of those … I stopped. The wood itself started bowing.'

'The feel, the experience of holding an album, reading the booklet and holding something of substance is simply a personal joy we all [in Rachel's] shared as art lovers and music listeners,' Rachel Grimes says. 'From the beginning, Jason was very interested in making the package feel like a personal piece of art. He worked with Greg King to design and photograph the duotone images in the *Handwriting* booklets, which Greg printed, and with creating the letterpress design of the cover from a gravestone rubbing and old-fashioned typeset.'

'A drop of our blood was added to each colour for authenticity,' Rachel's *Handwriting* proclaimed. ('The amounts were too small to harm anyone,' Noble said in 1996. 'Just enough to delight them.')

Handwriting, released in 1995, took 'Saccharin' and 'Seratonin', which Noble and Frederickson had recorded in 1991, added an even earlier piece Noble had worked on ('Southbound To Marion'), and included four more pieces recorded with Grimes, including 'M. Daguerre'. '[That one] had very few run-throughs before we captured it,' says Grimes. 'We had worked on the piece with just us, and then adding in Kevin Coultas [from Rodan] on drums, and then bringing in members of The Coctails on vibes, clarinet, bass and strings, and *then* Bob [Weston] on EBow bass. It was a juggle, and so much fun.' There was also 'Full On Night', a piece explicitly intended to capture the atmosphere of the blackest evenings, and which had calculated openings for improvisation within it.

'We have a semi-notated, semi-verbal way of playing,' Noble said in 1996, 'because half the people didn't read music. It's a bit of a free-for-all. The people that are from a straight academic background get a taste of rock'n'roll elements, but people from my background have to learn to keep up with their language and it's challenging.'

After *Handwriting*, Grimes says, Rachel's felt 'more like a band'; they booked a tour with June Of 44 for autumn 1995. 'Since we did not set out to become a touring band, but more of a writing and recording project,' she says, 'things did shift and develop, especially over the first couple of years.' In what has seemed to be a constant barrier for post-rock artists of whatever hue, Rachel's found that the practicalities of venues, and acoustics weren't always on their side. 'It meant having to work out the main touring ensemble, which songs worked to play live, and how to use things like live film and pre-recorded sample beds, and electronics as segues and components of songs. It was difficult to find the balance between loud and quiet instruments in soundcheck and in the show. Lots of patience. Lots of coffee and cigarettes.'

While Noble and Mueller were enjoying a mini-reunion on the joint Rachel's/June Of 44 tour, Tara Jane O'Neil—who had been the first to quit Rodan—was in New York. 'That was a really fun time in New York; everybody lived in the same neighbourhood, everyone was turning everyone else on to records,' says O'Neil. 'I can remember listening to Moondog for the first time at Sean [Meadow]'s apartment, somebody just came and gave him a record, and we were just … *What! Wow!* All these things were just coming and I think that did influence us. And I think the whole New York scene … even at that point some of the No Wave stuff was still in the waters there.'

O'Neil was part of Retsin with Cynthia Nelson, but she was also restless for something new. And it happened in collaboration with Sean Meadows—originally from Chattanooga, now living in New York and playing in June Of 44—and violinist Samara Lubelski, who had played with the German collective Metabolismus.

'The Sonora Pine was more intentional [than Rodan],' O'Neil says. 'Sean and I had very similar songwriting sensibilities. We were both pulling from lots of different places. I feel [The Sonora Pine] is a really endearing project, because we clearly had some ambitions and songwriting notions. We did it in a punk rock fashion, but a lot of the stuff we were writing doesn't fit so well into that. It would have been really great if we'd had more resources at that time, or people, or studios, to expand [into]. But at the same time, it's still super-cool, because it's just me and Sean and shitty amps and guitars, and writing all this stuff, and recording it in the way we knew how. Because we were punk rockers. Those were the tools we had at that point in life. We put that music through those instruments, and that's how it came out.'

The Sonora Pine's self-titled debut, Rachel's *Handwriting*, June Of 44's *Engine Takes To Water*; all three featured some combination of Rodan people (Kevin Coultas was on *The Sonora Pine* as well), but three more distinct projects made only a year or so after the demise of Rodan it would be harder to fathom. Since each album had its root in a post-rock originator, these three records contributed to how, for a time, the looseness of the term 'post-rock' would now be used.

Rachel's was developing as music for long attention spans, and putting down roots as a project. 'Even though we had just released *Handwriting*,' Grimes says, 'I just could not believe [Touch & Go] would want to release a straight-up chamber work. So grateful they did!'

Music For Egon Schiele had begun as a soundtrack Grimes wrote for a quasi-biographical play by Stephen Mazurek about the Austrian painter of contorted, long-limbed nudes. *Egon Schiele* combined dance and theatre, and initially Mazurek wanted Grimes to perform solo pieces from Schiele's era, the early twentieth century.

'I learned many of these pieces by Satie, Ravel, Schoenberg, but there was one piece that was way beyond my ability—Ravel's *La*

Valse,' she says. 'In talking about other options, [Mazurek] suggested that I write something. Once I started working with Stephen and the choreographer Brian Jeffrey, it became clear that writing a new score for the work would lend more fluid support to the whole piece.' Following Touch & Go's interest, Rachel's recorded the piece live to tape with Bob Weston in the summer of 1995 with Grimes on piano, Christian Frederickson on viola, and Louisville cellist Wendy Doyle. It was released the following year.

Contemporaneous to *Music For Egon Schiele* was the development of *The Sea And The Bells*. 'A concept album, for sure,' Grimes says. 'Jason and I started working on several songs at the piano, like "Lloyd's Register" and "Tea Merchants", way back in 1993. Along the way, we were sculpting the backstory for the album and how the songs would depict the various aspects of it. Jason brought the major themes and ideas, and wrote a long piece of prose that was published in the initial booklet printing included in the album. I think of it as a gothic tale of romance and longing, the main characters being a sailor and his wife. We used the nuggets from the story as departure points for the various songs, most of which are quite literal.'

Although *The Sea And The Bells* uses seventeen musicians, some of the most tender moments are found in 'With More Air Than Words'—just Noble, his guitar, and some groggy ambient noises—and 'Cypress Branches', which is overrun by flocking birds. It was followed by *Selenography*, named after the study of the moon's physical features. Recording of those tracks began in 1997, and only ended eighteen months later, in 1999. 'For *Selenography*, we wanted to create a whole different feel, a moonscape,' Grimes says, of its more rustic, decayed-civilisation feel.

The background of Noble and Mueller in hip-hop, laying somewhat dormant while they were in Rodan, made more philosophical sense in both Rachel's and June Of 44. 'I think hip-hop in particular makes me really question how to engineer and create songs,' Noble wrote in 2011. 'Hip-hop has advanced the way songs are recorded more than any genre, because DJs can draw on every style of music without getting hung up on tradition.' Noble revealed in 2001 that he and Mueller still regularly sent raps to one another.

Mueller, too, relished the confidence to shoplift from musical history that hip-hop had taught him. 'It was never specific,' Mueller says of June Of 44. 'It was always: we're gonna make a 70s revival song and put that right next to a Skinny Puppy–sounding song. And after that we'll throw in some King Tubby, and it'd just go on and on. We'll throw in some Scratch Acid. It just melts all these things to make something that seems identifiable as our music.'

'I think the EP [*The Anatomy Of Sharks*] and the first two records [*Engine Takes To Water* and *Tropics And Meridians*] were like: we learned the songs, we played them in the studio, Bob [Weston] made them sound great, and we were in and out of there in four days,' says Scharin. 'Record's done. No more than four, five, six days at the most. We didn't have a budget. We didn't *want* a budget. But on the later June Of 44 records we started to dabble around in the studio a little bit more, experimented.'

Jeff Mueller also remembers how, 'as June Of 44 aged, I guess, and cauterised and solidified as a group of people, there was a level of seriousness that replaced the [earlier] whimsy. At the onset of the project I was the principal guy trying to make it work. And then it was really, really awesome when all of a sudden everybody was [more] involved.' This is borne out on *Four Great Points* but in particular on their 2000 album, *Anahata*; a balance of closefisted guitar, rhythmic complexity, deft use of Fred Erskine's trumpet, and Doug Scharin's HiM dubs.

'For me, it was a lot of work,' says Scharin, 'and I had to choose sometimes between touring with either Rex or June Of 44. We toured together one time, which was cool, but it wiped me out. By the time we got from New York through the Midwest and out to Seattle, and started to head down the West Coast, I was sick as a dog. I would just be throwing up, and then I would go out to play, and then throw up, and then go out to play.'

The Sonora Pine, too, would be hit by differing priorities and conflicting schedules. Sean Meadows left after *The Sonora Pine*, and

O'Neil moved back to Kentucky from New York. Although there was a second record—*The Sonora Pine II*—the balance had gone. 'We were all so young,' she says. 'We were still trying to figure out just as people, how to do life. So that contributed to the band's shortlived-ness, more than anything else. By the second record, I was writing all the songs, and of course Samara, and Kevin, we worked on arrangement stuff together. By that second record, it felt very clear to me that it was not the band that had started in Sean's apartment two years earlier. There weren't big arguments. It was just impractical, because we were all over the place. So when I decided to move back to New York again, I was—*ahhhhh*. I think I'm just gonna make this a solo thing.'

That became *Peregrine*. 'With the solo records, and especially the first one, that was really fun in a way that first records and first bands can be,' she says, 'because it is just pulling from all these places, and seeing how it can fit.'

'It was really different back in the band days,' O'Neil continues. 'I think just being in bands there's more of a guard, and a protection, for sure. The singer-songwriter tag, like the others, [creates] expectations because there's an established formula, but also with that one there's a real thing about being a woman too that does set up an intimacy thing. The man singer-songwriter is writing for *everyman*. It's the archetype. The intimacy thing is really so much the woman's ghetto of music making. Because somehow that's become the expectation, and that's become the way that especially male listeners can receive this information. It has to be this exposure, this confessional intimacy of the woman doing this. I'm not sitting here on this *fuck the man* thing, but it is a real thing, and I've been dealing with it forever. But, male or female, if you're just using your name, or if you have a moniker but it's just mainly you, people project stuff, and want to know stuff, and you're really out there.'

Meanwhile, after *Selenography* and a radical remix/deconstruction of 'Full On Night' with Matmos, Rachel's decided to take some time off. 'We were exploring separate projects as well as looking at even more collaborative concepts like film scoring and making live theatre pieces,' Rachel Grimes says. Eventually, they joined forces with New York theatre group SITI Company to build a work for the stage: *systems/layers*. This was released as the final Rachel's album late in 2003, and includes string quartet pieces, sample-heavy sections, large band numbers, snippets of live improvisations with the acting company members, a vocal work with Shannon Wright ('Last Things Last'), and a number of field recordings submitted by fans.

June Of 44, too, were coming to a natural end, but one final act was to record an *In The Fishtank*. In a sweet causal nexus, they reclaimed the spontaneity of *Engine Takes To Water* (albeit in highly compressed form). Like Tortoise, June Of 44 were given two days in a studio; unlike Tortoise, who worked with The Ex, June Of 44 did it without collaborators. 'I can honestly say that the mess we recorded was *our* forty-eight-hour mess. We totally own that mess. It was all right then and there. However, it's interesting to bring that up, because the way that people approached the criteria for the *Fishtank* records informed one of the Shipping News records. We used that exact model to create a Shipping News record, with the principal difference being that we all lived in separate cities. So the idea was, within the shape of the same timeframe, we would all go into our own studios at home, and spend a day recording a song, and that song would end up on an EP.'

Shipping News brought Jason Noble and Jeff Mueller together once more. Mueller was friends with Alix Spiegal, a writer on the public radio show *This American Life*. 'They go into real-life circumstances and find the core person that is part of that circumstance,' explains Mueller. 'If they're trying to talk about children farm-hands, for instance, they'll find a farm somewhere in rural Midwest, go to the farm, pull out the kid, and say, *let's just walk around the farm and you show us the whole day there*.' Spiegal asked Mueller to score the music for a show on Tourette's syndrome. 'I thought, why don't I dial up Jason and see if he wants to work with me on it? He would *love* this. And that's sort of how Shipping News started.'

'He kindly asked me to help him,' Noble said in 2011, 'and we were like, hey, let's do this again and forever.'

'Once [Jason and I] started playing together again in 1996, 1997, we just kept going,' Mueller says. 'Shipping News was my longest-running project. It was kind of crazy. We were going for fifteen years.' From King G & The J Crew through Rodan and to Shipping News, the friendship and musical collaboration between Jason Noble and Jeff Mueller was an enduring one.

'I have to say, Jeff is one of my oldest friends and the only adult male I've ever walked with (naked) down Taylorsville Road in Louisville,' Noble wrote in 2010, when interviewing Mueller for *Magnet* magazine. 'I may have never played music without Jeff, 'cause I was far too conservative and scared and unsure to even start.'

'It was August 4th, 2012. That's when Jason passed away,' says Mueller. Noble died after a three-year battle with cancer, surrounded by family and friends. Musician friends had played benefit shows for him to help cover the costs of treatment, and the cassette *In Pleasant Company: A Mixtape For Jason* was another intimate tribute, echoing the way Jason had made mixtapes for *them* over the years.

'Then, months later, Jon [Cook], the drummer from Rodan passed away,' says Mueller. Cook died of pancreatic failure after long struggles with addiction and mental health problems. 'Within the shape of a few months, two of my favourite musicians had passed away. Because even when I was playing in June Of 44 without Jason, he was still this good-cop, bad-cop that was toggling around inside my brain. For a while, we were so involved with each other musically that every time I played a song I would try to think what his imprint would be on it, and all these different things. And so it's just … taken a little bit of time.'

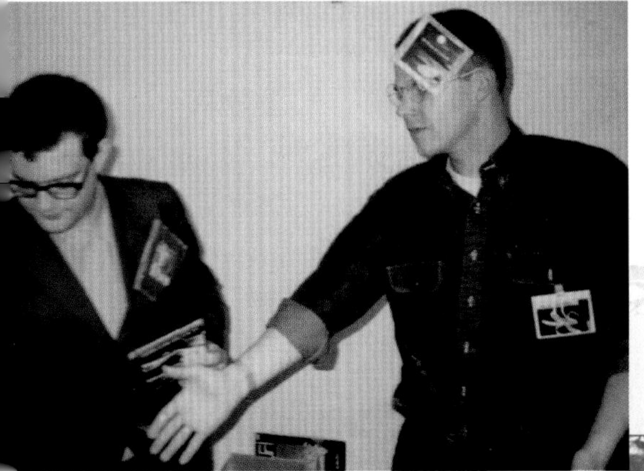

LEFT Gastr del Sol at the Musique Action Festival, Nancy, France, 1996. **BELOW** Tortoise's *Millions Now Living Will Never Die*.

BELOW Codeine's Stephen Immerwahr: 'Somehow we ended up doing a show with Pulp. And so we stuck, on the wall of the van, a countdown: Number Of Days To Pulp Show.'

ABOVE Rachel's pay homage to Slint in a sulphur hot springs pool situated in the Olympic Mountains, Washington state, 1997.

LEFT Jeff Mueller, about to play with June Of 44 at an all-ages show at Louisville's VFW Hall, 1998.

RIGHT The cover art for *The Epiphany Of Glenn Jones* by John Fahey and Cul de Sac.

BELOW Matt Elliott, aka Third Eye Foundation, performing in Camden, London, in 1997.

BELOW Mogwai at Bothwell Castle in South Lanarkshire, Scotland, March 2003.

LEFT Fridge in a Brighton car park, 1998.
BELOW A flyer for a 1996 Fridge Club Piao! performance, designed by Kieran Hebden's sister Leila.

ABOVE Test artifact from 2003 for the Bark Psychosis *///Codename: Dustsucker* cover. Weathered, buried, sandblasted logotype.

RIGHT A flyer for a 2003 show featuring Hangedup, Lightening Bolt, and Battles at the First Unitarian Church in Philadelphia.

FOLLOWING SPREAD Godspeed You Black Emperor! at the Royal Festival Hall, London, April 2000.

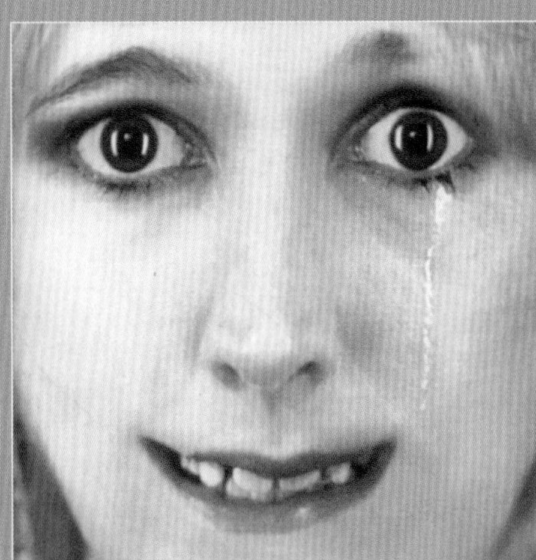

ABOVE Radiohead onstage at the Empress Ballroom, Blackpool, May 2006.

LEFT The cover art for the *Blue Jam* album, featuring edited highlights from Chris Morris's late-night BBC radio show.

CHAPTER THIRTEEN

badtimes

'I think we went from being quite light, and really happy, and doing well to … disappointed. Suffering personally with the whole thing. It wasn't the glorious thing, being a musician, that I thought it was going to be.' MARK CLIFFORD, SEEFEEL

'If you play early Eno records from the 70s and turn them up really loud,' Mick Harris of Scorn has said, 'there's a darker edge to it all. It becomes really quite unnerving.'

'An ambience is defined as an atmosphere, or a surrounding influence: a tint,' Brian Eno writes in the sleeve notes to 1978's *Ambient 1: Music For Airports*. 'Ambient music is intended to induce calm and a space to think.'

Post-rock shares a key sensibility with ambient. There is a lack of intentional narrative. Instead, narratives might emerge in pockets, peeping around the textural levees. Ambient, like post-rock, is decentred music, but in a more passive way. It evades its own presence and lets the listener contemplate or simply get on with his or her day.

But what Mick Harris and others also heard were the shadows cast by ambient. True, ambient defines itself as background music, but this calm could be ominous. Similar to a tranquiliser haze, it cocoons and nurtures, hollowing out an everlasting present; but just what is it protecting you from? That is the *really* interesting bit. Following this logic, there isn't the need to overlay dread onto ambient; it has been there all along, if anyone cared to mine for it (Tangerine Dream, on 1972's *Zeit*, certainly had a go at this, even before ambient had been named). Contemporaneous to Eno's series of Ambient works, artists like Throbbing Gristle and :$OVIET:FRANCE: began excavating the sounds of the surroundings, too; they linked what they found in its dark recesses with mechanised dread and their abject fascination about the body's many frailties. They saw Ambient as a noxious fug.

Later in the 1980s, chill-out music had become the *yin* to rave's hedonistic *yang*. Chill-out was a head-holder, mapping out a safe space in a communal experience. And it wasn't too long before it moved from a pragmatic music to something with its own artistry. 'People are questioning musical structures, the ambient boom has made them open to stuff that isn't song-based,' Kevin Martin of God, Ice, and Techno Animal said in 1994. 'But it needs to be taken a lot further.'

'[Main] want to embrace our environments, not retreat from it like Ambient Techno,' Robert Hampson said in 1993. 'Main music reflects the way we're surrounded by noise, all the hums and buzzes of traffic, planes, road drills, the constant clatter you can never really escape.'

Post-rock added two crucial, linked elements to all this: dub and pessimism. The way dub was ingested and disgorged into ambient was far from the exhilaration of, say, King Tubby, irresistibly alive with the sense of possibility; instead, this dub saw space as menacing, while the fluctuating instruments pierced the static like car alarms.

'I feel scarred for life by my first experience with soundsystems,' Kevin Martin has said. 'I can still remember vividly the first one I went to, which was in the East End of London. It was a horrible old warehouse and it was The Disciples and Iration Steppas having a face-off. There was no light apart from a bulb over each soundsystem, there were about fifty people there, no one clapped ... all of which was completely new to me. I was coming from a noise-cum-punk-cum-free jazz background and this was pretty radical—no stage show, no audience participation other than almost a complete *homage* or *faith* in the sound, and a total absorption in the frequencies. For me, it was incredible.'

It felt right that a cassette underground nexus of hardcore, noise, and metal had proved an entry point for many of these artists. 'I'm not ashamed of Napalm Death,' Mick Harris said in 1995. 'It's part of my history, part of my life. It's just another form of extreme music. Scorn for me is like Napalm, it's just the best way to express myself.'

Napalm Death's music was brutal and ultrafast, punk condensed and purifed. The drummer—Mick Harris—was of phenomenal importance, while guitar and bass were 'downtuned', in a Black Sabbath fashion. 'There's a certain pitch that's meant to be ideal for guitar and bass, called "concert pitch", and until a few years ago, that's what most musicians used,' guitarist Bill Steer has said. '[Downtuning] makes the sound deeper, and for that we're prepared to sacrifice a bit of clarity.' Napalm Death set themselves apart from others in the UK hardcore scene; they were not only concerned with speed, but in the specific power that comes from cavernous sound. Harris, while still in Napalm Death, told *Melody Maker* that he was keen on both Brian Eno and Cocteau Twins.

Napalm Death wrote politicised songs, and together with the grave mood they created (quite an achievement at whipsmart speed) they argued that suffering was inevitable and prolonged in this vicious world. From this context, Scorn emerged. Initially a duo, Harris and Nicholas Bullen (who had been Napalm Death's vocalist and bassist) claimed that Scorn was a 'rock'n'roll band' and on their 1992 debut, *Vae Solis*, this rings true—albeit one whose dub weight is plain. Yet beginning with the following year's *Colossus*, and accelerating after the departure of Bullen in 1995, Scorn increasingly abdicated all rock responsibility.

Harris was part of a heavy-*avant* triumvirate; the other two were Kevin Martin of God, and Justin Broadrick of Godflesh (who had also played in Napalm Death). 'There's no conscious decision of alienating an audience,' Kevin Martin said in 1990, of God. 'We just want to make music that's directly physical and, in a way, causes us a bit of pain for some reason. If a guitarist hits a chord that is painful to the ear, and it suits a feeling one of us has, then great, we build a piece around that. It's just a musical directness we're chasing, really.' The 1992 God album *Possession*, with its multiple drummers, bassists, and saxophonists (of whom Martin and John Zorn were two), was GBH for the senses: rafters of noise smacking the brain. It carried an air of lost empathy, chemical corrosion and *fin de siècle* communication breakdown. 'The best reaction is if people find [God] somehow therapeutic, if it cleanses them,' Martin has said. 'That's how *I* feel afterwards.'

Martin has been open about his difficult childhood, which was marked by upheaval and assault. 'My father was a cunt,' he said in 2014, 'he beat the shit out of [my mother] and he beat the shit out of me. It made no sense to me, why would someone spend their life with someone who's a sadist and selfish? He was in the navy and moved a lot when I was a child, so I never felt rooted to anywhere, and that's had a bearing on my view of everything.'

Originally built around the core of Martin and Shaun Rogan, God expanded in number, and, theoretically, expanded in possibility too. But Martin was cooling toward it. This crystallised at what turned out to be God's last live appearance. 'I had asked Boymerang to do their first show playing jungle, and I'd asked The Disciples to bring their soundsystem,' Martin has said.

'We played with God and people absolutely hated it,' Graham Sutton remembers. 'They were throwing bottles. We were projecting films at the same time and people were tearing down the screen.'

After Boymerang and God, The Disciples played, but virtually all the God fans in the audience left. 'It was everything that was crap about rock shows,' Martin recalled. 'So I stood in the middle of The Disciples' three *monoliths*, watching Russ [D] do his thing. On that night God had twelve people in the band—two electric basses, one double bass, two drummers, a troupe of African drummers, electric viola, two saxophones and myself screaming through an effects unit. But everything I wanted to do in terms of disorientation, groove *with* a tonality, confrontation with sound as well as excitation through sound—was done by this one guy, standing with his little box of tricks.'

Justin Broadrick had been involved with God for their inception, co-producing their first twelve-inch, *Breach Birth*, in 1990. '[Martin] was the first person to ever put on and promote Godflesh's first ever show in Brixton, London,' Broadrick said in 2009. 'He bought the first Godflesh album around the day it came out after hearing Godflesh on the John Peel Radio 1 show. We had our phone number on [the album] then, that was autumn 1988, and our relationship built from there since we shared a lot of common interests, musically and beyond.'

'We're a *true* heavy metal band,' Broadrick said at the release of Godflesh's second album, *Streetcleaner*. 'We're almost dub metal. World Domination [Enterprises] comes nearest to what we're trying to do, but they're more a trashtown ghetto sound. Dub and metal might seem like unlikely partners, but think about early PiL, too.' The heavy sound of Godflesh was, like God, always evolving; from the blackly severe *Pure* in 1991, through the dubby dark ambient of 'Flowers' from the 1994 album *Merciless*, to the cards-on-the-table statement *Love And Hate ... In Dub* in 1997.

'Justin is the only person I know who shares my taste for extremity,' Martin said in 1995. 'Not in a childish shock-value way, but in a genuine interest in everything that's full on.' Both of them seemed to emit an aura of solitude, too, despite being in group setups and engaging in frequent collaborations with others.

'From the beginnings of Techno Animal, I became more and more immersed in what I call the magical little zone which is the studio,' Martin said in 2015. 'For me, it's a way of almost constructing a parallel universe because the real one's so completely screwed.' It came from a similar impulse to that which gripped Can and Brian Eno in the 1970s; however, in the 1990s, artists didn't have to worry so much about a judgemental engineer or a fat invoice for squandered studio time. Digital technology, shrinking in size and expanding in power, was privatising the whole band process, shifting it into the home.

'Laika just evolved with the technology,' Margaret Fiedler says. 'It was totally different. In 1990, it was almost completely analogue; by

2000, everything was totally digital. People weren't using analogue tape anymore. You were just doing everything on your hard drive.'

For loners, perfectionists, and the impoverished (or all three) the new compact technology also bought time, while facilitating seclusion and control. 'He [Mark Clifford] would be on it day and night,' says Sarah Peacock of Seefeel, about the group's second album, *Succour*. 'Sitting there, clicking away. We were sharing a flat at the time, and *that* was a really bad idea. I said [to him], I would love to have a go on this, can't you just go out for an afternoon or something so I can have a play on it? I'd like to write something.'

'We'd totally moved on,' she continues, referring to Seefeel's composing and recording techniques following the fairly traditional studio album *Quique*. 'Mark [Clifford] had moved on in the way that he was constructing tracks. We weren't writing stuff in rehearsal—we weren't even rehearsing. We'd be writing stuff in the flat and I think necessarily with that you have to keep the volume down.'

Before Seefeel went to Moscow for the ill-starred Britronica festival in 1994, they had left Too Pure for Warp and released their first EP for the label, *Starethrough*. 'Warp offered me everything, really,' says Clifford. 'That was it. Warp was a shining light.'

'A dance label?' Warp co-founder Rob Mitchell chuckled in 1998. 'Well, you need to have quite an individual style of dance.'

The Warp roster at the time offers a good parallel example of how dance culture was also turning dour in the early-to-mid 1990s, following the rhapsody and elation of rave. 'We make music to listen to on headphones,' Sean Booth of Autechre, Warp's extraordinary flagship band, said in 1994. 'You need to concentrate on it.' A nerdy-but-cool label, Warp had attracted a cache of staunch electronica enthusiasts, and not everyone was happy that Seefeel had signed.

'We took a lot of flak when we joined Warp, just for the fact that we used guitars,' Clifford says. 'Because Warp at that point was a label for people who didn't like that stuff, didn't like guitar bands. And so for a lot of people, suddenly having a band on there with guitars, even though we didn't play them like normal guitars, was almost sacrilege.

Life was pretty hard for us to start with on Warp, and I think that's another reason why the music very quickly went quite difficult.'

Quique had exuded a downy, pretty quality. The *Starethrough* and *Fracture/Tied* EPs, and especially the 1995 album *Succour*, reject that serenity. Here was music from an automaton-ruled dystopia, while Sarah Peacock's vocals sound like the last human crying for its fate.

'There *are* tracks on *Succour* like "Cut" and "When Face Was Face"—they're kind of euphoric,' says Peacock, 'but there's other stuff on there that's darker, and probably the overall tone [is dark] because of the pacing, the starker electronicness of it. There's less of the wall of fuzzy analogue guitars, and effects and stuff that there is on *Quique*. Personally, I prefer it to *Quique*.'

'We were on the verge of really making it,' says Clifford, 'and if I'd had any sense of career, I wouldn't have released *Succour*. That put a massive full stop on it. There was definitely no compromise.'

The tension between 'band' and 'electronic project' that Seefeel had handled so effectively up until now was beginning to break down. Clifford was taking the increasingly hermetic path that the technology was offering him. 'I just wanted to be in the studio making music, and that wasn't going to be possible because I had to do everything else,' he says. 'I didn't enjoy touring at that time. I didn't enjoy doing interviews, any of that. I'd be quite happy for the record company to pay me to be in a big studio all the time. But clearly that's not going to happen.'

'The rest of us had our own issues with touring, but it was such a big part of why we needed to do it and why we needed to be in a band,' Peacock says.

It wasn't only Peacock who felt that way. 'I loved touring,' Margaret Fiedler of Laika says. 'I'm kind of weird that way. I really, really loved it. I love travelling and I love going places. I like staying in hotels. You don't have to make your bed and the towels are always clean. I do like playing live, although singing was always kind of difficult with Moonshake. We were quite loud, and I could never really hear myself. But it's gotten better over the years [with Laika]. I do really like it and, even when you have a shit gig, it's fine, you've got another one tomorrow.'

Laika had been conspicuously quiet since 1994's *Silver Apples Of The Moon*, which, considering its complexity, had come out remarkably soon after Moonshake had been guillotined. 'Sometimes I don't like the open-endedness of writing,' Fiedler explains of this period. 'It's *so* open-ended that I can shut down. I find it very difficult to write lyrics.' It would be 1997 before the next Laika record, *Sounds Of The Satellites*, emerged.

In the interim, Fiedler and Guy Fixsen—who were 'partners as well as a band, it was quite 24/7'—had been exploring home recording. This, as with others, led to an emphasis on introspection and fastidiousness, ultimately resulting in less, but a more precise *less*. 'We're not as dense now,' Fiedler said in 1997. 'One of the things we're trying to do on this new one [*Sounds Of The Satellites*] is to make more with less, just because I think half of the things we did on *Silver Apples* you can't even hear. We've spent more time trying to get the right thing, rather than building up the right thing over a period of time.'

The restraint and deliberation of the album is also there in Fiedler's lyrics. 'Breather'—'dead dreams dropping off the heart, like leaves in a dry season'—sums that feeling up, balancing mortality with a relentless, but not unsympathetic, percussive drive.

Laika's emphasis on rhythm and interest in micro-progress through repetition seems to reflect (at least in part) some of the ways Fiedler learned music from the youngest of young ages. 'The Suzuki Method,' she says. 'It does teach children as young as three the basics of cello, violin, and viola. It teaches you rhythm, and you start out playing "Twinkle Twinkle Little Star". That's the first thing you learn. And then as soon as you learn it, you do a concert in a group for your parents. You have this constant feedback, and performance, and it's not about soloing at *all*. Ever. They would never do that to small children. And then you do "Twinkle Twinkle Little Star" with eighth notes, and sixteenth notes, and do it with different rhythms, and stuff like that. But it's still "Twinkle Twinkle Little Star".'

Laika used a sci-fi smelt of programming and live instruments, but it conveyed more of a humanist-futurist concord and less of a brutal technological master/flesh slave dichotomy. However, the threat of electronic malignancy felt like a constant undercurrent, sometimes becoming blatant: 'Badtimes', on their next album, 2001's *Good Looking Blues*, details a malevolent email virus—one that quickly progresses from rewriting your hard drive to kicking your dog.

'This album [*Good Looking Blues*] in particular is much more like what we did live,' Fiedler said at the time of its release. 'It's something we've been meaning to do ever since we started, which was to play the songs live before going into the studio. I know it sounds like a very normal thing in terms of a rock band, but for a band that incorporates more electronic stuff, it tends to be that you make a very electronic album and then figure out how to do it live.'

What Laika did with *Good Looking Blues* was to record a programmed version of the songs first, play them live, and then bring them back to the home studio and re-record everything based on those live versions. 'Live, there was always more guitar,' Fiedler now says. 'Simply because it is a live instrument, it's more visceral. And we never, ever had a laptop on stage. Ever. I just won't do it. All the sampling was always triggered live.'

This was a time-consuming process, Fiedler says; there were also 'life things' happening at the time. 'Guy's mother died while we were making our third album. There was more of that started coming into our lives. Shit started happening.' Laika would release one more album—*Wherever I Am I Am What Is Missing*—although not until 2003. Fixsen and Fiedler's romantic relationship had ended by then. 'It was pretty painful,' she says. 'In theory, we were supposed to keep working together, but we weren't really making any money. It had sort of run its course.'

Seefeel, unsurprisingly, also ended. 'There was never a break-up as such,' Mark Clifford says. 'We never sat in a room and said, *This is it*.'

As a favour to their friend Aphex Twin, the following year Seefeel released (*CH-VOX*) on his Rephlex label ('it's just an EP of outtakes, really quite skeletal tracks from the *Succour* sessions,' says Clifford); by this time, however, Sarah Peacock, Daren Seymour, and Justin Fletcher had already teamed up again with Mark Van Hoen, Seefeel's first bassist, in Scala. Clifford remained at Warp, recording as Disjecta and, later, in a duo with Mira Calix (cliffordandcalix). Seefeel actually did demo some new tracks in 1997 and 1999, but Clifford claims they were 'just pastiches of what we'd done before'; nothing new came out until 2010, when Clifford and Peacock re-found their enjoyment in working with one another for *Seefeel.*

'Back then, it was like life and death,' says Peacock. 'I really felt like I was having my dream taken away from me. I wanted to write music and I didn't want to just be the singer. I didn't want to be the token girl at the front, singing. It felt like I had nothing else. We all wanted so much for it to succeed. We loved the music, we loved what we did. You're onstage and you see people grooving, and then they come up afterwards and tell you how much they loved it, and that's why you do it.'

Like Clifford, Robert Hampson was another artist who preferred the recording process behind closed doors. 'When I started Main, I insisted to my record company and also to my management that I needed my own studio,' he has said. 'Because I *did* want to take a lot longer … I'm very meticulous and very particular about what I do, and it does take a long time—which is something that I hope you can hear in the music. It's something that's had a lot of time spent on it, it's not something which has been knocked out in an afternoon. So it was very important to me to have my own studio, and ever since then I've never looked back.'

To start Main, Robert Hampson called time on his psychedelic band Loop in 1991; coincidentally, this was the same year that Spacemen 3 degenerated into civil war. The two groups had *not* gotten on. Asked in 1988 whether there was a link between Spacemen 3 and Loop, Sonic Boom replied, 'Of course! How can a band take another's music, right down to their record sleeves and things they say in interviews, and not expect there to be a link? They've gone out of their way to make a link. They're different, sure, but not enough to matter.'

'We find the whole scenario quite hilarious actually,' Robert Hampson claimed, somewhat unconvincingly, in 1990.

Internecine drone squabbles aside, both Sonic Boom and Hampson found themselves—again—in curiously similar territory once their respective groups ended. Hampson has said he felt Loop had 'exhausted all the ideas of what we could possibly do'; Main was conceived to push 'guitars to the point where it really was like, well, we don't know whether that was a guitar or not'.

'I just got bored of normal guitar,' Sonic Boom said of Experimental Audio Research (or EAR), which began in 1990. 'I mean, I love the guitar, but I just got bored with using it as a purely melodic instrument.' Sonic Boom kept his Spectrum alias for melodic and structured works; and, although the lines might smudge, he ringfenced EAR for experimental purposes.

EAR was the child of Sonic Boom, but it was always intended as an collaborative project; it quickly brought in My Bloody Valentine's Kevin Shields, AMM's Eddie Prévost, and Kevin Martin. Improvisation was the foundation of EAR, and this was not something Sonic Boom had had much experience of.

'The only improvisation I'd done before was in this club we [he and Jason Pierce] called the Reverberation Club in Rugby from about late '85 to mid '87, this thing we'd call freeform freakouts,' he recalled, 'where we'd take everything that you could bash, drag, pluck or whatever, and deposit them in a room.' This hippie-esque attitude to improv was in sharp contrast to the work of Prévost in AMM, where self-discipline had been as much of a priority as openness to experiment.

Sonic Boom acknowledged that he found that EAR 'flows a lot easier than actually having to write songs', and this was perhaps one reason why little happened in EAR's music. Sometimes there was a central concept on an album or EP, like the infiniteness of space in homage to the BBC Radiophonic Workshop (1996's *Phenomena 256*), or the circuit-bent Speak & Spell machine (2000's *Data Rape*). EAR's themes seemed to broadly relate to a machine's unblinking eye, and how humans might disrupt it.

Despite Robert Hampson's home studio, the early Main records were made without computers. Instead, Hampson took his whacking great twenty-four-track and exploited equalization (or EQing) in his setup to get the elevating interplay of, for example, 'Core' on 1994's *Motion Pool.*

'The way that the clarity and the separation of these sounds is achieved is through really meticulous EQing,' he has said. 'It was all done with parametric EQing on a mixing desk.' Hampson would make five or six versions of each Main track and then pick his favourite.

'We deliberately made *Motion Pool* to be half and half,' Hampson has said. 'It was the tail end of that very abstract song approach [in Loop], and then the rest of that was basically blowing that out of the water. It was a very definite and deliberate statement. I said to our then manager and record company, This is what it's going to be. It's literally the tail-end of what people know, and then it's a whole new ballgame after that.'

It felt logical that Main's guitar sound was in the process of becoming so blanched and wrecked that it would soon vanish completely. Main's conscious project to dissolve the guitar suggested that post-rock really *had* fulfilled a sort of evolutionary destiny; that it wasn't a genre tag with a definable sound but a way to hasten rock's extinction. *Firmament III*, released two years after *Motion Pool*, was almost a dramatisation of it. The record begins with an acid rain flash flood, one to warp circuits and burn flesh; the rest deals with the vapourous aftermath.

'The guitar finally went around *Firmament IV* when Scott Dawson [another former member of Loop] left and I really couldn't think of anything else to do with it,' Hampson has said. 'I just wasn't interested anymore. The more [*musique*] *concrète* and electroacoustic and field recording material had become much more prominent—it was a natural progression for me as I had just done everything I could.'

As for Justin Broadrick and Kevin Martin, they too saw Techno Animal and their other project, Ice (with two members of Terminal Cheesecake), as very distinct from their previous bands. Broadrick and Martin were becoming more enamoured with 'non-structural' music—dub, *musique concrète*, hip-hop. 'We wanted freedom to move and to express,' Martin has said. 'Bands can be really restrictive—both in good and bad ways.' Both Techno Animal and Ice were formed with no intent to perform live. Techno Animal was conceived of as a fully sampled-based project; Ice as half samples, half live playing.

Techno Animal started with *Ghosts*, released in 1991. '[*Ghosts*] was a direct reaction to the way we had been talked about in the press and all the shows we'd play where people would be shouting at us to turn it up,' Martin has said. 'That's why *Ghosts* has tracks at the other end of the spectrum, near silence. We thought, let's play it more psychologically.'

Techno Animal's most convoluted concept was 1998's *Techno Animal Versus Reality*, rooted in the culture of Jamaican DJ soundclashes. Five artists (Tortoise, Ui, Spectre, Porter Ricks, and Alec Empire) sent sound sketches to Techno Animal, who then created 'original' tracks from them. These versions were *then* sent back to the five artists, who remixed their own mangled work. Both the Techno Animal 'originals', and the artist remixes, were included.

Techno Animal, and Ice, were not well understood by their label paymasters, and were 'dropped almost album by album', Martin has said. It was particularly acute with Ice. Their debut, *Under The Skin*, was a kind of free-jazz, glum grindcore Public Image Ltd take on hip-hop; their second, *Bad Blood*, had its bastard sound hijacked by a series of vocalists, including underground rapper El-P (who would collaborate again with Martin and Broadrick on Techno Animal's *The Brotherhood Of The Bomb* in 2001). Rather than simply overlay a rapper onto a predetermined sound, however, Ice embedded hip-hop in the music, making use of Scott Harding, who had engineered Gravediggaz, Wu-Tang Clan, and Jungle Brothers. Still, making a hip-hop album was never really the aim. 'I was fucking with the backing tracks, making it more of a dub album,' Martin has said of *Bad Blood*. 'The label hated it and dropped us; and a lot of the musicians still hate it.'

'We had to find our own voice, and we found it through technology,' Broadrick said in 2001. 'That was our mission, to go past the conventional acoustic instrumentation that we'd both been brought up with. We were fascinated with the possibilities of technology but we wanted to mutilate it the same way we mutilated both rock and jazz, respectively.'

Kevin Martin was also a journalist. He wrote for *The Wire*, and it was he and colleague Biba Kopf who used the term 'isolationism' to characterise sounds that took from communal or community music—dub, hip-hop, even muzak—and ruthlessly stripped it off any sense of pleasure in the company of others. ('I dunno about that,' Main's Robert Hampson commented of isolationism in 1993, 'but I do feel isolated musically. Rock is getting really stale again.')

In 1994, Martin curated the compilation *Ambient 4: Isolationism* for Virgin Records, and used it to further develop its meaning. 'Dropping inwards instead of reaching out, this compilation's furtive music sounds as paranoiac as it does panoramic, and is in direct contrast to its mellow relative,' he wrote. 'Where New Ambient seeks to avoid discomfort, this Isolationist strain uses the studio as a monastic retreat to encourage self-confrontation.' *Isolationism* of course includes Techno Animal, Scorn (and Harris's other Ambient project, Lull), Seefeel, EAR, and Main. It also includes Jim O'Rourke and another American act, Labradford.

Joel Leoschke heard Labradford's first single, 'Everlast' / 'Preserve The Sound Outside', while working at Cargo distribution in Chicago. It struck him that here was a group standing almost wholly outside the conventions of indie-rock, having more in common with modern classical and minimalist electronica. The single had him so enthralled that it corralled him and his colleague, Bruce Adams, into implementing an idea that had been idly floating around for a good few years: starting a record label. 'There were no pre-formed ideas as to what the label would sound like, but it quickly developed into the intersection of the tastes that Bruce and I shared,' says Leoschke. Adams and Leoschke's new label, kranky (so named for Leoschke's temperament) released the debut album by Labradford as its first shot. *Prazision* was beatless and tenebrous, a secret dungeon of damp walls and forgetting.

Labradford grew from a kind of voluntary confinement and contemplation. Mark Nelson, Labradford's founder, spent hours sitting under a bridge in his hometown of Richmond, Virginia. It would be late at night, the undergrowth would squelch beneath him, and he listened to the sound of the traffic overhead. Maybe a band that sounded like that traffic, filtered through the bridge and his head, might be a good idea?

Nelson's friend Carter Brown, a church organist and a scholar of early classical music, was initially unconvinced but nonetheless strapped on his Moog and gave it a go. Labradford started out as improvisers, but after a few early gigs they soon put more emphasis on structure. Whenever Nelson's vocals appeared, they were a barely-there exhalation, condensing in the night air. The tracks on *Prazision*, taken together, form a woozy sea of sound.

'I wouldn't term our music "isolationist" so much as "introspective",' Mark Nelson said in 1995. 'The line of questioning always comes up. *Why do you make such dark music?* We don't see it as dark at all. It's strange that introspection is viewed as something depressing and melancholy.'

Nelson was right; such was the nature of the music press that extroversion was mostly valued and introversion overlooked. Post-rock artists felt this keenly, since they seldom shouted about how great they were; they could be chronically insecure and/or shy, and they also tended to be suspicious of hype. Even Simon Reynolds, who had proved his integrity time and time again to artists, nearly gave up when speaking to the reticent and self-effacing Tortoise in 1996. 'There were times during this interview when I'd have gladly traded my left leg to be interviewing any old bunch of Camden-based media-whore chancers, just for some rentaquote action,' he wrote. It therefore wasn't surprising that Labradford's extremely contemplative nature was, at the start, misunderstood as despondency.

Following *Prazision*, kranky became an ongoing concern. The label 'admired groups that were self-starters', Leoschke says, and its early releases reflect this: as well as Labradford having already put out a record, Jessamine and Bowery Electric had both self-released 7inch singles prior to their self-titled albums on kranky. It was also, and continues to be, a label that ardently dislikes the term post-rock. 'I abhor all attempts at grouping disparate artists together with tags because the minute some genre has been vaguely defined the phrase almost immediately becomes meaningless,' Leoschke says.

For their second album, *A Stable Reference*, Labradford added Robert Donne as a bassist. Donne had recently been in Breadwinner, a well loved and highly regarded 'math-rock' group (despite their tiny output of nine tracks). Theirs was a muscular and stressed sound, with the bass a firm weapon of tense attack; the addition of Donne's playing to something as drifting as Labradford was unexpected, but it was absolutely the right decision. 'We added a bassist because it would force a change,' Brown has said. 'With just me and Mark playing, we were so conscious of filling as much space as possible.' *A Stable Reference* had an almost sturdy feel to it; it was industrial music slowed and dissipated, losing the kinesis but keeping the power and perseverance.

Labradford also, notably, traded more in hope than other artists featured on Martin's *Isolationism* compilation. One song on *A Stable Reference*, 'El Lago', related to the space race—'a monument to the human spirit, a desire to see something fantastical,' Nelson has said. It was moments such as these that linked Labradford to their spacier companions on kranky, such as Jessamine.

The name Stars Of The Lid, another group to release albums on kranky, certainly also suggests a fascination for the astral. As did the manner of their connection with the label. 'I contacted Adam Wiltzie of the duo telepathically, and asked him to get in touch after I had heard their first album,' Leoschke says. 'True story.'

However, the droney Stars Of The Lid were less about the romance of space travel and more about soundtracking the small but grave shifts of galaxies burning up primordial hydrogen and moving toward extinction. 'What we do probably inspires some people to sit there and pay attention and wonder what's going on, but I'd hope that people would let go a little bit and just float downstream,' Brian McBride has said.

Stars Of The Lid formed in Austin, Texas, in the early 1990s. McBride and Wiltzie, like Labradford, were influenced by the minimalist Arvo Pärt and shared an ambient desire to slow processes of creation and of listening. McBride was a field recorder, hosting a college radio show where he integrated his own found minutiae over recorded work. *Music For Nitrous Oxide*, their first album, from 1995, includes sound art of all kinds, painstakingly mixed on a four-track, 'without keyboards', as the sleeve notes proudly state.

'We've always recorded at home,' Wiltzie has said. 'We're home recording kind of guys, 'cause we never had any money to record in studios. We've always had these old archaic four-track reel-to-reel cassette recorders that we recorded all of our stuff on 'cause that's all we could afford, and we made the best out of our predicament.'

Stars Of The Lid, Labradford, and Laika were at the lighter point of the post-rock/electronica/ambient nexus, but acts like Scorn and Techno Animal soundtracked a heart hardening and a pulse thinning. This music was pretty much *all* tension, with few moments of serenity. You were on your own, essentially; the instruments were intangible and there was no live expression. The physical community just wasn't there. It was a step further away even from post-rock's rejection of the band as a 'gang of mates' cliché.

There were a few difficulties with this approach. Firstly, a miserable ambient wash could provoke a kind of paralyzing wallow, particularly when the interplay of drums and bass was minimal (or completely absent). Secondly, the perceived lack of human agency could lead to music of dead frigidity, and a feeling that an abstract conceptual quest had been embraced at the expense of humanity. Perhaps all post- and no -rock could make Jack a dull boy—or at least a lonely one.

'I don't see anyone in Birmingham,' Mick Harris said in 1994. 'I don't go anywhere. I go to one dub club now and then. I keep myself to myself, have little involvement with people. Nick Bullen's the same. It has got a lot to do with things, the new album [*Evanescence*], how we feel with communication breakdown between people in Birmingham. We all fall out.'

'Working with technology,' Kevin Martin said in 1994, 'you become fond of machine time and fed up with the fallibility of human time.'

Main's disintegrating guitar, EAR's stasis, Techno Animal's apocalypse, Seefeel's change from optimism to nihilism: it all had a sense of finality to it. Even the way bands seemed to shrink, with the shedding of God members, and both Scorn and Main halving from duos to solo projects, felt forlorn. This was a post-rock endgame, where it had grown up and was now all alone in a barren landscape, because it had pushed too far and too quickly from the familiar.

CHAPTER FOURTEEN

young teams

'The best thing about the so-called post-rock thing was it had this brief moment where the concept of it was to make music that came from the indie scene but had no limitations. Any instrumentation would go, any song lengths, any format.' KIERAN HEBDEN, FRIDGE

'It was a really vibrant time. An exciting time,' says R.M. Hubbert—Hubby—a key player on the Glaswegian DIY scene of the 1990s, and a guitarist with El Hombre Trajeado. 'That realisation: why don't I just release my own records? or why don't I just put my own show on? We made our own zines. We had this really elaborate system for re-using stamps. Everyone did. And we would make up compilation tapes to give to people. We just set up our own system without realising it.'

As the first wave of Britpop ebbed, leaving its afterbirth of substandard follow-up albums and copyist bands, it seemed to spur evangelism within the UK underground of small labels, seven-inch singles, cross-promoting gigs, and *viva la punka* attitude. This new DIY was only united by its variety; its broad church had capacity enough for twisted pop, lo-fi mumblings, earnest wordsmiths—and new types of post-rock. These bands bore the imprint of A.R. Kane, of Tortoise, of Disco Inferno, of Slint, of Bark Psychosis. It was exhilarating and it was real. It was helped along firstly by fanzines, and then by the weekly music press who had picked up that something young and fresh was happening.

'In England, you could be completely crap, and you'd get booked, straight away,' says Kieran Hebden of Fridge. 'And you'd get in the *NME*. I remember Fridge opening for Elastica at the *NME* Awards or whatever—you'd just get booked for these things and it was so weird. We could barely keep our instruments in tune. I see the American thing, and think, these bands are *so* good, but they've got to prove themselves for three years before they can get going in any way. And in England you've got the opposite, where it's too quick, but you manage to capture that exciting, naïve moment.'

It also, usually, had a pro-active and defiantly local character, physically centered on enthusiast-run venues and record shops. This was certainly the case in Bristol. 'Roger Doughty, the guy who owned Revolver [Records] was a good teacher; he had an encyclopaedic knowledge of recorded music,' Matt Elliott of The Third Eye Foundation has said. Elliott worked at Revolver while he was still at Bristol's Cotham Grammar School; this meant that although he had a youthful zeal, he didn't have whole swathes of spare hours. More help was needed behind the counter.

In walked David Pearce. He was a country lad originally from Winchcombe in the Cotswolds, and he'd arrived at Bristol via art school in Cheltenham. Older than Elliott, Pearce had been involved in music for a while; he was part of the mid-80s group Ha Ha Ha and released their only single, 'Up & Down', on his own Hobby Horse imprint. More recently, he had been part of The Secret Garden while at art school. He got the job at Revolver and started working alongside Elliott.

'One day I went into the shop and there was this sort of racket playing,' Pearce has recalled. 'It sounded like badly recorded, very early Pussy Galore. I said, Oh blimey, what's this then? Matt [Elliott] said, It's our band practice I was telling you about. And I just thought, I can understand these people. This makes sense.'

The band in question was Elliott and fellow Cotham Grammar pupils Kate Wright, Rachel Brook (now Rachel Coe), and brothers Matt and Sam Jones. Wright once tried to describe their musical endevours.

'We had a band called Linda's Strange Vacation which sounded …'

'… like snooker cues hitting snooker balls, because that was the only equipment we had,' Matt Jones added. 'We didn't have a snooker table, though—just cues and balls. Very peculiar.'

Wright reflected some more. 'We used to shout down big rolls of carpet. Or use plaster casts.'

Linda's Strange Vacation was named after an obscure midcentury work of French erotica, and the band was in the fine tradition of playful noise bands, combining musical seriousness with arty knockabout. They started with a broken Casio keyboard, a cheap microphone, and a guitar; other instruments and objects were added as and when. Linda's Strange Vacation rehearsed a lot and recorded some tapes but never played live. 'We were sort of insular and had a little laugh at everyone else,' Coe has said. 'We were very judgemental about music and decided somehow that we were gonna make music ourselves.'

David Pearce soon joined Linda's Strange Vacation as a drummer. It was a shortlived addition. '[Pearce] wanted to kind of direct the band and we all split into kind of factions after that,' Elliott has said. 'We started taking things more seriously, although it was all amicable, we all collaborated with each other for a few years.'

Meanwhile, Brook and Pearce had begun a relationship. They spent a lot of time in Pearce's bedsit listening to records. Pearce liked then-obscure psychedelic folk such as COB, Comus, Pearls Before Swine; he had also come to a Nick Drake obsession via Loop's cover of 'Pink Moon'. '[It was] just Robert Hampson singing and an acoustic guitar, which he put a fucking repeat echo on to make it sound a bit drifty,' Pearce said in 2015. 'I don't think I realised until recently what a primary influence that was on me.'

However, Pearce *did* know at the time how much he appreciated A.R. Kane. 'When *Up Home!* came out, I thought, yes, this signals the start of something new,' he said in 1995. 'It's the way that the guitars had these free, random elements running against the structure. It was liberating to listen to, and yet there was such beauty of sound. I felt, wow, there is still work to be done with the electric guitar.'

One day in 1992, Pearce was 'round at Rachel's house, and her brother had just bought a Portastudio … a couple of hours later, the "Soaring High" single was born, although we never expected it to be a single at the time. Flying Saucer Attack is all an accident really. I had a whole load of songs and a whole load of ideas but I didn't know what to do with them or even if I wanted to do anything.'

Later, Pearce revised this perception a little. 'I had an idea in my mind of what the ideal band should sound like,' he said in 2015, 'but that was based on what little experience I had of life. I had an idea about this band that it should be VERY loud when it was loud, and hauntingly quiet when it was quiet. But my capabilities at that time extended to just about being able to hang in there on the bass and also personally being a bit of a pain.'

Pearce—as FSA records—self-released 'Soaring High', backed with 'Standing Stone', in 1993. It came in a photocopied sleeve with a fanzine-esque booklet in which he railed against 'clean' sound. 'Due to the perilous "wall of sludge" approach used in this recording, it has proven impossible to get an accurate cut off the original master cassette … (it's the only way to get *that* sound!) so, please adjust the volume to your ear.' Pearce would become known for his antipathy to digital recording and reproduction. 'Compact discs are a major cause of breakdown in our society,' ran the slogan on the CD version of 1993's *Flying Saucer Attack*.

'My problem with computers is … you seem to say that the digital way is the only way,' he said in 2001. 'I still can't agree with that. In music, there's a bit of a place for that. But there's still a place for the old-fashioned approach. The thing is you always have to adopt an apologist's position, and sometimes it doesn't have to be done digitally because the texture, either pictorially or soundwise, the digital way is different to the analogue way.'

Pearce was becoming more monomaniacal as regards Flying Saucer

Attack, and his partner was drifting away. 'I always felt I wasn't fulfilling myself in [Flying Saucer Attack],' Rachel Coe has said, 'and eventually I was just like, right, I am not doing any of this and we're not together, and that was that.'

'We were inspired by Sonic Youth, The Velvet Underground, Galaxie 500, and My Bloody Valentine, but also, for me, it was the Beat poets,' Kate Wright has said of the band she, Coe, Elliott, and the Jones brothers developed: Movietone. There was also jazz (the sleeve of Movietone's first single, 'She Smiled Mandarine Like' / 'Orange Zero', was a deliberate homage to the Blue Note label's artwork), and they also retained slivers of Linda's Strange Vacation's gung-ho am-dram.

'We'd recorded a song ['Mono Valley'] for the first album where we smashed bottles in a dustbin, and we tried to recreate that on stage,' Coe has said. Movietone had been invited to play the Sausage Machine (still being run by Too Pure); it was to be their London debut. 'We had all these dustbins, loads of bottles. And also Kate's mum had an old piano that we dismantled and took the frame out [of]. It was amazingly heavy and we took it to London. It all just fed back. We had no idea how to make things sound good, let alone the back of a piano.'

The first three Movietone singles and their debut album were all released on Bristol's Planet Records, alongside Flying Saucer Attack's 'Beach Red Lullaby' and various releases by Crescent (the other band of the Jones brothers). 'PLANET RECORDS IS COOL' was the legend heading up their 1995 list of releases. 'Correspondence only possible with SAE, otherwise tempers may flare.' Eventually, all these artists would release records on bigger labels—Domino, FatCat, Drag City—but the local Planet experience, run by Richard King and James Webster out of the back of Revolver, gave them essential nurture and shelter. It was an enclave from indie norms and sales pressure alike.

Bristol wasn't the only city that yearned for this. 'The only original music that was really happening [in Glasgow] in the late 80s, early 90s, was a kind of shit white-boy soul,' says Hubby. 'There had been things like Teenage Fanclub, but we weren't connected to that in any way. And there was nowhere for young, small bands to play and learn.'

A self-taught guitarist, Hubby was one-third of Me, Hubby & Thom. 'When we started, we were pretty shit,' Hubby says. 'But we were doing something a wee bit different.' The titular Thom—Thom Falls—was also in a band called The Blisters, with Alex Kapranos (known then as Alex Huntley, later of Franz Ferdinand). 'We were all friendly because we all practised in Thom's basement,' says Hubby. 'I think Alex had found out about a Tuesday night thing, a very DIY-friendly thing, that went on in this place [the Bogle Stone, soon to be renamed the 13th Note]. The guy that was there booked The Blisters for a show, their first or second gig. We all went down to see them. While we were there, we said, Thom's in another band, can we play next week? So the week after that there was The Blisters, and there was Me, Hubby & Thom. And then the guy running the night quit, on that very night. He'd been doing it for a while, and because nobody went to this club, he wasn't really getting paid much. So he quit and he said to us, Do you guys want to do this night instead? We said, Yes! Yes!'

Kapranos booked the bands; Hubby taught himself how to do the sound. They named their night the Kazoo Club. 'The booking policy was, anyone could play as long as they weren't morally offensive to us. So it started attracting all the other weirdos. It became a place where we could go and play, and fuck about, and basically play to the other bands. It became a scene where we helped each other,'

'I remember there being an almost defiant amateurism about the Kazoo Club,' says Stevie Jones (the 'Me' in Me, Hubby & Thom). 'The bands weren't slick. I don't ever remember there being a *sound*. It was wildly diverse. Folk were supporting it, and into it, and enjoying that variety.'

'I knew Alex,' says Stuart Braithwaite. 'When Mogwai started, he was the only guy who'd give us a gig.'

'I used to share a flat with Kanie, who I was in Eska with, and Geraldine, who was in Pink Kross,' Braithwaite continues. 'All the windows of the corner shop used to get smashed every weekend. But it, the music scene, felt like an oasis from normal Glasgow life. That's what everyone was doing, making their own sevens, doing their own fanzines. I actually started one but I was too lazy to finish it. I'd say I had a fanzine, though, to get into gigs for free.'

Mogwai formed in 1995. Braithwaite and Dominic Aitchison got on well, and when it became obvious that their current respective bands were moribund, the pair hung out, wrote songs, and got a temporary drummer to pitch in for a demo. It seemed clear, quite early on, that Mogwai was worth developing, so they recruited a friend of a friend from Braithwaite's old school, Martin Bulloch, on drums, and then—following a few shows at the Kazoo Club—John Cummings joined on second guitar. They rehearsed in Bulloch's bedroom.

'It might have been "New Paths To Helicon",' Braithwaite recalls. 'I remember us all playing, we'd play so loud, [Bulloch] had these jars of change that would just glide along the floor because we were playing so loud. And I remember having a bit of a moment thinking, *actually, this is quite good*.'

The first song Mogwai wrote was 'Summer'; the first seven-inch they released was 'Tuner' / 'Lower'; and one of Braithwaite's favourites, to this day, is their second single, 'Angels Vs Aliens'. 'I still really like it,' he says. 'It's a weird song and again it goes back to the whole, how did *that* happen? Starting playing a drum at the end. It's definitely full of youthful exuberance.' These three—plus the next two singles—were all seven-inches, all issued on different tiny labels.

The Kazoo Club, meanwhile, had branched out into releasing records. 'There's an album called *The Kazoo Collection*,' Hubby says. 'We basically recorded a weekend of live music at the Kazoo Club, with all the bands that were involved in that scene. I believe that Alex had most of *The Kazoo Collection* destroyed. And I would fucking help him. It's a terrible record.' Afterwards, Hubby started a label, Flotsam & Jetsam (releasing, among other things, the fifth Mogwai seven-inch, a live version of 'Stereo Dee').

'There were lots of people around that time starting to release their own seven-inches,' Hubby says. 'We found a pressing plant in the Czech

Republic. You could get five hundred singles for three hundred quid. You didn't get a test pressing, and sometimes it looked wonky. But they *were* really cheap.'

Glasgow's premier DIY label at that time was Chemikal Underground, founded in February 1995 by the band The Delgados, who released their own 'Monica Webster' as the inaugural seven-inch. 'We always had big ideas for Chemikal Underground,' Delgados drummer Paul Savage has said. 'We just used ourselves as guinea pigs. We wanted to see if we were capable of putting out our own stuff before we fucked up some other band's career.'

In fact, it was the opposite: CHEM 003 turned out to be a hit record. Bis's 'Kandy Pop' (from *The Secret Vampire Soundtrack* EP) reached number 25 in the UK charts, and was a strong indicator that an authentic DIY approach was indeed capable of crossing over into mainstream consciousness.

'Chemikal Underground were really, really good to us,' says Hubby. 'We'd been friends since the Kazoo Club and the 13th Note. One of my favourite 13th Note moments was when an absolutely pished Emma Pollock [of The Delgados], in 1995 or so, was like, *we just signed our second band ... it's these two mental guys from Falkirk, and I'm kind of terrified of them*. And it was Arab Strap.'

'These people are a disgrace to Falkirk, and everything they say about our town is wrong,' the leader of the local council said of Arab Strap in 1998. It was little wonder that Arab Strap attracted such approbation from a local councilor. Their music was a kind of Falkirk dispatch about the crusty stains left behind by provincial misery; it combined the emotional chill of Codeine with the everyday foulmouthed hostility of Big Black. Still, within their hangovers and battered romance, there was also a pop edge that seemed to draw from Tears For Fears, even The Human League. 'I think Arab Strap were victims of our time,' guitarist Malcolm Middleton has said. 'Me and Aidan [Moffat] had always grown up listening to really accessible music, but the actual climate we came out in was all lo-fi and American, stuff like Smog. That's why we sounded like we did.'

Glasgow, like Bristol, had a strong record-shop culture acting as a focal point for the initiated, particularly the second floor of John Smith & Son on Byres Road. Run by Stephen McRobbie of The Pastels, it would stock all the seven-inches from local labels such as Vesuvius, Flotsam & Jetsam, Modern Independent, Chemikal Underground; plus carry other small-scale releases from the UK and beyond. Some British labels had started to release one-off seven-inches by American artists, too, hastening along the exchange of ideas.

'I would go into Rough Trade Covent Garden,' says the London-based Kieran Hebden, 'and there were two guys working there: one ran this label Soul Static Sound, and another guy ran another label, Lissy's. And they released a record by Tortoise ["Why We Fight"], and one by The Sea & Cake ["Glad You're Right"]. We went in there, and they were on the wall and everything. These records look really odd and kind of different, and I get them, and they're the weirdest things I ever heard!'

Hebden and his friends Sam Jeffers and Adem Ilhan attended the liberal Elliott School in Putney. 'There were lots of bands,' Hebden says. 'Everybody was playing music at the school. Not because there was a good music department or anything like that, but because there were these rehearsal rooms, and we were just allowed to use them when we wanted.' Hebden had learned to play guitar in his early teens, and Fridge 'was the first band I'd ever formed where we decided we wanted to be in a band together because we liked the same type of music. Sam had never even really played drums, but at the time he did it because he wanted to'.

The type of music Fridge liked *was* the American end of things, but they also followed more scrappy British efforts. 'We discovered these promoters in London called Piao!—they're putting on a night somewhere with a band we like, and there's another band in that line-up called Quickspace Supersport.'

'I think being in Quickspace is a bit like doing a play and everybody's left their scripts at home,' vocalist and violinist Wendy Harper said in 1995. 'Everybody remembers it was a pretty good story, but you have to make it up as you go along.'

Quickspace Supersport formed at the very end of 1994 when Tom Cullinan—fresh from the break-up of Th' Faith Healers—and Harper met at a Christmas party. They had a label, Kitty Kitty, and put out their own singles; the seven-inches were sometimes festooned with tracing sheets or real wallpaper. There was a fair amount of press interest in them; the *NME* even, astonishingly, revived the Camden Lurch label for them (albeit suggesting it should now be called the Camden *Waft*, in deference to the more nebulous nature of Quickspace Supersport's music). They shared Th' Faith Healers' brink-of-collapse aura but incorporated repetition, a male/female vocal tension, and a *motorik* groove. 'Superplus', released in 1995, was their defining track; guitarist Barry Stillwell accurately claimed that it 'stays in the same place for ages and finishes in a bloody mess.'

'They were absolutely life-changing,' says Hebden, about Quickspace Supersport. 'They had a female singer, and two guitar players, and someone who just played analogue synths, which is kind of unusual as far as I'm concerned at that point. You've got to bear in mind I'd never heard Stereolab—even though Stereolab were going, *I* hadn't found them. But I'd found this band Quickspace Supersport, and they're playing twenty-minute krautrock-influenced things, and they have bizarre visuals. I saw them every single time I possibly could. They started releasing a few seven-inches, and this is the blueprint for what Fridge was interested in. Those messages: you can play records that you can't tell what speed it's meant to be played at, because it sounds good at both speeds. You can make records with no singing on. I didn't admit it to myself at the time, but I'm sure I was watching and thinking, *I could be part of this. This is obtainable.*'

Quickspace Supersport lasted barely a year. Three members—Harper, Stillwell, and drummer Max Corradi—left in a row over money and labels ('Bunch of cunts,' ranted Cullinan during a drunken interview in 1996). The new line-up, name shortened to Quickspace, went on to release several more singles and albums, characterised by a more guitar-oriented sound.

'I made a cassette tape of what I consider the *real* Quickspace

Supersport,' says Hebden. 'The new people they got in, the technical ability went down, and it lost something.'

Quickspace Supersport felt like a late-entry continuation of the 1992–1994 British post-rock scene. They had a bargain-bin early Stereolab aesthetic, a first generation Moonshake interaction, and they especially channeled a Pram-esque *la-la-la* sadistic glee. This was also true of fellow Kitty Kitty artists Novak, with their dubbed-down, sample-surfing 'Rapunzel' single from 1997, and Miss Mend's 'Living City Plan' (also released on the Piao! label and featuring former Stereolab / Th' Faith Healers drummer Joe Dilworth). Pram, too, were still going—a rare survivor from the 1994 carnage—consistently releasing records that were at least interesting.

Fridge were rehearsing at school, and soaking up their new influences. 'We've gone from where it's like guitar, bass, and drums, but now we're starting to try things,' Hebden says. 'We've got a walkman with recordings from TV, and we're playing that through effects pedals. We're playing these really long songs. And we're starting to do our first ever gigs, which would be at school assembly, and the Elliott [School] Summer Carnival. We're getting up and playing with ten-minute drones at these events. I was super-weird at that point, all my fingernails would be painted different colours and I'd wear women's clothes. At our school there was no uniform, so I'd turn up and be dressing as bizarre as I possibly could.'

They made a demo tape, and via a felicitous meeting with Luke Hannam—of the Acid Jazz-signed band Emperor's New Clothes—it found its way to Trevor Jackson, then making records under the name Underdog. Jackson was just starting up a label, Output. 'Trevor says, Well, what do you need? How can we make this happen? We'd never been in a recording studio or anything at this point. I'm like, well, I think we need some sort of multi-track recorder, and we need some microphones, and like a reverb unit. And he just arranged this with a rental company, to have all this stuff delivered to Sam's parents' house.'

Fridge put the lot into Jeffers's bedroom, upending the bed to make room. 'Then we just get in there, we make our first album [*Ceefax*] with this equipment that we'd learned to use by getting the manuals out. I think we'd got five days or something, and we recorded our first album and our first single ["Lojen"] in the summer holidays in the middle of our A-levels. The first record literally is recorded on cassette tape in a bedroom by these three seventeen-year-olds, learning how to use the equipment as we go along.'

From then, Fridge started to play the London indie toilet circuit: the Camden Monarch, the Laurel Tree, the Dublin Castle. 'We've got no money at all, we can't buy any equipment, we're really, really young,' Hebden continues. 'All our families are getting involved. Adem's grandfather, or my dad, is driving us to the gigs with all the equipment. We can't afford any synthesizers; we've got these children's synths and stuff. My dad used to go to car boot sales quite a lot, and he'd find amplifiers and things. One of the guitars we had was an old ILEA [Inner London Education Authority] one, from the 1970s, that the school had given me.'

Adem had also acquired eight school-issued antiquated cassette recorders. 'He decided if he recorded one droning note on each one, he could make like a keyboard where you played notes from the tape. And he had the eight tape recorders and they were all strapped onto an ironing board. We arrived at the Laurel Tree with this homemade thing, and he put microphones over them and it would drone away as he stopped and started the tapes. It sounded kind of good. But there are these eight things, with eight plugs. We put them all into the four-way, and we plugged this thing into the Laurel Tree and it blew the fuse on the whole venue.'

It seemed the challenge of performing post-rock live in an atmosphere that was practically and philosophically ill equipped to deal with it hadn't really gone away. 'Dave [Pearce]'s drones were very calm and introspective, with lots of space,' Sam Jones has said of Flying Saucer Attack, with whom he performed live. 'But when you have some young people on the stage and they're not pinned down to a regimented thing they have to reproduce, you end up with a big noise that's sort of belted out.' Evidence of this comes with the Flying Saucer Attack album *In Search Of Spaces*. As with Sonic Youth's *Sonic Death*, this was an unbroken and title-free live collage, collecting globules of performance mud from 1994 and splicing them together (without the aid of computers, naturally) to create a dirty eddy of guitar squall.

Mogwai, however, were different, right from their earliest gigs; their change-jar-shaking music filled small venues and, before very long, graduated to bigger ones. The tracks, too, were lengthening and gaining a self-conscious epic quality. 'I always liked long songs,' Braithwaite says. 'We always felt quite constrained by the seven-inches. So, as soon as we could have songs longer than four or five minutes, we kind of went to town a bit.' Their first Peel Session, recorded at the very end of 1996, opened up possibilities they hadn't thought of before, and was to have a profound effect.

'We were doing it in this massive orchestral room and the engineer, this guy Miti [Adhikari], was brilliant,' Braithwaite continues. 'He got into the orchestral side of what we'd been doing.' With shades of Talk Talk, Adhikari emphasised physical space, placing the microphones far away from the band. 'Miti said, I can hear Mahler in here, and he was just really getting into it. And no one had ever mentioned this stuff [to us] before, because we'd just been playing in bars.'

The songs on that Peel Session—'Superheroes Of BMX', 'Summer (Priority Version)', 'Waltz For Jo', and 'Mogwai Salute The Brilliance Of Steve Lamacq' [an instrumental version of 'R U Still In 2 It']—were a good indication of where Mogwai were heading.

They might have got there with their first album, *Mogwai Young Team*; they didn't. 'We were very rushed,' says Braithwaite, 'and we were still in a pretty hedonistic phase. We were getting drunk all the time and acting daft.' The band were stressed, doing too many festivals, too much press; concentration on the album was compromised. The track 'Tracy' depicts a fake argument between Braithwaite and Aitchison; although the specifics were false, the tense dynamic was all too believable.

Adding to the general chaos surrounding the recording of *Mogwai Young Team* was the recent addition of an extra member, Brendan

O'Hare. He had formerly been in Teenage Fanclub, but more importantly had been part of Telstar Ponies when they had recorded the episodic post-rock shimmer of 'Does Your Heart Have Wings?' Telstar Ponies also featured *Wire* writer David Keenan, experimental multi-instrumentalist Richard Youngs, and bassist Gavin Laird, who played with Rhys Chatham. 'When anyone ever compliments me on my past [with Teenage Fanclub], I just feel ... *dirty*,' he said in 1996. 'When people say they really like what I did then, I cringe. When I got to Telstar Ponies, I realised how fake and false my last situation was.'

O'Hare made his live debut with Mogwai in May 1997. 'We just thought Brendan was a great guy,' Dominic Aitchison reflected in 1999. 'A total laugh. He'd just get up in the morning and make sure we were completely pissed by the time it came to a gig. We were totally out of our faces every night. We thought we were playing the best gigs of our lives, but all Brendan was doing was taping down keys on his keyboard and putting poppers under girls' noses. We were just acting like total arseholes. All we ever did was drink.'

The final date of that tour was at London's Highbury Garage; by the end of the set, three guitars, a keyboard, and an amp were in ruins, destroyed by band and audience. O'Hare was finally ejected from the band after about a year when all these tensions reached a head. The final offence was his incessant chatter during an Arab Strap gig.

O'Hare contributed 'With Portfolio' to *Mogwai Young Team*, a delicate piano piece that morphs into an electronic cacophony. It is one of the more deconstructed moments on an album that too often relies on obvious signifiers in a short-cut to seeking an emotional response; nevertheless, 'Like Herod' and 'Mogwai Fear Satan' are awesome, slow-moving hulks, and the general air of innocence is appealing, especially on the much-misunderstood opening narration to 'Yes! I Am A Long Way From Home': 'Music is bigger than words and wider than pictures. If someone said that Mogwai are the stars I would not object. If the stars had a sound it would sound like this ... '

'That was a joke,' says Braithwaite. 'That was someone reading out a newspaper review that was so over-the-top that we just thought it was hilarious. And it became this mantra of how deep our music is. It's literally the opposite.' Similarly misconstrued was their use of *Mogwai Young Team* as a title, in reference to the terrifying Glasgow gang culture. 'We did an interview recently and someone asked us, So, what gangs were you in? and I was like, Look at us. Do you really think any gangs would want us? It was something we'd grown up around, so we referenced it, but not in a very serious way.'

Nevertheless, the Mogwai young team *did* feel like a rock group, a band of brothers: a gang in that sense. They shaved their heads for the making of *Mogwai Young Team*. They did not seem especially concerned, on that first album, with deconstructing rock music's hierarchies, erasing ego, or obfuscating the emotional centre of their music. Mogwai were the first major band to be tagged post-rock that unapologetically spoke the language of rock—a fact the band embraced.

'We're basically a rock'n'roll band,' Braithwaite said in 1997. 'We're an MC5 for the nineties. We just don't give a fuck about choruses. Or verses. Or bridges. Or notes.'

'We're more rock than half the bands that get in *Kerrang!*' Aithcison added.

'I think we were all a bit disappointed with *Mogwai Young Team*,' Braithwaite says now. 'I think we could have done better. We thought we could have written better songs. We *definitely* could have been better prepared. Because quite a lot of the *Mogwai Young Team* songs were written in the studio, written while the album was being recorded.' At the launch party for the album in 1997, Mogwai shut themselves in a toilet cubicle. They made a pact that the next album would be on a par with *White Light/White Heat* or *Spiderland*; if it was not, they wouldn't release it.

Meanwhile, as the early Fridge releases dropped—the album *Semaphore* followed *Ceefax*, also released on Trevor Jackson's label Output—they too dealt with some fairly intense press interest, and their shy charm was an asset.

'We were listening to a lot of lo-fi stuff when we started,' Hebden said to the *NME* in 1999, 'and my sister said, All these bands have stupid names, like Pavement. Why don't you give yourselves a crap name like "Fridge" or "Shelf"?'

'You could be talking to Shelf, right now,' added Ilhan.

The members of Fridge had left school. Hebden had gone to Manchester University to study computer science and maths. He used his student loan for a computer. 'We had been very limited by the equipment we had, and one of the things I couldn't do was sample anything. I couldn't afford a sampler; it was totally out of my reach. Suddenly I had a computer, and I could do that. At that point, I realised I had a million ideas to make electronic music that I'd never done, and that was when all the Four Tet stuff started.'

It was a strange time to be Hebden's student housemates. 'Suddenly, record companies are phoning up,' he says. 'I'd come home from college and there'd be notes on the wall, little stickers, saying Warp phoned. And then I remember Universal/MCA, calling up and offering Fridge a publishing deal, and me saying to them down the phone, *What's publishing?* It's all kind of crazy but I think that whole thing, the post-rock thing … why I think it was interesting is because of that naivitee. People wouldn't worry about it. People weren't worrying about *things*. It was very music-driven.'

Fridge eventually signed with the major label subsidiary Go! Beat. 'Because we'd just discovered jazz, we made quite a bonkers record for Go! Beat [1999's *Kinoshita Terasaka* EP] and we had all these ideas,' says Hebden. 'I remember, we had no management or anything, we just did everything ourselves, and I remember us going to meetings with them and us being, *we're going to do the album, we're going to do a single*, and they were, *well, which track on the album is the single?* And we were like, no we're not gonna use one of the tracks on the album. It'll be a separate single, because we've got a lot of music that we want to make and why would we release something twice? That was our thinking. The idea of doing *anything* that made it possible to promote a record didn't exist in our mentality. We saw it as if we release a single that's on the album, our fans will be completely pissed off, and they would think it was a rip-off if we released a song twice. We're not thinking about the fact that, at that point, we actually don't have any fans.'

Fridge stayed at Go! Beat for two EPs and the album *EPH*. The work was more sampler-oriented than their previous material, bringing in the experience Hebden was gaining in his Four Tet work. 'The roles in the band had evolved into this thing where Adem was this multi-instrumentalist that could write really great melodies, and things like that,' Hebden says. 'And I'd really got this producer type of role. I was going to make it sound a certain way and use all these tricks to get it to do certain things and work out how to record it all. And Sam's doing the drums, all the percussive stuff, and playing bits of synths. We were three people wanting to make the sound of fifteen people, and trying to do it with not enough decent equipment. We should have asked for help. We never asked anybody for help.'

Meanwhile, back up in Glasgow, Me, Hubby & Thom had petered out. In their place, Hubby and Stevie Jones, with Stef Sinclair on drums, formed El Hombre Trajeado. 'It was supposed to be a Spanish translation of "the man in the suit",' says Hubby. 'We all came from a really DIY, punk background, and we found it quite funny that we were in a band called "the man in the suit". I got a Spanish friend to translate it for me when she was really drunk. So I think it actually translates as "the suited man". We were just guitar, bass and drums in the first couple of years. The recordings of that really early stuff, it's very fast and very complicated. It's very jerky, and it's a lot weirder than the first album ended up being. Minutemen-type things. Quite technical but very aggressive.'

John Peel was interested in El Hombre Trajeado, and the band recorded the first of three Peel Sessions in 1998. 'I found out from somebody else who'd done a Peel Session that you actually get paid per member of the band,' Hubby says. 'At that time you'd get £120 per member. So we said, Shall we get Ben [Jones, Stevie's brother] to come down so we can get a wee bit extra money? It was a practical reason, but it sounded great, and he was in the band for the rest of the time.'

The addition of synthesizer—which Ben Jones played—made more explicit El Hombre Trajeado's links with 'dance music you can't dance to', as Hubby puts it. 'The idea was that the bass and drums were the main instruments, and the guitar should step back,' he says. 'It was all about the interplay between the drums and the bass. We started getting into a lot of Warp Records stuff, and Black Dog, and things like that. We started getting really interested in trying to emulate the structure and feel of those records, but within a traditional band set-up. We didn't want to make dance music. But we loved the intricacies you could produce in that stuff. It was very repetitive, but it develops in a subtle way. We liked that, and we liked the technical aspect of it, so the music started to move to that a lot more, which you can hear on *Saccade*, the second album, which uses a lot of electronics.'

Onstage, El Hombre Trajeado would employ live scratching, but 'we decided after the tour with Sebadoh never to do it again. I remember playing the Garage, in Glasgow, and basically the stage was too bouncy. Stevie and I used to jump about quite a lot, and every time we did it the decks would flip. We never had the most expensive gear so things would go wrong like that.'

El Hombre Trajeado would release three albums—the last, *Schlap*, was begun in 1999 but not finished and released until 2004. 'We had that great idea that bands have, that we didn't need to go and record it all in a studio. We could get a *home* studio and write, produce, do all the stuff ourselves,' says Hubby. 'Without the time constraint of a commercial studio we just fannied about. And we fannied about for four years. But the vast majority of El Hombre records were done at Chamber Records, with Jamie Watson, who we all really wanted to work with. He did the first Ganger album. And also the Long Fin Killie records. Long Fin Killie were a huge, huge influence on us.' Ganger were a krautrock-indebted act that had a Quickspace Supersport-style mass line-up change mid-career (and released their second EP, *The Cat's In The Bag*, on Bristol's Planet Records), while Long Fin Killie were a genre-shifting enigma, led by Luke Sutherland.

'What we would do is practise in this place called Jordanstone,'

Sutherland has said. 'There's this mansion house there owned by a lady by the title Lady Duncan of Jordanstone; she allows us to practise there in her stone-walled laundry, would you believe, in the heart of the Perthshire countryside for the last eight years. So what we basically do is go out there and jam, and we'll record these "grooves", if you like, and take out the bits we like best about them and hammer them into the shape of songs.'

Sutherland cited the Long Fin Killie track 'Heads Of Dead Surfers' on the debut album *Houdini* as emblematic of this method. 'The drums are vaguely tribal, vaguely hip-hoppish, classical-sounding violin, guitar that sounds like its sampled, bass that's played with a stick, three different types of voices. On paper it just sounds like junk basically, it's thrown together, but hopefully once it's arranged and set down and properly recorded you've got something coherent.'

Mogwai, despite their disappointment over *Mogwai Young Team*, came across in the late 1990s as confident, combative, competitive. 'Mogwai have always had an agenda,' Stuart Braithwaite said in 1999. 'It's simple really. We fucking hate everyone. I really believe in my heart that we're one of the punkest bands in the world. We deny convention and stand up against the system.' They were regarded as 'good copy' for journalists since, during this period, they were happy to pick fights with pretty much every band going.

'Loads of it was really stupid,' Braithwaite says now, 'but if you can't be stupid when you're young, when can you be? Like, I do remember one time, some guy from a band came up and said, Why are you slagging us off? and I said, I've never even heard your band. I'd just seen a CD on a journalist's table. Your band might be great; I've no idea. One of the reasons that the interviews were so ridiculous was because we were like teenagers, and people were buying us endless drinks. That was the motivating factor, and the reason for us talking so much crap.'

'I know those guys now,' says Kieran Hebden, 'but they slagged us off really badly in the beginning. They were on this mission to be anarchic.'

Mogwai's bravado peaked in the middle of 1999. 'I just really hated

Blur. I *really* hated them,' Braithwaite says. 'We were friends with the Super Furry Animals, and they were supporting Blur, so we went to see them. And in between the bands they had adverts for a bank. And we were all … wait a moment. This is not cool. This is not punk rock. Blur just seemed very contrived and business-oriented. It seemed the opposite of what we were into. To be fair, I think that over the years they kind of changed, and I know Damon Albarn does some really good stuff, he's done a lot of stuff promoting African music. They're not the worst. But, at that point, they *were* the worst!'

'The thing about the shirt is it's like a dictionary definition,' Braithwaite said in 1999, half-promoting, half-explaining the band's new T-shirt design: *Blur: are shite.* 'It's factual, and if there are any legal problems about it I'll go to court as someone who has studied music, so I can prove they are shite.'

'It wasn't even our idea,' says Braithwaite now. 'Our T-shirt girl, Valerie, said, What are the T-shirts for [Scottish festival] T In The Park? And she then just said, Write "Blur: are shite" hahahaha. And we did it. I don't think we expected there to be such a big fuss. Although why we didn't think there was going to be a big fuss, I've no idea. Again, we were young and naïve.'

'Basically, I think the band would say, It's a free country and everyone's entitled to their own opinion,' retorted a spokesperson for Blur.

Flying Saucer Attack had already—in a rather less direct fashion—criticised another Britpop-identified band, Suede, via their cover of 'The Drowners' in 1993. At the time, Pearce said, 'It wasn't a pisstake. I was just hacking around on a guitar and discovered that song has a really nice chord sequence—one that would sound good with a fair amount of extraneous noise.'

Later, Pearce disclosed a slightly different intent. 'The diplomatic thing to say is that I didn't entirely dislike their music, but it was really about this notion of announcing the best new band in Britain [Suede had been fêted as such by the *Melody Maker* in April 1992, before their debut single had even been released]. That seemed very strange. In retrospect, of course, that was the first attempted Britpop manoeuvre by the system. Up until that point, the idea of being the best new band in Britain was that they were going to make a racket like you've never heard before. That was the criteria for being the best new band. So that cover of "The Drowners" was more of a provocation, really.'

The final act to blossom directly from Linda's Strange Vacation was Matt Elliott in The Third Eye Foundation. Although he had been involved with the early Flying Saucer Attack, Elliott didn't see technology in the same way as Pearce did. 'On the first [Flying Saucer Attack] album, the tracks I was involved in were the weirder ones, not the song-y ones,' Elliott said in 1997. In strong contrast to Pearce, Elliott thought the sampler was 'the greatest musical invention: the technology has gone as far as it can. There's no excuse. I've never had an anti-keyboards thing; I'm up for anything. I can't stand people who say they can't listen to music made on a sequencer. There are things you can do with a sequencer you just can't physically do, no matter how good a musician you are.'

Elliott had started to record as The Third Eye Foundation with this mindset at the centre. He was inspired by the very English industrial mysticism of Psychic TV, Nurse With Wound, and Current 93, and utilised 'any old bits of equipment I had. I just used to wire them all up and see what came out. Then I'd just slow it down, and play it backwards. I listened to my first album [1996's *Semtex*] the other day and thought, why did I think anyone would be into this?'

Semtex—particularly the opening track, 'Sleep'—is wracked with junglist dread. 'I lived in Montpelier [an area of Bristol] and just walking to work every day in the summer … everyone's got their windows open. I'd walk along hearing this phat bass—no drums, hardly anything else—and some geezer going, *Whaaaa Whaaaa*. And I thought this was the real expression of the inner city.' In doctrine, it was very much the child of Disco Inferno.

'Bands like Disco Inferno had a massive influence on myself and Hood,' Elliott has said.

'We're obsessed with Disco Inferno to a degree that stops being funny,' the Leeds-based Hood confirmed, which wasn't surprising when you heard their cracked and creviced tape-spliced experiments, which they then soldered on to a strange heathen folk sensibility.

'I've got a Bark Psychosis CD,' says Howard Monk of Billy Mahonie. 'And that was given to me by Crawford Blair of Rothko. He was a big fan of Bark Psychosis. There is a circular thing within a circular thing. Us, The Monsoon Bassoon, and Rothko. North London post-rock. It was something I tried to coin the phrase of a couple of times.'

Howard Monk and Gavin Baker met at Middlesex University in 1996. 'Both myself and Howard had split up with girlfriends,' says Baker. 'He moved into my one-bedroom flat in Clapton. And we just started playing again. And I bought a little four-track, and I recorded us together, and we'd overdub. We just started fucking around with songs, nothing too major, no real plan. And it was at that point we started listening more and more to post-rock. The first Tortoise record. Mogwai.'

Monk and Baker then recruited another friend, Kevin Penney. 'Howard made me a compilation tape, a mix tape, to say, this is what we're into,' says Penney. 'Most of which was an eye-opener for me, musically. I'd never heard Slint at that point, so I was introduced to Slint, and Trans Am, Bundy K. Brown, Rachel's, The Sea And Cake's "Parasol". A lot of it was, *oh my god.* And then, there on the tape, too, were four of their home-recorded demos.' Penney, usually a guitarist, joined on bass; they then found another bassist, dub fan Hywell Dinsdale, via an advert in a Soho record shop.

'It wasn't originally the idea to have two bass players,' Penney says.

'When Hywell joined us, it seemed the most natural thing, to have that other rhythm, that bass,' Baker says. 'Essentially, [Dinsdale] was playing the melodies. I'm like the rhythm guitarist and he plays the melody, which just happens to be a deep, rhythmic melody, with Kev holding the thing down with the main bass parts. I play bass on a couple of songs, too, so at times all of us are playing bass. We are essentially three guitarists who play bass as well.' This emphasis on the low-end wasn't especially danceable; it wasn't even, as with El Hombre Trajeado, dance music you couldn't dance to. Rothko, with their three bass players, especially reveled in this dereliction of traditional bass duty, while simultaneously using the instrument's raw power.

The name Billy Mahonie was a character from the film *Flatliners*. 'I had just watched it a few nights before,' says Monk, 'and said, What about Billy Mahonie, the little kid in the film? The others knew it and said, yeah. And I think the name itself ... because it's not a "Bark Psychosis" or even a "Tortoise"—which is daft because it's an animal—but it still says something. Billy Mahonie is not anything remotely abstract or, dare I say it, pretentious. It's Billy Mahonie. I think Billy Mahonie as a name is kind of playful. And that is what we were.'

Like Mogwai, Billy Mahonie were a strong physical onstage presence; they were called the best live band in Britain by the *Melody Maker*. 'Live, we were so locked in,' Penney says. 'The intuition between us as musicians was just there, because we were living in each other's pockets.'

Although Billy Mahonie, Rothko, and The Monsoon Bassoon didn't have the same DIY community feel that the scenes in Glasgow and Bristol did, they still managed themselves and had control of most aspects of their presentation. 'All the artwork, flyers, T-shirts. Kev did those,' says Baker. 'We were quite used to being self-sufficient.' Billy Mahonie released their early seven-inches on a series of very small labels: Livid Meercat, Gold Hole, Stupidcat.

'My first experience of a DIY show was when Billy Mahonie had our first tour,' says Monk. 'We got to Leeds, we had no information [about the gig]. We were a bit nervous, thinking, *we could get shafted here*. But we didn't. They cooked us a big curry, it was the biggest sell-out show, and we got the most money. We got really looked after, and I think there's that element of trust that needs to exist.' However, Monk also points out other, less benign, forces he observed. 'In terms of "selling out", in terms of believing that you are "the source", or diverting from "the source" ... you get frowned on by other people.'

Bristol had been the first outside-London post-rock scene in the UK; it continued and expanded, with numerous other groups associated in some way. There was a gravitation toward spacerock psychedelia, as with AMP and Light, but more unusual was Foehn. The solo guise of Debbie Parsons, her isolationist collage from 1998, *Insideout Eyes*, looped found sounds and existential misery. Parsons also provided the ambient noise on The Third Eye Foundation's 1997 album, *Ghost*. 'I just go round, or Debbie did, taping hundreds of things—chairs, doors, anything—then listen back to tapes and take the stuff I like,' Elliott has said. On *Ghost*, Elliott mixed Parsons's samples of squeaky gates, creaking hinges and stormy weather with screaming wraiths and Eastern European folk music. *Ghost*, along with the folkier influences of Flying Saucer Attack and Hood, would coalesce into a distinctive new-old sound before too long.

The Third Eye Foundation was also the remixer-in-chief for pretty much all of the Bristol post-rock bands, and he collected some of these projects on 1996's *In Version*. Flying Saucer Attack's 'Way Out Like Dave Bowman' was especially piquant. 'Me and some friends did various percussion and flutes for [Pearce],' Elliott has said. 'I then went on to do drum machine programming and some other parts for him. I had more esoteric taste in instruments that Dave and I contributed various singing bowls and ritualistic instruments but Dave wasn't really happy with (as he said) the vibes associated with them, so he removed them. That's how ["Way Out Like Dave Bowman"] came about. I basically reassembled all the pieces that were missing into a remix.'

Elliott also remixed Mogwai, tackling 'A Cheery Wave From Stranded Youngsters' for Mogwai's *Kicking A Dead Pig* remix album. However, the highlight of that project was My Bloody Valentine's white noise treatment of 'Mogwai Vs Satan', which underscored what Mogwai had extracted from My Bloody Valentine *and* how Mogwai had added so much to that influence. Mogwai, too, were turning remixers, merrily profaning David Holmes's 'Don't Die Just Yet' in 1998.

'When the single came out, they wanted to do something different with the mixes rather than just getting techno guys in, so they got us and Arab Strap,' Braithwaite has said. Mogwai incorporated bits of an all-time favourite in their remix. 'The drums and bass from [Slint's] "Good

Morning Captain" are in it, slowed down a little,' Braithwaite added. 'I actually got to speak to Brian McMahan about that, and although he really didn't like [Holmes's] original song he didn't mind the remix. He's a nice guy.'

These new young bands were both cannibalising and emboldening post-rock; there was a certain cheekiness and sense of entitlement to them, and the go-getting spirit that led them to stage their own shows and put out their own records bred confidence.

'I hope we sell as many copies as we can,' Stuart Braithwaite said at the release of *Ten Rapid*, a collection of Mogwai's early, out-of-print seven-inch singles, which were then very difficult to get hold of. 'I want as many people to hear Mogwai as possible. I've never subscribed to any bullshit indie ethic.'

Shortly after *Mogwai Young Team*, Mogwai wrote a new, very impressive track: 'Xmas Steps', featuring Long Fin Killie's Luke Sutherland. '[It's] named after a street in Bristol,' Braithwaite has said. 'It's a street that has lots of steps in it. People thought it was about the build up to Christmas and the excitement of opening your presents and stuff like that. I mean, you call the songs something, and people expect it to have some attachment.'

'You've got to call it something, because you've got to write it down on a list,' says Kevin Penney of Billy Mahonie, on the challenge of giving an instrumental track its name. 'For a long time, things get called "Minor Jam in D". But there's usually something [that inspires us] at the time.'

'"Fishing With A Man For A Shark", I remember watching a documentary about someone trying to rescue, or pulling up from a helicopter, a bloke, rescuing him from a boat,' adds Gavin Baker. '"Nacho Steals From Work", we knew someone called Nacho, he was Spanish, he was a chef, and he used to steal stuff from work. So he'd come back with a massive bowl of pesto. "Simple Solutions Seldom Are", that was in a fortune cookie, "Keeper's Drive" is a street in Northern Rochdale where Howard grew up. "Bres Lore" was Kev's idea.'

'Because the song was big and bumbling and a bit stupid,' Penney says. 'It just made me think of Bernard Bresslaw.'

Often titles were off-the-cuff, but sometimes they were more pointed. The name of the EP Mogwai's 'Xmas Steps' first appeared on, *No Education = No Future (Fuck The Curfew)*, is a good example of this. 'It was either make it the title of an EP or go spray it on a wall,' Braithwaite told the *NME* in 1998, explaining that it related to a South Lanarkshire council directive stating that under-sixteens were not allowed out after dark. 'The scheme's just really snide,' Braithwaite said. 'It wasn't that long ago that this would have affected us, and it's going to affect people who go to gigs and the whole mentality of people who live here. People aren't going to be able to go out and practise with their bands or whatever.'

A small-scale example of how politics could be incorporated into post-rock. Expressing such sentiments via primarily instrumental music could be difficult. But that's not to say they were not there; and there was one city, one label, where they would become indivisible.

CHAPTER FIFTEEN

regret. desire. fear. hope.

'Simple acts of resistance could become a big thing.' ERIC CRAVEN, HANGEDUP

'Montreal was exciting and depressing at the same time,' says Efrim Menuck. 'It was a very cheap city to live in at the time, so it attracted a lot of people from other parts of Canada who weren't necessarily interested in having careers, or full-time jobs. But it was also a dark city. It was a little intense.'

The largest city in the province of Quebec, Montreal had also been the cultural and financial capital of Canada throughout the 1960s and 1970s. It had two main population groups—francophone and anglophone—and their separate-but-equal state was commonly characterised as 'two solitudes'. This lack of integration wasn't issue enough to threaten the wealth and status of Montreal itself until the francophone nationalist Parti Québécois (PQ) was elected in 1976. The PQ sought separatism for the province and passed a law stating that French was the *only* official language of Quebec. This rule was enforced with zeal, and anglophones voted en masse with their feet; they took their money, and businesses, to Vancouver or Toronto. The relationships between the remaining anglos and the dominant francos became more complicated in the light of a harder franco nationalism.

By the start of the 1990s, according to most conventional economic and social markers, Montreal was a city in slow decline.

However, it remained a city of educational excellence. 'The anglophone population here is partly fuelled by two universities, McGill and Concodia,' says Ian Ilavsky, co-founder of Constellation Records, and a musician in a plethora of Montreal bands. 'They are English speaking, and McGill is quite well known internationally. Concordia is highly regarded for its film and fine arts departments. Even in the darker years of the Québec economy and the province's culture wars, these schools continued to attract anglophone students from the rest of Canada, and at McGill in particular, lots of Americans and international students.'

Someone who came to Montreal to study was Efrim Menuck. 'Without getting too deep into personal biography, I left home at an early age and dropped out of high school, and had very many rough years,' says Menuck. 'I moved to Montreal because there was a university here that had a mature student program, so you didn't need a high-school diploma.'

Near to McGill University was the Mile End neighbourhood. It had big loft spaces and cheap rents—vacancies left by the anglophone flight—and was ripe for artists and activists. 'There was this feeling that there was a larger community—not just of musicians, but of writers, terminal grad-type people as well,' says Menuck. 'I guess the commonality was this commitment to try and figure out a different and easier way to live.'

The world knew of Montreal during the 1990s for its protest and its activism. It's where *No Logo* author Naomi Klein is from, and where the anarchist Jaggi Singh organised. 'I really can't emphasise enough that in that period Montreal, more than any other city in Canada, was a hotbed of the alter-globalisation movement,' says Ilavsky. He recalls a culmination of sorts in 2001, during the protests against the Free Trade Area of the Americas summit at Québec City: one of the largest anti-globalisation protests seen anywhere at that point. 'That shit was crazy,' he says. 'They put up fences, they turned downtown into a closed camp for world leaders, and it was essentially a pitched battle for three straight days, relentless tear gas, some rubber bullets, and all the rest of it, as protesters continually cut breaches in these miles of security fencing. I think for most of us, absolutely, this emerging critique, this fight against neo-liberalism, that was a huge dimension of what we cared about.'

One of the most immediate problems for musicians in Montreal at that time was finding somewhere to perform. 'It was a sad place to play music,' says Gen Heistek. 'It was getting more and more depressing during the nineties. A lot of clubs would charge for people to play, and there was a very limited range of places. So it just made sense for people to stop playing.'

'It was the post-grunge era, so most of the rock clubs were just shitty black boxes with bad sound systems,' says Menuck. 'The regular, playing-in-a-rock-club scene was just very depressing. Rehearsal spaces existed, though—Montreal has always had them, we call them "locals". At the time, because there was so much loft space for rent, it was the normal thing that five or six bands would get together and rent a small dry-walled basement, or some old warehouse, and share that as a jam space. So there were always places to rehearse, but in terms of places to play, it was so depressing, and for four or five years I just stopped playing music in that context completely. Because it just seemed like it wasn't going anywhere. The Godspeed thing started out of that, that dead period.'

Menuck was 'doing this four-track thing in my house, usually at three in the morning, coming home from a bar, just doing something quickly, and then trying to turn it into something the next day'. In 1994, as 'a young man's formal experiment', Menuck self-released a cassette, in an edition of thirty-three: *All Lights Fucked On The Hairy Amp Drooling.*

'The idea was this would be the last thing I would ever do,' Menuck says. 'A big dramatic gesture that nobody would care about. It was a private thing, *let's get this out of my system, and then figure out something else to do with my life*. It's pretty ragged, and there are some shared qualities with what Godspeed became, but I don't know if those similarities would be evident to anyone but those of us on the inside.'

The tape was mostly just Menuck, but Mauro Pezzente also plays on a couple of tracks; the biggest difference between this material and Godspeed, Menuck says, is, 'There's singing on it. I can't really listen to it objectively, and it's not like I listen to it a lot. I think the last time I listened to it was six years ago. I think it's interesting.' Despite many hoaxes, to date the cassette hasn't been leaked on the internet or offered for sale on the open market. 'For years, I've been saying it's gonna get out there someday, and people are gonna be pretty disappointed, because it's of the time,' Menuck says.

A friend of Menuck's liked the cassette and invited him to open for his band. 'That's when I got Mauro, and [Mike] Moya, who had just moved to Montreal. We played one show as a trio. Then it was eight of us, and we played a couple of shows like that. Dave [Bryant], the guitar player, was actually playing drums at that point. And then when I started playing with other people, trying to do that live, me and Dave, we had this idea that we would do this open callout to everyone we knew who didn't have a full-time job, or a serious relationship, or a kid, or commitments. Anyone who would be interested in actually doing this *for real.* So, because it came out of that at the beginning, it continues to be the case—that there are so many people who aren't musicians in the band. There was fifteen people in Godspeed at its height.'

'That was their trip, to some extent,' says Ilavsky. 'To get a lot of people together, and those earlier Godspeed performances, let's say 1995, 1996, were a bit more undifferentiated, incredible and visceral, big wall-of-sound type stuff.'

Godspeed saw themselves at 'year zero, which was super-liberating,' Menuck says. 'There was no earthly reason, no logical reason, no pragmatic reason, no functional reason, to function the way that most bands functioned. Because that just seemed like a dead end, a loser's game.'

The major space for those performances was the Hotel2Tango: a 'big, dirty old loft that a few of us were living in, and it was the rehearsal space. And, again, because playing in rock clubs just seemed a dead-end move, we just started putting on shows there. And then we built a little recording studio there. So for all those years, at the old Hotel, it was a dingy, polluted … it was above a car mechanics, so it was also toxic. It was a lot of work, but it was a good kind of work. So then, always at the end, like four in the morning or whatever, feeling exhausted, but triumphant. And, in a very boring practical way, for those of us who were putting on the shows, it was a good way for a learning experience, about doing things on your own.'

'It definitely was a community, there's no doubt about it,' says Eric Craven, who was playing in the band Shortwave. 'I wasn't part of the living arrangement thing, but a lot of people were living together; they were roommates, they were living in loft spaces, and I think everybody was pretty much in Mile End at that point.'

'We all saw each other all the time, because we lived really close together,' says Gen Heistek. 'The studio was literally across the street from Eric's house. I lived two blocks away. And then there was a load of people living in the studio. Proximity definitely has a lot to do with it.'

Heistek and Ian Ilavsky were part of the band Sackville, a group who made something akin to frayed folk music. 'Sackville had lost their drummer, and then lost another drummer, and then I was called upon to see if I could fit into that,' says Craven.

'Shortwave was, let's just say, not widely distributed as a phenomenon,' says Heistek. 'But it was amazing, and actually was definitely the most relevant predecessor to what we ended up doing.'

'I had a good buddy from high school—this is a long time ago—and he played bass, I played drums,' says Craven. 'We were both studying sociology at the time, and we wanted to disrupt our relationship with guitar playing, and so on. So that was the first time I started making instruments. I have this really primitive instrument that has strings on a skateboard, and the first time I did that was in Shortwave. We added a singer, who now lives in California, so it was just the three of us. Bass, drums, and we had a Dictaphone that we would record [into]. We had tape loops that we would record onto a cassette and then we used the foot switch. Everything was very primitive. And we did two cassettes and a seven-inch. We were invited to go play at the Knitting Factory [in New York] in 1995, and that was a huge deal for all of us at the time; that was what pushed me over the gap of wanting music as part of my life. It was No Wave-y ... it had all kinds of experiments with that kind of stuff. But it was very funky too, and that's Shortwave.'

Heistek, meanwhile, was playing in Pest 5000, a more straightforward indie-pop band with a Ut-esque fluidity. 'All four members wrote and sang songs,' she says. 'It was a bit unusual. It went all over the place, but there's a certain coherence to the sound of it.'

Sackville, Godspeed (now, through natural attrition, at about nine members), Sofa, Exhaust, the Shalabi Effect—and many more combinations and projects thereof—all started performing in Hotel2Tango, and at other 'locals'. It was clear some frighteningly intense music was brewing, along with a sense of community. 'People were learning,' says Ilavsky. 'We were all recording each other, and putting on shows in loft spaces and figuring out how to wire PAs, so in some way the label [Constellation] evolved out of that. I think it was marked by a very co-operative spirit and maybe—I like to think, looking back—that we had a fairly prescient understanding of finding terms for collective action, and co-operative action, while also understanding that certain people needed to take responsibility for certain things. So Constellation was always, bottom line, run by Don [Wilkie] and myself as co-founders. And the Hotel2Tango was a rehearsal space that eventually then evolved into more of a recording space. It was very much the work of Efrim and Thierry [Amar] from Godspeed, and a couple of others.'

The Hotel2Tango studio was an eight-track analogue setup, which, at that time, was reasonable, cost-wise, to run. Musicians who contributed to records (of bands that were not 'theirs') did so as shared labour, knowing the favour would be returned.

'*I need violin on this track.*'

'*Totally! I'm there!*'

'Why wouldn't I do that?' Heistek asks. 'I remember just loving the other bands, like Fly Pan Am and Exhaust.'

'For a while, it felt like it would be possible to only listen to the records Don and Ian were putting out,' adds Craven. 'That's a really privileged place to be, where you're mainly listening to music, that if you're not actually on the record, you have a relationship with them. And it's *building*. You feel like their success is part of your success.'

The label, Constellation, was explicitly run on the principles of co-operation, anti-consumerism, localism, and sustainability, and it was a thinking, analytical space for bands. But its founders were nobody's fools. 'I suppose we'd learnt some lessons, maybe not even directly in our own lives, but certainly by reading about things that had been forged structurally with a lot of idealism and that were so shortlived,' Ilavsky says. 'Whether it's the Rough Trade story, or any number of others' stories ... and I suppose we'd had some experience in our activist lives, our political and protest lives. The inertia of total consensus, and collective administration at all times, can be daunting. I definitely remember all of us talking about that at the time, too. So we tried our best to make a functional family out of things in those early years.'

Constellation was a 'political for-profit company'; although nobody went into it to make money, money was there because Wilkie and Ilavsky were studious and sensible operators, taking pride in spreadsheets and keeping on top of costs. Given the historic tendency for left-wing and collective endevours to go broke and implode, this emphasis on sustainability *in itself* was a political act. Constellation launched in 1997, and its first records were Sofa's 'New Era Building' seven-inch and *Grey* CD, and Godspeed You Black Emperor!'s *f#a#∞* LP.

f#a#∞ is like a Sphinx: it doesn't let you pass into it unless you carefully consider what it is asking of you. It draws power from mystery. It is didactic music, but far from the usual sense of that word: it doesn't tell you *what* to think, but it still rigorously demands that you do so. The narrations, crescendos and space in the album are challenges, pregnant with weighty discourse, and seem an honest effort to fully represent the complexity of Godspeed's multiple, sometimes contradictory, worldviews.

The blueprint included with the album gave some context of

f#a#∞'s riddle: 'infinity [∞] sweeping and falling away from you in all directions a dream you keep having where you are falling slowly or fast and there is no bottom never has been or will be and you will never ever land'. Along with other clues—like the recital that opens 'The Dead Flag Blues', blank-toned realism about the 'last days' and spontaneous societal collapse, and the mute, thudding locked groove at the end of 'Providence'—Godspeed felt final, cataclysmic, yet inevitable. The theories could run wild because the band generally did not give interviews or engage in any other promotional activities.

'No band photos, no cult of personality … at the end of the day, a band like Godspeed—no doubt they have limited their economic horizons in the name of maintaining their own sense of integrity and non-engagement with the media,' Ilavsky says. 'And I certainly can assure you that their principles were based on political and economic analyses. Never was there a conversation about anything as a strategic marketing exercise. But by the same token, the idea of maintaining mystery around stuff was important—and I think continues to be, for Godspeed, in an internet age of instant information and access.'

'When we came of age, you would go to the record store, and there would be some record with a crazy title, a crazy picture on the front, and you'd be like, I'll try that,' Menuck says. 'You'd bring it home and it'd blow your mind. And, again, this is pre-internet. You'd have to ask other people: *Who is this band? Have you heard them?* You'd have to fill in the narrative yourself. And there was space to fill in that narrative. And that's always what we loved about music, so that's how we wanted to function.'

'We were all really interested in the political aspect,' says Eric Craven. 'We were pretty militant about no band photos, and no T-shirts, and all that. It was really a privileged situation to have people supporting that, as well as in that context it was a chance to be a bit mischievous, to do your own thing and have some fun with that. And be part of a diverse aesthetic that was unified in a certain kind of way.'

All this meant that Constellation bands, and Godspeed in particular, had very little truck with 'post-rock' when it came knocking. 'Post-rock started to become almost a term of derision,' Ilavsky says. 'There was that. I think our larger concern with the term was that we were concerned that it was distracting from the kinds of conversation, the kinds of dialogue we were interested in seeing happen in the music media, the underground music media, which was to continue being engaged with questions about the terms of production: where are things coming from, what are the values underpinning this. It's not just about the music. We even wrote a little manifesto on it, and we included it in a CD compilation that we made of all the bands we had released up until 2001. And the little manifesto can probably be fairly summarised as: Fuck post-rock. We're punk rock.'

'I can't speak for everyone in the band, but the reason I didn't like it was we really, then and now, see ourselves as coming out of punk rock,' says Menuck. 'I see a line from punk rock to what we're doing, and again it had to do with this idea that we were living at a year zero. Everything was open. But at the same time, everything was denied. But definitely, at the time, we were listening to Tortoise, especially that first record. And, predating Godspeed, Slint. We were aware, especially of the stuff happening in Louisville and Chicago, and what kranky was putting out. But, for us, that just seemed like other punk rockers and hardcore kids coming to the same sort of conclusions that we were coming to.'

'The words we always used in the early years, and continue to deploy sometimes, is that we're excited by music that falls through the cracks of genre,' says Ilavsky, 'or that seems not just to blend genre as pastiche, but distills a lot of different genre influences into a new sound, or at least a vibrant toolbox.'

Godspeed's music, as they saw it, was 'a frame to give clues here and there, codified versions of whatever it is we're feeling in our lives in Montreal', as Menuck put it in 1999.

The next Godspeed record, *Slow Riot For New Zerø Kanada*, was released in 1999, 'all of it written in the empty space between tours', the sleeve noted. The front cover depicted the biblical Hebrew text **והת והבו** (*tohu wa-bohu*), found in the Books of Genesis and Jeremiah. The precise translation of **והבו והת** has been a source of much theologian angst over the millennia, but it can be thought of as something chaotic, desolate, vacant: a wasteland. Text from Jeremiah was included with *Slow Riot For New Zerø Kanada*, and gave **והבו והת** as 'waste and void'.

The EP's second track, 'BBF3', includes narration from 'Mister Blaise Bailey Finnegan The Third, taperecorded on a sidewalk in Providence, R.I.'. He discusses the shortcomings of 'the system' in terms both broad ('America is a third world country') and narrow (an argument over a speeding ticket). His ramblings become ever-more disquieting as he details the arsenal of weapons he carries, and then recites a poem—an approximate, semi-rapped version of 'Virus' by Iron Maiden, whose singer at that point was ... Blaze Bailey.

'If you ever get into a conversation with a homeless schizophrenic on the street, they usually have more to say about the unconscious reaction to living in this ridiculous power structure than most people do,' Menuck said in 1999. 'It's laid on the table, sometimes in a metaphorical fashion, sometimes in a literal fashion, but it's confirmation that it's there in everyone. It manifests itself in different pathologies, but it's there. That's the life we live, that's what we're stuck in and it's fucking ridiculous.'

This idea—of being trapped in the belly of the horrible machine, helpless within dysfunctional systems dictating lives—consciously or not evoked Greek myth, where unaccountable and whimsical Gods crushed a prostrate humanity. But always with Godspeed there was the will to fight, either through straightforward optimism ('the things we endure, soon they are distant bad memories,' they wrote on *f#a#∞*'s blueprint insert, 'we spent the last of our pennies on taxicabs and beer, stayed up all night hatching plans ... '), or through the more direct Molotov cocktail on the artwork of *Slow Riot For New Zerø Kanada*.

'It's amazing to me how many people misinterpret what it is we're trying to do,' David Bryant has said. 'People who play the record [*Slow Riot For New Zerø Kanada*] say it's depressing, defeated music, but that's not what I get from it. It's sad, but it's throwing out triggers like hope.'

'A thing a lot of people got wrong about us—when we did it the first time, a whole lot of what we were about was joy,' Godspeed said, in a collective voice, in 2012. 'We tried to make heavy music, joyously.

Times were heavy but the party line was everything was OK. There were a lot of bands that reacted to that by making moaning "heavy" music that rang false. We hated that music, we hated that privileging of individual angst, we wanted to make music like Ornette [Coleman's] *Friends And Neighbours*, a joyous, difficult noise that acknowledged the current predicament but dismissed it at the same time.'

Godspeed's 2000 album, *Lift Your Skinny Fists Like Antennas To Heaven*, seemed to represent this ideal visually, as well as sonically over its four movements 'Storm', 'Static', 'Sleep', and 'Like Antennas To Heaven'; the album's pilgrimage trail was set out in a diagram drawn by Menuck, with gradients representing individual parts' intensities.

Menuck drew on his filmmaking studies in constructing Godspeed tracks (the narration on 'The Dead Flag Blues' is from a screenplay he authored). 'The way that we were stitching things together, short pieces, long pieces, field recordings, tape loops, it felt the same as editing 16mm film,' he says. 'And also the idea too of not being afraid to have bad splices, we weren't too interested in the "invisible hand". The idea was that the music itself should be tactile. So if there's background noise, or distortion, it was fine. We wanted it to be smudged and fingerprinty.'

It was vital to all concerned that labels, studios, spaces, bands, should be consistent with the wider political arena; not promoting a specific ideology, but debating and challenging their roles. 'Even though every one was poor, if not penniless, we as musicians were certainly checking ourselves for privilege,' Ilavsky says. 'We had friends who were in the streets, or devoting themselves full-time to much more overt political battles, and we were trying to be true and respectful of that larger horizon in terms of music making, or art making. A number of manifestos and principles flowed from there, different kinds of speech coming from different kinds of people, and, also, I think as an artist on stage you can use a different kind of speech. But I think we were pretty hardcore about who we felt was in or out, really, on the level of ethics and politics. There were plenty of bands at that time that were all about trying to get their demos heard at Sub Pop, or to Matador, so even if a couple of those bands, in some ways, we might have imagined being interesting musically, it was always important to us what the musicians' career agendas were about, what their other values were about.'

The US company Southern were the first to distribute Constellation Records outside Montreal. This brought both financial stability and greater visibility, which came as the label released its first non-Montreal record, in 1998. 'The story there is that Godspeed had gone and played a show in Toronto, I think this was before Godspeed had even done their first European tour, it was early on,' Ilavsky remembers. 'And I think either Do Make Say Think opened for them, or ended up after the show talking to a couple of them. Dave [Bryant] was from Toronto originally, so I don't know if he knew any of those guys personally. Because a lot of the Do Make guys, they were playing in metal and hardcore. And so was Dave. Dave was actually the singer in a hardcore band before he became the guitarist in Godspeed.'

Do Make Say Think formed in Toronto in the mid-1990s, initially in a Tortoise-ish, sound project kind of way. 'We played so many times and didn't have a format,' Justin Small has said, 'just a few ideas that we jammed endlessly until we hit *that* part and *that* part would happen, and it would seem like we were composing things where in reality we were having such a good time. So we're just playing around and then the studio happened to us, and it was a new world, and some people in the band have just taken to the studio in such gorgeous ways and that's where their talents truly shine.'

Do Make Say Think had a Tascam 388—a massive reel-to-reel eight-track recorder—and got into the habit of constant recording from their earliest days. 'Having that eight-track around all the time, you just ended up using it as an instrument,' Small has said. 'You'd plug all sorts of things into it, you'd got the tape rolling, and just [do] one take of drones, and weird drumbeats coming from records, and loops, and you're using the faders as you would a piano.'

'It's basically built on relationships,' Ohad Benchetrit has said, of Do Make Say Think's early years. 'A lot of bands start with guys meeting for the first time and kind of growing together. For every member of the band, there's a history that goes way back before the band. Justin and Jimmy [Payment] have been together twenty years. Meeting Charlie [Spearin] and Dave [Mitchell], this is our fourth band together for eleven years. Everybody in the band has a history with somebody else dating back to three or four other bands for ten or fifteen years, so there was a real core and family thing going.' Their debut record, *Do Make Say Think*, was a lo-fidelity skank, mixing a clear affection for free jazz with 'an abiding love for *Master Of Puppets*-era Metallica'. They self-released it in 1997.

'Dave came back from Toronto,' continues Ilavsky, 'and he said, I think you'll really like this [*Do Make Say Think*], and we really did. So I can remember Don and I getting on a train, and going to Toronto, and meeting them, and it was the first time that we had a very different sort of process, where it wasn't just completely local and by osmosis in our own backyard. We were two label guys, going up to Toronto, to meet this band Do Make Say Think and see what they were about.'

The second Do Make Say Think album, *Goodbye Enemy Airship The Landlord Is Dead*, was a more ambitious, less patched-together affair. They had developed it in 57 Grange in Toronto, 'a really fun, weird slum that had a lot of people pass through the door', as Small put it. 'The rent was cheap; the stairs were sinking into the building. We had rats, and mice, and raccoons living there. We had a friend come back from a Korean prison (he was wrongly put there for four months!) to stay with us.'

Goodbye Enemy Airship The Landlord Is Dead was 'the sound of who we were at the time'. Most of it was recorded in a barn in rural Ontario, over a weekend in the summer of 1999, with a countrified ambience of crickets chirping and, as the instruments oozed into one another, an informality and intimacy.

'When we go out to a barn or a cottage to record there is a sense of freshness that we are looking for,' Spearin has said. 'When we get out there, it's a new place and there are none of the distractions of regular life, so our senses are open to what's around us a bit more; to what's new.

You sort of hope that that absorbs into the music a little bit, along with the smell of the manure in the next yard over. You kind of want the dirt of the experience to make it into the music somehow.'

But it was their third album, 2002's *& Yet & Yet*, where the combination of influences peaked. Do Make Say Think were very big fans of Tortoise. 'The first self-titled record,' Charles Spearin said in 2013, discussing the albums that had proved most influential to him. 'Justin went to see them and came home really excited. And then we just listened to the record again and again and again. And it had this amazing punk rock fearlessness to it, but it had this humble quality. It was this combination of being humble and fearless, and simple, and deep, at the same time.' Spearin also cited *Rhythms, Resolutions And Clusters* and said the albums ended up 'being one and the same in my mind'. Small added Talk Talk into the mix, stating that *Laughing Stock* was 'the greatest recording by human beings.'

& Yet & Yet offers, in a similar way to Talk Talk, an experience of hearing the dust settle and the lips chap. 'For one thing, when we listen to these so-called imperfections, accidents is probably more appropriate of a word, they have a human-ness to them when you listen to it that touches you, sometimes,' Spearin has said. 'We left a little laugh in on one of the songs, we left that in because it sort of gets you in the chest. It's not part of the composition, but it's definitely part of the composition now. All these little things, which are happy accidents, like the drummer putting down the sticks at the end of a song, they take it from just music to people playing music. You want to include the people; you want to keep it human.'

Montreal—and, more widely, Quebec—was in the midst of a particularly acute period of schism in the mid 1990s, stoked by a referendum on Quebecois independence from the rest of Canada. 'Non' won, but barely—50.6 percent to 'Oui' on 49.4 percent. And the majority of francophones voted 'Oui'. 'I don't want to say that our scene was strictly anglo, but there was a bit more of a divide back then,' says Ilavsky. Nevertheless, Godspeed and Exhaust both had francophone members at various points. And Fly Pan Am were an all-francophone band, influenced by French pop culture (and cultural theory), along with more electronic modes of expression. 'When we first started Fly Pan Am, we were interested in many different kinds of music, and krautrock, minimalism, and electroacoustic music were definite faves that still flow through my veins,' says co-founder Roger Tellier-Craig, 'but we were exploring these ideas through rock idioms and instrumentation, dabbling here and there with electronic sounds.'

Meanwhile, Eric Craven (drums) and Gen Heistek (violin) had veered away from Sackville. '[Hangedup] came from the spirit of playing, and the intensity of an individual, brought together with another individual, not something out front and something out back,' says Heistek. 'There *is* no back. You can be a drummer, but man, you're upfront. That's the way it is.'

Craven and Heistek shared an interest in Einstürzende Neubauten and The Ex. ('They're the biggest touchstone for us. Ever. That's it,' says Heistek. 'The Ex, in terms of their thinking, in terms of their music, in terms of their sonics, and their aspiration and their creation of space. They were massive for us.') Hangedup were also big New Order fans, and would go on to deconstruct 'Blue Monday' (as 'New Blue Monday') on their first album. 'It was about respecting the original, in hoping that a New Order fan would enjoy it,' Heistek says. 'It's been turned on its head, its been gutted, and its still dancing.'

There was also a corresponding interest in classical and minimalism, including Tony Conrad (who they would go on to work with in 2012) and the violinist, composer, and former actor Iva Bittová. 'I was exposed to classical music, and a lot of the ideas of classical music, without really caring so much,' says Heistek. 'But it was all in there, as an emotion, as a feeling, and I did enjoy it. I just wasn't going to get into the nitty-gritty of the practical. But I did enjoy the emotions and the feelings. And often, the repetition of it. As a classical musician, you played this, and you played this way, and … you're doing it wrong. I always played pretty badly. But you can push through it. The textures, and the sonics of the instrument rather than what it's supposed to do, what it's supposed to sound like, that's it.'

'It took us a combination of being reductive, finding the simple things and adding the complexity, about textures, sounds … and those things became melody,' says Craven. 'I play melody as much as Gen plays rhythm. But we're doing it in terms of the overall effect. Whatever complicated idea the process would be, we would have to reduce it so, say, Gen had a really interesting line that had several different keys in it, and a bunch of different notes … let's reduce it. It's all about reducing things. And, then once you have that chunk, then we can add different things to it.'

'One of our limits we would agree on, is if we're doing something, if we were working on something and it started to remind us of something you might want to play during a figure skating routine, we'd be … we gotta rethink this,' says Craven.

'It always seemed that the figure skating song was just lurking around the corner,' says Heistek.

Given this, it wasn't so surprising that Hangedup only released their self-titled debut album in 2001, long after they formed. 'It took us forever to get anything that sounded good,' says Craven. 'It took us a year of practising regularly. And we did have songs where Gen sang; we tried all kinds of stuff. The songs that we worked on for a year didn't even end up on our first record.'

'Definitely jettisoning things was key to the process,' says Heistek. 'The willingness to throw it all out except for that one little bit, instead of hanging on. It's finding the kernels.'

'I remember hearing Keith Jarrett say once, if he's any good at playing piano, it's only because he doesn't like his instrument, and he's always trying to push it into his zone, push it past,' says Craven. 'I identify with that, too. It's not that I don't like my instrument, but I definitely identify with trying to be engaged with that, those limitations.'

'All those things are political too,' Heistek adds. 'There are lots of things that are political, that are hard to write down. And if we can make something that creates a different space, a different headspace, maybe other things can happen.'

'A lot of what we did, it's relating back to the political idea, the idea of sound being political, there's so much struggle in our music in basic honest, hardworking—we hope—ways,' she continues. 'I think that's a lot of what we're working with, as a template: this idea of putting everything into everything, always. Like you give everything your absolute attention, you make sure that every little piece is—not the way you want it to be, in terms of controlling the sound at every moment—but that the intention is always there.'

'There's an interesting juxtaposition, in that there's a lot being offered to people in the records, and people really putting into it, but at the same time not being that accessible for interviews, and media,' says Craven. 'So we're generous on the one hand, but also being closed off. You can label us all as jerks for not talking to you, but here's the other ten ways that this music, and this production, is really generous.'

This was especially true of Constellation's artwork and packaging. The label's releases were produced *intensely* locally, even down to every copy of *f#a#∞* including a penny squished on the train tracks around the back of Hotel2Tango. Local visual artists and screenprinters would be commissioned for artwork. The musicians affiliated with Constellation would pitch up to fold and stuff inserts into new releases. It was all an extension of the help and support given on recordings, and made clear the kindness of spirit found within the Montreal community to the wider fans.

As the interest in Godspeed in particular grew, they did agree to two major British press interviews in 1999 and 2000: in the *NME* and *The Wire*, respectively. In a very rare act, the *NME* even granted Godspeed a cover without a photo of the band. It became a dramatic newsstand statement and was one of the handful of occasions when something underground genuinely reached a wider audience without compromise.

'There was a lot of back and forth between the editors and the band to figure out whether the band would do that [the *NME* interview], and what terms and conditions would make sense to them,' says Ilavsky. 'And I can remember the band also feeling like, *we don't want to come across as prima donnas*. We used to joke that, we have these political concerns but … are these just going to be perceived on the same spectrum as wanting no blue M&Ms backstage or something?'

'How much does any human being have to say at any point in time?' says Menuck, of the reluctance to talk to the press. 'Why the fuck would we talk to someone when we were busy doing other stuff? When we didn't necessarily have a point to make that week? But those decisions got blown up as these huge things. And for us—there was no grand statement. We weren't doing this stuff to be confrontational or to make any greater point. We weren't comfortable with this idea that we were presenting ourselves as special, in any way. I remember there was a lot of internal talking about that, when people started writing about us. There was frustration and confusion.'

The Wire's piece was a little more candid and found the group at a difficult juncture. 'I think the glory days are over,' David Bryant said. 'When we first started out, we pretty much knew everyone in the room. We knew why we were there and why they were there—you could talk to them afterwards and they told you why. Now we play in front of seven hundred people—they leave, you don't talk to anyone. It's more and more fucking alienating every time we come over here [to the UK] and it's less satisfying on a certain level.'

'There's barricades in front of the stage tonight,' cellist Norsola Johnson added. 'That's a fine example of lack of contact. That's really like "rock show".'

'I always thought that if we got to that stage we were going to find out ways to fuck with the space we played in,' Menuck said.

A Godspeed fan wrote in to *The Wire*, taking issue with this stance. 'I was stung by David Bryant's cynical assessment of the audiences the band had recently performed for,' he wrote. 'To an extent I agree that large venues can alienate both parties, but speaking as a fan in North Yorkshire where even good conventional rock gigs are scarce, I was delighted that they played here at all.'

The *Wire* piece did capture a brewing existential ambivalence in Godspeed, something harder to square than just worries over misrepresentation of the group. 'Do you know what I really think? My own opinion?' Menuck said in that interview. 'I think time is running short. I think time is running short. I think there are forces of evil in the world. I think that global capitalism is just, like, one inch away from being everywhere. I think now is not the time to be frittering away playing in a silly-assed post-rock band. I think everything you do in the face of this is inadequate.'

'Working in a true democratic process, with so many people, at a certain point ... I wanted to do something that's a little less personally intense,' Menuck says now. He founded A Silver Mt. Zion in 1999. 'Compositionally, [it's] a little less argumentative, and I don't mean argumentative in a bad way. It's a big ideal to live up to what we do in Godspeed, internally. And at some points, I just need a space over here in the corner. So that's what it started as. And when Godspeed went on its huge break, it just became the thing I did, and it turned into something else. It was in a lot of ways a response to the feeling that I got toward the first end of Godspeed, which was feeling a little ineffective, just sitting in a chair with my head down. Being able to have a microphone, and being able to have a back and forth with people every night. It was like a reaction to that. Yeah, that's all. And Silver Mt Zion is *definitely* not a post-rock band!'

Godspeed's final release, before an extended hiatus, was 2002's *Yanqui U.X.O.*, and the idea of 'hope' here, instead of being an ∞ possibility, was now drawn on a hammer's head. 'There was something about everything that happened after September 11, what the world turned into, that it seemed the trusting casual gesture, and trusting people to come to their own conclusions, it seemed a little lacking,' says Menuck. 'That was a very confusing time. There was a shift around that time, based on what our lived experiences were, especially touring in the States in the lead-up to the invasion of Iraq. There were definitely many moments when it felt a little strange just to get onstage and sit in a chair, and put your head down.' They signed off *Yanqui U.X.O.* with '&hope still, a little resistance always maybe, stubborn tiny lights vs. clustering darkness forever ok? thankslovegodspeedyou!blackemperorgoodbyexoxoxoxoxox'

'It's hard to explain, but our concerns a lot of the time are pretty basic, and from the beginning until now, a lot of what we're reacting to is pretty basic,' says Menuck. 'And what we're engaged with is pretty basic. It's got nothing to do with lecturing from the clouds on high, or presenting a romantic or idealised representation of youth, or beauty, or decadence, or anything like that. And I feel when anybody, regardless of what their trade is, talks honestly about the ins and outs of that trade, and the political and economic realities of that trade, there's something to be learned. Because obviously there's commonality in this world between all types of people. Godspeed's politics have always been rooted in that idea, of trying to find common cause with other workers.'

Constellation had laid solid foundations for its continued survival, notwithstanding the increased challenges of anyone remaining financially viable in the music game. The label have even mellowed *just a little* to the idea of post-rock being its own definable beast, and that Constellation had been an important part of making it so. Montreal itself gentrified, and those huge cheap lofts became increasingly unavailable to starving bands. Hotel2Tango moved in 2007; its facilities are now used by bands all over the world.

'Things change,' says Gen Heistek. 'It has to change. Things change and the world moves on. Things change and the world is different. But … I feel very special about that time in Montreal.'

CHAPTER SIXTEEN

there's a lot of dust in the air

'An image of something you can't quite remember, but that sounds like it should be familiar.' MARCUS EOIN, BOARDS OF CANADA

A 1998 review of The Notwist's album *Shrink* opened by saying, 'For the majority of post-rockers, the very idea of disorder is likely to bring them out in a fit of hyperventilation and a nervous rash. Repercussions and resonances are the air they breathe, the oxygen of a rarefied future where children are bred in bottles and production lines shine in the new dawn.' The reviewer, Victoria Segal, ultimately concluded that *Shrink* wasn't really like that, but the fact that this reviewer saw post-rock in 1998 as something safe and contained, ordered and formulaic—emphatically *not* fearless—was a telling moment. Was she right? And, if she was, how did we get here?

This era, in particular, saw a kind of elder exodus. More established post-rock bands tended now to emphatically rebel against the term, abandoning it sometimes via words, and sometimes by deliberately making changes to their intent and practice. 'I was more interested in the things that were less guitar-orientated, but then the guitar stuff started coming back,' Kieran Hebden of Fridge says. 'The concept of post-rock … it kind of changed from what I'd thought [it was]. It left me a bit. It turned into something else. All of a sudden, it was more drone-y; bands with bass guitar solos and things. It was less about electronics and bringing together dance music and all these things.'

'More compact, more visceral, and more rockin'—easier to grasp right away,' is how Dan Bitney described the 2001 Tortoise album *Standards*; it was the first Tortoise album for which the band trialed and tweaked the tracks on the road first (as opposed to laboriously working out how to play them live after recording). 'Seneca', *Standards'* first track, opens with a hiss of an amp and then fires up into a skuzzy garage-band jam.

'It wasn't a direct reaction against any of our other work, like *TNT* or whatever,' John McEntire has said, 'but there was this unspoken feeling that we wanted to do something really direct—shorter songs, more compact structures—something really visceral. With *Standards* there was a desire to get back to having at least three people playing live as the basic foundation of the songs.'

For one person who was there at the start but had long abandoned it, it was time to return. 'Post-rock, at that time [1994], didn't pay for my flat,' Graham Sutton says. His experience making drum'n'bass as Boymerang had proved different. 'I was flying all around the world doing this, that, and the other,' he says. 'I was remixing Metallica and I was remixing Goldie. I had signed a good deal with Parlophone, and it was great, knockout.'

Graham Sutton's late-90s tenure in drum'n'bass was not so different as to what was now happening to post-rock. 'It had solidified into something,' he says. 'It had become this thing; it was now a *genre*. It had become this bad techno, I suppose, and I just couldn't feel enthusiastic about it anymore. It was really quite overnight, as well. It was me switching off, like a lightbulb, at the end of 1999. Nah, it's not for me anymore. So when Parlophone wanted me to do the second Boymerang album, I went away and did a Bark Psychosis album.'

///Codename: Dustsucker had a long gestation period and was very different to the 'something really direct' of Tortoise's *Standards*. 'It started from a thing of, I'm not happy with this music [drum'n'bass], and it also

started from moving out of my flat, because I split with my wife,' Sutton says. 'Those things came concurrently. And it was a thing of, so I'm not happy with this music … what music *am* I happy with? It was starting, again, with a blank sheet of paper. You need rhythm there, don't you? I *think*. It was those sort of really basic questions, because working in drum'n'bass for that length of time, it's really hard to scrub [the idea] that you're dealing constantly in tiny little packets of sound, and animating those tiny little packets of sound. You're used to working on these tiny fragments, then you put them together, two of those, one of those, three of those. But, in isolation, they're just tiny, split-second things. It had completely broken my head in terms of anything longer than a blip, basically. You end up getting really, really critical about tiny bits.'

Sutton would test sounds and structures out, writing things down on his blank sheet of paper, testing them, then—as often as not—striking through. '*What sort of rhythms should it have? Should these rhythms be repetitive? Should they be free? Should it be like free jazz? Should it be completely free and open? No, I don't like that.* Questioning every little last thing. It was crazy. That's why the album took four years.'

One thing that became clear to Sutton from fairly early on in the process is that it would have vocals. 'I'm skeptical about instrumental music, because I feel it's a cop-out,' he says. 'Or it *can* be a cop-out. It's a thing of, if I was going to do this, which I clearly was, I wanted to put everything into it and not cop out. So, as good as a lot of instrumental music can be, it just felt that I'd be not really giving enough, for myself, not to do it. I'd have felt that I'd chickened out or something. I love the idea of words, and in some respects I thought about words more than anything else.'

Sutton used the 'Morning Pages' technique—three sheets, every day, of stream-of-consciousness writing—to find his way there. 'That was really fascinating. It doesn't cost anything. If it's indulgent, why not? I was being paid to be indulgent at that point in time. As a process, just getting in the mood for it, every day, for an extended length of time, doing nothing else but doing this. I loved it. It was great to get yourself in the zone.'

As Sutton began to slowly test, discard, and keep, he realised quite quickly that this music belonged to Bark Psychosis, not the Boymerang name, nor anything else. 'I thought about it for a little bit, but not very long. It felt the most natural thing,' he says. 'In my little mind, the band might have finished, but it became this thing that I did a certain sort of music under. While there was the four of us, everyone had complained about me being too this, that, and the other, so it just ended up being my thing, I suppose.'

The recording of *///Codename: Dustsucker* began with Talk Talk's Lee Harris setting down 'some basic drums, just to get some foundation of what we're going to work with,' Sutton says. 'But that was only the first two or three weeks. And the rest of the process was nothing to do with the band whatsoever.'

///Codename: Dustsucker is testament to the tiny fragments that Sutton assembled, in his mind and in the studio; the texture isn't simply a word used to describe its overall effect, but it relates specifically to the meticulousness of production; the blades of grass in a meadow. It's a harder album to grasp even than *Hex*, with thousands of concurrent parts flourishing and dying; still, that rhythmic base is always there, even when the album is fluid in everything else. Some songs seem to explicitly look back to *Hex*—the hushed brushfire of 'Miss Abuse' in particular recalls the concurrent cruelty and vulnerability of 'Eyes And Smiles'—and the tension, always as important as the quietude to Bark Psychosis, hasn't diminished over the ten years since *Hex*, with compresed nerve-endings of noise pervading the record.

'I hear it as one thing,' Sutton says of *///Codename: Dustsucker*. 'I was working on all the tracks at the same time, switching the album on, and I was working on the album, from beginning to end. But then I went and did a whole new track for it ['From What Is Said To When It's Read']. That was just done in one evening. Everything else had taken years, and then the main guts of that was just done in one night.'

Never lucky with the business end of the industry, Sutton irritated Parlophone by not delivering a drum'n'bass album; relationships broke down, and Sutton liberated a few (still unreleased) tracks from

///Codename: Dustsucker onto peer-to-peer filesharing. 'I was up on that from quite an early point,' he says. 'I love it. I think it's a really, really good thing. What an amazing distribution model. Because the music that I've been involved in, it's always been—to a greater or lesser extent—leftfield, which has always had very limited avenues in terms of exposure, in terms of radio, or the mainstream media. So the idea that your stuff can just get out there and people just access it … it's amazing.'

'*Hex* and *Dustsucker* very much relate to one another, as brother and sister relate to each other,' Sutton says. 'They look at each other with suspicion. With eyebrows raised. One's older than the other, but one's lived longer than the other. But they're very, very much interrelated.'

The influence of Bark Psychosis, of Tortoise, and of other leading post-rock artists on a newer generation was one reason for a more easily identifiable sound. If groups cited (say) The Sea & Cake, Slint, and Ui as influences, rather than picking from Lee Perry, Arvo Pärt, and Ut, almost certainly a narrowing of musical horizons would follow. After all, one of the foundational principles of post-rock was its ability to take ingredients that shouldn't work together and bake them into fresh bread. As good as The Sea & Cake, Slint, and Ui might be, there is much less of a musical and philosophical gap existing between the three of them; it follows that this left only small spaces for departures from what was quickly becoming a post-rock template. This reached something of an apex when some projects explicitly named themselves in tribute to post-rock artists they admired: After The Flood took from Talk Talk, Lockgroove from Stereolab ('Lock Groove Lullaby', on *Transient Random Noise Bursts With Announcements*), and Radarmaker were so named after a song on *Mogwai Young Team*.

More subtly—and surprisingly, given that most post-rock artists had until now prided themselves on being anti-retro—a new nostalgia started to creep in. However, and in its own way, it was at least a *fresh* kind of nostalgia. It combined half-remembered 1970s culture, the supernatural, rural melancholy, and, sometimes, a psychologically unsettling quest for a womb-like state. Like deconstruction, it was a phenomenon named by Jacques Derrida; like post-rock, its application to music was explored by Simon Reynolds.

'To haunt does not mean to be present,' Derrida wrote in his 1993 essay *Spectres Of Marx*. Here, Derrida combines this half-life of haunting with that of ontology—the study of a state of being—as Hauntology. (In the original French, *hauntology* sounds very close to *ontology*, making it less of a clumsy portmanteau and more of a written representation of how existence is suffused with ghostly presence.) Reynolds, in 2005 (and along with Mark Fisher), began to use 'hauntology' as a musical genre, initially to describe the work of artists on the UK's Ghost Box label.

Evoking indistinct feeling was hauntology's key, and shades had been there in Pram's repressed trauma, Hood's distorted folk-club aesthetic, and, especially, in the work of Flying Saucer Attack and Third Eye Foundation. It also took in a Butterfly Child-ish naturalness, a soil 'n' childhood air.

'There's a very silly story behind Butterfly Child,' Joe Cassidy says. 'When I was about six years old, we moved into this old house that everybody in the neighbourhood thought was haunted. It had very long grass. Literally, way higher than I was, as a kid. It was a weird imaginary place for a few months, until my mum and dad got it cleared up. But I would go out into that garden and write these little stories as a kid. And one of the stories I wrote was called "Butterfly Child".'

Later, when Cassidy came to his musical project, this feeling was at the heart of what he wanted to do. 'All my friends at the time were complete intellectual snobs,' he says. 'And they had band names like The Freudian Complex, just ridiculous. So I thought, screw all that. I wanted to name it the most innocent, naïve thing; something from my childhood, even though it's the worst band name of all time. I thought, I'll call it Butterfly Child.'

However, Cassidy has also said that his younger days were by no means idyllic; they carried a very hauntological threat of terror within them, which occasionally became tangible. 'I grew up in Belfast, and it's an interesting thing because my father was involved on the government front; he actually had a pretty dangerous job for a while dealing with the terrorists,' Cassidy says. 'It wasn't so much that I experienced the Troubles always firsthand—I would see it on TV like everybody else, but occasionally I'd run outside and grab my football and I'd have a British soldier put a rifle to my forehead and say, *F-off, you Taig* [a derogatory term for Irish Catholic] or something. It was definitely a difficult place, but it felt like a normal environment for me.'

Following the demise of H.Ark, Butterfly Child released the *Ghetto Speak* EP and *Onomatopoeia* album on Rough Trade. 'I think it was when *Ghetto Speak* came out,' Cassidy recalls, '[someone said] it literally sounds like a twelve-year-old playing with a Bontempi organ.' The giddy, spooky quality of Butterfly Child's music, especially in the Rough Trade era, was an unformed but effective precursor to the growing hauntological trend within post-rock.

Another influence came from an unlikely place: Warp Records. 'The source of all our music is that we've refused to accept adulthood,' Boards Of Canada's Marcus Eoin said in 1998. Eoin and his brother, Michael Sandison, were textural masters, seeing their music as folk music made electronically, saturating tracks in detail (little of it obvious). Their album *Music Has The Right To Children*, from 1998, is a hauntological landmark.

'When we were kids, a lot of our favourite TV programmes, particularly wildlife documentaries, were made by the Film Board Of Canada,' Michael Sandison said in 1998. 'We just loved the soundtracks. It's something people don't normally pay much attention to. Like the strings at the end of programmes, the corporate logos with a little flourish and a little happy melody. They're the ultimate in psychedelia, but no-one ever notices them or talks about them.' Boards Of Canada were an intricate net curtain cast over reality and, in this sense, were the absolute opposite to the isolationist trend. By contrast, artists like Main or Techno Animal had a single-minded determination to heighten every unpleasant sensation that life could throw at you.

That didn't mean that the two couldn't be combined, however, and this is what the later Labradford records achieved so effectively. On their

1996 self-titled album, unsettling psychological rumbles were mitigated by a spiritual serenity. 'We do shoot for an emotional feel with our records,' Mark Nelson said in 1997. 'I guess it's contented introspection. Most of life is a kind of chaos, whether it's jobs or relationships or travel. It's unfathomable and impossible to navigate, but there are moments, not of clarity, but of comfort and acceptance. When you get into our music, you don't worry about paying bills.'

'There's always that amazing lack of sound when it snows,' Carter Brown has said. 'And things that you thought were really ugly, like trash or run-down houses, become part of this really beautiful landscape.'

Labradford's fascination for 'drifting'—snow flurries, nomadism, weightlessness—inspired three events held between 1998 and 2000: their Annual Festivals Of Drifting. The first festival hosted Charlemagne Palestine and Tony Conrad (both huge influences on Labradford) alongside The Durutti Column, Mark Nelson's solo project Pan American, and the New York-based collective Bang On A Can, who performed Brian Eno's *Music For Airports*. It also featured the author Iain Sinclair, ruminating on the nature of drift.

Labradford, in the Festivals Of Drifting, were always keen to make links with modern classical; the composer Harold Budd felt especially close to what Labradford were exploring in this period. In 1998, *The Wire* magazine had played Budd a Labradford song ('Banco') as part of its regular 'Invisible Jukebox' feature, inviting the composer to comment. 'It's a great mood,' Budd said. 'It's not a threatening mood, it's not even sombre, but it's like that beautiful statue called *Religion* that's right next to Christina Rosetti's grave in Highgate Cemetry. It has a ghostly something about it that's pretty at the same time as being not quite of the real world somehow.' Budd was so impressed that he went on to remix Labradford's 'V' from their next, even calmer album, *Mi Media Naranja*.

It was Harold Budd's gentle solemnity that gazed serenely over the most commercially successful hauntological post-rock band of all, Iceland's

Sigur Rós. From their earliest days, Sigur Rós straddled prenatal purity and newborn scream. 'Being in the womb, there's so much peace and quiet, and when you get out, you just get into this madness,' guitarist and vocalist Jónsi Birgisson said in 1999. 'We like to think of it as something new. A new beginning. You're born into the chaos of this world, you die, and then you're born again.' This was sewn deep into Sigur Rós's fabric; they named themselves after Birgisson's baby sister, born a few days before the band formed at the start of 1994.

Their first recorded song, 'Fljúgðu', took them six hours to record and was a shoegazing plod, but by the time of their debut album, *Von* (meaning 'Hope'), three years later, their ambition was asserting itself. The long gestation time meant *Von*'s songs had undergone considerable change, and in order to pay their recording costs, the members painted the studio they worked in.

'I think we were out of everything when we started,' Georg 'Goggi' Hólm, bassist, said in 2001, 'and I think we've always been a bit outside of everything.' However, and despite the total audience in Iceland being small, there was a strong conglomerate at that time for DIY music: Kitchen Motors. It was a rallying point for all those outside of everything, and released records, staged events, supported artists, and promoted avant-garde diversity. 'I don't think it's enough to make music in your own little corner,' Kristín Björk Kristjánsdóttir of Kitchen Motors has asserted. 'I think it's very important to at least offer interested ears the chance.' Kitchen Motors galvanised those with open minds, putting tireless energy into projects that lacked obvious commercial crossover.

'Everybody in Iceland enjoys music and looks around for new bands,' Hólm said in 2001. 'I think people, when the band was beginning, at that time they didn't want to listen to Icelandic bands, but it's changing.'

On *Von*'s title track, Birgisson sings in an invented language, Hopelandic, a mixture of Icelandic, English, and hope. 'We have a song called "Hope" ["Von"], and once I sang it without words, and Hopelandic developed from this,' Birgisson said in 1999. 'Sometimes you can hear something in the vocals, but then it's gone, to emerge again later.' (Sigur Rós soon tired of being asked about Hopelandic, describing it as 'fucking bullshit' in an extremely surly NPR radio interview in 2007.)

Hopelandic was very much in keeping with Sigur Rós's brand of post-rock; it took the principle of decentred vocals, stripped it of tension, and injected it with unfettered optimism. And it wasn't just Birgisson's language. He sang in falsetto, drifting cloud-like above the music, his voice able to sweep from an infant's untutored yodel to the death-throes of a wailing unquiet spirit. In addition, he played his guitar with a violin bow, intensifying the drama of his vocals. The effect was 'immense' music that didn't sound overly bombastic; it could quite easily seep away down into crevices while the listener remained acutely aware of its presence.

Inititally, *Von* sold poorly in Iceland (and in infinitesimal qualities elsewhere), but it is a strong work; tracks like 'Sigur Rós' and 'Hún Jörð …' form the hitherto missing link between Mogwai and Labradford. Yet among the abstracted screams, gadabout indulgence, tape patchwork, and improvised guitars, there was also 'Myrkur'. For a still-young band, this was stadium-ready material, indicating a certain direction of travel both for Sigur Rós and for later post-rock.

After *Von*, and within a relatively short space of time, Sigur Rós gained the confidence—or at least the chutzpah—of a successful band. In 1999, on their website, they published a mission statement. 'We are not a band, we are music. We do not intend to become millionaires, we are simply gonna change music forever, and the way people think about music. And don't think we can't do it, we will.'

That year, they released *Ágætis Byrjun*. It took up residency in Iceland's album chart, spending eight weeks at number one. Sonically, it codified and strengthened the embryos of *Von*—retreat from adulthood, idealism, oceanic bliss-out—but added in an even stronger sense of the vistas in Iceland, a country high in natural beauty, low in population density. 'It's a subconscious thing, like with all Icelanders,' Birgisson has said. 'When you've travelled the world, you see more and more how much space we have. We've just come from New York, which is full of skyscrapers and endless straight roads, then you come back here and everything is so small. Of course this has some effect on you.' Their space was a paradox; the country was tiny, and relatively young in terms of human habitation, but the vistas per population head were enormous.

'Our music is affected by the landscape. Look at the rocks and stones; they're alive. I always get goosebumps in the country,' Hólm has said.

The lush scenery was an easy trope for the non-Icelandic press to pick up on, and pick up on it they did. 'Magazines always want to photograph us in front of a geyser,' keyboardist Kjartan Sveinsson has said. 'But it's a cliché to us: like photographing an English band in front of Tower Bridge.'

'We hate all the photos we did in front of Icelandic landscapes,' Birgisson griped in 2001. 'These pictures do not mean anything, only our music does.' Birgisson went on to say that 'the images cast by these handicapped persons, who are also in our video ["Svefn-G-Englar"], describe perfectly the honesty, sensitivity, and purity that we mean to represent. This is also the reason why we put babies on our covers. They represent a form of innocence that we are very attached to.'

This is a key insight into Sigur Rós at the time of *Ágætis Byrjun*. The 'handicapped' persons Birgisson refers to are the Perlan Theatre Group, actors with Down's Syndrome, who appear in the 'Svefn-G-Englar' video portraying angels in a lush green field. Without doubt, Sigur Rós were interested in promoting the work of Perlan (something Hólm has gone on the record about; Sigur Rós also made an 'Introducing Perlan' video to accompany 'Svefn-G-Englar', chatting to the actors involved), and Birgisson has direct experience of disability as he was born blind in one eye. Nevertheless, the unthinking stereotype of the video—denying the actors complexity by equating them with infants and angels—created a simple triumph-of-the-human-spirit narrative for the song and felt like a clear land grab for far more mainstream rock territory.

Another way Sigur Rós changed the working definition of post-rock was via their lack of interest in electronics; they claimed the only synthesized sound on *Ágætis Byrjun* was the 'ping' in 'Svefn-G-Englar'. This was a band thus able to claim a rock 'authenticity' in a way that Fridge—for example—could not (and nor did they wish to).

'I don't think the atmosphere around our band is the same,' Hólm said in 2001, referring to post-rock, but particularly to comparisons with Godspeed You! Black Emperor. 'I understand why people tend to categorise our music with their music, but I don't think we have much in common with them. It was very difficult touring with them. It was our first proper tour. Now we can look back—we have done several tours—but the Godspeed tour was really difficult. We had to have five minute soundchecks because they took three hours.'

The music of *Ágætis Byrjun* ran amok through film and television, starting with an extremely high-profile debut: the Tom Cruise/Penelope Cruz movie *Vanilla Sky*. 'We didn't like it at all,' Birgisson has said of the film. '[The director] Cameron Crowe asked for the songs. He used to write for *Rolling Stone* and listens to a lot of music, but it turned out to be a weird thing. It was too much Hollywood-like. We hope to have learned the lesson.' Their next significant soundtrack work was indeed more serious in intent: *Angels Of The Universe*, recorded in collaboration with composer and ex-Psychic TV member Hilmar Örm Hilmarsson. Sigur Rós's two contributions, 'Bíum Bíum Bambaló' and 'Dánarfregnir Og Jarðarfarir', felt especially hauntological; the former is based on an Icelandic lullaby, the latter on music that accompanies local radio announcements of funeral notices.

This relationship between post-rock and visual sources—directors, artists, TV producers, and (eventually) advertisers—was to increase substantially in the wake of *Ágætis Byrjun*'s success, contributing to the image of a tame and familiar post-rock. However, collaboration between post-rock and *auteurs* working in other media was an already-established trend. What seemed to really appeal about post-rock to visual artists was the time the sound took with texture and mood.

'It was an interesting process,' John McEntire has said of his 1998 soundtrack to the film *Reach The Rock*. 'I was composing directly to the cut, which was cool, 'cause I was doing it all on the computer, chasing the tape playback so I could spot things really precisely. Which is great to work out little pieces of music, like you calculate a tempo based on when you want a hit, when the door slams, and then you want another hit when somebody walks into the room, then go back and fill in the gaps. That kind of shit is fun.'

'Chris Fujiwara, our first bass player, is a film scholar,' says Glenn Jones of Cul de Sac. 'After leaving the band he wrote books on the filmmakers Jacques Tourneur and Otto Preminger. But at the time, he and his colleague, Scott Hamrah, were making original amateur films, so we started screening them at live shows. We didn't have a singer. As far as we were concerned, rock star-style posturing was an embarrassment, and something to be avoided at all costs, so there wasn't really anything for the audience to look at. So the films became a way of bringing a little bit of spectacle to what we did.'

The use of films in live settings was common, but was most effectively used by Godspeed You! Black Emperor, with images flickering as the musicians crouched over their instruments. Another interesting example is Insides. Julian Tardo and Kirsty Yates projected uncomfortable film of their faces, tight to camera, during their performances. 'It is quite weird, considering how shy we were, that that was the way we chose to play it: *OK, you'll have even more of us*,' Yates says.

Cul de Sac also performed a live soundtrack to F.W. Murnau's 1926 silent film *Faust*. 'We wrote two hours of original music for that,' Jones says. 'There'd be the major scenes where the whole band would play, and then there were scenes that seemed to call for only one or two instruments, or be a dialogue between instruments. It created all sorts of challenges. Whenever there was darkness and death and disease—cholera claiming the land, and those sorts of things—we loved it. We could really sink our teeth into that. But when we had to deal with humour, like when Marguerite is having her romance with the devil in counterpoint to Faust's romance with Gretchen—one is very tender, and the other is a complete farce. Having to go back and forth between the two was a real challenge for us. We may have grown as musicians by having to met those challenges, but I think it's safe to say that humour was not Cul de Sac's forte at all!'

Composing a soundtrack could provide a way around a creative block, as Stereolab's Tim Gane found. 'He [the artist Charles Long] was talking about this thing, and I said, Yeah, great, let me know. I'd just finished writing *Emperor Tomato Ketchup*, but we hadn't recorded yet, and then I get a phone call from him: "We're ready to go, it's two weeks' time, it's opening," and I'm like, two weeks! I haven't done anything!"

Charles Long's *The Amorphous Body Study Center* was an art installation that 'aimed to promote a better understanding between the body and the mind'. It consisted of a series of sculptures—the amorphous bodies—from which headphones sprouted, allowing people to listen to Stereolab's soundtrack. 'The audio program not only serves to establish a conducive mood for the mind to consider the public body,' Charles Long stated, 'but the headsets discourage the need to use the body to talk. This is a time to observe and be.'

'So … all right,' says Gane, picking up the story of the panicked Stereolab, 'We're going to write a series of melody loops, or try to. I had got dis-inspired again from *Emperor Tomato Ketchup*, and the thing that re-inspired me was listening to the very end of "Raindrops Keep Fallin' On My Head" by Burt Bacharach. It's got a bit right at the end, and I was just listening to it by chance where it kind of loops, and loops in a strange way. And I thought, this is what I've got to do, just get some really nice loops, and gradually add things on top. So [*Music For The Amorphous Body Center*] was recorded in a very short amount of time, just to radically do it. And it was really, really great. It was the perfect thing to do; and [the technique of looping] became a really big force in later Stereolab music, caused by just having to solve this problem.'

Looping, in a slightly different sense, was also part of *Thirty Minute Raven* by David Grubbs. 'It was an installation that was made for the Centre Pompidou for a group show that was called Elysian Fields,' he says. 'It was curated by *Purple* magazine in 1999. The piece, for me, kind of dramatised or represented the experienced of obsessive listening in the studio. The installation is on a sixty-minute loop. It starts at the top of the hour, so it really functions as a clock. At the top of the hour, and thirty minutes past the hour, you get the complete piece of music, which is this hard-driving, four-and-a-half-minute instrumental, with a dense arrangement. At fifteen minutes past the hour, and forty-five minutes past the hour, you get the coda to the piece, and then linking those moments in the hour-long cycle you have individual elements from the percussion track, scaled to the volume at which you would hear it if played acoustically in the space. There are some pretty long empty stretches. Let's call them *transparent* spaces!'

Between 1997 and 1999, the UK broadcaster Chris Morris created a radio show, *Blue Jam* (along with a television version, *Jam*), that simultaneously thrived on and undercut the hauntological elements of post-rock and electronica. According to Morris, it was about 'how your mind works in the middle of the night. It's designed to be hypnotic, so that it weaves itself in, and compelling, so that you stay with it. And quite often the jokes are going off underground—normally you're given a cue to laugh at things, and here there aren't any cues.' It was sinister, vicious, somnambulant, lawless and, indeed, fearless.

Labradford's 'P', Bark Psychosis's 'Pendulum Man', Stereolab's 'The Flower Called Nowhere', Brian Eno's 'Another Green World', and Third Eye Foundation's 'For All The Brothers And Sisters' were among the tracks used, but *Blue Jam* was more than its soundtrack. It actually felt like the radio equivalent to post-rock. Everything Chris Morris used seemed distorted: voices, images, samples, moralities, certainties; Morris benefitted from the new digital editing technology to fashion a crowded warren of surrealism that deconstructed the expected media tropes of radio, while simultaneously demolishing social hypocrisies and exposing interpersonal tensions.

Such instances of mining post-rock's seam of discomfort and disquiet became increasingly rare. More dominant was a trend to use the new kind of post-rock (as exemplified by Sigur Rós) in nature documentaries. This wasn't completely unheard of, for themes of the natural world and its discovery were present in Cocteau Twins' *Victorialand*, the post-Talk Talk band .O.rang, and an excellent if little-known 1993 album by The Ecstasy Of Saint Theresa: *Free-D (Original Soundtrack)*. However, works such as these tended to be part of the genteel overlap between post-rock and New Age, rooted in a shared interest in ambient. This new trend was different. Surging sounds met surging waves, and a kind of National Geographic post-rock sprung up.

Sigur Rós's 'Hoppipolla', from 2005's *Takk …* , was used to promote the David Attenborough documentary *Planet Earth*; the band also provided a re-recorded version for the 2016 *Planet Earth II*. 'In Iceland we are blessed with a seemingly inexhaustible supply of wild and untamed places,' the band said, in a statement for *Planet Earth II*. 'But even here, in the very furthest flung corners of Europe's largest wilderness, the scars of human industry are visible, the plans for future encroachments, by dam and smelter, legion. If lost the Icelandic highlands are not recoverable. Around the world the story is the same; the traffic, literally, going in one direction. Sigur Rós are proud to be associated with *Planet Earth II* and its all-important mission to hold us rapt in understanding of, and respect for, this endlessly fascinating, utterly surprising and ultimately fragile place we are lucky enough to call home for a short while.'

In the wake of *Planet Earth*, 'Hoppipolla' became extremely well known (at least in Britain), and was often used without the band's consent. '"Hoppipolla" has been raped on British TV,' Jónsi Birgisson said in 2010. 'In some weird way, the national TV here in Britain doesn't have to ask permission to use songs if it's in the background of TV shows or whatever. So they can just take it and use it, and that happened a lot with "Hoppipolla".'

Sigur Rós were asked in 2000 what would happen if people didn't believe their over-confident website mission statement—the one about changing music. 'Oh, fuck 'em,' Goggi Holm responded. 'We'll get them in the end … Like we say on our website, *we will*.'

They did. At least, they changed the way people thought about post-rock; they were the final ingredient in allowing post-rock to be re-integrated into mainstream rock sensibilities, appealing to a far wider audience in the process. 'We play pop, future pop,' Birgisson said in 2001. 'We hope that pop in the future is going to be like this.'

CHAPTER SEVENTEEN

the national anthem

'Post-rock had become kind of... trendy.' STUART BRAITHWAITE, MOGWAI

The attentive reader may remember Tony Wadsworth, Capitol and Parlophone Record's General Manager, chatting awkwardly about artistic integrity while trying very hard to fill in the long interview silences left by Mark Hollis's 'promotion' of *Spirit Of Eden*. Twelve years on, Talk Talk may well have been at the back of his mind. Now the president and CEO of EMI in the UK, Wadsworth was in charge of another bunch of unusually experimental musicians on a major label: Radiohead. But, this time, he wasn't panicking. He was gloating. 'The message is clear for UK record companies,' he said. 'Take risks, ditch the formulae, and support creative artist development, because it pays off.'

In a way that would have seemed almost unbelievable five years previously, post-rock had become a part of music's mainstream vocabulary. But it wasn't a straightforward co-option. Sometimes it was the philosophy that was taken up; sometimes the effects pedals. Post-rock-rock—rock music that could only have existed in post-rock's wake—was often as ill-at-ease as its parent had been.

It was around 1999 that the trend started to gather pace. One of the first examples of a powerful post-rock-rock sound came, appropriately enough, from emo. Emo—emotional hardcore—had its roots, as the name suggests, in hardcore, just as post-rock did. But where post-rock largely ditched or muddied the role of vocals, emo embraced and championed them; it was characterised by confessional, often introspective lyrics. The band American Football were one of the earliest bands to re-adhere post-rock to emo, making a striking statement—their 1999 self-titled album—that would be much-copied during the subsequent decade.

In an example of how most genre tags are unwelcome for artists, whatever they may be, American Football did not try to make an emo record. 'It was never something that any of us were interested in,' Mike Kinsella, the guitarist, vocalist, and bassist of the band, has said. 'Steve [Lamos], the drummer, was into a lot of jazz, and me and the other Steve [Holmes, guitarist] were into punk, and hardcore, and bands that were just sort of spastic and loud. When we played together, though, we were just making it all about the interplay between the guitars. The practices ended up involving a lot of counting, and we didn't have a vocal PA, so the other dudes didn't know any of the lyrics or the vocal melodies until we actually went out and played a show. For a couple of songs, I don't think they'd ever even heard the vocals until we went into record.'

Kinsella's lyrics were an axis, but they weren't there all *that* often. Tracks like 'The Summer Ends', and especially the instrumental closer, 'The One With The Wulitzer', are vulnerable in a much more cryptic way, with Steve Lamos—a trumpeter as well as a drummer—exuding languid and sorrowful tones that complicate the directness of Kinsella's heartfelt words. American Football's method of composing was influenced by Steve Reich, in the sense that Kinsella and Holmes would 'both have patterns going on, and we tried to see how we could let them overlap; have one move on while the other stays, then flip it the other way on the next section. So, it was never verse-chorus-verse-chorus; it was always to do with musical cues.' The group's rehearsal and demo material—such as 'Untitled #3 (Boombox Practice Session, 1999)'—lays bare the mechanics of the repetitive, shifting interplay that underpinned the album.

Like Slint and *Spiderland*, or Bark Psychosis and *Hex*, American Football split up virtually concurrently with their album's release. They had almost made *American Football* as a graduation present to themselves, and then in 1999 they quietly disbanded, leaving few mourners outside of their immediate community. But, as with *Spiderland*, *American Football*'s reputation grew. Listeners were drawn not just by Kinsella's stark memoir—after all, rock isn't short of lyrics like that—but because it combined with such patient textural subtlety. Although at the time it was an obscure release, *American Football* showed that post-rock characteristics themselves could be taken apart and refashioned into something that, once again, resembled rock music.

Also in 1999, and with what seems like similar emotional intent to American Football, a 'Sad Triumphant Rock Band' formed (or so read the advert planted in a record shop in Austin, Texas, by the drummer Chris Hrasky). This was Breaker Morant; they soon renamed themselves Explosions In The Sky. The group—Hrasky, and three guitarists, Michael James, Munaf Rayani, and Mark Smith—did as much as Sigur Rós did to change and develop the meaning of post-rock for the 2000s. 'We don't consider ourselves post-rock at all; we consider ourselves a rock band,' Munaf Rayani has said. They too were a post-rock-rock band; it is hard to imagine them without their post-rock forbears.

'I really like the idea of taking an individual story and translating it musically,' Rayani said in 2001. 'I don't know if you remember the Russian sailors that crashed into the bottom of the ocean about a year ago. The Russian submarine or whatever. Well, we wrote a song around that which hopefully will show up on the next record.' It did: 2003's *The Earth Is Not A Cold Dead Place* contains 'Six Days At The Bottom Of The Ocean', so named because that is 'how long they were alive down there'.

A lot of the stories that Explosions In The Sky mined in their early days had unusually militaristic themes ('All the songs we'd been doing up until that point seemed like they were about … war,' Michael James bluntly claimed in 2001). This was especially true of their 2001 album *Those Who Tell The Truth Shall Die, Those Who Tell The Truth Shall Live*

Forever. Its artwork relates to the Angel of Mons fable, evoking the pity of war, as Hrasky explained.

'In World War I, there was a group of French troops in a trench. In trench warfare, there's not much movement except back and forth through the trenches. And one night, after a really fierce battle, they all looked up at the sky and they thought they saw an angel in the clouds. They all reported seeing it, or at least a significant portion of them did, but the official military story is that it was a plane's lights.'

The mottos in the album's booklet related to the Angel of Mons: the words 'this plane will crash tomorrow' and 'help us stay alive' are juxtaposed with the silhouettes of soldiers against a blood-red sky. Released on September 4, 2001, *Those Who Tell The Truth Shall Die, Those Who Tell The Truth Shall Live Forever* earned the band brief notoriety in the light of events in New York just one week later.

Explosions In The Sky might have preferred to be called rock music, but they were the prime example of how the tag post-rock was now the default for instrumental music—the lazy option for writers that had begun, really, with Dirty Three. It was also clear that Explosions In The Sky—like Mogwai and Godspeed You! Black Emperor—were emphatically a *live* act, indicating how the idea of post-rock had moved far from those who would retreat from performance at the first opportunity, or stumble cantankerously through sets. Now, post-rock was more associated with musicians revelling in the effect their music had, much like My Bloody Valentine had done. Explosions In The Sky left audiences (and themselves) glassy-eyed. 'All of us get so lost while we're playing that I truly don't know where I am,' Rayani has said. 'We've ended shows where we're just toppled over on each other. When that last note ends and I look up, it's like I haven't been there the whole time.'

Explosions In The Sky were signed to the (then) Baltimore-based Temporary Residence; Fridge, unhappy at Go! Beat, had also joined up with the label. 'This must be 2000, 2001,' Kieran Hebden says. 'And I remember arriving and hearing all the music on Temporary Residence and being kind of confused by it in some ways. Because it was *all* post-rock. It was all post-rock in this melodic, chiming guitars [way]. I realise, in hindsight, for loads and loads of people, this was the beginning. And for me it was the end.'

The 2001 Fridge album released on Temporary Residence, *Happiness*, had been brewing for a while. 'We'd kind of been working on the record for ages and we had recorded loads of material that wasn't right,' says Hebden. 'We went back to it and we were experimenting to a point where we were making some stuff that was not very good. Just because we were trying to do something really different. I think we were trying to do stuff that was more with these big arrangements and lots of instrumentation and stuff, and it sounded over-convoluted.'

Fridge were gifted a chance to whip the tracks into shape when their publishers, Universal, got access to the Island Records studios. 'We were allowed to use that and they would pay for it,' Hebden says. 'So we went into the studio there and did a bunch of stuff and that was a turning point for the record, I think. We went through this whole process and discarded a bunch of stuff and then wrote all this other material. We had that combination of not having much baggage and being particularly open-minded, but also we'd actually acquired more technical ability at that point.'

One of Fridge's final acts as a band—bar an underwhelming reunion album in 2007, *The Sun*—was to tour as Badly Drawn Boy's live band. 'For me, it got something out of my system,' Hebden says. 'The idea of being in a rock band or whatever. It made me more interested in focusing on my electronic music stuff [as Four Tet], where I could be more anonymous. But then after that, Adem … I don't know what the exact reason was for it, but then he started writing songs. He'd always sung a bit and I think he wanted to get more into singing, and maybe for him he was watching it and thinking, I want to do *my* songs. Not this other dude's songs.'

'I collect silly little instruments,' Ilhan has said, expressing the same urge that had led him to tape down eight cassette recorders onto an ironing board at the start of Fridge. 'I get them from flea markets;

I can't really afford to get them from anywhere else. Or friends give them to me when they find them in attics. I have an Autoharp, which is basically a box with strings across it and some mechanics to make it work. I took it home and found out to play it and how it shouldn't be played. I hit it with a paintbrush and it made a good sound, so I decided to make a track based on that. It was an acoustic instrument and I thought, *that's nice*. Let's try to record some acoustic instruments and try not to use any electronics.' The result was the Adem album *Homesongs*, released in 2004.

'Sam then got interested in a lot of computer programming,' continues Hebden. 'Designing websites and things. And he started getting work doing that, and he was building websites. And now the three of us do completely different things.'

Fridge had been in demand as collaborators during their purple period, not only as live musicians but as remixers and producers. This development was another important way in which post-rock infiltrated the mainstream. On this occasion, Fridge had been headhunted by Arthur Baker. 'He hears Fridge on [London alternative radio station] XfM, and contacts Output,' Hebden says. 'He was working on this record with Bernard Sumner and Johnny Marr—they had this project called Electronic—and he says, These guys need some fresh blood, new people to come in and work with. So he hires Fridge to come in. He's in Rak Studios, and that's the first time I ever went in a recording studio. And we walk in, and these guys have got pretty much the whole studio booked out. And we walk in and … we're in charge. Me and Adem and Sam. And we walk in with our rubbish keyboards under our arms, and all our equipment, and we didn't worry about anything, we just got right stuck in to it. I'd just be there in a swivel chair at the mixing desk. I think what was interesting to me is that we worked there for a couple of days and the stuff we were coming out with didn't really sound much different to what we'd been doing in our bedrooms. It was all this lo-fi, distorted mess.' The two tracks Fridge worked on, 'Haze' and 'Late At Night', appeared on the 1999 Electronic album *Twisted Tenderness*.

Mogwai, too, found they got more remix offers following their defilement of David Holmes's 'Don't Die Just Yet'. One was for the Manic Street Preachers ('You Stole The Sun From My Heart' in 1998); Mogwai also supported them on the 1999 *This Is My Truth, Tell Me Yours* arena tour. 'They were lovely boys, as well,' said the Manics' Nicky Wire. 'They were sweet. Uncorrupted. Very rare.' (Manics fans didn't always agree; Mogwai were pelted and heckled on numerous occasions, but always gamely played on.)

Mogwai had taken the bathroom pact that they had made following *Mogwai Young Team* very seriously, and, moreover, listened to their critics as well as their admirers. 'I think a lot of people—and this shows how young and touchy we were—had criticised that there were so many effects [on *Mogwai Young Team*]. And that it was all pedals and stuff. So I think we wanted to make a record that almost didn't have any,' says Stuart Braithwaite. Mogwai were also keen to not fudge together songs in the studio for this album, as they had done with *Mogwai Young Team*.

'The noisy songs were ones written when we still doing *Mogwai Young Team*, or very close to it,' Braithwaite says. 'And really the songs we wrote specifically for *Come On Die Young* were in a certain style. We wanted it to be like The Jesus & Mary Chain did on *Darklands*; I'd never actually thought about that [at the time], but they were very much about the music and not the sound. And also I think I was getting really into quite minimalist music, like Phillip Glass, and Low, and The For Carnation, and the last Nick Drake album, *Pink Moon*. It was very much a less-is-more kind of thing. And also films, like *The Exorcist*. We wanted to be very prepared, and we wanted it to be *not* the same as the first one.'

Mogwai carefully demoed and incessantly rehearsed, in a bid to stave off the shortcuts of last time. They started recording in Glasgow, but then capitalised on the friendly relationship their label Chemikal Underground had with Dave Fridmann, who had just produced Mercury Rev's *Deserter's Songs* at his Tarbox Road studios. Fridmann had completely altered that band's approach, augmenting their sound with orchestral instruments rather than guitars. '*Deserter's Songs* is a brilliant sounding record,' says Braithwaite, 'and again, probably because we were young, we said [to Chemikal Underground], We can go to America! And you'll pay for it!'

Tarbox was out in the wilderness, wolves and wild dogs circling, presumably kept back by the swelling of 'Christmas Steps' or the enmity of 'May Nothing But Happiness Come Through Your Door'.

Come On Die Young opens with 'Punk Rock:' and an Iggy Pop sample. 'It was on a bootleg video that my girlfriend at the time had borrowed from someone. Me and Dominic saw it and we were just, *that's amazing*. I was always worried over the years that Iggy Pop was gonna try and sue us, but apparently he'd heard it and thought it was cool. So that's good.'

'It's a term that's based on contempt,' Iggy Pop opines in the sampled dialogue. 'It's a term that's based in fashion, style, elitism, Satanism, and everything that's rotten about rock'n'roll.' The analytical type might pull out parallels between what Iggy Pop said about punk and what was now the feeling—Satanism aside, perhaps—for post-rock.

'I don't know if we were even thinking about it that deeply,' Braithwaite says. 'I think we just thought it was cool!'

Come On Die Young is a ravishing experience, a huge leap from *Mogwai Young Team*, and a clear attempt by Mogwai to cleave deeper in terms of finding the inherent emotion and tension within a track. There is far more ambient patience: the drip-drip of 'Chocky', the distorted piano balladry of 'Oh! How The Dogs Stack Up'; these are hues that had not been present on *Mogwai Young Team*. 'We've avoided a lot of the quiet/loud element of things because we've managed to do that to death,' Braithwaite said at the time of *Come On Die Young*'s release. 'It's kicking the fuck out of it to keep doing it. I guess it's downbeat, a bit more thoughtful.'

For *Rock Action*, Mogwai's third album, they returned to Fridmann and Tarbox. 'We'd moved to a big label,' says Stuart Braithwaite. 'So there was a bigger budget. And we were going to spend all the money we could! We spent ages and ages and ages in the studio.' Multi-instrumentalist Barry Burns—who joined in the middle of making *Come On Die Young*, and had contributed 'Oh! How The Dogs Stack

Up'—was now more central to the band. 'We had access to a lot of different instruments that we'd bought,' Braithwaite says—these included a vocoder, and a synthesizer, as well as brass and banjos—'and I think we wanted to make as different a record as possible.'

The greater emphasis of vocals on *Rock Action* was also a point of difference. Braithwaite sings in several places (and was vocoder'd on 'Two Rights Make One Wrong'); David Pajo's burr is audible on 'Take Me Somewhere Nice'; and Gruff Rhys of Super Furry Animals is the most prominent presence, on 'Dial: Revenge'. Using so many words was a gamble for Mogwai, as they were so associated with their lack, but Braithwaite sees it partly as a reaction to post-rock's development. 'In this period, our style of music, the instrumental post-rock, had become quite commonplace,' Braithwaite says, 'and I think we wanted to do something very different, very different from that.'

'Embarrassing. Embarrassing but necessary,' Braithwaite said at the time, when asked about his vocals on *Rock Action*. 'Singing a song is like stopping the car on a motorway, jumping out, doing a pee behind a tree and seeing that a family's having a picnic and they can see you.'

But one thing didn't change. Although many might think that the title *Rock Action* was a statement of a new direction, it was actually a continuation of Mogwai's now-proud tradition of piss-taking. 'This guy John Niven, who's now a writer, had signed us [to Southpaw],' says Braithwaite. 'And I think we wanted to annoy John, and annoy Colin, who was our old manager. It was this guy Mark Mitchell who was involved in putting the record out. And I remember him writing this massive email [about] why it shouldn't be called *Rock Action*, and why it wasn't a good title, and I think the more we realised it was annoying people, the more we wanted to keep it. That was kind of our philosophy back then.'

Mogwai remained a very busy live band. As well as the Manics tour, in 1999, they played at a new festival-of-sorts—the Bowlie weekender, in Camber Sands, on the Sussex coast. It was organised by the band Belle & Sebastian and, rather than having its punters camp in a muddy field with lots of corporate logos, Bowlie lodged them in holiday chalet accommodation and banned sponsorship. The acts on the bill were all indie-and-proud, and although more than a few erred on the side of twee, Mogwai and Godspeed You Black Emperor! were two notable exceptions.

Stuart Braithwaite was asked at the time how punk rock Bowlie was. 'At the moment, pretty much zero,' he said. 'It's all duffle coats and hairgrips. But there's definitely an anti-chart feeling.'

The Bowlie weekender was a success, and its creators built on this anti-chart feeling to spawn All Tomorrow's Parties. The first ATP took place in 2000 and was curated by Mogwai; the second, in 2001, had Tortoise at its helm. ATP remained extremely supportive of post-rock into the 2000s, with future curators including Slint and Explosions In The Sky. ATP promoted successful events for fifteen years (until financial mismanagement ruined first its reputation and then its business), and there was usually a good proportion of post-rock artists past and present on the bill.

'We've gotta give a shout out to Mogwai, because they asked us to do ATP multiple times,' Stephen Immerwahr of Codeine says. 'We turned them down multiple times. And they kept asking! And when it was time to do the reunion shows and we *could* say yes, and we did, they were incredibly generous to us. Their generosity in sponsoring us, and getting us on to ATP shows, really made a lot possible.'

As important as all these developments were in terms of exposing post-rock to a wider audience and cross-fertilising with rock, it was the act of one band—almost unique in their position of having a huge and trusting audience that were willing to hear pretty much any output from them—that provided some kind of benchmark for a post-rock rock.

Ironically, while bands who were unblinkingly tagged post-rock primarily by being instrumental fought against it, Radiohead had a hard time getting recognition for just *how* post-rock *Kid A* and *Amnesiac* really were. Because, while most of the bands that had helped make post-rock over the previous decade-and-a-half picked and chose a few of its central tenets, these two Radiohead albums contained every one of post-rock's primary attributes: guitars as texture, lack of group hierarchy, spaciousness, deconstruction, incorporating disparate influences, distorted or abstracted vocals, dizzying flexibility, anti-nostalgia, using the studio's outer limits, colourful timbre, incorporation of sampling and electronic technology, an obsessive focus on packaging and tactility; all were ticked off. That's not to say that *Kid A* and *Amnesiac* are the *best* post-rock albums, but they do represent a culmination of sorts.

'It's like, how do we start this—when we made our last three albums, there were time restrictions—we no longer have these,' Ed O'Brien, Radiohead's guitarist, reflected in his online diary on August 4 1999. Two days later, he summed up the terror and glory of being in the position they were in: 'It's taken us seven years to get this sort of freedom, and it's what we always wanted, but it could be so easy to fuck it all up.'

If Britpop had helped assassinate the British post-rock class of 1994, Radiohead certainly got a little bit of revenge on their behalf a few years later. In 1997, their third album, *OK Computer*, left Britpop looking shallow and outmoded. It caught a pensive, destabilised mood (also present in Spiritualized's album of the same year, *Ladies And Gentlemen We Are Floating In Space*), was instantly deified, and turned indie music in the UK toward the simultaneously epic and despondent. Stripping down to a clipped, riff-y sound wasn't cutting it any more; the grandiose was in, even for milquetoast Radiohead imitators like Muse, Travis, and Coldplay.

But for Radiohead personally, the most immediate effect of *OK Computer* was the insatiable demand for them: to play live, to 'perform' in interviews, and (for Thom Yorke especially) to absorb crippling character judgments. The documentary *Meeting People Is Easy*, which follows them on their 1997 tour, shows a band compelled into endless repetitive tasks, reeling off radio idents and recording acceptance speeches as *OK Computer* racks up gongs, while leaving the band exhausted, hostile, and cut off from the music that was now sung back to them every night by thousands upon thousands of other people.

'The more concerts we do, the more dissatisfied we get with trying to reproduce the live sound on a record,' Jonny Greenwood said in 2001, expressing one of many post-rock ideas which would influence their 1999 recording sessions. 'In a way it can't be done, and that's a relief really, when you accept that, and recording just becomes a different thing.'

'What were those reasons [for starting a diary]?' O'Brien asked himself at the start of October 1999. 'A mixed bag really, a bit of an attempt to de-mythologise this whole process of making a new record. It might be of interest to some to hear from one of the horses' mouths (or arses) what is going on. And it's actually pretty interesting for us if only to reassure me / ourselves that there are patterns which emerge.'

Since *OK Computer*, a few influences had come into Radiohead's ambit; while not exactly new to the band, they seemed to present themselves in a different way now. Yorke had long had an ear to Warp Records—he had been impressed by how the label's 1990 release, Sweet Exorcist's 'Per Clonk', 'sounded really amazing coming out of an enormous PA system. All that Warp stuff made the bass bins blow with their turbo sounds.' Post-*OK Computer*, he splurged on the label's entire back catalogue. Jonny Greenwood, with a solid place in riff history for the guitar-as-carving-knife of 'Creep', was now more interested in an obscure electronic instrument, primarily used in modern classical: the ondes martenot. Ed O'Brien revealed the explicit influence of Hank Shocklee's work with Public Enemy, and of Mark Hollis's 1998 solo album. The group frequently spoke of Can, of the Polish composer Krzysztof Penderecki, and of free jazz.

In the background, Yorke was struggling with his own words and voice. Writer's block plagued him after *OK Computer*, and he only broke through it by using the technique of cut 'n' paste. Instead of crafting lyrics, he slashed through them with sudden, destructive, unpredictable actions; he gladly incorporated accident, and by severing his words from linear meaning, he consciously liberated them from a duty of care.

As to his voice, the glut of Yorkian imitators had affected him, and cut him off from his own distinctiveness. He now 'got really into the idea of my voice being another of the instruments, rather than this precious, focus thing all the time'. Blessed with vocal dexterity, Yorke was able to reassess his own voice, reaching similar conclusions to those of Scott Walker on *Climate Of Hunter* and *Tilt*. 'There's an unhealthy obsession with death going on, and also the absolute opposite of hopeless,' Yorke has said of the lyrical threads of *Kid A* and *Amnesiac*, and they shone through despite the cutups (and sounded another echo of *Tilt*).

The members of Radiohead had known one another for twenty years and had played together for more than fifteen, but, all of a sudden, that history felt meaningless. Their musical positions were overturned, acoustic sounds rejected in favour of electronics, and sometimes a member's regular instrument wasn't required at all. O'Brien has said that they all needed to learn 'how to be a participant in a song without playing a note'. Unlike bands such as Godspeed and Ut, who had anti-hierarchy intentions from their beginnings, it was psychologically difficult for Radiohead to erase the accumulation of inter-band dynamics in this way, and none of the band have ever suggested these sessions were easy in that regard. They even—in a Rain Tree Crow-ish break from established identity—toyed with a fresh band name.

'If you're going to make a different-sounding record you have to change the methodology,' O'Brien has said. 'And it's scary—everyone feels insecure. I'm a guitarist and suddenly it's like, Well, there are no guitars on this track, or no drums. Jonny, me, Coz [Colin], and Phil had to get our heads round that. It was a test of the band, I think. Would we survive with our egos intact?'

'It's a return to where we were at school and we couldn't play our instruments very well,' Colin Greenwood noted.

O'Brien, according to his online diary, was finding that certain band behaviour—for instance, taking lots of breaks—meant they were in worried mode; or that when things 'came to a head' (as O'Brien diplomatically terms one of the *Kid A/Amnesiac* arguments), he could console himself with a bottle of wine and the knowledge that, when the same thing had happened a month earlier, an intense period of creativity followed. O'Brien later said that the band thought 'long and hard about whether we wanted to continue at all' during this period. 'We had a meeting, and there was a scary, unspoken sort of fear. We were really serious. I mean, why not go out on top?'

O'Brien's diary reveals the fairly standard pains and joys of making a new album. However, when analysing how these sessions differed to *OK Computer*, he notes that Radiohead now paid far more attention to the studio environment. 'The way we worked on the last record was to rehearse everything to such a standard, where most of the parts have been so finely tuned, that recording was largely a matter of capturing the best performance,' O'Brien writes. 'And that's fine, but recording in this way tends to mean that the songs have a certain way of sounding, i.e. pretty good in a live/band context.'

Several songs were started at once, and then left in stasis; although it was an effective way to break through the capturing-a-performance method of recording, it could leave the band feeling skittish and unfulfilled. To re-galvanise them, producer Nigel Godrich—as important to Radiohead as Tim Friese-Greene was to Talk Talk at this point—suggested *Oblique Strategies*-esque tactics, including separating the members into two sub-groups. Another Godrich method was to insist on building experimentation in as a studio process rather than a technological add-on.

'Nigel Godrich is very into the idea that if you're going to do something weird with the track, you make it weird there and then, rather than doing it in the mix afterwards, because the effect changes the way people play,' Yorke has recalled. 'They'll play to it, and that's really inspiring, because it's like having a new instrument. If you've got an incredibly cool reverb or something on your voice, suddenly you're really excited about what you're doing again.'

The band looked for coincidence or fate, and would embrace it. 'Like Spinning Plates', for example, had its seed in an earlier song, 'I Will'; it was only when 'I Will' was played backward that the potential for 'Like Spinning Plates' was revealed.

The studio came to the fore in several other related ways, often with conscious reference to Can. 'It was incredibly boring,' Yorke said of editing 'Dollars & Cents' down from an eleven-minute improvisation, 'but it's that Holger [Czukay] thing of chop-chop-chop, making what seems like drivel into something coherent.' It also had shades of the *Laughing Stock* sessions, panning for gold among the inevitable bagginess of instant creation. The other Talk Talk tint was in Radiohead's use of lesser-spotted instruments and gear; although Jonny Greenwood's ondes martenot is the obvious example, there was also its palm speaker for reverb, and ribbon microphones channelled through an egg box on 'You And Whose Army'.

Greenwood later reflected on the false dichotomy between the 'artifice' of electronic instruments and the 'authenticity' of acoustic ones. 'I see it like this: a voice into a microphone onto a tape, onto your CD, through your speakers is all as illusory and fake as any synthesizer—it doesn't put Thom in your front room. But one is perceived as 'real', the other somehow 'unreal' … it's the same with guitars versus samplers. It was just freeing to discard the notion of acoustic sounds being truer.'

It also disrupted the expected sound of a band with five members in it. While (for instance) 'Kid A' might sound smaller than the sum of its parts, 'The National Anthem' sounds much larger; it was this Tortoise-style flexibility that formed an important part of facing down the band's pre-existing dynamics.

Thom Yorke was used to—if not always happy with—having his lyrics scrutinised for meaning. Although the cut 'n' paste method of *Kid A* formed some defence against this, the band's politics were often invoked in terms of *Kid A*, especially since O'Brien had recommended that Radiohead fans read Naomi Klein's *No Logo*, and as Yorke was publicly engaged with the alt-globalisation movement. *Kid A* evoked a pitiless system of subtle oppression.

'If there is a devil at work, then he rests in institutions and not individuals,' Yorke has said. 'Because the beauty of institutions is that any individual can abdicate responsibility,' He wasn't unaware of the irony of a millionaire rock star issuing such pronouncements, and of how it might not settle well in certain quarters—Efrim Menuck, for example.

'We don't know Radiohead, we've never met them or communicated with them in any way, some people in Godspeed like their music, others don't ... ' Menuck wrote in an open letter in 2001. 'The fact remains, Radiohead are owned, part and parcel, by a gigantic multinational corporation, and their critique of global corporatism is tainted by that one harsh reality.' (It's important to note that Menuck was not holding Godspeed up as a paradigm of consistency by comparison. 'Anyone wants to punch holes in our politics, go ahead; you wanna say that we don't properly address the paradox of a "political" band making money off of compulsive shoppers or victims of fetish capitalism—guess what, YOU'RE RIGHT! We haven't properly addressed that paradox at all, and we know it and we kinda know why too,' he added.)

Radiohead *do* attempt to deal with these contradictions through a very post-rock strategy—abstraction over many levels. Walking over Yorke's cutup words was his mutilated voice, obfuscating his intent further via vocoder and autotune. On 'Packt Like Sardines In A Crushd Tin Box' and 'Pulk/Pull Revolving Doors', Yorke used autotune by giving 'the machine a key and then you just talk into it. It desperately tries to search for the music in your speech, and produces notes at random. If you've assigned it a key, you've got music.' The effect is dislocation, reflecting the atomisation that Yorke saw happening in wider society; of tiny, invisible, powerful structures guiding everyday thought and movement while, concurrently, political and environmental systems undergo terrifying lurches.

Radiohead decided to separate the sessions into two distinct albums, rather than putting the lot out at once. *Kid A* came first, in 1999, released on the cusp of two industry eras. The band embraced the potential of the internet, offering *Kid A* as a stream to fans from their website, but they were also protective of their new album, playing it to the press only at hermetic listening sessions. 'I think the one serious regret we have ... the one mistake we made is that we didn't give the record to journalists a longer time away from the release,' Colin Greenwood reflected, very soon after *Kid A*'s release. 'I think it's a problem a lot of bands are going to have, how to deal with it getting onto the internet. But I think that [holding the album back] definitely hurt us. But I think a lot of people are into it now they've lived with it for a while, because it's a great record.'

Not long after *Kid A*, and sometimes with a palpable edge of relief, it was reported that there was a 'Kid B' in the can: another Radiohead album from the same sessions. *Kid A* might be all arms-as-windmills, flailing out to punch the casual Radiohead fan, but *Amnesiac* would be the 'reward' for those who still stuck around. It was a plausible theory. A lot of the more 'song'-type tracks—'Knives Out', 'You And Whose Army', 'Dollars & Cents', 'I Might Be Wrong', and 'Pyramid Song' (aka 'Egyptian Song', aka 'Nothing To Fear')—had already been played live, and were more obviously within a rock lineage. (In fact, for *Kid A* to lose moments like 'Pyramid Song' was another very post-rock move; rejecting the too-beautiful, the too-moving, in pursuit of an overall mood.)

'I think the artwork is the best way of explaining it,' Yorke reflected, on the difference between the two releases. 'The artwork to *Kid A* was all in the distance. The fires were all going on the other side of the hill. With *Amnesiac*, you're actually in the forest while the fire's happening.'

Amnesiac is, indeed, a warmer work, and the deconstructed moments—the guitar scrabble of 'Hunting Bears', after John Fahey or Jim O'Rourke; the reverse-shot 'Like Spinning Plates'—seem more human. Reflecting on the closing track, 'Life In A Glasshouse', a sort of despairing piece of dinner jazz, Yorke said, 'I'm desperate for people to understand the words because they're really important. It began after I read this interview with the wife of a very famous actor who the tabloids completely hounded for three months like dogs from hell. She got copies of all the papers with her picture and she pasted them up all over the house, over all the windows, so that all the cameras that were outside her lawn only had their own images to photograph … I thought that was brilliant.' Finally, *Amnesiac*'s packaging was of a hardback library book, complete with stamped dates, bringing in the recent hauntological trend in post-rock.

Asked why people shouldn't just listen to Aphex Twin rather than Radiohead, Ed O'Brien said, 'Well in that case, why listen to a Bowie album? Why not go to the sources that he was listening to? If you're creating and doing something new, you're absorbing influences. It's that age-old thing of taking on new things and making them your own. You find your own path, and that's what makes it interesting.'

That was what post-rock did, and it had now been made; it was as solid as the awkward bastard would ever get.

'It's definitely about finding your own voice,' says Graham Sutton.

'I guess you just let all these things come out, for better or worse, and then you figure out what to do with them,' says Tara Jane O'Neil.

'We didn't understand it. I don't know who does understand it,' says Efrim Menuck.

Now, nothing left to fear.

ACKNOWLEDGEMENTS

Thank you: Aaron, Anita, Coral, Dan, David, Howard, Ian, Jude, Judy & David, Ken, Lauren, Louis, Louise, Lucy, Naomi, Nik, Noshee, Phil, Stephen C., Stephen D., Vinita.

My interviewees: for time and inspiration; for sharing viewpoints, memories, archives, and the occasional drink.

My brilliant editor: Tom.

Special thanks and love, for support above and beyond: Andrew, Gladys, Heather, Kathryn, Paul, Rupert, Tim.

And most of all: love to my fearless husband, Graham.

NOTES AND SOURCES

INTERVIEWEES

Fearless includes original material from interviews with the following people:

Gavin Baker
Stuart Braithwaite
Gary Bromley
David Callahan
Joe Cassidy
Mark Clifford
Ian Crause
Eric Craven
John Engle
Dan Erickson
Margaret Fiedler
Tim Gane
Mimi Goese
Rachel Grimes
David Grubbs
Jacqui Ham
Kieran Hebden
Gen Heistek
RM Hubbert
Julian Hunt
Ian Ilavsky
Steven Immerwahr
Glenn Jones
Stevie Jones
Noel Lane
Joel Leoschke
Gary McKendry
John McEntire
Efrim Menuck
Howard Monk
Jeff Mueller
Tara Jane O'Neil
Jeff Parker
Sarah Peacock
Kevin Penney
Doug Scharin
Graham Sutton
Rudy Tambala
Julian Tardo
Richie Thomas
Kirsty Yates
Sally Young

All quoted material is from original interview sources unless stated below.

BOOKS

Martin Aston *Facing The Other Way: The Story Of 4AD* (Faber, 2013)
Michael Azerrad *Our Band Could Be Your Life: Scenes From the American Indie Underground 1981–1991* (Little, Brown, 2001)
Stephen Blush *American Hardcore: A Tribal History* (Feral House, 2010)
David Brown *Goodbye 20th Century: Sonic Youth And The Rise Of The Alternative Nation* (Da Capo, 2008)
Joe Carducci *Rock And The Pop Narcotic* (Redoubt, 1995)
Jeff Chang *Can't Stop, Won't Stop: A History Of The Hip-Hop Generation* (Macmillan, 2005)
Chuck D. *Fight The Power: Rap, Race And Reality* (Dell, 1998)
Jacques Derrida *Of Grammatology* (John Hopkins, 2016)
Jacques Derrida *Spectres Of Marx* (Routledge, 1994)

James Doheny *Radiohead: The Stories Behind Every Song* (Carlton, 2012)
Kim Gordon *Girl In A Band* (Faber, 2015)
Marvin Lin *Kid A* (Bloomsbury, 2011)
John Lydon *Rotten: No Irish, No Blacks, No Dogs* (Picador, 1993)
John Lydon *Anger Is An Energy: My Life Uncensored* (Simon & Schuster, 2014)
James Marsh, Chris Roberts, Toby Benjamin *Spirit Of Talk Talk* (Rocket 88, 2012)
Marc Masters *No Wave* (Black Dog, 2007)
Mike McGonigal *Loveless* (Bloomsbury, 2007)
Mick Middles *Factory: The Story Of The Record Label* (Penguin, 1996)
Erik Morse *Dreamweapon: Spacemen 3 And The Birth Of Spiritualized* (Omnibus, 2004)
James Nice *Shadowplayers: The Rise And Fall Of Factory Records* (Aurum, 2010)
Michael Nyman *Experimental Music: Cage And Beyond* (Cassell, 1974)
Ranaldo, Lee *JRNLS 80s* (Soft Skull, 1998)
Simon Reynolds *Rip It Up And Start Again* (Faber, 2005)
Ann Scanlon *Those Tourists Are Money: The Rock'n'roll Guide To Camden* (Trista, 1997)
Tom Seabrook *Bowie In Berlin: A New Career In A New Town* (Jawbone, 2008)
David Sheppard *On Some Faraway Beach: The Life And Times Of Brian Eno* (Orion, 2008)
David Stubbs *Future Days: Krautrock And The Building Of Modern Germany* (Faber, 2014)
Scott Tennent *Spiderland* (Bloomsbury, 2007)
David Toop *Ocean Of Sound: Aether Talk, Ambient Sound, And Imaginary Worlds* (Serpent's Tail, 1995)
Michael Veal *Dub: Soundscapes And Shattered Songs In Jamaican Reggae* (Wesleyan, 2007)
Tony Visconti *Bowie, Bolan And The Brooklyn Boy: The Autobiography* (Harper, 2007)
Dean Wareham *Black Postcards: A Rock 'N' Roll Romance* (Penguin, 2008)
Valerie Wilmer *As Serious As Your Life: John Coltrane And Beyond* (Quartet, 1977)
Paul Woods *Scott: The Curious Life And Work Of Scott Walker* (Omnibus, 2013)
Christopher E. Young *On The Periphery: David Sylvian—A Biography* (Malin, 2015)
Rob Young (ed.) *No Regrets: Writings On Scott Walker* (Orion, 2013)

VISUAL

Breadcrumb Trail (dir. Lance Bangs, 2014)
Come Worry With Us! (dir. Helen Klodawsky, 2013)
Brian Eno: Another Green World (dir. Nicola Roberts, 2011)
Half-Cocked (dir. Suki Hawley, 1994)
Jam (TV series) (dir. Chris Morris, 2000)
Lonely Is An Eyesore (dir. Nigel Grierson, 1987)
Meeting People Is Easy (dir. Grant Gee, 1998)
Put Blood In The Music (*The South Bank Show*, March 12 1989, dir. Charles Atlas, 1988)
Swans: A Long Slow Screw (1988)
Too Pure special on MTV's *120 Minutes* (c. late 1993)

AUDIO

Blue Jam (BBC Radio 1, 1997–99)
Brian Eno and Alan Moore on *Chain Reaction* (BBC Radio 4, January 2005)
Mark Hollis Talks About Laughing Stock (promo, 1991)
The Mogwai Story (BBC 6Music, February 8 2015)
Vini Reilly in conversation with Dave Haslam, at Manchester Town Hall (March 3 2013)

MAJOR ARTICLES

Kevin Adickes, 'Explosions In The Sky', *Pitchfork*, November 1 2001
Steve Albini, 'The Problem With Music', *Maximumrocknroll*, June 1994
Maddy Costa, 'Godspeed You! Black Emperor: The Full Transcript', the *Guardian*, October 11 2012
Byron Coley, 'John Fahey: The Persecutions And Resurrections Of Blind Joe Death', *Spin*, November 1994
Christoph Cox, 'Jim O'Rourke: Studies In Frustration', *The Wire*, November 1997
Ronald Hart, 'Tortoise's Pioneering Debut Album: An Oral History', Red Bull Music Academy, June 20 2014
Glenn Jones liner notes to *The Epiphany Of Glenn Jones* (Thirsty Ear, 1997)
David Keenan, 'Techno Animal', *The Wire*, October 2001
David Keenan, 'Godspeed You Black Emperor!: Life Stinks', *The Wire*, May 2000
I. Khider, 'Do Make Say Think', *Perfect Sound Forever*, September 2002

Neil Kulkarni, 'A New Nineties' (series), *The Quietus*, 2011
Steve Lamacq, 'Too Pure: Little Cred Roosters', *NME*, October 3 1992
Kevin Martin, liner notes to various artists, *Ambient 4: Isolationism* (Virgin, 1994)
Mike McGonigal, 'Galaxie 500: Temperature's Rising', *Pitchfork*, May 3 2010
Mike McGonigal, liner notes to Codeine, *When I See The Sun* (Numero Group, 2012)
Phil McMullen, 'Flying Saucer Attack', *Ptolemaic Terrascope* #16, 1993
Jason Noble, 'Concrete and Crawdads: A Short Conversation with Jeff Mueller', *Magnet*, November 16 2010
Paul Oldfield, Simon Reynolds, 'Oceanic Rock', *Melody Maker*, December 24/31 1988
Ned Raggett, 'Disco Inferno', *Pitchfork*, January 23 2012
Simon Reynolds, 'Ambient: Easy Lizzzning', *Melody Maker*, October 2 1993
Simon Reynolds, 'It's A Jungle Out There', *Melody Maker*, January 21 1994
Simon Reynolds, 'Shaking The Rock Narcotic', *The Wire*, May 1994
Simon Reynolds, 'R U Ready To Post-Rock?', *Melody Maker*, July 23 1994
Simon Reynolds, 'Radiohead: Walking On Thin Ice', *The Wire*, July 2001
Victoria Segal, 'Godspeed You Black Emperor!: The Last Great Band Of The Century', *NME*, July 24 1999
Joseph Stannard, 'Bristol UFOs', *The Wire*, August 2015
John Tatlock, 'The Noise And How To Bring It: Hank Shocklee', *The Quietus*, February 4 2015
Wyndham Wallace, 'I Put A Spell On You: The Story Of Bark Psychosis And *Hex*', *The Quietus*, August 14 2014
Rob Young, 'Sigur Rós: Desolation Angels', *The Wire*, January 2001

ONLINE

Fodderstompf: PiL fansite archive (fodderstompf.com)
Electric Audio forum (Steve Albini) (electricalaudio.com)
Green Plastic Radiohead (greenplastic.com)
r/postrock (reddit.com/r/postrock/)
Sigur Rós (sigur-ros.co.uk)
Snow In Berlin: A Mark Hollis and Talk Talk resource (snowinberlin.com)

ENDNOTES

INTRODUCTION

'Open-ended yet precise' Simon Reynolds, *The Wire*, May 1994
'One cannot get around …' Jacques Derrida, *Of Grammatology*

CHAPTER ONE

'A lot of musicians …' Edward Blackwell to Valerie Wilmer
'consisted of holding …' John Cale to Jim Condon, 'Angus Maclise And The Origin Of The Velvet Underground', *What Goes On #3*, 1983
'Does group direction …' Liner notes to *AMMMusic*, 1967
'essential prerequisite for …' Cornelius Cardew, quoted by Michael Nyman
'AMM music existed …' Eddie Prévost quoted by Rob Young, *The Wire*, February 1995
'Concern about what …' Eddie Prévost, liner notes to AMM's *The Crypt*, 1988
'We were proud …' Godspeed You! Black Emperor to Maddy Costa, *Guardian*, October 11 2012
'The players could …' Eddie Prévost, liner notes to AMM's *The Crypt*, 1988
'I used to take things …' Keith Rowe to Rob Young, *The Wire*, February 1995
'[*Coconut Hotel*] is both thoughtful …' Mayo Thompson to Edwin Pouncey, *The Wire*, January 1999
'We set out …' Mayo Thompson to Richie Unterberger, published on richieunterberger.com, 1996
'Prog rock with crippling …' *Word*, May 2004
'The prog rock, jazz …' Michael Karoli to Simon Reynolds, *Melody Maker*, July 15 1989
'The more you learn …' Holger Czukay to Paul Mather, *Melody Maker*, January 31 1987

'If the idea was spontaneous …' Holger Czukay to Simon Reynolds, *Melody Maker*, July 15 1989
'With a cyclical rhythm …' Jaki Liebezeit to David Stubbs, *Future Days*, 2014
'Every little noise …' Irmin Schmidt to David Stubbs, *Future Days*, 2014
'[*Cream*] was part of this wave …' Michael Karoli to Edwin Pouncey, *NME*, August 5 1989
'It was political …' Jaki Liebezeit to David Stubbs
'The idea was …' John Weinzierl to David Stubbs
'Outside the stage door …' Brian Eno to Robert Sandall, *Q*, November 1990
'Eno would appear …' Chris Salewicz, *NME*, December 7 1974
'What happened in Roxy …' Brian Eno to Caroline Coon, Ritz, 1977
'In talking so much …' Brian Eno to Ian McDonald, *NME*, November 26 1977
'We are no longer interested …' Brian Eno to Frank Rose, *Creem*, July 1975
'The way rock music is traditionally …' Brian Eno to Vivien Goldman, *Sounds*, February 5 1977
'I tried all kinds of …' Brian Eno to Miles, *NME*, November 27 1976
'Swing the microphone …' Brian Eno to Alan Moore, *Chain Reaction*, BBC Radio 4, 2005
'His initial guidance …' Percy Jones, quoted by Geeta Dayal in *Another Green World*, 2009
'until it made …' Brian Eno, 1977, quoted in David Sheppard
'The problem is that people …' Brian Eno, 1977
'I read a science fiction …' Brian Eno to Ian McDonald, *NME*, November 26 1977
'Life in LA …' David Bowie to Chris Roberts, *Uncut*, October 1999
'fuck with the fabric of time' Tony Visconti
'Brian had talked David into …' Tony Visconti to Tom Doyle, *Melody Maker*, March 19 1994
'to the zeitgeist' David Bowie to Chris Roberts, *Uncut*, October 1999
'I couldn't express …' David Bowie to Charles Shaar Murray, *NME*, November 12 1977
'[*Low*] is an act …' Charles Shaar Murray, *NME*, January 22 1977
'When it came out …' Stephen Morris to Stephen Dalton, *Uncut*, April 2001
'A big tom-tom riff …' Stephen Morris to Simon Reynolds, *Rip It Up And Start Again*
'At that time, [Hannett] wanted …' Stephen Morris to Anton Spice, thevinylfactory.com, January 27 2016
'That was the big joke …' and 'I grew up playing jazz …' Andy Summers to Paul Lester, teamrock.com, December 18 2015
'I thought it was …' Vini Reilly to Dave Haslam
'I can't understand …' Vini Reilly to Mick Middles
'I first felt funny …' and 'When you don't care …' Vini Reilly to Dave Haslam
'Those gigs taught me …' and 'I distinctly remember …' Vini Reilly to Mick Middles
'Dreadful pretentious and portentous …' Vini Reilly to James Nice
'I thought, who needs …' Tony Wilson to Mick Middles
'I'll never forget …' Vini Reilly to Mick Middles
''There's definitely a connection …' Vini Reilly to Paul Oldfield, *Melody Maker*, April 8 1989
'This was the first letter …' John Lydon, letter to fan c. 1978, viciousriff.com
'Reggae was the only other …' John Lydon, *Rotten*
'The technique of dub' Richard Williams, *Melody Maker*, August 21 1976
'The studio must be …' Lee Perry to David Toop
'I'd opened up …' John Lydon, *Anger Is An Energy*
'We used to fuck about …' Jah Wobble to Simon Reynolds, *The Wire*, November 1991
'We mixed it to …' John Lydon to Robin Banks, *ZigZag*, December 1978
'They all slagged …' Keith Levene to Mikal Gilmore, *Rolling Stone*, May 1 1980
'We take a silly …' John Lydon to Trevor Dann, *Rock On*, BBC Radio One, December 1980
'compromising the vocal' and 'The idea of [*Metal Box*] …' John Lydon, *Anger Is An Energy*
'a limited company …' John Lydon to John Shearlaw, *Record Mirror*, May 18 1981
'post rock' Paul Morley, *NME*, 17 October 1981
'All sorts of garbage …' Green Gartside, to Chris Roberts, *Melody Maker*, March 2 1991

CHAPTER TWO

'The film [is] …' Melvyn Bragg, *Put Blood In The Music*
'I don't know if …' Lee Ranaldo to Simon Reynolds, *Melody Maker*, March 11 1989
'We borrowed a couple …' Thurston Moore, *Put Blood In The Music*
'That was one …' Lee Ranaldo, *Put Blood In The Music*
'loud, violent, non-stop energy' Lydia Lunch, *Put Blood In The Music*
'New York is the grandest …' Alan Vega to Lisa Jane Persky, *New York Rocker*, May 1976

'I get really heavy welts …' Alan Vega to Lisa Jane Persky, *New York Rocker*, May 1976
'We weren't really …' John Lurie to Paul Bradshaw, *The Wire*, March 1987
'You're glad someone's …' Brian Eno to Robert Sandall, *Q*, November 1990
'We very deliberately …' Arto Lindsay to Jason Gross, *Perfect Sound Forever*, November 1997
'We didn't …' Glenn Branca to Marc Masters
'After working pretty much …' Rhys Chatham to Rob Young, *The Wire*, April 1999
'Depending on where you are …' Rhys Chatham to Rob Young, *The Wire*, April 1999
'I had no desire …' and 'When I first started …' Glenn Branca to Marc Masters
'I felt negatively …' John Cage to Wim Mertens, *Chicago '82: A Dip In The Lake*, 1982
'One concert we did …' Rhys Chatham to Rob Young, *The Wire*, April 1999
'The way the band composed …' Kim Gordon
'It gave us an …' Lee Ranaldo to David Browne
'It opened up' Lee Ranaldo to Michael Azerrad
'Because of our experience …' Lee Ranaldo to Biba Kopf, *The Wire*, December 1988
'Next to our friends …' Kim Gordon, *The Village Voice Rock 'N' Roll Quarterly*, Fall 1988
'It was raining …' Kim Gordon, *The Village Voice Rock 'N' Roll Quarterly*, Fall 1988
'I thought the music …' Michael Gira to Ian Penman, *The Wire*, July 1999
'I started working out songs …' Michael Gira to Marc Masters, *No Wave*, 2007
'I just basically …' Michael Gira to David Browne
'It just seems to me …' Michael Gira to Biba Kopf, *NME*, March 8 1986
'It was a long …' Michael Gira to Howard Wuelfing, *Addicted To Noise*, January 6 1997
'found total abjection …' Michael Gira to Kory Grow, *Rolling Stone*, May 26 2015
'It describes how …' Paul Smith to Jack Barron, *NME*, October 22 1988
'I wanted to play' and 'killed those songs' Thurston Moore to Michael Azerrad
'We do not try to pinpoint …' Lee Ranaldo
'They were phoning us …' Ollie Smith to *Melody Maker*, October 31 1987
'What it reinforced …' Lee Ranaldo to Michael Azerrad
'We use three guitars …' Robert Poss to Paul Oldfield, *Melody Maker*, October 15 1988
'Blast First would have …' Thurston Moore to Ted Mico, *Melody Maker*, November 13 1989
'I saw Ut's very first gig …' Thurston Moore to Mark Sinker, *The Wire*, February 1993
'We're not into pacification …' Jacqui Ham to Dave Jennings, *Melody Maker*, October 28 1989
'Why don't these bitches …' Michele Kirsch, *NME*, October 21 1989
'Me and Hahn …' Tim Sommer to Simon Reynolds, *Melody Maker*, October 24 1987
'We tend to think …' Hahn Rowe to David Stubbs, *Melody Maker*, July 16 1988
'It seems bizarre …' Tim Sommer to Joy Press, *Melody Maker*, May 23 1987
'neither the dancing feet …' *Melody Maker*, December 23/30 1989
'Hip-hop may have started …' Chuck D to Frank Owen, *Melody Maker*, March 21 1987
'Bill had the willing …' Chuck D to Danny Kelly, *NME*, 8 October 1988
'It was never …' Hank Shocklee to John Tatlock, *The Quietus*, February 4 2015
'What does Flavor *do*?' Rick Rubin, recalled by Chuck D
'I wasn't interested …' Chuck D
'Chuck's voice is so powerful …' Hank Shocklee to Jeff Chang
'I wanted to do something …' Hank Shocklee to John Tatlock, *The Quietus*, February 4 2015
'Shocklee, on *Fear* …' Kevin Martin to Simon Reynolds, *The Wire*, May 1994
'They seem to have …' Kim Gordon to Harold Demuir, *Melody Maker*, February 13 1988

CHAPTER THREE

'The intention of …' Ivo Watts-Russell to Chris Roberts, *Melody Maker*, July 4 1987
'disappointing, because of …' Elizabeth Fraser to Chris Roberts, *Melody Maker*, July 4 1987
'It really pissed us off …' Miki Berenyi to David Stubbs, *Melody Maker*, July 24 1993
"We're thoroughly fed up …' Robin Guthrie to Chris Roberts, *Sounds*, January 4 1986
'We never talk about …' Simon Raymonde to Andrew Collins, *NME*, September 22 1990
'they could have asked …' Simon Raymonde to Martin Aston
'[New Age] is a music …' Harold Budd to Brian Morton, *The Wire*, February 1988
'shambling bands' A.R. Kane to Simon Reynolds, *Melody Maker*, February 7 1987

'You can get really ...' Alex Ayuli to Simon Reynolds, *Melody Maker*, February 7 1987
'A.R. Kane have an ...' Martyn Young to Stuart Cosgrove, *NME*, September 12 1987
'I just got involved ...' C.J. Mackintosh to Robin Gibson, *Sounds*, September 19 1987
'Our claim is that they ...' Pete Waterman to *Melody Maker*, September 26 1987
'There's sampled stuff ...' Alex Ayuli to Andrew Catlin, *Melody Maker*, July 25 1987
'For us, where the sampler ...' Kevin Shields to Mike McGonigal
'We really hated the reputation ...' Kevin Shields to Steve Lamacq, *NME*, February 25 1989
'We had this frequency ...' Kevin Shields to Chris Roberts, *Melody Maker*, April 28 1990
'I once spent ...' Bilinda Butcher to Chris Roberts, *Melody Maker*, April 28 1990
'It's just a guitar ...' Kevin Shields to Paul Oldfield, *Melody Maker*, August 20 1988
'With the open tunings ...' Kevin Shields to Mike McGonigal
'Usually, people would experience ...' Kevin Shields to Aaron North, *Buddyhead*, January 19 2005
'We like to play ...' Kevin Shields to Stuart Maconie, *NME*, April 21 1990
'The *Isn't Anything* phase ...' Kevin Shields to Mike McGonigal
'I'm being totally honest ...' Sonic Boom to Push, *Melody Maker*, October 24 1987
'When we first started ...' Jason Pierce to Caren Myers, *Melody Maker*, February 2 1991
'[Drugs were] fundamental ...' Sonic Boom to Edwin Pouncey, *The Wire* March 1996
'It's the same principle ...' Sonic Boom to David Stubbs, *Melody Maker*, June 13 1992
'The maximal effect ...' and 'Uuuuuuuurrrgh!' Sonic Boom to Ian Gittins, *Melody Maker*, August 20 1988
'The new kind of rock 'n' roll ...' Kevin Shields to Chris Roberts, *Melody Maker*, April 28 1990
'It all happened last ...' Alex Patterson to Paul Oldfield, *Melody Maker*, March 10 1990
'It actually all started ...' Jimmy Cauty to Paul Oldfield, *Melody Maker*, March 10 1990
'We always try ...' Bill Drummond to Paul Oldfield, *Melody Maker*, March 10 1990
'it sounds like something loud ...' Kevin Shields to Ben Thompson, *NME*, September 10 1988
'Over in the States ...' Kevin Shields to unnamed journalist, *Melody Maker*, March 14 1992
'I think bands like us ...' Neil Halstead to David Stubbs, *Melody Maker*, August 31 1991
'It's the kind of track ...' Kevin Shields to David Stubbs, *Melody Maker*, January 26 1991
'Once I would have said ...' Alex Ayuli to Simon Reynolds, *Melody Maker*, October 7 1989
'"Oceanic" rock ...' Simon Reynolds and Paul Oldfield, *Melody Maker*, December 24/31 1988
'It was extreme ...' Kevin Shields to Paul Oldfield, *Melody Maker*, August 20 1988

CHAPTER FOUR

'One note ...' Mark Hollis, *Mark Hollis Talks About Laughing Stock*
'I could see my label ...' Alan McGee to Simon Reynolds, *Spin*, August 2008
'£250,000 in debt ...' Lee Harris to John Howard, *The Standard Recorder*, April 13 1984
'the math [to] explain ...' Steve Albini, *Maximumrocknroll*, June 1994
'false attribution ...' *Melody Maker*, April 11 1992
'Once upon a time ...' Betty Page, *Record Mirror*, September 17 1988
'What I like about Shostakovich ...' Mark Hollis to Marianne Ebertowski, *Zig Zag*, July 1982
'I hate synths ...' Mark Hollis to Cliff Jones, *International Musician*, November 1991
'We try to use ...' Ian Curnow to Sean Rothman, *Electronic Soundmaker & Computer Music*, July 1984
'Traffic, King Crimson ...' Mark Hollis to Hans van den Heuvel, *Oor*, September 24 1984
'*Spirit Of Eden* shines ...' Mark Hollis to Hans van den Heuvel, *Oor*, September 24 1984
'Me and Lee have ...' Paul Webb to Betty Page, *Noise!*, November 11 1982
'rambled and got nowhere ...' Simon Napier-Bell to Sylvie Simmons, *MOJO*, April 1999
'What I feel about ...' David Sylvian to Simon Dudfield, *NME*, 30 March 1991
'We were in Pete ...' Holger Czukay to Sylvie Simmons, *MOJO*, April 1999
'It is quite a rare ...' Tim Friese-Greene to Neville Unwin and Tim Goodyer, *Home And Recording Studio*, April 1986
'It sounds ...' Mark Hollis to Richard Walmsley, *International Musician & Recording World*, April 1986
'In "It's Getting Late" ...' Mark Hollis to *Record Mirror*, February 1 1986
'are three months ...' Mark Hollis to Hans van den Heuvel, *Oor*, September 24 1988

'sort of electro-boffin synth …' Lee Harris on the .O.rang website
'As soon as you start …' Hugh Davies to Rob Young, *The Wire*, February 1988
'We learned over the …' Tim Friese-Greene quoted in James Marsh, Chris Roberts, Toby Benjamin
'The story about how [Hollis] got …' Phill Brown to Cliff Jones, *Melody Maker*, October 26 1991
'We're doing something that's …' Mark Hollis to Cliff Jones, *Melody Maker*, October 26 1991
'Talk Talk are not …' Tony Wadsworth to Adrian Devoy, *Q*, October 1988
'I've been going …' David Sylvian to Steve Sutherland, *Melody Maker*, March 30 1991
'I got the idea …' David Sylvian to Christopher E. Young
'We spent a few months …' David Sylvian to Sylvie Simmons, *MOJO*, April 1999
'At the end of the day …' Steve Jansen, quoted in *David Sylvian: The Last Romantic*, 2004
'My relationship with the boys …' David Sylvian to Simon Dudfield, *NME*, 30 March 1991
'I find it very difficult …' David Sylvian to Steve Sutherland, *Melody Maker*, March 30 1991
'I may as well …' Jim Arundel in *Melody Maker*, September 7 1991
'It's never a thing …' and 'It's just about virtue …' Mark Hollis to Steve Sutherland, *Melody Maker*, September 7 1991
'The studio was oppressive …' Mark Hollis to Cliff Jones, *Melody Maker*, October 26 1991
'the first time …' Mark Hollis
'So much of what …' Mark Hollis to Cliff Jones, *International Musician*, November 1991
'I remember thinking …' Tim Friese-Greene quoted in James Marsh, Chris Roberts, Toby Benjamin
'I like cross-referencing …' Mark Hollis to Christophe Basterra, *Magic*, January 1998
'I only know …' Mark Hollis to *Intro*, March 1998
'He asked to meet up …' David Sylvian to Sylvie Simmons, *MOJO*, April 1999
'He did say …' Scott Walker to Richard Cook, *The Wire*, May 1995
'I've been writing the same …' Scott Walker interviewed on *The Late Show*, May 10 1995
'People expect a lot …' Scott Walker to Richard Cook, *The Wire*, May 1995
'We wanted to record …' Scott Walker to Simon Williams, *NME*, May 20 1995
'Everything comes from …' and 'It comes from silence …' Scott Walker to Richard Cook, *The Wire*, May 1995
'Essentially, I'm really trying …' Scott Walker to Sean O'Hagan, *Guardian*, November 9 2008
'By the time I get …' Scott Walker to Richard Cook, *The Wire*, May 1995
'They're agony …' Brian Gascoigne to Sean O'Hagan, *Observer*, October 9 2008
'Can we have a lighting change, please?' Jools Holland on *Later …*, 1995
'I haven't heard *Tilt* …' Paul Woods
'I worked at it …' Scott Walker to Richard Cook, *The Wire*, May 1995
'I think there's an amount …' Mark Hollis

CHAPTER FIVE

'Basically, fuck all that …' Steve Albini on www.electricalaudio.com
'I like noise …' Steve Albini in *Forced Exposure*
'Warning!' Sleeve to *Headache* by Big Black, 1987
'As we got bigger …' Steve Albini to Simon Reynolds, *Melody Maker*, November 21 1992
'[Big Black] had an …' Steve Albini to Simon Reynolds, *Melody Maker*, November 21 1992
'We wanted to have …' Ian MacKaye to Stephen Blush
'Everything [hardcore] set out …' Jesse Malin to Stephen Blush
'You couldn't really do …' David Pajo in *Breadcrumb Trail*
'I started getting …' David Pajo to Scott Tennent
'Slint was casual' Drew Daniel, *Conqueror Worm #3*, Summer 1987
'Personally speaking …' Britt Walford to John Calvert, *FACT*, March 12 2014
'They were all really conscious …' Steve Albini in *Breadcrumb Trail*
'This was our first recording …' Ethan Buckler to Scott Tennent
'I can't hear you …' Steve Albini onstage at London Mean Fiddler, as reported by Jack Barron, *NME*, October 22 1988
'Having been raised male …' Steve Albini to Evelyn Morris, *LISTEN*, May 2 2016
'I don't think …' Brian McMahan in *Breadcrumb Trail*
'It was all about …' David Pajo to Scott Tennent
'One thing that seems like …' Britt Walford to John Calvert, *FACT*, March 12 2014
'The way the writing …' Todd Brashear in *Breadcrumb Trail*

'It made for some really ...' Brian McMahan in *Breadcrumb Trail*
'I felt like there wasn't ...' Brian McMahan to Bram E. Gieben, *The Skinny*, April 3 2014
'I was a geeky kid ...' Brian McMahan to Andrew Male, *MOJO*, March 26 2014
'We wanted to ...' David Pajo in *Breadcrumb Trail*
'I guess that ...' Brian Poulson in *Breadcrumb Trail*
'"Washer" has my ...' David Pajo to Michael Wojtas, *Under The Radar*, October 15 2014
'Brian came to ...' David Pajo to Scott Tennent
'That was a huge ...' Britt Walford to Robert Cooke, *Drowned In Sound*, March 11 2014
'I really couldn't ...' Jason Noble in *Breadcrumb Trail*
'Two thumbs up ...' Lee Ranaldo to Jim Arundel, *Melody Maker*, April 2 1994
'It's not a premeditated ...' Jason Noble to Angela Lewis, *NME*, May 21 1994
'Oh Louisville!' Everett True, *Melody Maker*, May 21 1994
'We were certainly ...' Jason Noble to Michael T. Fournier, *Cabildo Quarterly*, January 26 2009
'It came out of a joke ...' Jason Noble to Angela Lewis, *NME*, May 21 1994
'Rodan was the one ...' Jason Noble to *Melody Maker*, October 22 1994
'Even though *Spiderland* ...' Britt Walford to John Calvert, *FACT*, March 12 2014
'ten fucking stars' Steve Albini, *Melody Maker*, March 30 1991
'*Please* tell me everything ...' Nick Wrigley, *Melody Maker*, February 20 1993
'the most dropped ...' Jim Arundel, *Melody Maker*, May 14 1994
'home to the Care ...' Mark Sutherland, *NME*, July 23 1994

CHAPTER SIX

'The nineties start here ...' Jonathan Selzer, *Melody Maker*, January 20 1990
'There was the fragile ...' Simon Reynolds, *Melody Maker*, December 19/26 1992
'I wouldn't say ...' Nick Allport to Jonathan Selzer, *Melody Maker*, April 7 1990
'The moods and the ...' John Ling to Simon Reynolds, *Melody Maker*, October 20 1990
'The only thing ...' Ian Crause to David Stubbs, *Melody Maker*, May 30 1992
'It's quite simple ...' Franz Treichler to the Stud Brothers, *Melody Maker*, June 20 1987
'To me, rock ...' Franz Treichler to Simon Williams, *NME*, February 4 1992
'When we play ...' John Ling to Jim Arundel, *Melody Maker*, September 26 1992
'Lee would disappear ...' Graham Sutton in James Marsh, Chris Roberts, Toby Benjamin
'If I were to put ...' Ian Crause to Rob Young, *The Wire*, April 1994
'When Ian bought ...' Rob Whatley to Ned Raggett, *Pitchfork*, January 23 2012
'Rough Trade had ...' Ian Crause to Ned Raggett, *Pitchfork*, January 23 2012
'"From The Devil" ...' Paul Willmott to Ned Raggett, *Pitchfork*, January 23 2012
'It's tension-release ...' John Ling to Sally Margaret Joy, *Melody Maker*, April 18 1992

CHAPTER SEVEN

'Enter Camden Lurch ...' Simon Williams and Steve Lamacq, *NME*, February 21 1991
'The whole point ...' Joe Dilworth to Ann Scanlon
'melody with a tense ...' Simon Williams and Steve Lamacq, *NME*, February 21 1991
'[It] was basically just ...' Steve Lamacq to Ann Scanlon
'I got Richard ...' Paul Cox on MTV's *120 Minutes*, c.late 1993
'If we sign ...' Richard Roberts to Everett True, *Melody Maker*, April 17 1993
'There isn't a Too Pure ...' Richard Roberts to Steve Lamacq, *NME*, October 3 1992
'I'm taken by ...' Tim Gane to Michael Bonner, *Melody Maker*, June 1 1991
'Stereolab we came across ...' Richard Roberts to MTV's *120 Minutes*, 1993
'Young enthusiastic people ...' Tim Gane to MTV's *120 Minutes*, 1993
'We know that we're ...' Richard Roberts to Steve Lamacq, *NME*, October 3 1992
'I could write a nice ...' Laetitia Sadier to Ted Kessler, *NME*, July 16 1994
'Pram have some fine ...' Ian McGregor, *Melody Maker*, February 3 1990
'There was never any ...' and 'we were never ...' Matt Eaton to Neil Kulkarni, *The Quietus*, December 22 2011
'There is a theme ...' Rosie Cuckston to Dave Jennings, *Melody Maker*, May 25 1991

'When you're a kid ...' Rosie Cuckston to Dave Jennings, *Melody Maker*, February 6 1993
'It used to be ...' Rosie Cuckston to Dave Jennings, *Melody Maker*, May 25 1991
'The new Too Pure signing ...' Mig Morland to Dele Fadele, *NME*, November 7 1992
'film, animation, children's TV ...' Sam Owen to Neil Kulkarni, *The Quietus*, December 22 2011
'I've always liked music ...' Matt Eaton to Dave Jennings, *Melody Maker*, February 6 1993
'The music is more ...' Rosie Cuckston to Dave Jennings, *Melody Maker*, February 6 1993
'A typical day ...' Matt Eaton to Neil Kulkarni, *The Quietus*, December 22 2011
'Typical Pram clutter ...' Sam Owen to Neil Kulkarni, *The Quietus*, December 22 2011
'It was just the cost ...' Matt Eaton to Neil Kulkarni, *The Quietus*, December 22 2011
'using technology as a live instrument' quoted by Ngaire-Ruth, *Melody Maker*, April 3 1993
'We are a remix ...' Mig Morland to Kevin Martin, *The Wire*, August 1993
'post-rock and post-rave ...' Simon Reynolds, *Melody Maker*, September 25 1993

CHAPTER EIGHT

'diamante detonations ...' Simon Reynolds, *Melody Maker*, June 8 1991
'What to call ...' Simon Reynolds, *The Wire*, May 1994
'The future of rock ...' Simon Reynolds, *MOJO*, March 1994
'collective toil'; 'authenticity'; 'palette of textures' Simon Reynolds, *The Wire*, May 1994
'given up the idea ...' Simon Reynolds, *Melody Maker*, July 23 1994
'What happened?' Jim Arundel, *Melody Maker*, February 19 1994
'The album is about ...' Graham Sutton to *Melody Maker*, December 18 1993
'I am a little upset ...' Margaret Fiedler to *Melody Maker*, October 2 1993
'ambient music where ...' Ian Crause to Rob Young, *The Wire*, April 1994
'We had great fun ...' Paul Willmott to Ned Raggett, *Pitchfork*, January 23 2012
'We slogged our ...' Paul Willmott to Ned Raggett, *Pitchfork*, January 23 2012
'Sid James, proper football ...' Andrew Harrison, *Select*, April 1993

CHAPTER NINE

'People make ...' Dave Rowntree to The Stud Brothers, *Melody Maker*, September 25 1993
'Grunge—the fusion of punk and metal ...' Simon Reynolds, *Artforum*, February 1996
'We got to kind of ...' Bruce Pavitt to Leslie Michele Derrough, *Glide*, February 26 2014
'We've played a lot ...' Damon Krukowski to Everett True, *Melody Maker*, February 17 1990
'I think if people ...' Naomi Yang to Steve Lamacq, *NME*, December 2 1989
'I like people who ...' Damon Krukowski to Ian Gittins, *Melody Maker*, October 6 1990
'To be perfectly honest ...' Kramer to Mike McGonigal, *Pitchfork*, May 3 2010
'We had been listening ...' Damon Krukowski to Mike McGonigal, *Pitchfork*, May 3 2010
'Our sound is a Hegelian ...' Dean Wareham to Everett True, *Melody Maker*, February 17 1990
'the way they focus ...' Dean Wareham to Bob Stanley, *Melody Maker*, November 18 1989
'I always thought ...' Naomi Yang to Mike McGonigal, *Pitchfork*, May 3 2010
'To play less notes ...' Dean Wareham to David Pais, *The Drone*, January 10 2012
'Quick doesn't do ...' Damon Krukowski to Mike McGonigal, *Pitchfork*, May 3 2010
'Outside the music ...' Damon Krukowski to Phil McMullen, *Ptolemaic Terrascope* (#27), 1997
'The lighting director ...' Dean Wareham
'No explanation ...' Damon Krukowski to Phil McMullen, *Ptolemaic Terrascope* (#27), 1997
'It really felt like ...' Naomi Yang to Phil McMullen, *Ptolemaic Terrascope* (#27), 1997
'The suggestion is ...' Dean Wareham
'We find the power ...' Jon Fine to Ian Gittins, *Melody Maker*, January 5 1991
'I hadn't played ...' Chris Brokaw to Mike McGonigal, liner notes to *When I See The Sun*, 2012
'Chris came to a ...' John Engle to Mike McGonigal, liner notes to *When I See The Sun*, 2012
'For the last year ...' Chris Brokaw to Everett True, *Melody Maker*, March 28 1992
'some intense states ...' Stephen Immerwahr to Mike McGonigal, liner notes to *When I See The Sun*, 2012
'headphone music ...' Curtis Harvey to Mark Luffman, *Melody Maker*, November 1 1997

'We just really worked ...' Bubba Kadane to Matt Gallaway, liner notes to *Bedhead 1992–1998*, 2014
'Originally, [playing slow] was ...' Alan Sparhawk to Stephen Dalton, *NME*, August 10 1996
'a week-and-a-half ...' Alan Sparhawk to April Long, *NME*, May 15 1999
'I guess we do take ...' Dean Wareham to Simon Reynolds, *Melody Maker*, August 19 1989
'We're more interested ...' Michael Gibbons to Jon Selzer, *Melody Maker*, September 30 1995
'It's peculiar ...' Damon Krukowski to Keith Cameron, *NME*, July 20 1991

CHAPTER TEN

'I guess the air ...' Johnny Herndon to Martin James, *Melody Maker*, March 28 1998
'The lyrics must ...' David Grubbs to Ian McGregor, *Melody Maker*, February 10 1990
'Tortoise is about ...' Doug McCombs to John Robinson, *NME*, December 17 1994
'Things really changed ...' Johnny Herndon to David Keenan, *The Wire*, February 2001
'Where with Gastr ...' Bundy K. Brown to Ronald Hart, Red Bull Music Academy, June 20 2014
'I had never played ...' Dan Bitney to Ronald Hart, Red Bull Music Academy, June 20 2014
'Last year, when we ...' Johnny Herndon to Dele Fadele, *NME*, 13 April 1996
'It's alright taking these kids ...' Goldie to Simon Reynolds, *The Wire*, September 1994
'I don't think any ...' Bundy K Brown to Ronald Hart, Red Bull Music Academy, June 20 2014
'When we did those ...' Tim Gane to Mike Barnes, *The Wire*, October 1997
'I think I tried ...' David Pajo to A.D. Amorosi, *Magnet Magazine*, 2014
'It was weird' and 'I don't know' Bundy K. Brown to Christoph Cox, *The Wire*, February 1997
'We went into the studio ...' Doug Scharin to Mike Barnes, *The Wire*, December 2000
'The whole basis ...', 'it wasn't until ...' Jim O'Rourke to Christoph Cox, *The Wire*, November 1997
'I was afraid ...' Jim O'Rourke to David Keenan, *The Wire*, November 2001
'When you're ...' Jim O'Rourke to Peter Margasak, *Chicago Reader*, September 12 1997
'I remember being taken ...' Laetitia Sadier to Mike Barnes, *The Wire*, October 1997
'I don't think he remembers ...' Jim O'Rourke to Rob Young, *The Wire*, January 1999
'It's about the spaces ...' Jan St Werner to David Hemmingway, *Melody Maker*, September 2 1995
'The album's not a very ...' Tim Gane to Andy Crysell, *NME*, September 6 1997
'Maybe that's why ...' Laetitia Sadier to Andy Crysell, *NME*, September 6 1997
'When I was young ...' Sasha Frere-Jones to Peter Shapiro, *The Wire*, March 1996
'[Reynolds] wrote ...' Sasha Frere-Jones to Andy Mulkerin, *Pittsburgh City Paper*, April 24 2008
'There's so much good ...' Tim Gane to Mike Barnes, *The Wire*, October 1997
'were in this band ...' Sam Prekop to Chris Ruen, *Tiny Mix Tapes*, January 30 2006
'Each record has been ...' Sam Prekop to Mark Luffman, *Melody Maker*, April 26 1997
'I was buying a jacket ...' Johnny Herndon to Victoria Segal, *NME*, July 25 1998
'It's not an easy record ...' John McEntire to Joshua Klein, *AV Club*, March 24 1999
'Tortoise, in many ways ...' Dan Bitney to Martin James, *NME*, March 28 1998
'the guys manage to play samba ...' Tom Zé, *The Wire*, July 1999

CHAPTER ELEVEN

'It's interesting ...' Warren Ellis to Cathi Unsworth, *Melody Maker*, May 6 1995
'At the level of ...' Drew Daniel to Carlos M. Pozo, *Perfect Sound Forever*, September 1999
'Fahey's weirder tunings ...' Thurston Moore to Byron Coley, *Spin*, November 1994
'Wine And Roses' Elijah P. Lovejoy (John Fahey), liner notes to *Dance Of Death And Other Plantation Favorites*, 1965
'I bought every album ...' Glenn Jones, liner notes to *The Epiphany Of Glenn Jones*, 1997
'I've always really thought ...' John Fahey to Byron Coley, *Spin*, November 1994
'I spent so many years ...' Jim O'Rourke to John Fahey, *The Wire*, October 1996
'We're kind of opposites ...' John Fahey to Jim O'Rourke, *The Wire*, October 1996
'actually started that ...' Jim O'Rourke to David Keenan, *The Wire*, November 2001
'For a week of ...', 'no interest in making ...', 'In scrapping what ...' Glenn Jones, liner notes to *The Epiphany Of Glenn Jones*, 1997

'That one recording session …' David Pajo to Bram E. Gieben, *The Skinny*, April 3 2014
'a non-profit …' The For Carnation to David Hemingway, *Melody Maker*, August 2 1997
'I would never think …' Brian McMahon to Dave Christenson, *fakejazz*, October 6 2000
'I think you can hear …' David Pajo to Sharon O'Connell, *Melody Maker*, January 31, 1998
'the first and last …' David Pajo, liner notes to *Hole Of Burning Alms*, 2004
'I chose …', 'like most Midwesterners …' David Pajo to Christoph Cox, *The Wire*, February 2000
'If you consider the …' Drew Daniel to Carlos M. Pozo, *Perfect Sound Forever*, September 1999
'There's a hybridness …' Drew Daniel to Jim Haynes, *The Wire*, April 2001
'We never really had...' Warren Ellis to Mike Barnes, *The Wire*, October 1995
'It's celebratory …' Warren Ellis to Everett True, *Melody Maker*, December 9 1995

CHAPTER TWELVE

'It's probably something …' Jason Noble to *Melody Maker*, October 22 1994
'People talk of the …' Jason Noble on publicnoise.blogspot.co.uk, May 2012
'It's not rock music …' Jason Noble to *Melody Maker*, October 22 1994
'Around the time …' Lisa Gerrard to Fred H. Berger, *Propaganda Magazine*, Spring 1994
'We started working …' Lisa Gerrard to Jonny Mugwump, *The Quietus*, September 4 2012
'I remember very …' Jason Noble to Michael T. Fournier, *Cabildo Quarterly Online*, February 9 2009
'I was looking for …' Bruce Licher to James Nice, www.ltmrecordings.com
'We started with …' Jeff Mueller, published email, www.discogs.com
'The amounts were too …' Jason Noble to Mark Luffman, *Melody Maker*, March 2 1996
'We have a semi-notated …' Jason Noble to Mike Barnes, *The Wire*, February 1996
'I think hip-hop …' Jason Noble to Joseph Lord, *Velocity*, March 9 2010
'He kindly asked me …' Jason Noble to Joseph Lord, *Velocity*, March 9 2010
'I have to say …' Jason Noble, *Magnet*, 16 November 2010

CHAPTER THIRTEEN

'If you play early Eno …' Mick Harris to Simon Reynolds, *Melody Maker*, October 2 1993
'An ambience is defined …' Brian Eno, liner notes to *Ambient 1: Music For Airports*, 1978
'People are questioning …' Kevin Martin to Simon Reynolds, *Melody Maker*, July 23 1994
'[Main] want to …' Robert Hampson to Simon Reynolds, *Melody Maker*, October 2 1993
'I feel scarred …' Kevin Martin to John Eden, *Uncarved* blog, undated
'I'm not ashamed …' Mick Harris to Tommy Udo, *NME*, August 5 1995
'There's a certain pitch …' Bill Steer to Paul Spence, *NME*, 16 July 1988
'rock 'n' roll band' Mick Harris to Simon Reynolds, *Melody Maker*, July 23 1994
'There's no conscious decision …' Kevin Martin to Biba Kopf, *The Wire*, September 1990
'The best reaction …' Kevin Martin to Chris Roberts, *Melody Maker*, March 24 1990
'My father was …' Kevin Martin to Luke Turner, *The Quietus*, August 29 2014
'I had asked …' and 'It was everything …' Kevin Martin to John Eden, *Uncarved* blog, undated
'[Martin] was the first …' Justin Broadrick to Klaus Kinski, *Brooklyn Vegan*, September 21 2009
'We're a *true* heavy …' Justin Broadrick to Paul Oldfield, *Melody Maker*, June 3 1989
'Justin is the only person …' Kevin Martin to Neil Kulkarni, *Melody Maker*, July 8 1995
'From the beginnings …' Kevin Martin to Guy Odey, *The Arts Desk*, June 8 2015
'A dance label?' Rob Mitchell to Victoria Segal, *NME*, July 11 1998
'We make music to …' Sean Booth to Jon Robb, *Melody Maker*, September 3 1994
'We're not as dense …' Margaret Fiedler to Louise Gray, *The Wire*, March 1997
'This album …' Margaret Fiedler to Joshua Klein, *A.V. Club*, January 17 2001
'When I started Main …' Robert Hampson to Kiran Sande, *FACT*, July 20 2012
'Of course! How can …' Sonic Boom to Ian Gittins, *Melody Maker*, August 20 1988
'We find the whole …' Robert Hampson to Andrew Collins, *NME*, January 27 1990
'exhausted all the ideas …' Robert Hampson to *FACT*, July 10 2015

'I just got bored ...' Sonic Boom to Tony Wilson, *Melody Maker*, May 18 1996
'The only improvisation ...' Sonic Boom to Mike Barnes, *The Wire*, May 1997
'flows a lot easier ...' Sonic Boom to Carrie Hourihan, *Ptolemaic Terrascope*, 1996
'The way that ...' and 'We deliberately ...' Robert Hampson to Kiran Sande, *FACT*, July 20 2012
'The guitar finally ...' Robert Hampson to Jonny Mugwump, *The Quietus*, November 19 2008
'We wanted freedom ...' Kevin Martin to Guy Odey, *The Arts Desk*, June 8 2015
'[*Ghosts*] was a direct reaction ...' Kevin Martin to David Keenan, *The Wire*, October 2001
'dropped almost album by album' Kevin Martin to John Eden, *Uncarved* blog
'I was fucking with ...' Kevin Martin to David Keenan, *The Wire*, October 2001
'We had to find our ...'' Justin Broadrick to David Keenan, *The Wire*, October 2001
'I dunno about ...' Robert Hampson to Simon Reynolds, *Melody Maker*, October 2 1993
'Dropping inwards instead ...' Kevin Martin, *Isolationism* liner notes, 1994
'I wouldn't term our music ...' Mark Nelson to Julie Taraska, *The Wire*, February 1995
'There were times ...' Simon Reynolds, *Melody Maker*, February 3 1996
'We added a bassist ...' Carter Brown to Julie Taraska, *The Wire*, February 1995
'a monument to the human ...' Mark Nelson to Julie Taraska, *The Wire*, February 1995
'What we do probably ...' Brian McBride to Ian Maleney, *Resident Advisor*, November 18 2015
'We've always ...' Adam Wiltzie to Christopher R. Weingarten, *Rolling Stone*, July 21 2015
'I don't see anyone ...' Mick Harris to Jakubowski, *The Wire*, July 1994
'Working with technology ...' Kevin Martin to Simon Reynolds, *The Wire*, May 1994

CHAPTER FOURTEEN

'Roger Doughty ...' Matt Elliott to Joseph Stannard, *The Wire*, September 2010
'One day I went ...' David Pearce to Joseph Stannard, *The Wire*, August 2015
'We had a band ...' Kate Wright and Matt Jones to Mike Goldsmith, November 1995
'We were sort of insular ...' Rachel Coe to Joseph Stannard, *The Wire*, August 2015
'[Pearce] wanted to ...' Matt Elliott to Joseph Stannard, *The Wire* [online], September 2010
'[It was] just Robert Hampson ...' David Pearce to Joe Clay, *The Quietus*, September 2 2015
'When *Up Home!* ...' David Pearce to Simon Reynolds, *Melody Maker*, October 14 1995
'round at Rachel's ...' David Pearce to Phil McMullen, *Ptolemaic Terrascope #16*, 1993
'I had an idea ...' David Pearce to Joe Clay, *The Quietus*, September 2 2015
'Due to the ...' Liner notes to *Soaring High*, 1993
'My problem with computers ...' David Pearce to Fred Mills, *Ptolemaic Terrascope #29*, 2001
'I always felt ...' Rachel Coe to Joseph Stannard, *The Wire*, August 2015
'We were inspired by ...' Kate Wright to Joseph Stannard, *The Wire*, August 2015
'We'd recorded a song ...' Rachel Coe to Joseph Stannard, *The Wire*, August 2015
'It might have ...' Stuart Braithwaite to Mary Anne Hobbs, *BBC 6Music*, 8 February 2015
'We always had big ideas ...' Paul Savage to Jade Gordon, *Melody Maker*, April 5 1997
'These people are ...' Provost Alex Fowler to *Melody Maker*, May 2 1998
'I think Arab Strap ...' Malcolm Middleton to Nicola Meighan, *The Quietus*, May 21 2012
'I think being in ...' Wendy Harper to John Mulvey, *NME*, August 5 1995
'stays in the same place ...' Barry Stillwell to John Mulvey, *NME*, August 5 1995
'Bunch of cunts' Tom Cullinan to Everett True, *Melody Maker*, June 1 1996
'Dave [Pearce]'s drones ...' Sam Jones to Joseph Stannard, *The Wire*, August 2015
'When anyone ever ...' Brendan O'Hare to Jennifer Nine, *Melody Maker*, May 18 1996
'We just thought Brendan ...' Dominic Aitchison to James Oldham, *NME*, April 3 1999
'We're basically a ...' Stuart Braithwaite to John Robinson, *NME*, May 24 1997
'We're more rock ...' Dominic Aitchison to Keith Cameron, *NME*, October 25 1997
'We were listening to ...' Kieran Hebden to Kitty Empire, *NME*, 12 June 1999
'What we would do ...' Luke Sutherland to *Vacant*
'Mogwai have always ...' Dominic Aitchison to James Oldham, *NME*, April 3 1999
'The thing about the shirt ...' Stuart Braithwaite to *NME*, 10 July 1999

'Basically, I think the band ...' Blur spokesperson to *NME*, 10 July 1999
'it wasn't a pisstake ...' David Pearce to Stephen Dalton, *NME*, 26 November 1994
'The diplomatic thing ...' David Pearce to Joe Clay, *The Quietus*, September 2 2015
'On the first ...' Matt Elliott to Simon Hopkins, *The Wire*, May 1997
'any old bits ...' Matt Elliott to James Oldham, *NME*, October 26 1996
'I lived in Montpelier ...' Matt Elliott to Simon Hopkins, *The Wire*, May 1997
'Bands like Disco Inferno ...' Matt Elliott to Joseph Stannard, *The Wire*, September 2010
'We're obsessed with ...' Hood to Mark Luffman, *Melody Maker*, June 29 1996
'I just go round ...' Matt Elliott to Simon Hopkins, *The Wire*, May 1997
'Me and some friends ...' Matt Elliott to Joseph Stannard, *The Wire*, September 2010
'When the single came out ...' Stuart Braithwaite to Jonathan Greer, *Weedbus*, 1998 [unpublished at time; published on *Slow Thrills*, November 1 2011]
'I hope we sell ...' Stuart Braithwaite to Neil Kulkarni, *Melody Maker*, May 10 1997
'[It's] named after ...' Stuart Braithwaite to Kika Johnson, *Nothing But Hope And Passion*, February 27 2014

CHAPTER FIFTEEN

' ...infinity [∞] sweeping ...' Godspeed You Black Emperor! blueprint, *f#a#∞*, 1997
'a frame to give ...' Efrim Menuck to Victoria Segal, *NME*, July 24 1999
'all of it written ...' Liner notes to *Slow Riot For Zero Kanada*, 1999
'If you ever get into ...' Efrim Menuck to Victoria Segal, *NME*, July 24 1999
'the things we endure ...' Godspeed You Black Emperor! blueprint, *f#a#∞*, 1997
'It's amazing to me ...' David Bryant to Victoria Segal, *NME*, July 24 1999
'A thing a lot ...' Godspeed You! Black Emperor to Maddy Costa, *Guardian*, October 11 2012
'We played so many ...' Justin Small to I. Khider, *Perfect Sound Forever*, September 2002
'Having that eight-track ...' Justin Small on *The Sound It Resounds*, March 2013
'It's basically built ...' Ohad Benchetrit to I. Khider, *Perfect Sound Forever*, September 2002
'an abiding love ...' James Payment to I. Khider, *Perfect Sound Forever*, September 2002
'a really fun ...' and 'the sound of ...' Justin Small to Rob Hollamby, *The 405*, November 27 2012
'When we go out ...' Charles Spearin to Jon Bosworth, *EU Jacksonville*, September 20 2007
'the first self-titled record ...' Charles Spearin on *The Sound It Resounds*, March 2013
'the greatest recording ...' Justin Small on *The Sound It Resounds*, March 2013
'For one thing ...' Charles Spearin to Jon Bosworth, *EU Jacksonville*, September 20 2007
'When we first started ...' Roger Tellier-Craig to Jakub Adamek, *Weed Temple*, February 2 2015
'I think the glory days ...' David Bryant to David Keenan, *The Wire*, May 2000
'There's barricades in front ...' Norsola Johnson to David Keenan, *The Wire*, May 2000
'I always thought that ...' Efrim Menuck to David Keenan, *The Wire*, May 2000
'I was stung ...' Kevin McCaighy, letter to *The Wire*, July 2000
'Do you know ...' Efrim Menuck to David Keenan, *The Wire*, May 2000
'&hope still ...' Liner notes to Godspeed You! Black Emperor, *Yanqui U.X.O.*, 2002

CHAPTER SIXTEEN

'An image of something ...' Marcus Eoin to Toby Manning, *NME*, April 18 1998
'For the majority ...' Victoria Segal, *NME*, October 3 1998
'More compact ...' Dan Bitney to David Keenan, *The Wire*, February 2001
'It wasn't a direct ...' John McEntire to David Keenan, *The Wire*, February 2001
'To haunt does not ...' Jacques Derrida, *Spectres Of Marx*
'The source of all ...' Marcus Eoin to Toby Manning, *NME*, April 18 1998
'When we were kids ...' Michael Sandison to Toby Manning, *NME*, April 18 1998
'We do shoot ...' Mark Nelson to Ian Watson, *Melody Maker*, March 22 1997
'There's always that ...' Carter Brown to Ian Watson, *Melody Maker*, March 22 1997
'It's a great mood ...' Harold Budd to Mike Barnes, *The Wire*, January 1997

'Being in the womb …' Jónsi Birgisson to Ian Watson, *Melody Maker*, January 5 2000

'I think we were out …' Georg 'Goggi' Hólm to Rob Young, *The Wire*, January 2001

'I don't think it's enough …' Kristín Björk to Rob Young, *The Wire*, January 2001

'Everybody in Iceland …' Georg 'Goggi' Hólm to Rob Young, *The Wire*, January 2001

'We have a song …' Jónsi Birgisson to Neil Thompson, *NME*, September 25 1999

'fucking bullshit' Jónsi Birgisson to Luke Burbank, *Bryant Park Project*, May 10 2007

'We are not a band …' quoted by Andy Crysell, *NME*, January 6 2000

'It's a subconscious …' Jónsi Birgisson to *Fökus*, 2002 [*translated by Björn Erlingur Flóki Björnsson*]

'Our music is …' Georg 'Goggi' Hólm to Ian Watson, *Melody Maker*, November 10 1999

'Magazines always want …' Kjartan Sveinsson to Danny Eccleston, *Q*

'We hate all the photos …' Jónsi Birgisson to *Trax*, February 2001

'I don't think the …' Georg 'Goggi' Hólm to Rob Young, *The Wire*, January 2001

'We didn't like it at all …' Jónsi Birgisson to *El Mundo*, October 2002

'It was an interesting …' John McEntire to Mike Barnes, *The Wire*, January 1998

'aimed to promote …' and 'the audio program …' archived at adaweb.com, 1995

'how your mind works …' Chris Morris to Robert Hanks, *Independent*, April 19 2000

'In Iceland we are …' Sigur Rós to BBC Press Office, *BBC Media Centre*, October 11 2016

'some weird way …' Jónsi Birgisson to Scott Colothan, *Gigwise*, February 21 2010

'Oh, fuck 'em …' Georg 'Goggi' Hólm to Andy Crysell, *NME*, January 6 2000

'We play pop …' Jónsi Birgisson to Rob Young, *The Wire*, January 2001

CHAPTER SEVENTEEN

'The message is clear …' Tony Wadsworth to *NME*, October 21 2000

'It was never …', 'both have patterns …' Mike Kinsella to Joe Goggins, *The Line Of Best Fit*, June 5 2014

'We don't consider …' Munaf Rayani to Juliet Eilperin, *Washington Post*, September 25 2006

'I really like …' Munaf Rayani to Kevin Adickes, *Pitchfork*, November 1 2001

'All the songs …' Michael James to Kevin Adickes, *Pitchfork*, November 1 2001

'In World War I …' Chris Hrasky to Kevin Adickes, *Pitchfork*, November 1 2001

'All of us get so lost …' Munaf Rayani to Michael Chamy, *Austin Chronicle*, October 24 2003

'I collect silly …' Adem Ilhan to Steve Bittrand, *Prefix*, January 1 2000

'We've avoided a lot …' Stuart Braithwaite to *NME*, January 9 1999

'Embarrassing …' Stuart Braithwaite to Sylvia Patterson, *NME*, May 5 2001

'At the moment …' Stuart Braithwaite to Stephen Dalton, *NME*, May 1 1999

'It's like how …' Ed O'Brien, radiohead.com

'The more concerts …' Jonny Greenwood to Simon Reynolds, *The Wire*, July 2001

'What were those …' Ed O'Brien, radiohead.com

'sounded really amazing …' Thom Yorke to Simon Reynolds, *The Wire*, July 2001

'There's an unhealthy …' Thom Yorke to Sylvia Patterson, *NME*, May 19 2001

'how to be a participant …' Ed O'Brien to Simon Reynolds, *The Wire*, July 2001

'If you're going to make …' Ed O'Brien, quoted in James Doheny

'It's a return to …' Colin Greenwood to James Oldham, *NME*, September 30 2000

'long and hard …' Ed O'Brien to *Spin*, quoted in *Melody Maker*, October 25 2000

'The way we worked …' Ed O'Brien, radiohead.com, 1999–2000

'Nigel Godrich is …' and 'It was incredibly …' Thom Yorke to Simon Reynolds, *The Wire*, July 2001

'I see it like this …' Jonny Greenwood to Simon Reynolds, *The Wire*, July 2001

'If there is a devil …' Thom Yorke to Sylvia Patterson, *NME*, May 19 2001

'We don't know …' and 'Anyone wants to …' Efrim Menuck, www.brainwashed.com

'the machine a key …' Thom Yorke to Simon Reynolds, *The Wire*, July 2001

'I think the one serious regret …' Colin Greenwood to *NME*, November 21 2000

'I think the artwork is …' and 'I'm desperate for …' Thom Yorke to Nick Kent, *Mojo*, June 2001

'Well in that case …' Ed O'Brien to James Oldham, *NME*, December 23/31 2000

INDEX

PHOTO CREDITS

The photographs used in this book are from the following sources, and we are grateful for their help. If you feel there has been a mistaken attribution, please contact the publisher.
Author photograph by Leonie Morse © The Simple Things magazine (thesimplethings.com). 'Citywide Action Plan' designed by Efrim Manuel Menuck and screenprinted by Leyla Majeri, 2005. PiL by David Corio/Redferns. Hugo Largo by Adam Peacock. Ut by Dave McFall. Ut poster photograph by Peter Anderson. A.R. Kane, Cocteau Twins photographs from 4AD promotional material. Mark Hollis by Martyn Goodacre/Getty Images. Papa Sprain by Peter Morris. *Spiderland* cover photograph by Will Oldham. Bark Psychosis by Phil Nicholls. Seefeel by James Bignell. Stereloab, Margaret Fiedler, and David Callahan by Greg Neate (neatephotos.com). Gastr del Sol courtesy of David Grubbs (photographer unknown). Codeine by John Engle. Rachel's and Jeff Mueller by Rachel Grimes. Third Eye Foundation by Greg Neate (neatephotos.com). Mogwai by Eva Vermandel. Fridge by Jason Evans. *Codename: Dustsucker* artwork by Victoria Browne. Godspeed You Black Emperor! by Eva Vermandel. Radiohead by Mick Hutson/Redferns.